LONDON FROM PUNK TO BLAIR

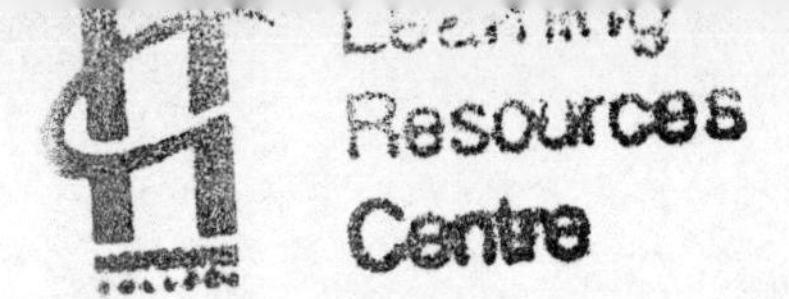

LONDON

FROM PUNK TO BLAIR

SECOND EDITION

EDITED BY JOE KERR
& ANDREW GIBSON

REAKTION BOOKS

Published by
Reaktion Books Ltd
33 Great Sutton Street
London EC1V 0DX, UK
www.reaktionbooks.co.uk

First published 2003
Second edition 2012

Printed and bound in Great Britain
by Bell & Bain, Glasgow

British Library Cataloguing in Publication Data

London from punk to Blair
1. Street life – England – London – History – 20th century
2. Subculture – England – London – History – 20th century
3. London (England) – Social life and customs – 20th century
4. London (England) – In literature
I. Kerr, Joe, 1958–
II. Gibson, Andrew, 1949–
942.1'085

ISBN 978 1 78023 049 8

Contents

POLITICS/ECONOMICS 95

INFRASTRUCTURE 159

INTRODUCTION TO THE SECOND EDITION

London from Blair to Boris

Joe Kerr

London from Punk to Blair was originally conceived to cover a 'a very small and very recent slice of London's long and complex history', a mere quarter-century in the life of a city that is not far short of celebrating its 2,000th birthday. This new edition follows less than ten years later, a mere blink of the eye in terms of historical perspective; so one could well imagine that my task of updating the book by means of this new Introduction would involve no more than a simple archiving of a few new architectural additions or subtractions, and the sketching in of a few significant or eye-catching events.

But that would be a profound mistake, for the London in which I write today has been convulsed by change on a seismic scale in the intervening years. This old, old city has been transformed by events so profound and permanent that they really seem to constitute a rupture with the immediate past, and are not merely the latest episodes in the relentless continuum of reconstruction and renewal that London has undergone without pause or retrenchment for at least the last two centuries. While of course the first edition of this book also embraced an era that we claimed had undergone a 'dramatic and traumatic process of change', nonetheless the narrative of London in the early years of the twenty-first century seems even more fast-paced and violently dramatic than that of the dying decades of the old millennium.

Indeed, I find it hard to imagine any other subject that would require the same degree of revision or demand as profound a challenge to received understanding than the one under review here, except perhaps if it was a new and fast-growing field of scientific research . . . or another major city, one that is as enmeshed as is London in the web of global finance and trade. For of course the cities that count are no longer merely complicit in events at a local or national level, but are themselves major players in the process of globalization, and for that reason alone, we should expect and plan for them to transform at an unprecedented rate and scale.

It is not my intention to map out a detailed historical timeline of the short span of years that concerns us here, for that would best be done for a wider compass of time and at a greater distance from the present day; instead I wish to concentrate on those particular events and activities that seem at this moment, and without the benefit of hindsight, to have forged a wholly new London that could not have been imagined or anticipated by the original contributors to this book nor by its very first readers. I have also chosen to omit those recent events that might seem to have had a major impact on London right now, but whose influence is less certain to prove of lasting consequence when reviewed in future years. Thus while two successive electoral defeats for Ken Livingstone, whose success in becoming London's first directly elected mayor was cited in the original Introduction, have signalled the retirement of the city's best-known and most enduring politician (and have also marked the rise of a politician, in the shape of his victorious opponent Boris Johnson, whose career may well carry him far beyond this city), my instinct is that political developments in this period will form little more than a footnote in future histories of London.

There have been greater forces at work on the fabric of London than those at the disposal of its elected representatives, as I hope to demonstrate by focusing on four key episodes during the brief time period under examination. I have not attempted a hierarchy of importance or significance in the narratives that follow, nor attempted to order them chronologically; instead I have grouped them thematically, not least because that's how I have come to understand them myself.

'The Winner is London' . . . the Loser was London

We start with a brace of resounding disasters, neither of them the kind of physical cataclysm – fire, flood or warfare – that periodically punctuates the history of cities, and most obviously effects dramatic physical change in them. Instead, there have been two profound episodes in the recent history of London that were both the consequence of deliberate and carefully planned and coordinated actions by closely allied groups of people; neither was remotely predicted by anyone else (although in both cases arguments have raged since about whether they should have been anticipated by those whose jobs it was to prevent such calamities).

Given that this survey represents such a minute examination of a microscopic slice of London time, it seems only fitting to start with an extremely precise set of dates; however, we pick up the story not in London but in Singapore, and with an apparent triumph rather than a tragedy. At a special meeting of the International Olympics Committee on 6 July 2005, anxious delegations from Moscow, New York, Madrid, Paris and London waited to hear which of these cities would be awarded the honour of hosting the 2012 Olympics. When at 7.30 pm local time IOC President Jacques Rogges finally announced the result, there was a slight pause as the news sank in before the delegates representing firm favourites Paris sank to their seats in disbelief, while the apparent outsiders from London commenced their joyful celebrations. London's success in winning the Olympic bid has undoubtedly had the most profound effect on London in the seven years since, and I will return to this, but the carnival mood that descended on the city was cut short dramatically and without forewarning by a devastating event merely a day later.

Towards the end of the morning rush hour on 7 July 2005, confused and contradictory news stories began rapidly to emerge about sudden major disruptions on the London Underground. Initial reports of a power surge that had left trains stranded on a number of tube lines quickly escalated into suggestions of an incident on a far larger scale and of far more sinister intent. Amid the chaos of screaming sirens and bewildered commuters spilling out onto the streets, stories quickly circulated of smoke and explosions erupting from Underground stations and of injured passengers emerging coughing, choking and bleeding from below. Suspicions of a major terrorist attack spread inexorably, preceding the eventual confirmation that three bombs had been detonated virtually simultaneously on the Underground system, and one slightly later on a bus, with the inevitable consequence of significant casualties.

London – including much of its transit system – quickly ground to a confused halt as shocked and disbelieving inhabitants attempted to digest the awful news and to assess the immediate consequences. Despite the wails of emergency vehicles speeding to the bombing sites, and from there to London's many hospitals, an eerie calm descended on the city as stranded citizens began the long walk home, chatting to each other and offering assistance as they only did at times of great crisis. Almost immediately comparisons with the fabled 'Blitz Spirit' were suggested both by those caught up in the grim event and more significantly by the news media who were by now broadcasting the unfolding drama in real time around the world (although inevitably other local reports of less than heroic behaviour gained a significantly smaller circulation: the more nuanced truth is a predictable casualty in the aftermath of such tragedies). What followed was familiar from the bombings in Madrid the previous year, and from New York in 2001; an anxious wait for news of friends and relatives, in some instances an agony that was prolonged for days as official information flows and media networks were overwhelmed by the scale of the crisis. In the case of London this was made doubly difficult on the morning of the bombings by the mobile phone network being switched off temporarily, and by the emergency information line repeatedly crashing – the first of many hints that perhaps London was not as well prepared as it might be to cope with unexpected disaster. But by nightfall on that awful day, most people had learnt whether they could expect good news or bad.

In retrospect, the final tally of 52 dead (excluding, naturally, the four suicide bombers) and several hundred seriously injured was by a wide margin less severe than might have been expected, given the potential impact of detonating four bombs on London's crowded transport network, but that was no consolation to the bereaved or to those who suffered devastating physical and emotional wounds; and anyway, it was the deadliest attack since the Second World War on a city that prides itself on its safety and on its tolerance.

The blow-by-blow narrative of what are now widely known as the '7/7' bombings has been detailed exhaustively elsewhere and need not be repeated, but it is important here to try and assess the consequences for London, both in the short term and as time has distanced us from the most notorious incident in its recent history. Naturally the implications of such a high-profile attack on an internationally important metropolis extended far beyond the city itself; the London bombings can be placed in a long trajectory of violent episodes that have punctuated the 'War on Terror', a highly emotive catch-all for the global campaign against militant Islam originally coined by President George W. Bush. Indeed, it was subsequently alleged by many opponents of the invasion of Iraq only two years earlier, which was led by the USA and the UK (or more specifically by Bush and by Blair), that military conflict inevitably leads to terrorism, in exact opposition to its intended effect: an argument that as yet remains unresolved.

The fact that the four suicide bombers (the first such ever to strike in Europe) were actually born and bred in the UK – 'home-grown' terrorists, as they were routinely referred to by press and politicians – sparked off a sustained bout of national hand-wringing and recrimination, and an intensification of the surveillance of British citizens by the domestic security services. But what of the consequences of the 7 July bombings for London itself? Most visibly, there are the physical, infrastructural interventions introduced around the city's most significant monuments, government and judicial buildings, foreign embassies and a myriad of other sensitive or vulnerable 'targets', although this was in reality an acceleration and intensification of the ongoing process of fortifying London's centres of power and wealth that marks a much longer decline in public security, and the emergence of any number of external threats. Initially the brutal tank traps and hulking great concrete barricades crudely disguised as flower tubs that were piled up alongside such symbolic sites as the Palace of Westminster and the US Embassy provided unequivocal reminders, reinforcements even, of the growing climate of fear and paranoia. But now the field of counter-terrorism design is so sophisticated and understated that sometimes it takes a cultured eye to realize that the robust but elegant bollards, the discreet metal plates in the roadway, the tasteful planters and classical balustrades that surround such sensitive sites are actually unbreachable barriers for car bombers and the like. The design of major buildings and public spaces now routinely embodies elements that are intended to prevent or at least deter potential terrorists, much to the dismay of some prominent architects who believe that this is a disproportionate response to a highly improbable threat.

However, the possible outcome that was perhaps most widely feared by Londoners, and no doubt desired by the ideologues who planned such attacks, seems not to have materialized: namely a degrading of London's proudly upheld capacity for accommodating and celebrating cultural and ethnic diversity and difference. Mayor Ken Livingstone was quick to emphasize the fact that no mosque was set alight or even had its windows broken in the immediate aftermath of the bombings, the type of unpleasant reaction that was indeed experienced in other communities elsewhere, and the fact that London's great tradition of tolerance held firm in face of this threat is highly commendable. It has to be said though that relations between the police and certain ethnic minorities have deteriorated in the years since, and the serious outbursts of rioting that caught London by surprise in the summer of 2011 were a warning sign that combustible tensions have built up in large swathes of the city where optimism and opportunity are in short supply, and that our much-cherished adherence to a diverse and heterogeneous society cannot and must not be taken for granted.

Those riots, which spontaneously erupted in Tottenham in early August following the fatal shooting by police of a local man, and over several successive nights spread to Wood Green, Hackney, Brixton, Chingford, Peckham, Enfield, Croydon, Ealing and East Ham, were characterized less by violence – as with many previous riots – than by the widespread and indiscriminate looting that quickly became the sole common cause of those involved. However, while a year later the riots are pretty fresh in London memories, and the anger and frustration that most citizens felt towards the rioters is still seething, it is highly probable that in retrospect they will seem of little consequence: although that is just the kind of speculation that historians, journalists and politicians alike can often come to regret!

'Iceland on the Thames'

It is time though to turn our attention to an equally momentous disaster that fell within our chosen decade, and one that will undoubtedly be accorded privileged status in future historical accounts of London (and that's a prediction based on cast-iron certainty), not least because this epochal episode has not just shaken London, nor merely the country or the continent, but has sent shock waves across the globe that to date show no sign of diminishing. If only it were something of which London could be proud . . .

The banking crisis that has gripped the global financial system since 2008 did not begin in London, nor does London hold primary responsibility; the blame for the whole disaster lies originally with American financial institutions and American systems of financial regulation. However, as far as the rest of the world was concerned, the City played an unparalleled role in the unfolding drama, and as the world's top financial centre it suffered greatly from the consequences. Following a string of high-profile failures, mergers or government buyouts of such internationally renowned US names as Lehman Brothers, Bear Stearns, Merrill Lynch and Citigroup, all of which took their toll on London's markets, it was the turn of their British counterparts, and a string of banks, including many of the familiar high-street names such as Northern Rock, LloydsTSB, Royal Bank of Scotland and HBOS, were either forced into hasty and ill-planned 'shotgun' mergers or propped up by massive government intervention, much to the growing indignation of taxpayers.

To understand London's role in what is undoubtedly the worst financial crisis since the Wall Street Crash of 1929, and by some estimates the worst ever, we have to look back as far as October 1986, to the event known as the 'Big Bang'; this was when the Thatcher government introduced mass deregulation of the City, alleging that overregulation and the predominance of elite 'old-boy' networks were to blame for London's perceived decline as an international financial centre, and thus liberalization of financial markets, based on free-market principles of unfettered competition, would provide an immediate stimulus to financial trade. The consequences were immediate and spectacular, and were largely responsible for restoring London's pre-eminent position as a global financial centre.

Over the quarter-century since, and through successive changes of government, the basic assumptions that 'light-touch' regulation of financial business was essential to London's status as world banking capital, and that the interests of global finance were far more important to our national economy than the traditional bedrock of manufacturing, remained unchallenged by those in power. This concentration on money over making was closely allied to the American neo-liberal economic policies pursued by President Reagan and his successors, and thus it was that New York and London were able in tandem to pursue the disastrous, high-risk and devious financial strategies that ultimately led to the current crisis. Thus while the shockwaves of the banking crisis continue to spread across the globe, and have helped to distract attention away from the City as a major player in the crisis, it would be reprehensible if its shameful and irresponsible role in sparking international financial meltdown were to be glossed over or forgotten when markets recover and the task of long-term restructuring and reregulating commences.

While such crises are always serious and damaging, it's clear in retrospect that no one predicted quite how far this one would lead, or how devastating its consequences would be. London never faced outright bankruptcy, despite the opportunistic predictions of its international competitors; for example, the German newspaper *Der Speigel* dubbed it 'Iceland on the Thames' in reference to one of those unfortunate and improvident countries that did indeed go bust. Nor was it directly hit by the woes that have more recently befallen the European single currency, although it will not avoid the fallout from across the Channel. Indeed, despite the short-term spectacle of mass redundancies in the City, and of the government austerity measures that have devastated public sector employment, London has not suffered as badly as many other financial centres around the world. But that's not really the point, for what is important to acknowledge is the share of the blame it should carry.

London over London

While at the time of writing it is far too early to predict accurately the long-term consequences for the City of London of this spectacular mess, nevertheless it comes as an extraordinary shock to stand on Waterloo Bridge and look eastwards to the Square Mile, and to realize that far from seeing any obvious evidence of financial failure – stalled construction projects, say, or greatly diminished streams of workers flooding into the financial district – the very opposite seems to hold true, and the City displays every sign of boom rather than bust. Indeed, the most dramatic visible change to London in the last decade has been the revived onslaught on its skyline.

Thus while the episodes described previously have left precious few visible signs on the city, whatever their consequences have been for its citizens, we have witnessed dramatic changes to London's physical fabric over the last ten years, and in particular the vertiginous vertical expansion of its skyline, which *en masse* are so profound that it is no understatement to claim that they have altered its appearance and character permanently and irrevocably, and in the process have divided Londoners sharply on their merits or otherwise. Writing a decade ago, I referred to controversial plans that were already in the pipeline to resume the construction of tall office towers in central London after a lapse of twenty years or more, but it was uncertain which or if any of these would actually make it through planning, despite widespread support from interested parties. In fact, within a few years work had started on a whole range of extravagantly high buildings, largely designed by internationally renowned architects, on each of which was bestowed a jolly nick-name derived from its distinctive form – the walkie-talkie, the helter-skelter, the cheesegrater, the pinnacle – as if somehow these cartoonish references to much smaller objects would reduce the crushing impact of what are ultimately no more than speculative commercial developments, however wild and eyecatching their shapes might be.

However, by the end of the decade most of these schemes were put on hold as the recession gripped the financial district, no doubt raising hopes among their opponents that common sense would prevail, and that these monuments to the folly and hubris of our bankers would be scrapped. If that was their belief then they were soon disabused of it, and with the extraordinary rapidity of modern construction techniques a new generation of City towers have already risen to completion, or are close to topping out. It is as if there had never been a banking crisis, and once again high finance is calling the shots in shaping the future of our city.

Towering over them all is the behemoth that now stands at its full height over London Bridge Station. Designed by the Italian architect Renzo Piano, underwritten by the fabulous wealth of the Qatari royal family and universally known as The Shard, its 72 habitable floors now reach to 310 metres over London, allowing it for a brief time at least the title of the tallest building in Europe. Despite Piano's confident assertion that this elegant tapering pinnacle of steel and glass will 'disappear into the sky', it shows no signs of doing so as yet, and one can only imagine the added strain that such concentrated nodes of employment and habitation will have on London's already overstretched transport infrastructure. Also, given that it is shards of glass that cause the most severe injuries in the wake of a bomb being detonated in an urban environment, it is perhaps an unfortunate name to give a building so soon after a major terrorist attack.

Ludic London

But it is not just the City that is witnessing a frenzy of construction, for to the east a different order of monument now rises out of the flat former marshland of the lower Lea Valley; the *ArcelorMittal Orbit*, as it is officially and awkwardly titled, is a sculpture on a colossal scale. Designed by sculptor Anish Kapoor and engineer/architect Cecil Balmond, at 115 metres it is the tallest work of public art in Britain, and its purpose is to mark the site of the 2012 London Olympics and to represent part of the permanent legacy of that event. In many respects it seems to serve as a highly appropriate symbol to the London Olympics given that in some eyes it encapsulates the ambition and glamour of this eagerly anticipated spectacle, while to others it stands as testimony to the huge cost and pointlessness of an extravaganza that has utterly transformed one of London's most socially and economically challenged areas, but with no obvious benefit as yet to its indigenous population.

It is almost impossible at present to speculate confidently on the long-term legacy of the Olympic Games. Battle has commenced between eager developers, interested sporting concerns and self-interested local politicians, all of whom will pick over the Olympics site to extract whatever benefit they can usefully salvage from it. One hopes at least that the future offers more than the empty and abandoned facilities that remain from the previous Beijing Games, and particularly from the Athens

Olympics before that, where the useless monuments that survive are slowly sinking into decay.

Past, Present and Future

Undoubtedly there will be those readers who will accuse me of over-egging this narrative of wholesale transformation over such a short span of London's recent past; much of the city is little changed, and many of the additions, amendments and subtractions to the physical fabric have had little impact on the mass of daily lives. But it's not just the effects wrought on London by the passage of time that make a difference to our perceptions of life here, for of course we have aged as well, and inevitably that transforms our relationship with the city around us. The span of time embraced by this book matches precisely the years that I have spent living here. The London I first knew, the one that became established in my mind as the 'authentic' London, and against which all subsequent iterations have unconsciously been compared, has gone forever, and the London of today is the authentic city of other peoples' perceptions and ambitions. I cannot help but mourn the loss of that place, and the people and objects that populated and animated it, while remaining fascinated by witnessing such a rapid and brutal pace of change and development over more than three decades.

Having lived in a place for that long, the real, tangible place that I inhabit has also been colonized by the ghosts and traces of all those other Londons I have lived in, and to be honest that leaves it feeling a little crowded and claustrophobic. Perhaps this means, that like so many previous residents of the Great Wen, I have fallen a little out of love with the place, but I'm still not tired of it yet. I sincerely hope that when I am called on to write the next new Introduction to this book a decade hence, I will still be capable of mustering the depth of passion and engagement that has tied me to this ancient city throughout the years that I have written about here.

INTRODUCTION
to the First Edition

Joe Kerr

This book is concerned with a very small and very recent slice of London's long and complex history. It covers slightly less than a third of the average lifespan of one of its 7 million-odd citizens. The longer history of London in the late twentieth century will eventually come to be written and re-written many times, each new version applying a progressively finer filter to the available data, and so eventually a sharper picture will emerge of what has endured and what has changed between the dreary, angry London of the late 1970s and the buoyant, bullish city of the early years of the twenty-first century. In retrospect, it will become evident that some of the transformations referred to here – the closure of the London Docks and the dismantling of the post-war consensus – were finite and final episodes, while others – the growth of a mature post-colonial, multicultural society and the adaptations that the city has made to accommodate the forces of globalization – will continue to shape London for decades to come.

But while the general contours of metropolitan history might eventually appear more fixed and readable, what will disappear from the future charting of the period will be a dynamic sense of what it was actually like to live in London in the dying years of the last century. It is precisely this, the vividness of everyday experience during a precisely delineated period of London time, that this book attempts to convey. The tentative and transient quality of the subject – the life of the city as it appears to us now – is reflected in its treatment here, for the fragmentary and discontinuous character of this ensemble of writing and image parallels our own limited ability to make sense of both the time in which we live and the environments that we inhabit. Cities can cease to appear confusing and chaotic only in retrospect, and this book is retrospective to a very limited extent indeed.

We can only guess at any final verdict that a future generation will pass on the London of our period, but it is nonetheless immediately obvious that over the last quarter of a century this city has undergone a dramatic and traumatic process of change. It is true that London has never stagnated at any time in its modern history, and every generation of its citizens has witnessed and experienced the consequences of continuous transformation, but there have also been crucial moments in its history when that process has greatly intensified, with the result that, within the span of only a few years, the city has fundamentally changed in character. Sometimes, rarely perhaps when compared to many other European cities, that change has been the consequence of a cataclysmic disruption to the physical fabric, such as the Great Fire of 1666 or the Blitz of 1940–41. But, more often, the catalyst for an intense phase of development has been as a result of social or economic transformations, as in the years of peacetime prosperity following the Battle of Waterloo of 1815, or, a century later, after the Armistice of 1918.

Even before the dust has settled on the recent past, it is evident that just such a phase of accelerated progress has occurred in London over the brief period of time examined here, one that is possibly unprecedented in character and scope. For since the late 1970s the metropolis has stood at the epicentre of an extraordinary political revolution that has not only transformed the social landscape of London, but has subsequently helped to shape the future of many other cities around the world. The successful counter-attack by laissez-faire Conservatism against the seemingly permanent post-war social democratic settlement, launched from Downing Street in 1979, in a few short years swept away both the ethics and the institutions of the interventionist, welfarist state. Other cities may have experienced the consequences of this resurgence of unfettered and unashamed capitalism in a more dramatic fashion – Berlin, Moscow, Shanghai – but it is hard to think of anywhere else that has been reshaped more comprehensively than London in response to this new ideological vision. On the one hand deregulation of the City's financial markets has elevated London to the elite status of World City and concentrated untold wealth in the hands of a privileged few, and on the other hand wholesale privatization has altered every aspect of daily life for its ordinary citizens, leaving in its wake social distress and inequality of the kind that the proponents of the Welfare State had once mistakenly thought it possible to eradicate.

In a city that was until very recently wholly accustomed to universal municipal supervision and regulation, it is truly remarkable just how far the power of the local state has been eroded. Over the last two decades the ownership of buses, railways and the Underground, of houses, utilities, buildings and telecommunications have all passed from State to private ownership, as has the administration of many public services and benefits, including even some school and health provision. The theory behind this policy of rolling back the influence of the State was that years of public under-investment and mis-management would be counteracted by a massive injection of private funding and the introduction of commercial discipline and acumen. However, the reality is that in most cases the promised benefits have yet to materialize, and by and large Londoners still have to pay exorbitant prices for indifferent or inadequate services. It has become a favoured cliché of critics of privatization to claim that the capital's transportation system is now no better than that of a Third World country, even though more measured experts have pointed out that most developing countries are perfectly capable of providing a much better public transport service than London, at a fraction of the cost.

Taking the longer view, it would be premature to assume that the legacy of this monetarist coup is any more permanent than that of the Welfare State that it so successfully attacked. Nonetheless, the consequent transformation of the political landscape has proved to be so comprehensive that nearly two decades of Conservative administration were only finally ended by a Labour government that could prove itself equally committed to the task of pursuing the dream of economic liberalization, while at the same time also attempting to ameliorate the worst excesses of Thatcherite reform. Thus London has entered the twenty-first century uneasily facing the prospect of further privatization – most controversially the entire Underground system – but it is also armed with a new mayor and a new plan for its future. Neither of the last two would be considered particularly unusual events in the life of a major city were it not for the fact that London, at the start of the new millennium, lacked any form of municipal government, and consequently any means for planning on a city-wide basis.

So extraordinary is it to think that London was until recently the only great city in the Western world without any significant democratic supervision that it is also worth remembering that London had previously enjoyed a long and successful tradition of effective and independent local government. The very first elected city-wide authority, the London County Council (LCC), was created in 1889 and almost immediately faced calls for its abolition from suspicious politicians, but remained in control of the capital until it was replaced in 1965 with the Greater London Council (GLC), whose much larger geographical area reflected the city's growing influence over the surrounding region. London's unique influence on the political and economic life of the country as a whole meant that its municipal government, ruling from County Hall on the south bank of the Thames, was always capable of mounting a challenge to the authority of central government administered from the Palace of Westminster on the opposite side of the river, much as the merchants and guildsmen who ruled the medieval walled City had traditionally maintained a healthy independence from the power of the Crown at Westminster. Indeed, the old Greater London Council eventually proved such an effective obstacle to the ambitions of the Thatcher Government that they simply abolished it in 1986, leaving the city effectively defenceless against the free-for-all, laissez-faire commercial exploitation unleashed on it in the same decade.

When Tony Blair's new government, elected to power in 1997, legislated for a new London-wide municipal authority, it took great care to create a body that had significantly less control over the lives of its electorate than the old GLC, and a greatly diminished ability to defy central government. Nonetheless, so ineptly did the Government handle the process – in particular by attempting to deny Londoners the chance to vote for a universally popular left-wing candidate who had led the fight against the abolition of the former GLC – that when the new Greater London Authority (GLA) assumed control of the capital in July 2000, it was already set on a collision course with Westminster. Furthermore, the Government's attempts to influence the election came to naught when the candidate they had so vigorously opposed successfully stood as an independent. Consequently, the new American-style executive mayor Ken Livingstone has been nearly as painful a thorn in the side of the Blair administration as the former leader of the GLC, the same Ken Livingstone, had been for Thatcher's Government nearly two decades ago.

While he remains a controversial figure, the politician once christened 'Red Ken' by a hostile Tory press speaks with authority about the city that he has twice been elected to serve, and it would be unwise to dismiss his views on it. Thus whatever else his citizens might think of him, they would find it well nigh impossible to disagree with the conclusion he presented in his preamble to the recent *Draft London Plan*, that London is simultaneously a grand and a ghastly city, both the beneficiary and the victim of its own success. This is of course hardly an original thought, and indeed countless critics across five centuries or more have delivered more or less the same verdict on London, and one could certainly speculate that Livingstone himself would have made a similar diagnosis when he was previously in office, albeit delivered in slightly more inflammatory prose. In that respect at least London remains unchanged across the period. But in every other respect imaginable the city feels very different indeed, and anyone who has lived through the fourteen years between the demise of the Greater London Council and the creation of the Greater London Authority would not consider this period to have been an insignificant hiatus.

However, merely acknowledging that significant change has taken place is not sufficient, and we must also attempt to measure and to analyse that change. The truth is that neither the constant tinkering with the systems of local democracy, nor the ramifications of wider political change, can on their own account for the absolute certainty that London is now a profoundly different city to inhabit than it was a quarter of a century ago. Ultimately it is material rather than ideological change that shapes the experience of urban life. The challenge then is to convey convincingly a sense of the wholesale physical transformations that have also taken place between then and now.

To attempt this we could do worse than to borrow a brilliant device from one of the most evocative historical accounts ever written of the city. In Sir John Summerson's Georgian London of 1945, written as the bombs rained down on its subject, the author took inspiration from the established scientific technique of time-lapse photography and then transposed it to the relatively new perspective offered by aerial reconnaissance, to convey vividly the scale of London's growth and development during that long historical epoch:

> I ask you to imagine yourself suspended a mile above London; and to imagine yourself staying up there for a period of time proportional to two centuries, with the years speeding past at one a second. The spectacle below you proceeds like those nature films which accelerate into immodest realism the slow drama of plant life. The life of a city, condensed so, would be dramatic.

Dramatic indeed. While the readers of this book need only to imagine themselves suspended above London for a comparatively brief period of time, the conceit will serve equally well to demonstrate the wholesale changes wrought in London's fabric in the last 25 years. Imagine then viewing the metropolis of the late 1970s from a similar height. A vast, shapeless mess of a city sprawls outwards almost to the horizon from the same meandering curves of the Thames that Summerson's Georgians would have looked down on – although since the nineteenth century the river has been rigidly confined and embanked as it passes through the centre of London. Further east the crowded riparian strip has long been ruptured by the great artificial docks carved out of the poorest quarters of the city, although now only a very few large, rusting ships are unloading there, in dramatic contrast to the forest of wooden masts that had huddled into the cramped confines of the Pool of London two centuries earlier.

As we move forward a couple of years, the freight ships disappear altogether from the city-bound reaches of the river, which is now straddled by an imposing flood barrier, while newer, gargantuan container ships dock 20 miles or so downstream at Tilbury. At an equivalent distance from the city's centre, and connected to it by the relatively new but already overcrowded motorway network, dramatic expansion is visible around the major airports of Heathrow to the west and Gatwick to the south, and later also at Stansted to the north-east.

While the overall shape of London remains largely unchanged – constricted for the first time in its modern history by the post-war imposition of the Green Belt – one can see a vast engineering project in hand some distance beyond the outer perimeter of inter-war suburban development. The M25, or London Orbital Motorway to give it its proper name, which had been dreamed of since the early years of the twentieth century to divert traffic away from London, is finally completed in 1986. However, it soon becomes clear that the capital's older roads remain as clogged as ever, despite the removal and relocation from central London of its docks, breweries and wholesale markets.

The M25 itself quickly acquires an unenviable reputation for congestion and delays, despite a hastily planned widening programme. Regardless of its notorious overcrowding, the new outer ring road soon starts to attract its own specialized forms of development, most visibly two enormous shopping malls built close to either end of the motorway's spectacular bridge downriver at Dartford. Ironically, rather than keeping cars out of central London, the M25 is drawing business and retail trade away from the capital. By the time we draw close to the present day, every major intersection on the M25 is ringed with a variety of vast, windowless distribution sheds, gleaming lorry parks, generic commercial hotels, campus office developments set in neatly manicured landscapes, and highly priced luxury housing complexes, each a small but cumulatively significant encroachment on the old Green Belt. From this distance at least, the many new fringe developments surrounding

London seem indistinguishable from the American conurbations that inspired them, a stark demonstration of the homogenizing effects of globalization.

It would be wholly misleading, however, to conclude from this that London as a whole has been transformed into anything remotely resembling an imitation Houston or St Louis, for the truth is that the London that most people know today is still markedly different in character from any other city anywhere else. Here the limitations of adapting Summerson's method to our purpose and our times become apparent, because London's significant growth is no longer exclusively outwards, but upwards and even downwards as well, making it difficult to read from the air alone. Instead, we might usefully update his visual device by thinking in terms of a cross-section across the city, cutting above and below ground level to reveal the true scale of redevelopment that has taken place across the metropolis.

If we were once again to imagine the London of 1977 from this new perspective, we would be witnessing the unmistakable evidence of a recent building boom, one that has transformed the appearance of the city in an unprecedented manner. For we see silhouetted against the skyline a considerable number of recently completed tall buildings, predominantly housing blocks in residential areas and commercial towers in the centre, and also the tower cranes and skeletal structures that mark the location of yet more high-rise construction. As an indication of how rapidly this wave of redevelopment has altered the face of London, St Paul's Cathedral was still the tallest building in the capital as recently as 1958, but less than 20 years later at least a dozen towers have risen higher. As our period begins, the NatWest Tower in the City is approaching its final height of 183 metres, leaving it a full 72 metres higher than Wren's masterpiece. But just as Britain's tallest tower nears final completion in 1981, the economic cycle makes its periodic shift from boom to bust, ensuring that it is actually the last tall tower of its generation, and to this day it remains the highest structure to rise from the densely packed confines of the City.

It is no surprise, though, that within a few years a new construction frenzy has gripped the Square Mile, spurred on by financial deregulation in 1986. Popularly known as 'Big Bang', this is the most important change to the workings of London's money markets in its entire history. What the city now requires are large, open, highly serviced dealing floors, and the tall slender towers of the previous generation are superseded by massively broad, squat office complexes, increasingly built over railway lines and other large undeveloped areas. Something approaching 20 per cent of the City is rebuilt during the 1980s, before recession once again brings new construction to a halt. This time, however, it is not the traditional business district within the square mile of the former city walls that is worst hit by the economic downturn. For during the same decade a new rival has appeared to challenge the City's commercial dominance.

If we shift our viewpoint a few miles further eastwards, we can see among the abandoned and derelict remains of London's former docks the first results of an extraordinary economic experiment taking shape. In 1981 the new Conservative Government decided to remove eight and half square miles of the former docklands area from local planning control and place it under the supervision of the London Docklands Development Corporation, whose brief was simply to enable the rapid regeneration of the area. Within a few years huge swathes of derelict land have been brought back into profitable use, covered not with the low-rent public housing and small businesses called for by local communities, but in the main with exclusive private housing developments and office complexes. At its heart stands the 35-hectare Canary Wharf development on the Isle of Dogs, whose 50-storey central office tower becomes briefly the tallest inhabited structure in Europe at 244 metres when completed in 1991. Initially conceived by its Canadian developers as a new financial centre for London, the economic downturn in the late 1980s bankrupts the scheme. The initial failure of this hugely ambitious development establishes it as a popular symbol of the folly of free-enterprise planning, but it soon recovers and has continued to expand to the present day.

The ultimate success of Docklands depends on the completion of the Jubilee Line, London's first new Underground railway for nearly 30 years, opened just in time to participate in the Millennium celebrations. Built to the designs of a string of Britain's most famous architects, although using the outmoded technology of the existing system, it now provides a vital link between the old city and its new commercial enclave. London continues to develop beneath the ground with a new railway currently under construction on a route beneath north and east London as the last link in the new high-speed rail link between St Pancras Station and the Channel Tunnel. Initial work has also begun on the Crossrail project, which will enable railway trains to cross between west and east beneath the capital. Like most major London initiatives, however, this has been dogged by years of uncertainty and delays. Even today it is still unclear whether it will actually progress further, and the recent pronouncement by a Government minister that 'there has been no decision not to proceed' has hardly helped to clarify matters.

From our imaginary viewpoint we can see the pace of change continuing to quicken as we near the present day. The advent of the new millennium has prompted a rash of new cultural developments along the river, including the conversion of the former Bankside Power Station opposite St Paul's into the new Tate Modern gallery, while upriver the London Eye, at 135 metres the world's largest revolving passenger wheel, has made an idiosyncratic but highly popular addition to the skyline.

The future character and direction of London development remain a subject of controversy. While it is likely that the further regeneration of the Docklands area will continue unabated, London is now faced for the first time since the start of this period with a range of proposals to build more tall towers within the central area. At the time of writing a grand new tower in the heart of the City (popularly known as the 'gherkin' on account of its startling bulbous form) is nearing completion, and has already made a substantial impact on the London skyline. But this and other schemes yet unbuilt pale in comparison with the most spectacular and thus controversial proposal for a new tower adjacent to London Bridge Station, designed in the form of a soaring shard of glass: rising to 310 metres, it would be the most elegant skyscraper in London, and the tallest building in the whole of Europe. Firmly supported by the Mayor and most of the architectural establishment, but vehemently opposed by many conservation and environmental groups, the outcome of its forthcoming planning enquiry will undoubtedly have a profound impact on the nature and scale of future proposals for the capital.

There is no question, then, that the physical appearance of London has been transformed by the political and economic convulsions of the last 25 years. Indeed, the pace of redevelopment seems to be accelerating, driven by the demands of the City and the ambitions of City Hall alike. However, it will be the task of other historians in the future to gauge the full extent of their efforts. We in the meantime are presented with a more immediate challenge, for in truth our privileged vantage point has merely indicated the general contours of change, and has placed us at too great a distance to focus on the individual lives of any of London's multitude of citizens. Yet, ultimately, it is the minuscule shifts and adjustments in daily experience that should matter most to us. In reality it is the view from the pavement rather than from far above it that is most revealing about the ways in which the city is actually changing.

So let us once again attempt to imagine the London of 1977, this time not from the vantage of an abstract, disembodied viewpoint, but instead from an actual and precise location within the city. To do this we must relinquish the fiction of a detached, dispassionate view of the whole city, the view of politicians, planners and financiers. So let us take a walk through the heart of the West End, in the early summer of 1977. Walking up Charing Cross Road from Leicester Square Station some time after dusk, we pass buildings that have changed very little in the previous century, save for the dense blanket of grime that has over time subdued the intended variety of brick, stone and cement into a homogenous, dull grey. The sombre and dilapidated sense of a post-war city still pervades here, except where the subsequent settlement of a thriving Chinese community adds a little colour and bustle to the streets leading off to the West. The pavements quickly empty of people as the daytime inhabitants and evening theatregoers are turned out of pubs and restaurants and head away from the city centre. Long before midnight the city is virtually deserted, until we cross Cambridge Circus and bear left into Soho.

Here the shabby activities of the sex trade, half-seen through discreet, red-lit doorways obscured by a thin strip of ribbons that are occasionally parted by a furtive passer-by, and vaguely heard through the hurried exchanges of flesh or drugs in the entrances to dark alleys, ensure that this part of London never fully sleeps. Otherwise, only a few small knots of punks hurriedly pass by, keeping to the shadows and nervously scanning at each street corner for ambushes by the gangs of patriotic Teddy boys who have come up west from East Ham or Homerton to rid the streets of perverts and misfits. Depending on which night of the week, these groups might be heading up to Wardour Street or to Dean Street, in search of the few small clubs that support or at least tolerate their aggressively anti-social music and clothes.

Tonight, though, it is Covent Garden, and following this tatty tribe of cultural outcasts as they head away from the eerie half-life of Soho, past the squatted mansion blocks on Shaftesbury Avenue, we enter a dark and wholly lifeless netherworld of abandoned warehouses and derelict market halls shuttered away behind temporary hoardings. Suddenly a door opens and shuts at the foot of murky basement stairs, the brief escape of noise, light and the mingled fumes of smoke and sweat, betraying the semi-secret gathering place for these social refuseniks. Rather than follow them down, we carry on to explore the uncanny landscape that rises up out of the orange-tinted gloom. For here, at the heart of this great capital city, we are surrounded by a dead zone, a great swathe of the West End that lies empty and useless since the closure of London's principal wholesale market for fruit, vegetables and flowers. Facing an uncertain future at the hands of municipal planners and commercial developers, for the time being at least it provides a nocturnal shelter for London's shifting subcultures.

Similar strange pockets of silence and stillness,the spaces vacated by unwanted trades and industries, still abound in central London, contributing to the general atmosphere of slow decline that pervades so much of the metropolis. The air of hopelessness that seems to have fallen over the whole city is exacerbated by the daily evidence of growing disaffection, from the angry posturing and mutual antipathy of suburban punks, East End bovver boys, black youth from Brixton and Ladbroke Grove, and the police Special Patrol Groups, to the pickets' braziers outside fire stations and bus garages and the mounting piles of rubbish at the side of the street that mark the increasing militancy of public service workers fighting for their livelihoods. The mounting frustration and alienation that fuel such demonstrations of discontent culminates the following year in the notorious 'winter of discontent', so-called for the widespread industrial unrest that marks the final months of the failed Labour Government of James Callaghan. As a controversial advertising campaign announces in the spring of 1979 from billboards around the city, 'Labour Isn't Working', and in May of that year Margaret Thatcher is triumphant in the first of four consecutive election victories that will keep the Conservatives in power for the next eighteen years. All of London knows that radical change is on the way, but not one of its seven million inhabitants could predict the extent to which their city, and their daily lives within it, will be transformed over the next two decades.

As its older industries decline, and its financial markets grow ever more powerful, there is a sharp divergence in the fortunes of its citizens. Increasing unemployment combined with the 'rolling back' of state regulation and support, and exacerbated by the inexorable rise in the cost of living in the city, intensify the economic inequality and social stratification that had once appeared to be permanently diminishing. It also creates two wholly incompatible perceptions of the future of the city, one convinced that London has had its day and is now sinking into irreversible decline, the other equally certain that it has successfully cemented its place as a centre of the new world economy. As London leaves the twentieth century, however, it is this latter view that has prevailed, and any contemporary visitor to the city can hardly fail to be impressed by its sheer self-confidence, despite the daily evidence that its overburdened infrastructure is close to collapse, and the constant proof provided by every transaction that this is now arguably the most expensive city in the world.

Let us take that same walk again through London in the spring of 2003. An immediate impression is that everything is as it was, yet everything has changed. We find little difficulties in retracing our steps, for in this part of the West End the street patterns remain familiar, as indeed do many of the buildings that line them. But we can now no longer stroll uninterrupted along the pavement, for even at the same late hour there are throngs of people everywhere; emerging in droves from the Underground station and fighting their way into the glitzy nightclub directly beside it, or doubling back to join the crowds of revellers gathering in Leicester Square; packing the pavement cafés and bars that form an almost continuous ribbon alongside the street; queueing in the brightly lit souvenir shops, convenience stores and fast-food restaurants that barely close at this time of year; or even browsing (or as likely drinking coffee) in the nearby branch of an American bookshop chain that is only just thinking of shutting up after twelve hours or more of continuous trading. Indeed Soho and its environs are now busier at this time of night than during the earlier evening rush hour, as the city effortlessly swings from work to leisure. London is now routinely described as a 24-hour city, caught up in an unceasing cycle of consumption.

Remarkably, London has shed its drabness; the dinginess and dirt that once coated its every surface have been scraped away from its older structures, or else they have been replaced with sleek, hard facades of steel and glass. Only in the darkest piss-smelling doorway or sunless back alley do traces of its past sordidness linger.

As we push through the tourists emerging from the musical that has played at the Palace Theatre on Cambridge Circus for the past nineteen years, we turn up to Old Compton Street, and are abruptly confronted with the most compelling evidence of London's cultural transformation. In place of the shabby shops and seedy cafés, and the furtive life that once accumulated around them, the street is now lit up like a fairground with a dense throng to match that spills off either pavement and merges in the middle of the road. Brushing through the crowd – which is no easier than swimming upstream, as we avoid the odd moped or cycle rickshaw – we pass gawping, but slightly ill-at-ease tourists, who are self-consciously rubbing shoulders with large, loose groups of predominantly young men clearly dressed for display. As any tourist guide will explain to you, Old Compton Street is London's premier 'gay quarter', a community self-defined by its sexuality that has supplanted a former community devoted to sex as a commodity. Fetish clothing shops abound here, but they are wholly legal operations selling to customers who don't hide their faces as they enter. The hardcore sex trade has not been eradicated from Soho, nor probably ever will be, despite the best efforts of Westminster City Council to homogenize the West End into one vast, trouble-free tourist zone, but you have to penetrate a little further into the dense tangle of streets and alleyways if you desire to purchase something that the law does not permit.

Escaping this diverse gathering that has so self-confidently assumed ownership of its own patch of the city, we head eastwards towards Covent Garden, temporarily diverting into the gutter to skirt the boisterous overspill from a hot, noisy bar. We weave through the traffic across Seven Dials, once the heart of Victorian London's most notorious rookery, but now just a brief spatial interruption in a jostling procession of shops and restaurants that sweeps us onwards towards the heart of the old market district. The warehouses and market halls have survived largely intact, but any trace of their temporary abandonment has been eradicated by the expensive boutiques, skateboard shops, wholefood stores, ethnic restaurants, exclusive delicatessens and handcraft stalls that have since made their (often temporary) home in this concentrated zone of consumption. Covent Garden exemplifies the new 'heritage' London in which the familiar local landscapes have been subtly reconfigured to accommodate the new imperatives of global capitalism. It has gone the way of all those many dark and empty places that had once lingered on in the midst of London's principal commercial enclaves. The successive redevelopment booms that have swept across the city in the last two decades have gradually filled in all these blanks on the property map. The last of them, the great sprawling remnants of the railway industry surrounding King's Cross and St Pancras stations, is now finally succumbing to the onslaught of the developers, as the tell-tale forest of tower cranes that has sprouted there visibly reminds us. Within a few years high-speed trains from Paris and Brussels will be arriving at the new terminus now under construction behind its Victorian predecessors, and passengers will disgorge into the new Underground station being built in front of them. As the old industrial landscape is stripped away, the prostitutes and drug dealers that have blighted the area for years will be displaced to other less favoured London neighbourhoods. But as the relentless cleansing of the capital continues apace, it is becoming increasingly difficult to imagine where its black economy, and its poorer populations, will settle. Amidst the apparent evidence of increasing diversity and heterogeneity, the truth is that contemporary London is simultaneously moving towards greater uniformity and homogeneity.

Summerson famously wrote that his account of an older London was a 'story made up of topography, biography and architecture, and I shall try and weave these three together'. The essays that follow on the city's recent past offer both more and less than his elegant model. On the one hand they embrace a far wider range of perspectives and experiences than he would have thought possible or desirable, as befits a portrait of a more complex and intriguing era of metropolitan history. But on the other hand they are not accompanied by a comparable ambition to stitch these various stories together into a single, inclusive narrative, and nor should they be. London can no longer be usefully defined as a single entity even on a map, for surely Heathrow, Tilbury and the South Mimms junction of the M25 and M1 are all legitimately part of the city they serve, despite falling outside its administrative boundaries. We cannot now claim to know London, and to imagine we could would be to miss the point, for otherwise what would impel us to endlessly explore and re-explore a place that has in reality grown beyond our understanding?

ETHNICITY / IDENTITY

In a speech delivered in March 2001, the then Labour Foreign Secretary, Robin Cook, tackled the highly contentious issue of Britishness, a subject he acknowledged was normally only broached by right-wing politicians bemoaning the demise of traditional ideas of national identity. In the course of mounting a robust defence of multiculturalism, he portrayed London's ethnic diversity in terms that the majority of its citizens would recognize:

> Today's London is a perfect hub of the globe. It is home to over 30 ethnic communities of at least 10,000 residents each. In this city tonight, over 300 languages will be spoken by families over their evening meal at home. This pluralism is not a burden we must reluctantly accept. It is an immense asset that contributes to the cultural and economic vitality of our nation.

His views were widely reported in the British press, but this was not because of the strength of his carefully worded and cogent analysis of the relationship between ethnicity and identity. Rather it was the crude analogy he employed to illustrate his argument – 'Chicken Tikka Massala is now a true British national dish' – that proved a godsend to tabloid hacks and opposition politicians alike. This was particularly unfortunate because it simply served to reinforce the pervasive but banal assumption that an enriched national cuisine is the primary benefit to be derived from a successful multicultural society. This may be a common misunderstanding, but it's a damaging one, because it perceives the most valuable contribution that immigrant communities make to their new host culture to be an essentially passive one: their role is simply to cook the exotic dishes which the rest of us can then happily consume. With 'authentic' ingredients and even pre-cooked Thai, Chinese and Indian meals now readily available in the local supermarket, even that role is potentially redundant, and so to measure the successful assimilation of such communities simply in terms of their influence on popular taste sayslittle for their long-term prospects.

The idea of *building* a multicultural society needs to be taken a little more literally, for the point is that the culture of contemporary London really is being constructed collectively. Only the most die-hard Little

Englander could fail to acknowledge the active contribution made by London's immigrant communities to its intellectual and cultural life in fields as diverse as politics, painting, music, architecture, literature, journalism . . . Given this, it would seem perverse to see cultural diversity in any but the most positive light.

As Cook rightly argued, a modern notion of national identity cannot be based on race and ethnicity alone, but must embrace shared ideals and aspirations. London cannot yet claim to offer that to all of its citizens, irrespective of cultural or ethnic origin. While fewer individuals may experience open and blatant discrimination on the grounds of ethnicity than they might have done a quarter of a century ago, none the less the contemporary experience of multicultural society for some people still includes having excrement and burning rags anonymously pushed through the letterbox, or suffering muted hostility from public officials and publicans. Furthermore, the increasing disparity between wealth and poverty in London threatens to create a dispossessed and alienated underclass that will inevitably draw some of its numbers from immigrant communities who have struggled to establish themselves economically, thus helping to fuel tensions between those communities and the forces of authority.

Nevertheless it is possible to believe that London will build a genuinely equal and tolerant society, and one that can continue to sustain its recent cultural renaissance. It is without doubt the diversity of its population that has helped London to resist the creeping homogenization that is an inevitable by-product of a globalized economy. Suspicion of multiculturalism is still an easy card for politicians to play, as the growing furore over current immigration policy starkly illustrates. Resisting such cheap demagoguery is a necessity and a duty for us all, not as a selfless act on behalf of other less fortunate citizens, but as a self-interested affirmation of ownership of a common culture that we all both draw from and enrich.

LONDON AND LANGUAGE

Katie Wales

IN THE 1970S, Doncaster and District Development Council produced a caricature of Londoners' perceptions of the North, out of a wry realization that firms were reluctant to relocate from the capital. Potters Bar, the northern limit of the Greater London Council established in 1963, was the 'End of Civilization' (and Manchester certainly the 'End of Railways'). 'North of Potters Bar' may have entered the language of Londoners before the comparable satirical phrase 'North of Watford' (first recorded by the *Oxford English Dictionary* in 1973), Watford marking the last stop northwards on the Metropolitan Underground line; but both phrases testify to the common image of London as being the only significant city in cultural, social, political and economic terms. Indeed, as the 1970s turned to the 1980s, such satirical references stung sharply, as Conservative Government policies exacerbated the so-called North–South Divide, another popular phrase, the 'South' largely synonymous with the Metropolis. From 1981 to 1989 the phrase recurs frequently in headlines and research papers from such groups as the Town and Country Planning Association and Centre for Economic Policy, as London far outpaced other cities in the price of housing and the expansion of employment.

London's status as the national 'centre of gravity' for business, finance, media, politics and also fashion is reflected in the trendy vocabulary that circulated in the City and Westminster in particular. Although the Big Bang rocked the City in 1986, and Black Monday in 1987, this was a period of flaunted consumption, following the push for an 'enterprise culture' from Margaret Thatcher the 'leaderene' (a term coined by Norman St John Stevas in 1980, and much used by *Private Eye*). There were certainly plenty of successful 'young urban professionals' (yuppies) and 'dual income no kids' (dinkies) with 'loadsa money' in the mid- to late 1980s. They tended to live in the Tower Bridge area, at the same time that Docklands and the Charing Cross area were being subjected to 'yuppification'.

As befitting the capital of the country and the seat of government and the monarchy, the political and cultural prestige of London has been assured since late medieval times. So too has its linguistic prestige, at least in terms of the speech and usage of the court and aristocracy. But what is particularly interesting about the last quarter of the twentieth century and the early twenty-first is the way in which that traditional prestige has shifted and also diversified, at the same time as the rich variety of London's dialects and even languages has come more and more to be recognized and respected.

The 'Monarch's English', currently the 'Queen's English', has been a model of usage with the highest social status since the Tudor period. But in the last 25 years or so, the Queen's own pronunciations and even those of her children have come increasingly to be perceived as 'old-fashioned' or 'affected' and are no longer influential. Indeed, in the 1990s, particularly following the Queen's own public statement that 1992 had been an 'annus horribilis', with the collapse of the marriages of Charles and Andrew and the fire at Windsor Castle, there was an increase in the media both of speculation on the 'fall' of the 'House of Windsor' and also of satirical representation of the speech of the elder royals. The distinctive vowels in particular were easy targets for TV's *Spitting Image*: 'hice' for house; 'hellay' for hello; 'tar' for tower; and the use of the pronoun 'one' for 'I' in tabloid headlines: NOW ONE IS ONE (when Princess Anne was divorced); ONE'S WON (when the Queen's horse won the Derby in 1993); ONE'S BUM YEAR (1992).

Media awareness of the conservative nature of the speech of the aristocracy was heightened in the early 1980s by the 'Princess Diana effect', and what was dubbed as the 'Sloane Ranger' phenomenon. Here social class met urban space as the young upper and upper-middle classes like Diana herself tended to settle as singletons in the 'muesli belt' round Sloane Square on the border of Belgravia and Chelsea, but also down the King's Road into Fulham and Wandsworth ('Fergie's pre-marital territory). 'Sloanies' became cultural icons in the capital for a time, marked by dress, cultural pursuits and language. Words were either drawled ('jah' for yes; 'she's rairly rairly [really] nice'), or shortened ('Rods' for Harrods; 'Fred's' for Fortnum and Mason's). Hyperbole was rife (frightfully, ghastly, appalling), but there were also signs of an influence from the more demotic speech of the capital, at the other end of the King's Road. Word-final glottal stops were noted in the speech of both Diana and

Prince Edward ('There's a lot of it about'); and vocoids for 'l' as in 'miu(l)k', milk; and words like 'bog' (lavatory) and 'yonks' (a long time).

To many middle-class Londoners, however, the speech of the Sloane Rangers was most probably deemed as 'marked' or 'affected' as the Queen's, so closely identified was it with a particular social group: the 'rah-rah' accent, as it was dubbed in 1982. Educated Londoners tended for most of the twentieth century to gravitate in their pronunciation towards what is most popularly known as 'BBC English', or, more technically, 'Received Pronunciation' (RP). This is not strictly a regional variety, since it is typically spoken in public schools and certain elite professions throughout the UK and is used as a model for foreign learners of English, but nonetheless it is popularly perceived as being spoken most regularly in London and the Home Counties, and as being broadcast world-wide from Bush House in The Strand and from Great Portland Street. For those living north of Birmingham, it is certainly marked by two 'Southern' vowels, the long 'a' in words like 'bath' and 'grass' and the centralized 'u' in words like 'butter'.

Londoners themselves, however, recognize subtler distinctions, and in the past twenty years RP has itself come to be seen as a 'marked' variety socially. So much so that it is probably best to see 'London English' or 'Englishes' in terms of a continuum, and roughly corresponding to different areas of London as well as socio-economic groups. Just as RP can be distinguished from the conservative variety of the aristocracy and the once 'trendy' Sloane-speak, so there is a London or South-East 'regional standard', itself increasingly influenced by the well-established city variety traditionally known as Cockney. So much so that this blended or blurred variety was called 'Estuary English' in 1984, a term that rapidly caught the media imagination, reflecting the social and geographical fact that many aspiring and nouveau-riche East-Enders moved out to Essex and north Kent suburbs along the Thames Estuary.

Despite derogatory terms like 'Essex Man' and 'Essex Girl' at the beginning of the 1990s to describe the beneficiaries of Thatcherite entrepreneurship, it is noteworthy that their linguistic habits have made their mark on general London English: the increased use of final and also medial glottal stops ('Ga[t]wick'); l-vocalization as in 'Muswe(ll) Hi(ll)'; and pronunciations like 'two(w)' and 'Estchery' (Estuary), and 'real' and 'reel' as homophones; and even initial h-dropping as in ''Arry'. There are also characteristics of grammar and vocabulary: 'you know what I mean?', 'cheers', 'mate', 'innit', 'right?'. Estuary English became popularly associated with TV and 'mee-jah' presenters and personalities such as Ben

Elton, Paul Merton, Janet Street-Porter and Harry Enfield, and politicians as ideologically opposed as Norman Tebbit and Ken Livingstone. If Margaret Thatcher spoke with the voice of the Establishment, John Major represented the 'new' London voice. Not that the metropolitan press always liked what was seen as the 'Cockneyfication' of London English, a symbol of its 'degeneration'. But nor did they like those personalities who seemed to adopt Estuary English as a trendy accessory: Emma Thompson (1993) and Mick Jagger (1994); and notably the prime minister Tony Blair on the Des O'Connor Show in 1998. 'Islington Person' may have replaced 'Essex Man' following the General Election of 1997 but the latter's linguistic influence persists.

What is generally very interesting to observe is how Cockney, characteristically and historically a localized (East End) working-class variety and traditionally much stigmatized, has become more and more influential on the strata of language perceived as socially more superior, as the cultural vogue for the 'downmarket' rather than the 'upmarket', for the demotic and the 'streetwise', has generally intensified since the 1980s. Indeed, it is a matter of dispute amongst linguists whether working-class London English generally, or 'popular London English' as it is sometimes called, is having an effect on sound changes beyond the capital, notably with t-glottalling and also th-fronting: words such as 'thrush' and 'feather' pronounced 'frush' and 'fevver', and particularly in the speech of young people, especially adolescent males. It is generally certainly the case, however, that Cockney is consistently rated more highly in attitudinal surveys of accents in terms of 'friendliness' than BBC English, if lower than BBC English (the highest of all) in terms of 'intelligence': indeed, lowest of all English accents for this rating. Associations of bigotry and foul language from your TV-sitcom, Alf Garnett-figure of the 1960s have gradually been replaced by those more endearing and communalist from the wiles of your Arthur Daley type based on Thames TV's *Minder* ('[h]er indoors' entered the language in 1979), and from your average domestic wrangles of Walford Square's *EastEnders*. Cockney is unusual amongst London Englishes, however, in being very marked not only in terms of its typical pronunciations ('fice' for 'face', 'abaht' for 'about') and general nasalization, but also in its grammar, which is largely non-standard and therefore identified with being 'uneducated'. There is, for instance, the use of double negatives ('I aint got no money'); relative 'what' ('the boy what's coming over') and demonstrative use of 'them' ('them apples').

Traditionally, the most obvious linguistic marker of the Cockney as an icon of London has been 'rhyming slang', often nowadays regarded by the public at large as being outmoded and as obsolescent even as the Pearly kings and queens. Its origins are obscure, but seem deeply embedded in the street-trading and music-hall entertainment of the nineteenth and early twentieth centuries. Certainly phrases like 'dog and bone' for 'phone', and 'frog and toad' for 'road' seem part of a Cockney caricature, but many phrases entered London English more widely and are still heard and used in colloquial speech from Stanmore to Staines: 'skin and blister' for 'sister', and 'currant bun' for 'sun'. The City of London police accuse those arrested of telling 'porkies' ('pork pies' = lies); Fleet Street journalists are 'sniffers' ('sniffers and snorters' = reporters). Television series like Steptoe and Son in the 1970s helped to disseminate phrases like 'Brahms and Liszt' (= pissed) more widely, but rhyming slang is part of the fabric of the language itself ('raspberry [tart]' = fart), and not all of it may be due to Cockney influence.

The essential creativity of rhyming slang has not gone unappreciated in the City, however, and new terms have been coined in recent years amongst the young trendsetters: for example, 'George Michael' for cycle, 'Glen Hoddle' for doddle and 'Bill and Ben' for yen. In 2001 Stella McCartney launched a range of clothes decorated by rhyming slang slogans such as 'raspberry ripple' (nipple). Since one theory has it that Cockney rhyming slang may have originated in the London underworld, it is interesting to note that an extremely creative source of rhyming slang in the 1980s and '90s was drug use amongst the middle- and upper-class London youth, with a prominent witty exploitation of the names of sporting, media and political personalities: 'Niki Lauda' (powder), 'Damon Hill / Jimmy Hill / Pebble Mill' (pill), 'Beryl [Reid]' (weed), 'Janet Street-Porter' (quarter [ounce]), 'Gary Abletts' (tablets), 'John Selwyn [Gummer]' (bummer). 'Vera Lynn', in traditional usage denoting 'gin', was reassigned to 'skin' (cigarette paper), and 'King Lear', once 'queer', to 'gear'.

Thus far London presents itself in this period in linguistic terms as a multi-dimensional physical space, where different voices and argots jostle with each other in different kinds of London 'Englishes' according to class, age, profession and postcode. But as with other great cosmopolitan cities of the world, the picture is complicated by the necessity to map onto this grid the languages of the non-Anglo-Saxon peoples and their descendants who have made London their home, particularly since the late 1940s and early 1950s. Current estimates of the number of languages spoken in London range from 170 to 700. About 25 per cent of schoolchildren speak something other than English. In 1980 the educationists Rosen and Burgess identified 55 languages and 24 'overseas dialects' of English as being spoken by schoolchildren in the Inner London Education Authority area. One in 60 pupils were plurilingual, speaking two or more languages as well as English. The Sikhs and Hindus from the Punjab tended to settle in Southall, the Guyanese in Tottenham, the Cypriots in Camden Town and the Bengalis from East Pakistan in Spitalfields.

Immigration from the West Indies in particular has made the linguistic picture more complex, and indeed the concept of a 'London Black English' is best seen in terms of a 'continuum', as with 'London English' above, and these continua themselves interlocking. Jamaican immigrants tended to settle after the Second World War south of the Thames in Brixton and Stockwell, the Trinidadians and Barbadians to the west in Notting Hill, so maintaining their differences in dialect and culture to some extent in their new locations. Second-generation non-whites went to schools where London English was the medium, but at the same time they nurtured what for them was their 'Black English', a multi-ethnic vernacular. Inspired also by reggae music and the songs of Bob Marley, its political or ideological reference point was 'patois' or Jamaican Creole, the most influential of the Caribbean creoles generally on British Black English. The veneration of Jamaican Creole, along with the cult of Rastafarianism, reached its height in the 1980s, as unemployment amongst West Indian youths rose to 40 per cent. By 'code-sliding' they could vary the intensity of the Creole features, so replacing 'to eat/come' by 'fe com/eat', for example, the degree of Creolization varying from speaker to speaker and situation to situation.

With the intermingling of black and white adolescents in the school environment, however, Black English tended to merge at one end of the spectrum into local forms of London English. Indeed 'ax' for ask is probably now more likely to be used in Black London English than Cockney, as traditionally it has been, and 'Yo China' means 'hello China [plate]' = 'mate'. Phrases like 'innit', and 'you know what I mean' have been variously identified as having either Cockney or Black English origins (and 'innit' even London Indian English). Conversely, Black English has brought new phrases into the speech of London's white youth who 'talk black' out of solidarity and who listen to the same music: 'wicked' and 'bad' as terms of approval; 'seen!' (right on!), 'tief' for steal. In the 1980s, a new form of pop music idiom was created for the moment by 'Smiley Culture', a British black MC (master of ceremonies) who mixed Cockney and Creole for the benefit of his black and also white audiences.

Influential too has been the Black English of the United States, again via the intermediary of musical genres such as soul and disco: words like 'posse' and 'respect!', for example.

As the century drew to an end, however, such phrases and others became inextricably associated in the media with the cult television figure of 'Ali G' from Staines, as created by the comedian Sacha Baron Cohen: a parody of white and Asian adolescents trying to get access to black street culture. His formulaic vocabulary, truncated syntax and gangster rapper accent ('These unemployed – they just chillin', innit man?') might be sounding the death-knell of ethnic code-crossing; alternatively they may be an implicit testimony to the heterogeneous blending of London's languages. In the words of the black British Rastafarian poet Benjamin Zephaniah:

> I love this concrete jungle still
> with all its sirens and its speed,
> the people here united will
> create a kind of London breed.

THE METROPOLITAN PLAYGROUND: LONDON'S CHILDREN

Jenny Bavidge and Andrew Gibson

ONE OF THE more intriguing ways of trying to get the flavour of London culture at any given time is to look at what people are reading on the Tube, especially the books. We mean the Tube in particular, rather than just public transport, because the Tube has the singular effect of cutting people off from the airwaves, and therefore from electronic communication. One of the truly resonant figures of the contemporary metropolis is the desolate Tube-rider forlornly fingering a dead keypad. In the Tube, if anywhere, people are driven to read. Not many, it's true, especially if we leave out the newspaper readers; and along with them, too, we should leave out the exceptions: the occasional preposterous creatures seemingly absorbed in books on Nietzsche or deconstruction held at 90-degree angles; the belated undergraduates and diligent self-improvers clutching their Austen or their Dickens, even, occasionally, their James or Conrad. There are always much more normal readers than these, and much more representative authors. In the 1980s, the representative authors tended to fall into two camps: bluff, masculine heavies (Jeffrey Archer, Frederick Forsyth) and feminine sentimentalists (Jilly Cooper, Joanna Trollope). Both are still around, but there is no doubting the rise to prominence of a new 'literature of the Tube'. It is contemporary children's literature. In the subterranean world of the Tube, *Harry Potter* reigns supreme, with Philip Pullman, Eoin Colfer and Lemony Snicket gaining ground.

Our argument here is this: considered specifically as a feature of London life, the *Harry Potter* phenomenon is indicative of a major current shift in the culture of the metropolis, a shift that is best understood through the figure of the child. On the one hand, London is increasingly taking on the appearance of a vast, twenty-first-century playground. The pleasures and freedoms that the city offers Londoners and visitors alike seem more and more closely to resemble those classically associated with childhood. Or, to put the point differently: in a number of different respects, life in the city seems at present to be subject to a progressive infantilization. Yet, on the other hand, the metropolitan play zone is perceived as ever more dangerous and threatening to children themselves. In one way or another, the culture is obsessed with connections between children and criminality. We goggle with appalled fascination at the latest account of abduction or disappearance, paedophilia or child murder. We fear for our children in new and unprecedented ways. As a result, children have been increasingly marginalized and excluded from public space. As potential victims, they occupy anxiously guarded and separated zones. They do as real criminals, too. Children must now be the objects of social and technological surveillance. This is clear enough from the Crime and Disorder Act of 1998, which issued precise directives on child curfews, tagging and tracking. We try in this essay to elicit just a little of the weirdness of a historically very specific metropolis where, more and more, the only children who can enjoy the freedoms of urban life are no longer (legally) children at all.

The beautiful and useful British Airways London Eye appeared in 2000. In its form and function, it seems the very symbol of funfair London. Paris also has its Ferris wheel. As Tori Smith has shown, the European capitals once imitated and emulated each other in imperial pomp and grandeur. Now, as competing wonderlands displaying a seemingly boundless array of consumer pleasures, hedonistic phantasmagorias and freedoms personal and sexual, they vie over fairground trappings. But be advised: the pleasures come with warnings attached. Children under 16 are not allowed on the Eye unless accompanied by an adult. This reasonable demand is also precisely symptomatic: in the great new metropolitan theme park, children must not go unsupervised.

The capital's children have long been the stuff of legend. In the section of his biography of London devoted to children, Peter Ackroyd tries to hear the voices of London's children themselves as they ring through street games, rhymes and riddles. But he also cites a range of sources from the eleventh century onwards that show how far London's children have repeatedly been both sanctified and demonized. As rogues, victims, ragamuffins, urchins or little angels, metropolitan children have always been mythic figures, and, as such, a source of adult disquiet. Henry Mayhew even produced a typography of them. This has its present-day equivalent: the tabloid system of categories (thugs, darlings, innocents, 'angels', 'monsters', etc.), a system, so the geographers tell us, that maps quite neatly on to concepts of 'pure' and 'polluted' places.

The situation of London's children is currently the subject of a range of vigorous debates. These debates partly follow established patterns. They particularly resemble nineteenth-century arguments about the presence of women in public spaces, and are similarly fraught with anxieties about moral geographies, the dangers supposedly inherent in movement around the city. Colin Ward has suggested that children now make less use of the city than their predecessors did, because their parents are more afraid for their safety. We are more and more concerned for the vulnerability of London's children. By contrast, the city itself might be best represented in that potent symbol from the 1980s, the Rottweiler in full career towards the toddler's face. The question of the particular places in the city that children should and should not occupy has become an intensely moral one. According to Gill Valentine, current research on the urban geographies of childhood suggests that, for many, the wider urban environment is no longer a 'childhood domain'. However inadequate as a substitute, institutionalized, tightly regulated (and commercialized) 'spaces of play' appear to be the only option.

If urban environments are often aggressively anti-child, as Stuart Aitken argues, adult fears for city children are leaving them more and more confined. The United Nations Convention on the Rights of the Child of 1989 gives children the right 'to engage in play and recreational activities' (as well as the related right to speak on their own account). In direct response to this, in 2000, the Office of the Children's Rights Commissioner for London conducted a survey into children's opinions and experiences of London. It found that children were 'more and more restricted as their place to play gets smaller'. Increasingly, children take to the streets and parks only with a watchful adult by their side. Another figure for our present metropolitan culture is the child peering out wistfully at the city world from the shaded windows of a Range Rover, 'people carrier' or similar armoured car. As Aitken says, it is hard not to read the loss of small freedoms for children – walking to school, playing on commons – as part of a wider failure of creativity or imagination in metropolitan living.

Bachelard has written of a 'passionate liaison' with particular places that occurs in childhood and informs our later relationships with the surrounding world. This affective geography – an intimate closeness with the texture of the city – is denied to the school-run child of today. Instead, he or she is likely to end up spending more time in a new set of precisely circumscribed (and often expensive) spaces, most notably virtual worlds. As Henry Jenkins says, whilst contemporary video games may seem to provide children with deregulated, even limitless pleasures, they are actually largely based on the rigid narrative patterns of a long-established 'boy-culture'. The interactive pathways they offer are pre-structured. Enticing as may be the prospect of hypertextual 'wild spaces', the games effectively function as safe versions of the playgrounds and city parks for which, more and more, they are substitutes.

The freedom and mobility of the child in the city thus seem progressively more circumscribed. But if this is the case, it is not just because innocence has to be protected, but also because the little monsters have to be watched. In Ackroyd's terms, again, over the past few years the metropolitan child has been demonized as much as sanctified. From the murderers of the 10-year-old Damilola Taylor in 2000 to the uncontrollable 'children from hell' on inner-city estates to the 13-, 12-, 11-year-olds increasingly suspected of a whole gamut of crimes from rape to robbery with violence, London seems to be spawning ominous and sinister children, perhaps as never before. In this context, the James Bulger case of 1993, in which a toddler was murdered by two young boys, has been particularly significant. A series of government-sponsored policies followed in its wake. Most of these sought to exert greater control over children through schemes such as 'truancy watch'. The keepers of London's corner stores were already desperately intent on policing their own particular space, insisting that it could tolerate only 'two schoolchildren at a time'. Now they were also asked to keep an eye on the activities of children escaping the constraints of the classroom for the freer life of the street. The Criminal Justice Bill of 1994 – once described as 'a great moral crusade against children' – was followed by the Crime and Disorder Act of 1998, which partly extended its measures. In September 1998 a scheme was introduced that permitted local authorities to impose curfews on the under-10s. In fact, this measure was only taken on a single occasion. Yet, in 2000, the curfew laws were extended to under-16s. Both the local authorities and the police now have the power to apply a curfew (9.00 p.m.–6.00 a.m. for a maximum of 90 days) to 'a known trouble spot', such as a particular estate. There have been other initiatives experimenting with various forms of surveillance, tagging and curfew. All these measures have come under persistent fire from human rights and civil liberties groups: the London Fair Play group, for example, whose website monitors the rights of London's children, has attacked the curfew laws of 1998 as not only draconian and repressive, but as damaging to community relations. The liberal perspective, however, holds little sway. Reasonability has little purchase on the myths; not least because, for the moment at least, the myths appear to serve multiple if partly contradictory purposes quite successfully.

Meanwhile, the big wheel keeps on turning. One of the purposes served by the myths may well be the current adult usurpation of metropolitan childhood. ('The city is a playground', says the car ad, 'go play!') For some time now, urban fashion has been appropriating toys, games and other accoutrements of the child. We live in a culture of 'infantile chic', and what de Certeau called the practice of everyday (metropolitan) life is changing accordingly. At a peripatetic club night, School Disco (copied by the more Molesworthian 'Skool Disco'), London clubbers dress in school uniform, dance to 1980s pop and play at being high-school children again. The 'sound and vision' department on the fourth floor of Harvey Nichols has started to call itself 'The Playground'. Besuited businessmen pedal silver scooters to work. Outsize boys and girls career through the city on rollerblades, wearing Shaun-the-Sheep backpacks and Winnie-the-Pooh pouches. More strikingly still, where, but a few years ago, the only socially sanctioned vehicle on the pavement was the kiddies' bike or tricycle, adult cyclists now scare the wits out of the London pedestrian. The pavement cyclist can sometimes be the contemporary bully par excellence: out of order in a supposedly protected space but fearful of the larger space beyond it, daunted by the adult bustle of traffic. Of course, children themselves were long ago bullied off the roads.

Mobile phones are the walkie-talkies that children always wanted. You can use them, like Millwall supporters, to set up the next rumble with the other gang (aka the Metropolitan Police). You can use them to set up the evening's play. ('Are you coming out to play tonight?', says a young man from Sotheby's to a young woman from Merrill Lynch.) Play, or 'recreation': once closely connected with school life, the concept of 'recreation' has now migrated to adult spheres, as in the case of 'recreational drugs'. Or think of fireworks: Guy Fawkes Night was never a one-off, not in London. But the 'fireworks season' stretches back ever earlier. Hot summer nights can sound like November 5th. Cross Clapham Common in mid-June, and you may find grown-up kiddies firing rockets at a bright blue sky. The point is partly that Thatcher's children have become Blair's babes; and who, indeed, could better preside over them than our first conspicuously boyish Prime Minister who, like any shrewd goodie-goodie, knows when it's prudent to say 'sorry' (Irish history, comprehensive schools)?

London is probably not the most obviously infantilized contemporary metropolis. In Tokyo, for example, the signs of delayed adulthood are everywhere. If *Harry Potter* rules on the London Tube, cartoons and comic strips are the staple of the Tokyo subway. (This suggests that urban infantilism may partly be connected not only to affluence, but to life expectancy, higher in Japan than anywhere else.) But there are also more adult cities: London, of course, is not the only city where it is easy for the pedestrian to find him- or herself being run down by a cyclist. But if it happens to you in Copenhagen, a city still more liberal than neo-liberal, it will probably be because you have misjudged the speed with which the riders sweep down the ample and ubiquitous cycle lanes. It may be no coincidence that, in the Tivoli, Copenhagen has a special, beautiful, licensed but delimited space for adults to return to childhood. In other, still more serious cities, childhood itself is in scarce supply. Istanbul, for example, is strewn with devastated, unusable playgrounds. They were wrecked by the recent earthquake. Not surprisingly, when funds are tight, renovating playgrounds is not a priority.

In *Passagen-werk*, Walter Benjamin suggests that modernity under the rule of advanced capital functions as a dream-world. We have yet to know how we might awaken from our collective trance. Capital does not strip the world of its magic, as the German sociologist Max Weber and many since Weber have argued. It casts a spell over the world. In Benjamin's phrase, it 'reactivates the mythic forces'. The paralysis it inflicts is inseparable from its powers of enchantment. For all the appearance of ever-increasing mechanization and systemic rationalization, the modern world is gripped by a daemonism. Benjamin aimed to start dispelling the dream, and the figure of the child was crucial to his efforts. For children, he insisted, are not interested in the preformed world or in the given meanings of things. They are essentially creative: they take hold of objects with established functions and put them to new uses. The child's chest of drawers holds 'an arsenal and a zoo, a crime museum and a crypt'. 'Tidying up' means demolishing a world where prickly chestnuts are spiky clubs and tinfoil hoarded silver. The child transforms the world, or asserts the fact that it can be transformed. It maintains the link between perception and action that, in the adult world, is characteristic of the revolutionary mind. The enchanters have not yet hypnotized the child. It is rather precisely in the child that we may observe a kind of imaginative life that is radically unlike that of the dream-world.

Benjamin could not have foreseen that childhood itself would become part of the enchantment. He did not anticipate the power of advanced capital to hoover up, commandeer or make over spheres of life that seem to threaten it with radical difference. Even as it co-opts existing sites of resistance, however, capital also creates new ones. On the one hand, we've suggested, the spaces that London offers the child are currently more and more confined and regulated ones; on the other hand, metropolitan 'childhood' is becoming a more and more widely marketed commodity. But city life is never wholly reducible to such neat formulations. What cuts across this particular structure? We'll look briefly at two figures, the skateboarder (who resists confinement) and the prophet (who resists infantilism).

Here and there, some of London's children struggle to keep their activities free from regulation. In doing so, they maintain a sense of city space that is directly opposed both to current adult geographies and to current preconceptions of the place of the urban child. Iain Borden's account of skateboarding brings this out clearly. Borden traces the development of what was, in the 1970s, a fashionable suburban children's sport into an irrepressibly disruptive feature of '80s and '90s metropolitan culture. Skateboarding brings children into the city in distinctive ways. As Borden argues, the purpose-built skate-parks or organized 'super-architectural spaces' of the '70s – Mad Dog Bowl, Skate City – were practical but unexciting. Skaters refused to be screened out of city life. They insisted on sharing the city with others. They took over neglected or unused buildings, streets and zones, or pressed already occupied parts of London into service (Liverpool Street Station, Canary Wharf). Like the Huns, Goths and Vandals, they also transformed the spaces they invaded. Most famously, in Borden's phrase, under the calm lines of the high-culture bastion of the South Bank lies the 'heart and mother of English skating', its gloomy, cavernous slopes alive with yelling and clatter and transformed into an alternative spectacle of social practice. The skater invasion of city space is no abstraction. As Borden makes clear, skaters lay specific claim to a host of particular concrete features of the metropolis, to 'streets, ledges, window sills, walls, roofs, railings, porches, salt bins, fire hydrants, bus benches, water tanks, newspaper stands, handrails, barriers, fences, banks, skips, posts, tables and so on'. Moreover, they do so without paying for the privilege. Not surprisingly, city authorities quickly tried to clamp down on them. The police chased them from the spaces they had made theirs. The urban planners sought to 'manage them away', as in the case of the benches in the Bishopsgate frontage, where dividers were introduced to keep the skaters off. The struggle continues – and what continues with it is a sense of the city as disputed territory rather than organized playground, as a place vitalized by conflict, the ways in which cultures (and subcultures, including children's subcultures) negotiate or squabble over spaces.

Finally: the period that has witnessed the growth of metropolitan infantilism has also witnessed the re-emergence of a figure who might seem to serve as a standing rebuke to it, the London prophet. Paradoxically, perhaps even guiltily, we have recently become more and more attentive to a number of grave and powerful voices – Iain Sinclair, Michael Moorcock, Patrick Keiller, Patrick Wright – that are concerned to remind us of the seriousness of London, its extraordinary history, its myriad forms of life. In *Mother London*, perhaps above all, Moorcock presents the city's most significant children as the 'children of the Blitz'. The central characters are such children. Haunted by memories, troubled by visions and plagued by voices, they cannot forget the wartime devastation of London, or the ideals that, for a while, it bred. They scan later London in anger, sorrow and mute disbelief. Moorcock unfashionably insists on the profoundly traumatic dimension to London's recent history, a dimension that the London of the present appears to want to forget or erase. He insists, too, in the teeth of all the transformations that the cityscape is currently undergoing, that the traces of trauma and loss lurk in innumerable metropolitan nooks and crannies, that we ignore them at our peril. But the losses are also ours:

> We children of the Blitz are not to be pitied. We are to be envied. We are to be congratulated because we survived . . . we are happier than any generation before or since. We were allowed to play in a wider world.

The 'wider world' at stake here will have little or no meaning for those used to para-gliding in the Philippines. But it may have more for their children, who are currently so largely kept apart from it.

GAY LONDON

Mark W. Turner

A LOT HAPPENED in 1979. The nightclub Heaven opened its arches and became the biggest gay disco in Europe. The queer artist and activist Derek Jarman moved from a south London warehouse to Soho. Margaret Thatcher was elected Prime Minister and her radical free-market, individualist revolution began. These seemingly incongruous events are all significant markers for understanding Gay London in the late twentieth century. First, the gay political and social movements that came out of the 1970s led to increased visibility for lesbians and gay men, in particular, who were in celebratory, liberatory mode, and needed a glamorous disco to prove it. Secondly, Thatcher began her malign reign, with all the socially repressive – and specifically anti-homosexual – measures that were to follow, and which provided the political context in which gay Londoners organized themselves in the 1980s. Finally, Jarman's move to Charing Cross pre-empted the symbolic rise of Soho as the centre of Gay London, which was firmly established by the early 1990s. Jarman is such a significant 'Gay Londoner' because of the way that his art and life were increasingly bound up with the politics of gay life in the capital during this period, from Gay Pride marches to activist protests to nights spent cruising Hampstead Heath. Furthermore, he was an astute commentator on the fortunes of the city, and his work takes us straight into the complexities of Gay London in the 1980s.

Jarman's film, *The Last of England* (1987), marks a turning point in his cinematic vision, and introduced the autobiographical presence that would appear in virtually all of his later films. Yet this film, which merges the personal with the political, is also his finest cinematic statement about the condition of England in the late twentieth century and the 'Thatcher Terror', as he calls the 1980s in his journals. The state of the nation is imagined as a bleak, dissolute urban landscape, a city of violence in decline, a city of ruins in which the future can be imagined only as a departure or leave-taking, like the boat setting off at the end of the film (an allusion to a painting of 1855 in the Birmingham City Museum and Art Gallery by Ford Madox Brown, which provided Jarman with his title). The most poetic and haunting images from the film – of warehouses ablaze, of gay sex on the Union Jack,of a modern-day Pan playing his pipes atop a pile of rubble – point to the discontent of urban dystopia that represents both life under Thatcher and the condition of England at the end of the century. As Michael O'Pray put it in his study of the film-maker, Jarman 'uses the wasteland of London's docklands to create an atmosphere of hysteria, paranoia and pessimism'.[1] It's a vision that we see in the music videos that Jarman made for The Smiths, those sullen but inspiring miserablist spokesmen for 1980s discontent, in which flames consume the same abandoned warehouses that were used in *The Last of England*.

In another helpful coincidence, *The Last of England* was released in the same year that Margaret Thatcher was re-elected for a third term. For Jarman, Thatcher and her 'ism' held nothing of social value; indeed, she stood for the fragmentation of society into rich and poor, haves and have-nots:

> I wouldn't wish the eighties on anyone, it was the time when all that was rotten bubbled to the surface. If you were not at the receiving end of this mayhem, you could be unaware of it. It was possible to live through the decade preoccupied by the mortgage and the pence you saved on your income tax.[2]

The critique of the state of the nation in *The Last of England* – symbolically imagined as a decaying city of the marginalized – was linked to the political disengagement that Jarman felt resulted from the economic boom of the 1980s. As O'Pray observes, 'Jarman's allegiances in the film are with outsiders – the cast-offs, junkies, refugees and homeless who populate England's margins'.[3] Nineteen-eighty-seven was, interestingly, also the year that saw the building agreement to construct Canary Wharf Tower, the centrepiece of Thatcher's vision of a satellite city on the Isle of Dogs. At a time when the virtues of enterprise zones were being espoused by the London Docklands Development Corporation (LDDC) to revive the abandoned docklands of the East End, Jarman builds into his video for The Smith's song 'Panic' images of graffiti reading: LDDC ARE BLOODY THIEVES and LOCAL LAND FOR LOCAL PEOPLE.

In *The Last of England*, soldier-terrorists menacingly police these rough edges of London. As a consequence, through much of the film there is a pervasive sense of danger and repression, of violence about to break out. And yet, anger about social divisions and market-driven economics was not Jarman's only cause for rage. In 1986 he learned that he was HIV+, and I don't think we can help but read part of the angry vision of the film in relation to the AIDS epidemic. As Jarman records it:

> AIDS showed up an inheritance for a confusion. Faced with the prospect of writing about it, I faltered; there were too many stories I wanted to record. There had been no disease since syphilis so trapped in preconceptions and sexual stigma; exaggerated by the (erroneous) perception that it was only transmitted between homosexual men – 'AIDS, AIDS, AIDS,' shouted the kids in the playgrounds, 'Arse Injected Death Syndrome'. In the first few years of this epidemic, your neighbours were cast out of the city.[4]

It is reasonable to imagine that the transgressors and castaways on the marginalized and deserted docks and wharves of the Thames – the very same docks that would become the site of such aggressive gentrification over the next decade – owe something not only to Jarman's dissatisfaction generally with Thatcher's Britain, but also to a raw anger at the state of Gay London in the time of AIDS.

Of Communities, Ghettos, Scenes, Lifestyles . . .

Arguably, at the time that Jarman moved from his warehouse on the Thames to Soho in 1979, there was no such thing as Gay London. For decades, there had been small clusters of gay-frequented bars, clubs and backrooms – The Gigolo, The Casserole and The Hustler in 1960s Chelsea, for example, or, later, the nightspots around Earl's Court – but there was nothing to compare with what we might understand Gay London to mean twenty years later. By the turn of the twenty-first century, Gay London can be talked about in diverse ways – as a range of commercialized, vibrant gay/lesbian/queer scenes; as a global tourist destination and the gay capital of Europe; as one of the centres of gay politics of all persuasions – but in the year that Thatcher came to power and Heaven opened, Gay London occupied the margins rather than the centre, whether considered geographically or imaginatively. In the early 1980s, the focus for many gay Londoners was on 'Building the London Gay Community', as the title of a pamphlet of 1982 by the London Gay Workshops Collective put it. Gay London, according to Bob Crossman of the Collective, had yet to be built. He acknowledged from the outset that:

> there ain't no such animal as a gay community – but there is a series of gay villages, either in the head or on the ground (and sometimes just below it). Ten years of Gay Liberation in London has not created a 'Gay Vote' like San Francisco's, there are no recognizably gay ghettos – 2 pubs and a couple of clubs within 100 yards of each other in SW10 don't make a ghetto – and gay people in public life are still pussy-footing around, lying or arguing that 'the time is not yet ripe'.[5]

While there was no clearly defined gay community in 1982, the pamphlet firmly argues that there ought to be, and that with a little more visibility, political organization, lobbying and help from trade unions and local government, there certainly could be.

What exactly is meant by the term 'gay community' is, unsurprisingly, difficult to define. That there were large numbers of queer people (gay men, lesbians, transsexuals and others out of the mainstream) in London by 1979 is obvious enough; even if there hadn't been before (and there were), then the post-1967 gay urban migration and the legalization of homosexuality ensured that small-town boys (and girls), to borrow from Jimmy Sommerville, made it so. And, as I've noted, there were venues where queer people gathered – legally or illegally, here and there throughout the city. Furthermore, there were Gay Pride marches, however small (16,000 in 1987), and a range of political activism, more or less visible. The point isn't that there weren't a lot of 'us' in London, it's that there was no 'community', no bringing together of all of us, no collectivity.

It ought to be said that the notion of any community (like the notion of any city) is in part a fiction, and, arguably, there is nothing tangible about the 'Gay Community'. Yet a notion of community does have its uses; drawing on the work of Benedict Anderson, Kath Weston argues that a symbolic, or fictionalized, community is an important conceptual notion in allowing us to imagine and consolidate our identities:

> As 'members' of an imagined community, people feel an attachment to a necessarily fictional group, be it nation, race, gender,

> class, or sexuality. In the process they interpret themselves *through* that attachment, so that their subjectivity becomes inseparable from constructions of 'we-ness'.[6]

Through attachment to the Gay Community – whether as pink triangle wearers in the 1980s or rainbow-flag flyers in the '90s – 'I' can attain some much-needed definition and empowering clarity through identifying with others. So while we tend now to take phrases like 'Gay Community' with a pinch of salt (if not downright postmodern scepticism), in the 1970s–80s, especially, the term was far more politically necessary and poignantly uplifting, even in a city as large and diverse as London. Indeed, it may be precisely the vast sprawl and loose shape of London that made calls for a focused 'community' all the more necessary. At any rate, Gay London found a communal room of its own in 1985 when, after a number of years of mutterings, the London Lesbian and Gay Centre (LLGC) opened in Farringdon. Part café, part drop-in centre, part information centre, part nightclub, the LLGC finally provided a one-stop gay shop, a 'centre' around which the community could assemble itself.

What tended to happen quickly in the 1980s was a slide in terminology, from an emphasis on 'community' to an emphasis on 'scene'. In fact, the importance of establishing a locatable and identifiable gay scene – of bars, clubs, cafés and other hangouts – began as another aspect of community building. Already in 1985, only three years after the London Gay Workshops Collective's pamphlet pointing out the paucity of gay venues in the city, a *Gay Times* feature article entitled 'The Big City Ghetto' warned that 'the booming commercial scene, centralized in London and a few other cities, has blunted gay radicalism'. But this commercial scene, the article continues, was not yet perceived as fully above ground:

> On the whole London's gay scene, although widespread, is not visible; it remains largely a secret world hidden from public view. London's gay pubs are still fringe establishments, where the police are free to hassle at will with no fear of media criticism. Illicit sex is tucked away after dark on Hampstead Heath, where it doesn't offend straight sensibility, and where it can be ignored except from the occasional reminder of vice-squad raid. The majority of gay sceners still live a double life; straight or very discreetly gay during the day, 'night-hawks' after sunset.[7]

So while the gay scene in London (and we're talking largely about the gay *male* scene, and the gay *white male* scene, at that) is said to be booming, it was still a twilight gay culture, a city of night and shadows, akin to those we read about in 1950s pulp fiction. In 1984, when that hottest of hot new megaclubs, The Hippodrome at Leicester Square, launched its Monday gay nights – the moment the gay scene became absolutely fabulous, in New York mode, you might say – in that same year, the highly popular, more alternative gay pub, The Bell in King's Cross, was raided several times and the Gay's the Word bookshop in Bloomsbury, a sort of gay community *centre manqué*, was also raided. The booming expansion of Gay London had growing pains, and harassment of this sort and gay bashing were still very much a part of the gay experience in London.

Locating Gay London

Mapping Gay London across the years is a useful way of reading the city, not only as a way of demonstrating the extraordinary growth of queer life in the capital, but also as a way of understanding shifts in perception about what Gay London might actually mean. Take, for example, *Kennedy's Gay Guide to London* of 1987. Brian Kennedy, the man behind the guide, begins with a short introduction called 'The Gay Life', in which he tells us that he has 'watched with interest as what some would call a ghetto has grown into a lifestyle': 'Fortunately, young gay people today have few of my hang-ups, and have embraced a gay lifestyle which is diverse, continuous and fulfilling. And that's how it should be. Why should we cower and suffer?'[8] From gay community to gay ghetto to gay lifestyle – the terminology keeps us on our toes. In Kennedy's guide, the scene – where one goes out, gets drunk, cruises, has sex – becomes the defining feature of what Gay London is. The emphasis on lifestyle – even lifestyle as a kind of lived politics – continues throughout the guide, which notes that 'the evolving gay lifestyle is becoming increasingly visible in the press, on television, in films, books and pop music, and your options are probably wider than ever before'. That may be true, but those options can still be contained on a single (often empty), two-page spread map. It interestingly provides an overview of the whole of gay London, from Hammersmith to West Ham, from Tufnell Park to Tulse Hill. The attempt to provide such a cartographic overview, one that suggests that *all* of London is, in fact, interpretable as Gay London, is only partial. Even on the page a detailed insert of the West End more or less admits that Gay London has a centre, but it's not located in the LLGC in Farringdon, rather in the lifestyle scene of Soho and the pleasures of WC1.

Kennedy's Gay Guide of 1987, like most gay guides until very recently, caters far more for gay men than lesbians. There are a number of more or less complicated reasons for this, not the least of which has to do with economics and the gendering of wealth. Historically, men have always earned more money than women, and gay men are no exception. Rose Collis, writing about lesbians in London in *Kennedy's Gay Guide*, notes that 'one of the world's largest cities has no women-only café or restaurant, or a bar, club or disco where every night is "ladies' night"'.[9] It wasn't always thus in London, and, at the time she was writing, there were women-friendly spaces, in particular places like the First Out café near Charing Cross Road, but the rapid pace of expansion of the commercial gay scene in the late 1980s was clearly aimed at men rather than women. There is a hopeful resolve in Collis's account of lesbian London – 'wherever two or three of us are gathered together in our own names, we'll always try and persuade owners to let us have their venue on one of their quieter nights'[10] – but the fact is that the burgeoning scene that led to the queering of Soho in the early 1990s was largely a 'boy's own' story.

Soho's tranformation into the symbolic and material centre of Gay London is a complicated story, but it is true to say that it would not have been possible without the wider socio-economic shifts that were taking place under Thatcherism. As Frank Mort has noted, 'if the growth of shopping and other services seemed to shift the community away from activism and politics, it also stimulated a self-confidence in urban, public space. The consumerist ethos was encouraging homosexual men to stake a greater claim to ownership of the city.'[11] Voracious consumerism and a desire to create niche gay markets were not the only reason for the queering of Soho, in and around Old Compton Street in particular. The late 1980s and early '90s saw a renewed vigour in gay politics, and an increasing imperative for visibility, in the face of the challenges brought about by AIDS, most significantly, but also by reactionary and repressive social measures such as Clause 28. Both of these factors helped to harness energy and anger, and focused gay politics on something more specific than community building, but something that made the notion of community perhaps even more important than ever before. One of the great ironies of the AIDS era, as a number of commentators have noted, is the way that it brought queer people together in a single-minded solidarity. There were, naturally, vast political differences in the way different lobby or activist groups approached the epidemic – the formation of the moderate, reform-minded Stonewall group and the first demonstration by radical ACT-UP both took place in 1989 – but there was no dispute that AIDS was *the* political point, above all others. Gay London, the 'community', could come together, not only in acts of mourning, but in acts of defiance, large and small.

Three things coalesced, then, by the early 1990s, when Soho was increasingly imagined as a gay village in the heart of the capital. First, there was the desire for community-building that was so much a part of the dream of Gay London in the 1980s. Secondly, there was the heady consumerism of the late 1980s, in which the gay community, in the eyes of business, was seen as an untapped market. Thirdly, there was an invigorated political commitment in which gay visibility and presence were an important dimension in a world in which SILENCE = DEATH. Soho – where in the space of a very few years a spate of Continental-style bars and shops catering for gay men opened – in some sense became the centre of that much longed-for thing, the gay community, and, paradoxically, the wish-fulfilment of the Thatcherite desire for consumerism.

Leading the way in establishing Soho as the centre of the commercial scene and the centre of the community, at least initially, were the Village bars, which opened on Wardour Street at the end of Old Compton Street (still open) and on Hanway Street, just north of Oxford Street (now closed), in the early 1990s. Mort suggests that:

> The aptly named Village Group, a chain of local gay businesses, strove hard to portray Soho as London's very own homosexual quarter, through carefully targeted advertising. Specially commissioned market research pointed to the growing demand for a distinctly gay milieu in the centre of London, especially among younger men. Taste preferences were believed to be specific: the choice was for a 'continental-style' café-bar culture.[12]

The marketing campaign for the Village Group's bars, particularly the advertising images for the bars by TradeMark (king of the gay ad and club flyer in the early 1990s), was extremely effective in addressing the desires of the moment and capturing the gay male imagination. Take, for example, the back-cover advertisement for the Village bars and a

Village-sponsored gay night called 'Youth at Limelight' in *Gay Times* in May 1992. On the one hand, the image suggests the gay pornographic fantasy of the corn-fed farm boy. On the other, it depicts the fantasy of a gay community with a playful rural pastoral, complete with church spire (a nod to the Limelight venue on Shaftesbury Avenue, which was housed in a former church) and piles of hay in which to roll. The gay night at Limelight is 'new', it's 'fresh', and it's 'sexy', just like the boys from the village/Village. New TradeMark adverts of this kind were eagerly awaited for their combination of wit, confidence and good old-fashioned horniness, but the image that such adverts promoted helped to define and perhaps delimit the breadth of the community in Soho. Although frequently savagely ironic, these ads, like the bars, suggested very specific virtues: youth, maleness and whiteness as defining qualities of the Soho scene. Largely, those are the qualities that continue to define gay Soho today.

'Here, Queer and Always Shopping'?

Exploiting a Thatcherite vision for the purposes of gay lifestyle has not sat well with many gay commentators, who think that Gay London is one consumerist lifestyle venture too far. One of the sharpest critics of gay Soho, Chris Woods, suggests that the promotion of the gay ghetto in the centre reduced and redefined, for the worse, gay life outside the centre:

> Success in the West End was at the expense of outlying bars. Gay men were being drawn away from old-style 'community' haunts and into the soulless commercialism of Soho. A particular form of homosexual venue was being killed off by the new bar and club culture. Gay men in London were rejecting old-style gay pubs, modelled on a pre-1967 style of drag, spit and sawdust and blacked-out frontages, and instead seeking identity through the 'new' commercialism with its brash confidence, designer interiors and showcase windows. Gays still wanted local bars, but they wanted them re-invented to match the novelty of Soho.[13]

Paul Burston makes the point that many others have also made, that the centralization of gay Soho has led to a less politicized gay public sphere. It's Boyztown, but one in need of a town hall:

> . . . the same faith in emancipation through consumerism that kept the aspirational working class voting Tory throughout the

> 1980s seems to have persuaded the 1990s gay generation that the most important thing in life is to be here, queer, and always shopping, and that the only rights worth fighting for are the rights to look good and party.[14]

Woods and Burston certainly have a point. While the centralization of Gay London in Soho has clearly done wonders for gay confidence in the city (is there anywhere else where gay couples can feel so completely at ease holding hands or kissing in the street, for example?), the transformation of the gay scene has undoubtedly taken its toll in a less fully engaged, less radical politics. Like many others, I recall the incredible vitality of Pride marches in the late 1980s – so politically rousing at the time, when Clause 28 was passed and AIDS was devastatingly immediate – but Pride has now gone the way of corporate sponsorship. Indeed, the whole 1970s concept of 'Gay Pride' has recently been dropped in favour of Mardi Gras and Summer Rites, whose target audiences are undoubtedly different from Pride marches and festivals, since the gay scene is increasingly populated by and designed for young men and women who were only ten years old when Thatcher was so unceremoniously ousted from office. 'Gay Pride' to them sounds as quaint as 'Make Love Not War'.

Yet, it's almost too easy to criticize and to overstate the dominance of the Compton Street Catwalk with the benefit of hindsight. For one thing, there were important alternatives to the mainstream Soho scene, even when gay Soho seemed at its most dominant. To take one example, the establishment of the queer indie scene in clubs such as Popstarz and Club V (originally Club Vaseline, until the makers of that *de rigeur* gay-1970s product objected strongly to such an appropriation) provided spaces outside the gay centre where those disaffected with the scene could imagine their own alternative queer community. And plenty of Gay Londoners – whether spending their time in S/M bars, or straight bars, or at home, or wherever – continue to have nothing to do with the commercial scene. But even in Soho, things were not only, not always, about selling out to the breweries in pursuit of gay abandon. Along with those empowering Pride marches, I also recall the extraordinary excitement of gay Soho in the early 1990s, and the Valentine's Day festival in 1993 when Derek Jarman, patron saint of the new Queer London, presided over the renaming of Old Compton Street as Queer Street. The celebration didn't gather massive crowds of tens of thousands, but this was a local, even communal, act of appropriation – a playful and high-camp taking to the streets, that seemed an inspiring and reaffirming thing to do. Frank Mort writes about this event as 'the deliberate attempt to fuse together a new upsurge of radical sexual politics with the celebratory style of the street festival'.[15] It may have been gay Soho's finest moment, a perfect fusion of community, politics and lifestyle, the moment when our terminology converged.

There were much darker times to come. One of the distinct disadvantages of communities establishing centres is that they also fix targets for the hatred of others. Just after 6.30 p.m. on the evening of 30 April 1999, a bomb exploded in the Admiral Duncan pub in Old Compton Street. Three people died and more than eighty were injured. It followed bombs in Brick Lane (a centre for the Bengali community) and in Brixton (a centre for Afro-Caribbean cultures). The Soho bombing was a painful reminder of the risks of visibility, for, like the other bombs, this was a hate crime against a minority group on a horrific scale. At a moving vigil in Soho Square for victims of the Soho bombing, Jeremy Joseph, the club promoter of the largest and brashest of Soho's gay nightclubs, G-A-Y, appealed to a sense of community to help financially: 'The gay scene must take on the duty to raise money for the victims and continue to support the victims'.[16] It was up to us to look after our own. This was particularly true, given that a number of mainstream press reports inaccurately reported, or played down, the fact that the Admiral Duncan was a gay pub in the heart of the gay village. As Vicky Powell argued in *Gay Times*,

> there is a renewed sense that we are in some way a community. We have all hurt together over the bombing, because we all know that what happened in the Admiral Duncan could as easily have happened in any gay pub anywhere in the country; and that we have all experienced, in one way or another, the homophobia which lay at the heart of such an attack.[17]

And there is the paradox. The centralization of Gay London in Soho created a celebratory space of confidence, a pocket in the city where gay presence was (and is) absolutely taken for granted. But it also created a target. The violent, menacing sense of the city that Jarman imagined in those soldier-terrorists in *The Last of England* had left the margins and come to the centre.

Is the transformation of Soho the single most significant aspect of Gay London since 1979? I think it is. Not because the creation of the gay scene, the gay lifestyle, the gay village, the gay ghetto is in and of itself a necessarily great thing. Maybe it is, maybe it isn't. Rather, because in the move to establish a 'centre' to Gay London, we see many of the most important political and social issues related to queer people coming into focus. In the twenty-first century, Gay London isn't *only* gay Soho – and it never was. While it's still true that the West End remains a symbolic centre, Gay London has spread, and gay neighbourhoods and local gay scenes have emerged and coexist (Vauxhall, Stoke Newington, Clapham, Brixton), providing richer and more diverse opportunities than a decade ago. The rather empty map of London in *Kennedy's Gay Guide* of 1987 continues to be filled in.

WILD WOMEN, WILD MEN

Hanif Kureishi

WHEN I SAW them waiting beside their car, I said, 'You must be freezing.' It was cold and foggy, the first night of winter, and the two women had matching short skirts and skimpy tops; their legs were bare.

'We wear what we like,' Zarina said.

Zarina was the elder of the pair, at twenty-four. For her this wasn't a job; it was an uprising, mutiny. She was the one with the talent for anarchy and unpredictability that made their show so wild. Qumar was nineteen and seemed more tired and wary. The work could disgust her. And unlike Zarina she did not enjoy the opportunity for mischief and disruption. Qumar had run away from home – her father was a barrister – and worked as a stripper on the Soho circuit, pretending to be Spanish. Zarina had worked as a kissogram. Neither had made much money until they identified themselves as Pakistani Muslims who stripped and did a lesbian double-act. They'd discovered a talent and an audience for it.

The atmosphere was febrile and overwrought. The two women's behaviour was a cross between a pop star's and a fugitive's; they were excited by the notoriety, the money and the danger of what they did. They'd been written up in the *Sport* and the *News of the World.* They wanted me and others to write about them. But everything could get out of hand. The danger was real. It gave their lives an edge, but of the two of them only Qumar knew they were doomed. They had excluded themselves from their community and been condemned. And they hadn't found a safe place among other men and women. Zarina's temperament wouldn't allow her to accept this, though she appeared to be the more nervous. Qumar just knew it would end badly but didn't know how to stop it, perhaps because Zarina didn't want it to stop. And Qumar was, I think, in love with Zarina.

We arrived – in Ealing. A frantic Asian man had been waiting in the drive of a house for two and a half hours. 'Follow my car,' he said. We did: Zarina started to panic.

'We're driving into Southall!' she said. Southall is the heart of Southern England's Asian community, and the women had more enemies here than anywhere else. The Muslim butchers of Southall had threatened their lives and, according to Zarina, had recently murdered a Muslim prostitute by hacking her up and letting her bleed to death, *halal* style. There could be a butcher concealed in the crowd, Zarina said; and we didn't have any security. It was true: in one car there was the driver and me, and in another there was a female Indian journalist, with two slight Pakistani lads who could have been students.

We came to a row of suburban semi-detached houses with gardens: the street was silent, frozen. If only the neighbours knew. We were greeted by a buoyant middle-aged Muslim man with a round, smiling face. He was clearly anxious but relieved to see us, as he had helped to arrange the evening. It was he, presumably, who had extracted the thirty pounds a head, from which he would pay the girls and take his own cut.

He shook our hands and then, when the front door closed behind us, he snatched at Qumar's arse, pulled her towards him and rubbed his crotch against her. She didn't resist or flinch but she did look away, as if wishing she were somewhere else, as if this wasn't her.

The house was not vulgar, only dingy and virtually bare, with white walls, grimy white plastic armchairs, a brown fraying carpet and a wall-mounted gas fire. The ground floor had been knocked into one long, narrow over-lit room. This unelaborated space was where the women would perform. The upstairs rooms were rented to students.

The men, a third of them Sikh and the rest Muslim, had been waiting for hours and had been drinking. But the atmosphere was benign. No one seemed excited as they stood, many of them in suits and ties, eating chicken curry, black peas and rice from plastic plates. There was none of the aggression of the English lad.

Zarina was the first to dance. Her costume was green and gold, with bells strapped to her ankles; she had placed the big tape-player on the floor beside her. If it weren't for the speed of the music and her jerky, almost inelegant movements, we might have been witnessing a cultural event at the Commonwealth Institute. But Zarina was tense, haughty, unsmiling. She feared Southall. The men stood inches from her, leaning against the wall. They could touch her when they wanted to. And from the moment she began they reached out to pinch or stroke her. But they didn't know what Zarina might do in return.

At the end of the room stood a fifty-year-old six-foot Sikh, an ecstatic look on his face, swaying to the music, wiggling his hips at Zarina.

Zarina, who was tiny but strong and fast, suddenly ran at the Sikh, threateningly, as if she were going to tackle him. She knocked into him, but he didn't fall, and she then appeared to be climbing up him. She wrestled off his tweed jacket and threw it down. He complied. He was enjoying this. He pulled off his shirt and she dropped to her knees, jerking down his trousers and pants. His stomach fell out of his clothes – suddenly, like a suitcase falling off the top of a wardrobe. The tiny button of his penis shrank. Zarina wrapped her legs around his waist and beat her hands on his shoulders. The Sikh danced, and the others clapped and cheered. Then he plucked off his turban and threw it into the air, a balding man with his few strands of hair drawn into a frizzy bun.

Zarina was then grabbed from behind. It was the mild, buoyant man who had greeted us at the door. He pulled his trousers off and stood in his blue and white spotted boxer shorts. He began to gyrate against Zarina.

And then she was gone, slipping away as if greased from the bottom of the scrum, out of the door and upstairs to Qumar. The music ended, and the big Sikh, still naked, was putting his turban back on. Another Sikh looked at him disapprovingly; a younger one laughed. The men fetched more drinks. They were pleased and exhilarated, as if they'd survived a fight. The door-greeter walked around in his shorts and shoes.

After a break, Zarina and Qumar returned for another set, this time in black bra and pants. The music was even faster. I noticed that the door-greeter was in a strange state. He had been relaxed, even a little glazed, but now, as the women danced, he was rigid with excitement, chattering to the man next to him, and then to himself, until finally his words became a kind of chant. 'We are hypocrite Muslims,' he was saying. 'We are hypocrite Muslims,' – again and again, causing the man near him to move away.

Zarina's assault on the Sikh and on some of the other, more reluctant men had broken that line that separated spectator from performer. The men had come to see the women. They hadn't anticipated having their pants pulled around their ankles and their cocks revealed to other men. But it was Zarina's intention to round on the men, not turn them on – to humiliate and frighten them. This was part of the act.

The confirmed spectators were now grouped in the kitchen behind a table: the others joined in on the floor. Qumar and Zarina removed their tops. The young and friendly man who owned the house was sitting next to me, exultant. He thought I was the women's manager and he said in my ear: 'They are fantastic, this is out of this world! I have never seen anything like this before – what a beef! Get me two more girls for Wednesday and four for Saturday.' But things were getting out of hand. The centre of the room was starting to resemble a playground fight, a bundle, a children's party. The landlord, panicking, was attempting to separate the men and the two women. He told me to help.

An older man, another Sikh, the oldest man in the room, had been sitting in an armchair from which he reached out occasionally to nip Zarina's breasts. But now he was on the floor – I don't know how – and Zarina was on his head, Qumar was squatting on his stomach with her hand inside his trousers. It didn't seem like a game any more, and people were arguing. The landlord was saying to me. 'This man, he's a respectable man, he's the richest man, one of the best known in Southall, he's an old man . . .' Zarina and Qumar were stripping him. Other men, having lost their tempers, were attempting to drag the women away.

The old man was helped to his feet. He was breathing heavily, as if about to have a seizure. He was trying to stop himself from crying. His turban had been dislodged and chicken curry and rice had been smeared over him, which he was trying to brush off.

There was still the final part of the show. For this, the men sat cross-legged on the floor to watch the women pretend to have sex with each other. One man got down on his knees as if he were checking his car exhaust-pipe – and peered up Zarina's cunt. Beside me, the landlord was passing comment once more. Our Muslim girls don't usually shave themselves, he said. He disapproved of the neatly trimmed black strip of hair over Zarina's cunt.

The show lasted over two hours. 'It wasn't difficult,' Qumar said. They were exhausted. They would ache and be covered in bruises. They did two shows a week.

FROM *Dreaming and Scheming* (2002)

AN UNIMPORTANT FIRE

Salman Rushdie

THERE WAS AN unimportant fire in the London Borough of Camden on 20 November. Nothing spectacular; just a cheap bed-and-breakfast establishment going up in flames. The fire was at 46 Gloucester Place, owned by London Lets, whose proprietor is one Mr J. Doniger. When it started, no alarm rang. It had been switched off. The fire extinguishers were empty. The fire exits were blocked. It was night-time, but the stairs were in darkness, because there were no bulbs in the lighting sockets. And in the single, cramped top-floor room, where the cooker was next to the bed and where they had been housed for nine months, Mrs Abdul Karim, a Bangladeshi woman, and her five-year-old son and three-year-old daughter died of suffocation. They had been housed in London Lets by Camden Council, at a cost that one councillor estimated at £280 a week. Death-traps are not always economical, it would appear.

Those of us who do not live in slum housing get used with remarkable ease to the fact that others do. It is by now reasonably well known that councils all over the country are putting people into substandard B&B accommodation. The councils admit that this accommodation is way below their own standards, and conforms to just about no public health and safety regulations. They will even admit, if pressed, that black and Asian families are far more likely than white ones to be placed in such 'temporary' places. (I use the inverted commas because I have met many families who have been in these slums, without hope of a move, for well over a year.) Hard statistics are not easy to come by, but it seems safe to say that between a third and a half of all families put into London Lets-type establishments are black. We know all this; and sighing sympathetically about the problem, we pass by on the other side. This time, however, the maltreated families have decided not to make things so easy for the council, or for us. On 22 November, they came to Camden Town Hall to ask for a public inquiry. When it was refused, they occupied the council chamber. As I write this, they are still there, and intend to remain until kingdom come, if need be, although they would prefer just to be rehoused in safe, decent, permanent accommodation.

The occupying families are representative of the eighty or so families housed by Camden in London Lets properties. They are demanding a commitment from the council that it cease to use such accommodation. And there are plenty of horror stories, if you want them. One mother told us how her baby died of infections contracted because they were living in a room into which sewage kept pouring. Another told us that she had been stuck in a B&B for three years now. Two pregnant mothers, past their due dates, have been sleeping on the council chamber floor for over a week, thinking it preferable to, and safer than, their appalling homes. And, over and over again, I was told of staircases with rotten floorboards, of toilets that did not flush, of damp and mould, and of infestation by insects. In their single room at 42 Gloucester Place, Mr and Mrs Ali and their son are obliged to share their quarters with large numbers of 'whitish, crawling insects, like earthworms'.

It gives me no pleasure to attack a socialist local authority like Camden Council, already high on Nanny's hit list. But nor do I derive much pleasure from the way I have seen supposed socialists behaving and talking over the last week or so. I asked Councillor Bob Latham, Chair of Camden's Race Committee, what would happen if the families in the slums took the council to court for being in breach of their statutory duty to house the citizens of the borough according to public standards. He said that many of the B&B places were in fact outside Camden; so he didn't think Camden could be sued. Councillor Sandy Wynn, Deputy Leader of the council and a woman with an unfortunate, high-handed manner, loudly proclaimed that the homeless families were being 'manipulated by people with other things in their minds.' Councillor Richard Sumray has implied in his media interviews that the occupation is part of an attempt by Bengali families to jump the housing queue. (It's worth pointing out that by no means all the families involved are black.) Presumably not enough people have been burned to death yet. Priorities are priorities, after all. How does the old song go? *The people's tape is deepest red . . .*

On the second night of the occupation, the families formed a ring around a group of councillors who were trying to walk out of a discussion. Camden's radical response was to send in the police. While a police superintendent was negotiating with the families' lawyer, his men took matters into their own hands and stormed the council chamber. There are three entrances to this room. Two were completely unguarded and unlocked. By the third, there was a crowd of people. The police came in by the crowded entrance, and they came in roughly. One young man had to go to hospital and returned with his arm in a sling. I asked Sumray what had happened. 'Somebody grazed an elbow,' he told me.

The police are now treating the deaths of Mrs Karim and her children as a murder investigation. There is apparently evidence that the fire was started deliberately. And at once the hints and innuendoes have started flying: the homeless families started the fire themselves, the insinuations say, to force the council to rehouse them. It sounds like the New Cross fire all over again: how much neater life gets when you make the victims responsible for the crime.

Since the deaths and the beginning of the occupation, there have been numerous stories of an increase in the harassment of slum-housed families by their landlords, and by the police, under the cover of 'investigating the Karim murders'. There has been an attempt by councillors to divide and rule: they offered to rehouse the families actually in the council chamber, and leave it at that. But solidarity still means something in Britain, even if Labour councillors have forgotten the word: the occupiers refused to negotiate except on the basis that all eighty families should be considered together.

And there has been one very moving moment. On Wednesday 29 November, the Leader of the council, Phil Turner, came to listen to the families describing the horrors of their lives, and to discuss what the council could do; and he burst into tears, an honourable man driven to weeping by the frustrations of his position. The occupying families believe Turner to be sympathetic to their case. They say his problem is that he is not getting much support either from the housing department's officers or from the majority Labour Group. So the families have been offered, and rejected, a whole series of vague promises and inadequate new homes, that is, more B&B housing or more 'temporary' accommodation.

This is why the council is so nervous of giving the eighty families the commitment they are asking for: London Lets is by no means the end of the story. I have heard people describing many other B&B establishments which sound even worse. Again, it's hard to be certain about the figures, but there may be as many as 700 families – about 2,000 human beings – housed by Camden in disease-infested firetraps. No wonder the councillors are nervous. The mice have started biting back.

Let me say again, at the end, it's no fun to bash Camden. Many members of the council, and many of its employees, are dedicated folk doing their best. Think how much worse the plight of the homeless must be in less 'enlightened' boroughs.

The trouble is, Camden's best has been nothing like good enough. It is time people stopped having to die to prove to local authorities that they live in hideously unsatisfactory conditions. If the deaths of Mrs Karim and her children are to be treated as murders, then many of us would say that the murderers are to be found in Camden Town Hall; and no, I am not talking about the families occupying the council chamber to protest non-violently and to demand their long-denied rights.

FROM *Imaginary Homelands* (1991)

COSMOPOLIS: LONDON'S ETHNIC MINORITIES[1]

Panikos Panayi

IT IS IMPOSSIBLE to understand the development of London without examining the history of immigration. However far back we go, whether to the Romans, the Anglo-Saxons, the medieval period, or the expansion of the modern city during the nineteenth and twentieth centuries, immigration is an essential element in its history. Perhaps the most dramatic transformation occurred at the end of the Second World War, when settlers from beyond Britain's shores made their way to the heart of the Empire.

Immigrants have entered the capital in particularly large numbers during the past 150 years. One of the most significant streams of all came in the middle of the nineteenth century, as a consequence of the Irish famine. In 1851, Irish settlers made up 4.6 per cent of the population of London, concentrated in the areas of St Giles, Whitechapel and Southwark.[2] Further influxes of immigrants, including Germans, followed.[3] The next major stream of settlers, in the years before the First World War, consisted of Jews from central Europe, who overwhelmingly focused on the East End of London; subsequently, they moved to suburbs in the north-east and north-west, where many still remain, playing a major role in the life of the city.[4] Because of the tight immigration policy that Britain operated between 1918 and 1945, no significant permanent settlement occurred in this period.

New patterns of immigration emerged after the end of the Second World War. Before 1945, most foreign settlers had come from Europe, and only a handful from Africa, the West Indies and Asia.[5] While some of the major streams immediately after 1945 also came from Europe – including Poles, who settled predominantly in west London; Irish, who moved mostly to the north; Italians, who expanded their historical core of Clerkenwell, which dated back to the nineteenth century; and Cypriots who settled in north London – the most visible newcomers were from the West Indies and South Asia. They moved into parts of London with little previous experience of immigration, notably Lambeth, Ealing, Haringey and Brent, transforming vast areas in these boroughs. It is now impossible to conceive of London without the presence of these immigrants and their descendants; without them, its physical appearance, demography and culture would be completely different.

In many ways, the year 1979 represents an artificial watershed in the evolution of multicultural London. Although Margaret Thatcher talked tough about controlling immigration and introduced legislation to lessen it, she had a fairly limited impact, for several reasons. In the first place, most of the measures that kept out non-white Commonwealth immigrants had come into operation between 1962 and 1971; her British Nationality Act of 1981 essentially formalized these. Secondly, there were still a number of avenues open to those who wished to settle in the capital. Workers in areas of labour shortage could obtain a work permit, and some people could claim asylum under the United Nations Refugee Convention of 1951. There are no limitations on certain groups: European Union citizens can move freely among member states, and white Commonwealth citizens with grandparents born in Britain are also able to enter the country freely, since they are exempt from the legislation of 1962, 1968 and 1971. The Conservative governments of 1979–97 had no monopoly on the rhetoric of racism and the implementation of immigration controls – the Blair government has carried on both traditions.[6]

Nevertheless, there have been changes in the immigrant populations of London since 1979. The Commonwealth minorities already present have continued to grow, mainly through births, while new inhabitants have appeared, most notably various groups from the Balkans, fleeing from the collapse of the former Yugoslavia during the 1990s. Some European groups, such as Germans, who have a long tradition of settlement in London, have also increased, while white Commonwealth groups, particularly Australians, have become much more noticeable. In addition, the number of illegal immigrants has increased dramatically, to the extent that some occupational activities in London would collapse without them.

Since 1979, the presence of immigrants in London – and in Britain as a whole – has become increasingly accepted. This is partly due to the increasing self-confidence of ethnic minority groups and their refusal to accept the status of second-class citizens, as the public disorders that occurred in Brixton and Tottenham in 1979 and 1984 respectively testify.

The furore over the murder of the black teenager Stephen Lawrence in 1993 provides the clearest indication of the changing position of ethnic minorities. These changes have not necessarily affected the position of immigrants in the social and economic hierarchy of London, however, since some still remain at the bottom, especially illegal migrants.

There have been dramatic changes to the demography and geography of immigrants in London since 1979. The most useful and detailed information comes from the census of 1991,[7] which not only asked people where they were born – as previous censuses had done since the nineteenth century – but, for the first time, asked them what they considered their ethnic identity. By far the largest group of foreigners in 1991 consisted of the Irish (214,033) followed by Indians (151,619). Of people born outside the United Kingdom, there followed Jamaicans (76,445), Kenyans (56,993), Bangladeshis (56,567), Cypriots (50,684) and Pakistanis (44,741). Germans and Italians each counted more than 30,000. The census also revealed that 79.8 per cent of the population of London described itself as 'white' (this figure would include the hundreds of thousands of people of European origin). Other groups included Indians (5.2 per cent), black Caribbeans (4.4 per cent), black Africans (2.4 per cent) and Pakistanis and Bangladeshis (1.3 per cent each).[8] The Yugoslavs and Sri Lankans have been among the main settlers since 1991, the former making an impact throughout the city.[9]

The different ethnic groups are concentrated in particular areas, and a journey from one part of the cosmopolis to another would suggest that these statistics of ethnicity underestimate the true figure. From the Greek Palmers Green in the north to the Indian Southall in the west, to the Afro-Caribbean Brixton in the south and the Bangladeshi Bethnal Green in the east, the high streets of London abound with different ethnic populations, and there is Chinese Soho and Gujurati Wembley. Official statistics tend to confirm these patterns. Irish London lies primarily in the north-west, with pockets in the south. Cypriot London is focused on the north, and has become increasingly suburban since the first immigrants moved to Camden Town during the 1950s. Likewise, Turkish London lies in the north, especially in Dalston and Stoke Newington. Indian London has its main concentration in the west, while Pakistanis and Bangladeshis reside mainly in the east. African Caribbeans, meanwhile, live in both the north and the south. The south-east is the only area lacking ethnic minorities.[10] In 1991 sixteen of the twenty districts in the UK with the highest percentage of ethnic minorities were in London. At the top was Brent, with 44.9 per cent ethnic minorities (17.2 per cent Indian), followed by Newham. The other boroughs were Ealing, Lambeth, Hackney, Haringey, Tower Hamlets, Croydon, Waltham Forest, Barnet, Southwark, Harrow, Wandsworth, Lewisham, Hounslow and Redbridge.[11] By 2001, 45 per cent of ethnic minorities lived in London, where they made up 29 per cent of all residents. They formed the majority in two London boroughs, Newham and Brent.[12]

Since post-war immigrants and their descendants can be found in virtually every occupation and social bracket, from the underclass to the aristocracy, it is difficult to generalize about the employment patterns of ethnic minorities in London. Self-employment is a prominent characteristic of many of the groups that have settled here. Indians and Pakistanis have focused on small-scale retailing, including the ownership of newsagents and grocery stores. Bangladeshis dominate the 'Indian' restaurant trade, and the Chinese also depend largely on catering. Ethnic concentration has also facilitated self-employment, since many ethnic minorities service their own communities, as the many food and clothes shops throughout the capital testify. The Greek Cypriots, for example, have had a high rate of self-employment since first arriving in Britain. At the opposite end of the social scale, the unemployment rate among Commonwealth minorities seems to be higher than among whites.[13] Anyone who spends a day in London will probably also come across illegal immigrants from all over the world carrying out the jobs that most others shun, such as car washing and waitering in restaurants.

Every aspect of life, from food to schooling and clothing to spiritual needs, is catered for in the areas in which minority populations are concentrated. Southall represents a classic 'ghetto' in this sense, although in fact it contains a variety of immigrants, both in terms of their areas of origins (India and East Africa) and their religion, which encompasses Hindu, Sikh and Muslim. A visit to Southall Broadway and the surrounding streets reveals shops selling all manner of South Asian products, including jewellery, clothes and delicacies, with places of worship for the different religious groups in the immediate vicinity. Throughout London, numerous mosques, temples and churches unconnected with the white English represent the centre of life for many first-generation immigrants. According to the UK Directory of Mosques, for example, there are 166 Muslim places of worship scattered throughout the capital.[14] By the early 1990s, there were 32 Greek Orthodox churches.[15]

The diverse inhabitants of London probably communicate in thousands of different languages and dialects from all over the world. This has led to the emergence of newspapers and radio and television stations in both foreign languages and English, as well as the development of diasporic literature and theatre groups. By the 1980s, even the Greek Cypriots, one of the smaller communities, had one major newspaper, *Parikiaki*, and numerous community centres, educational and youth groups, village societies, professional groupings, women's organizations, a Thalassemia Society and at least one theatre group, Theatron Technis. London Greek Radio broadcasts from Haringey on a broad range of topics.[16]

Immigrants in London have deeply impacted on people of native British origin. Intermarriage has not only helped to break down ethnic barriers but has altered the appearance of the 'average' Londoner to a darker hue than that possessed in the nineteenth century.[17] Immigrants and their offspring, especially those from the Commonwealth, have also transformed British popular culture, particularly in London and especially in the years since 1945. South Asian dress is one example, influencing retail chains such as Accessorize. More importantly, African-Caribbean migrants have had an impact upon music and the London club scene, where many disc jockeys are of black origin.[18] Black footballers have also become commonplace. Originally they tended to consist of people of West Indian origin born in the city, notably Ian Wright of Crystal Palace and Arsenal. By the 1990s, however, they included international stars from throughout the world.[19] The immigrant populations have also changed the food of Londoners. Guides to eating out list a wide variety of restaurants all over the city, notably the ubiquitous Chinese, Indian (mostly Bangladeshi), Greek and Italian.[20]

The minorities from former British imperial possessions that arrived after the end of the Second World War have become increasingly self-confident, while continuing to face racism. Whereas in the first post-war decades hostility towards them was manifested in overt ways, notably violence, which peaked in the Notting Hill Riots of 1958,[21] negative attitudes towards first- and second-generation immigrants later tended to become more subtle. This change is largely due to the introduction of legislation attempting to outlaw discrimination, notably the Race Relations Act of 1976, but the presence of non-whites is increasingly regarded as normal. Black and Asian ethnic minorities have increasingly played a role in the media, for example, especially television news. The return of black and Asian MPs in London constituencies since 1983 has also had a positive affect, despite the fact that they remain unrepresentative vis-à-vis the proportion of ethnic minorities in London. Councillors and mayors from Commonwealth countries have held office in numerous boroughs.[22]

The descendants of Commonwealth immigrants have refused to accept the sort of treatment meted out to their parents. Instead of becoming the victims of racist riots, in the late 1970s and early '80s inner-city youths (of all ethnic origins) decided that they had had enough, and took the law into their own hands in urban riots, particularly in Brixton and Tottenham.[23] Within the bounds of the law, such self-confidence manifested itself in a remarkable way in the case of Stephen Lawrence. His West Indian family in south London refused to accept the way that the police had treated them after their son's murder and decided to take on the entire British establishment in an ultimately unsuccessful attempt to bring his killers to court.[24]

The events surrounding the Stephen Lawrence case point to the more overt manifestations of racism in London. The inquiry and report into his murder revealed the presence of institutional racism within the Metropolitan Police, despite the fact that the Scarman Inquiry into the Brixton riots of 1981 had also pointed this out and had made recommendations to eliminate it.[25] Furthermore, Stephen Lawrence was certainly not the only person to have come under attack by racists in London over the last two decades. While rioting against ethnic minorities may have disappeared, small-scale attacks have not. In 1986, one in four black residents living in the London borough of Newham had been 'victims of some form of racial harassment' in the previous twelve months.[26] In the reporting year 1997–8, reports of racial attacks to the Metropolitan Police totalled 5,862.[27]

The most disturbing aspect of contemporary cosmopolitan London concerns the plight of asylum seekers. Media attacks and Government attitudes have led to their becoming fair game for abuse, and groups such as Yugoslavs have not yet developed the strategies of resistance common among the non-white Commonwealth minorities from the West Indies and South Asia, who have lived in London for much longer.

At the start of the twenty-first century, London has become the global multicultural city par excellence. In the former heart of the British Empire, less than half a century after its demise, a city has emerged that would not exist without the contribution of immigrants and their offspring. They have become part of the geographical, social, economic, cultural, sporting, culinary and political landscape of the only true global city in the British Isles. London without its ethnic minorities would be London without blood.

WHITE HAIR RIGHT NOW: STYLING THE LONDON MAN

Caroline Cox

IN AN ARTICLE for the *Hairdresser's Weekly Journal* of 1949 entitled 'Barbers out of Bondage', the historian and hairdresser J. Stevens Cox described the status of the barber thus:

> In hotels and on railway stations, a common situation for the 'barber's shop' is adjacent to the men's convenience. An hotel in the West country . . . has the 'barber's chair' actually *in* that place. If that is the considered opinion of the hotel management as to where the hairdresser should be relegated, it is quite clear that many other members of the public share the same view, and are satisfied that the hairdresser is then in his natural environment. A few more inches and he would be in the public sewer . . . The ladies' side has never had such an indignity thrust upon it.[1]

Stevens Cox was lamenting the status of the barber and concomitantly men's hairdressing in the immediate post-war years in the urban south. By the early twenty-first century, however, it seems that an important cultural shift had occurred. In 2002, The Refinery of Brook Street, London, sold itself as a new 'one stop grooming and spa experience for men', offering facials, shaves and massage in a 'holistic health and beauty retreat', a site more familiar to female than male consumers. The boundaries cannot be blurred too far, though, and, anxious to avoid any hint of femininity, treatment rooms at The Refinery were given names with an almost hysterical embracing of traditional male pursuits, including 'Turbo Boost' and 'Pit Stop'. There is not a hint of postmodern irony here.

The apparently new project of The Refinery, however, has its antecedents in the 1970s, when hairdressers tried to appeal to a modern man who was prepared to be a little more up-front about his personal grooming habits than his forebears. Hairdressers were prepared to offer something a little more sophisticated than the average barber's chair and its 'something for the weekend' aesthetic. Indeed, in 1970, Rodney Bennett England, a fashion writer specializing in men's fashion and grooming in London, had written:

> the old barber's shops resembled sheep-shearing shacks in the Australian bush, with hair clippings all over the floor. In them haircutting was a dull routine, if sometimes chancy, operation. You were in and out in under fifteen minutes, the wiser for a smutty joke or two, lighter of a few shillings, and relieved that the dreary session would not have to be repeated for a couple of weeks or so. The décor was often decidedly shabby, with uncomfortable chairs to wait on, drab linoleum floors, and display cases full of faded hair creams and contraceptive products. Today's salon presents a very different picture. A man's attitude towards his hair is almost summed up by whether he still talks of his barber or his hairdresser. Many salons now resemble gentleman's clubs with deep, comfortable armchairs, wood panelled walls and pictures or prints. Others are close-carpeted, with chandeliers, potted plants and piped music. In some you can order gin and tonic or coffee and soft drinks; in others you can easily while away a complete half-day having your hair heightened, lightened and brightened, your hands manicured and your tired face cleansed and patted back into new vigour.[2]

Bennett England recognized the change that was taking place vis à vis men's hairdressing and hairstyles in the 1970s. Men were wearing their hair longer and with more variety, a breakthrough helped by the gradual acceptance of the long-haired androgyny of hippie counterculture. Traditional hair greases such as Brylcreem were no longer being used by a younger generation who had been inspired instead by the dry cut 'Continental' techniques of Italian barbers and their assimilation into mainstream mod culture in the mid-1960s. The rock star shag exemplified in the rooster cut of the singer Rod Stewart and the proto-mullet of David Bowie by the London stylist Susie Fossey were longer styles worn by many young men on the streets of London by the mid-1970s, a major change, since for most of the twentieth century men had preferred the short back and sides or 'normal' done as quickly and efficiently as possible at the local barber. Time and money spent on hair spelt vanity, and that was supposedly a female trait. The new 1970s hipster eschewed the drab barber's saloon in favour of Leonard's of Upper Grosvenor Street, Mayfair, or Samson and Delilah, a salon off Bond Street run by Denise Karen, which had two female cutters attending to their male customers in black bikini tops and matching loincloths.

By the mid-1970s, men were also prepared to enter the female domain of the open-plan salon if it was marketed under the term 'unisex hairdressing', with its tones of a more inclusive 'swinger' sexuality. Bennett England recognized that part of the draw of the unisex hairdresser was the possibility of a wholly heterosexual erotic encounter as much as a fashionable haircut. He described:

> women's salons . . . providing a his 'n hers service [where] men and women sit side by side at the washbasins or under the dryer and nobody seems unduly conscious or bothered by the presence of the opposite sex. You are just as likely to have an attractive blonde or appealing brunette easing comb and scissors through your hair. You may even date her afterwards.[3]

New male hairdressing establishments were also booming: Philip Kyriacou at the Green Park Hotel, Mayfair, and the Mandeville Hotel near Oxford Street; Vidal Sassoon's new male salon in Knightsbridge run by Frank Cheevers in 1968; and that most infamous new haunt for the modern man, Sweeny's of Beauchamp Place, and its sister salon, Todd's of King's Road, Chelsea. Named after the demon barber of Fleet Street and run by Gary Craze, this happening salon was

> in a basement furnished with antiques, noisy and often full of well-known personalities: actors, dress designers, pop singers, various peers and a duke. You can buy a groovy Herbert Johnson hat and even eat there. Todd's is in a row of Georgian-type houses, presently being renovated near World's End. Gary lives there as well, and when pop or Eastern music – the air is heavy with incense – doesn't satisfy you, it is possible you may find Mick Jagger or another star sitting in the next chair.[4]

By the late 1970s, however, a veritable hair revolution had occurred with punk. In a reaction against hippie values and styles (one of the slogans of punk was 'Never Trust a Hippie'), the mid-length 'rock dinosaur' styles were rejected in favour of an aggressive urban 'hedgehog' style as sported by the lead singer of the Sex Pistols, Johnny Rotten. On the King's Road, a do-it-yourself cropped and spiky look began to emerge that had young men rejecting the expense of the hairdresser's salon for their own concoctions. As Tony James of the punk band Generation x explained, to get the vertical effect he used a combination of lemon juice, spit and orange juice: 'I used to walk round smelling like a carton of Kia-Ora.'[5] James's hair was styled vertically rather than down to the collar, an 'in your face' look that was both tribal and deliberately anti-natural, culminating in the ubiquitous spiked Mohican of the late 1970s. Unnatural colours added to the performative artificiality of the look, helped by the use of Crazy Color, a range of lurid, neon colours, as in the work of Ray Bird of Alan Hairdressers in the King's Road, who worked leopard print and text into punk hair. Punk hairstyles continued to inspire looks throughout the next decade, providing the basis for the teased, dyed, androgynous black hair displayed in the Goth movement whose adherents haunted Camden Market and the infamous Batcave.

By the late 1970s, the punk notion that a haircut could be a walking work of art on the streets of London was pushed even further by the New Romantic subculture, whose shock value rested on a deliberate confusion of gender seen in clubs such as Blitz and Taboo. Kevin Ryan of Antenna, Kensington Church Street, was responsible for some of the most exciting developments in male hairstyling of this period, and used extensions in his session work for singers such as Boy George. A whole host of retro references began to influence men's styles, such as the brushed flat top – Andy's Cut and Blow Dry of Tulse Hill was reputed to do the best flat top in London, followed closely by Atlas Associates of Fulham Road.

As ever, some young men were prepared to be quite experimental in the 1980s. Long, moussed and blonded locks, which required a fair degree of upkeep, were worn by many, and greased-back 1950s-inspired styles became so popular that the manufacturers of Brylcreem re-launched their product, a traditional mixture of brillantine and cream. A slicked-back look became associated with the Young Urban Professional, or yuppie as he was colloquially known in London, a new stereotype of masculinity stalking the corridors of moneyed power, who supposedly lived in a loft apartment in Docklands and spent his easily earned cash on Italian furniture and hair highlights. In a special issue of *Hair* magazine entitled 'Hair for Men' (*c.* 1983) and centred on London style, the editor Norman Bloomfield wrote that:

> the trend in men's hairstyles is towards a cleaner, stronger and more manly look, with more men asking for shorter haircuts, but not the traditional short back and sides of years ago. Hair is now left fuller on the crown, is frequently given extra volume by being lifted with the fingers or the brush while being blown dry, or is combed through loosely, with a wide-toothed comb, for an 'un-hairdressed' look. Perming, highlighting and colouring services are increasingly sought after and men are showing greater care in choosing the right shampoos and conditioners for their hair care.[6]

According to the magazine, 'quiffs, colours and curls' could be seen on 'Park Lane and Piccadilly, Oxford Street – highways [that] link to enclose the fashion heart of London, Mayfair', and Mayfair style itself could be identified by hair that was 'short and easily combed, dressed into shape with the fingers' and that 'must fall into place when the occasion merits'.[7] This look was associated in the issue with Panache of Maddox Street, Mane Line of Savile Row, Robert Fielding of Regent Street and Vidal Sassoon's Barbershop in Sloane Street.

The metropolitan 'London-ness' of 1980s hairstyles was disregarded by one section of London men by the early 1990s. A grungy downbeat style inspired by the look of the American singer Kurt Cobain of the band Nirvana, with his styled 'unstyled' mid-length look, could be spotted hovering around market stalls in Camden Market and Portobello Road. Some environmentally aware men wore a white version of the dreadlocks of black Rastafarian culture, a variation of the artificial extensions of the 1980s. London-based squatters, anti-capitalist rioters and festival goers deliberately mismanaged their hair to create a matted, more 'natural' look, and when eventually appropriated by the fashionable rather than inspired by eco or religious belief, a new moniker was created: the Trustafarian. With income supposedly derived from a personal trust fund, Notting Hill was the favoured haunt of this young white black-wannabe male, an irony since this formerly poverty-stricken black area, the scene of a series of race riots in the 1950s, was becoming the centre of a housing boom that was driving out many of its former inhabitants in favour of media and pop celebrities.

A more mainstream style began to be seen in London by the mid-1990s, a variation of the Caesar cut that had been popular since the 1950s. This Roman-inspired look reappeared in the midst of a reputed 'crisis of masculinity'. Concerning this, the cultural critic Jonathan Rutherford wrote that the structures and institutions that enforced men's dominant positions in the workplace and public culture were being threatened by socio-economic and political factors, such as the changing nature of work. The decline of manufacturing industries and the reliance on new technology had led to a de-skilling of traditional male jobs, causing a 'crisis' as 'traditional working-class masculinities' were 'undermined'. The subsequent high levels of male unemployment and the increasing employment of women in the part-time jobs sector had changed the face of the family. As Rutherford saw, 'These developments and other structural changes have all contributed to the questioning of taken-for-granted assumptions about man's role and function in life.'[8]

This reputed 'crisis in masculinity', even if a media construction, has affected the nature of fashionable male consumption. One such change was the rise of the lad movement around 1993–4. Redhead sees the genesis of the lad movement in the 'lager lout' of the late 1980s, 'a young male with too much money to spend and too much lager inside him',[9] who by the early 1990s had 'shed his more violent qualities and was transformed from folk devil into a consumer category . . . The New Lad was middle class (or trad-rock *nouveau riche* like Oasis), but in love with working-class masculinity and irresponsible hedonism. New Lads included pop stars (Blur), comedians (Baddiel and Skinner's *Fantasy Football League*) and most importantly journalists. They even had their own sitcom to confirm that they were *Men Behaving Badly*.'[10]

The lad was another version of masculinity based on nostalgia with its roots in Northern culture, but its style appropriated by the creative and media industries of London. New Lads looked to alcohol, football and 'birds', and one of the nostalgic markers of the fashionable 'lad' was a new version of the Caesar haircut. Perhaps rather surprisingly, the most image-conscious politician of his generation, the British Prime Minister Tony Blair, adopted a Caesar haircut for a brief period in 1997, a fashionable choice that was extensively commented on in the metropolitan press. His new haircut was dubbed the 'Antonius Caesar', and Blair became a target of much criticism from journalists, who made no comment when the haircut was worn by thousands of young men on the streets of London. His lad haircut seems to have been another aspect of the 'rebranding' of London as the centre of a 'Cool Britannia', which had been part of the New Labour government's political agenda, and had led to invitations to Noel Gallagher of the Britpop band Oasis (at that time sporting a Caesar haircut) and his wife Meg Matthews to Downing Street. The look, however, was judged unsuccessful and Blair quickly returned to his 'frizz-prone bouffant'.[11]

By the year 2000, men, although left with more styles to choose from than ever before, tended either to shave their heads or crop their hair very short. There are a number of reasons for this – an incorporation of a look from black male hairdressing practice and associated with American hip hop culture and, of course, a disguise for male pattern baldness. Once the province of the 'bruiser', a stereotype of thuggish working-class masculinity, the shaven head has become acceptable at all social and political levels. This look is widespread in London and, as one Clapham hairdresser put it, 'All men have their hair the same these days, it's very boring . . . all number 2 or number 3 or French crop'.[12] A similar observation had been made in 1947 by Stevens Cox, who remarked that: 'The barber appears to have lost the initiative with his client. Where the woman says to her hairdresser: "What new style do you recommend?" the man says to his barber: "As short as you like, but leave a bit on the crown."'[13]

Here some connections can be made with 2002. Stevens Cox talks of a period of ornamentation occurring in the fashion cycle, when simple looks are overtaken by the ornamental, and, coincidentally in his writing, generically inspired London place names are used to describe the new looks. Coincidentally or not, since 2000 many young men, inspired by the catwalk looks of the London-based session stylist Guido Palau for Gucci and Karl Lagerfeld and Gianni Scumaci of Vidal Sassoon, have begun sporting a series of styles, variants of what was later dubbed the 'Hoxton fin', so-called because of its associations with a burgeoning area of the East End of London, which was being gentrified by artists and media professionals.

The Hoxton fin was a variation of the punk Mohican of the late 1970s (which by the 1990s had become a conventionalized symbol of rebellion) mixed with the 1980s mullet, a bi-level style cut short at the sides, spiky on top and kept long at the back. The mullet was a look that combined the spikiness of post-punk styling with the addition of long hair at the back as a psychological safety device. It had been enormously popular, surviving in various guises throughout the late 1970s and 1980s. By the early 1990s, it had become hopelessly outdated and thus reviled, reputed to be worn by ageing stand-up comedians on the pub circuit, middle-aged football managers and cheesy Country and Western music fans. The Hoxton fin incorporated the mullet as an ironic gesture, toughened with the inclusion of the Mohican-derived centre fin but with the sides cut longer rather than shaved. It is beginning to become as commonplace as the Caesar cut of the mid-1990s and has spawned its own stereotypical wearer, as described in a chatroom devoted to London style. 'Vishnoo' saw Hoxton fin wearers as 'typically called Floyd or Sebastian, [with] really overpaid easy jobs in media, buy all their clothes from Newburgh Street, and have the latest copy of Sleazenation sticking out of the back pocket of their ridiculously low slung Evisu jeans. And they all ride micro scooters too.'[14]

As the Caesar cut was popularized on a more mainstream level with the footballer Paul Gascoigne, so the England striker David Beckham has been instrumental in the more widespread appeal of the Hoxton fin and its variants, such as the shattered Mohican. Originally styled by Tyler of Vidal Sassoon, London, Beckham has achieved notoriety as much for his hair as his footballing skills. In the masculine arena of football, it appears that men with exceptional incomes can experiment with fashionable looks with none of the usual aspersions of effeminacy being passed upon them, because, of course, in British culture the relationship between football and heterosexual masculinity has been secured for some time. On the streets of London, many young men sporting the fin cited Beckham as a role model, although they stressed the DIY nature of their own haircuts, referring to original punk philosophy and a masculinized attitude to their hair.

THE LONDON SUIT

Christopher Breward

IN MARCH 1977, during the year of punk and the Royal Silver Jubilee, the style journalist Peter York identified the existence of a hitherto unrecognized social type. As the author was well aware, the reactionary characteristics of his obscure subject were to shape future representations of London-based fashionable style in a manner that was just as pervasive as the more generally acknowledged and radical impact of the safety pin (recently used as a decorative accessory to the monarch's face in Jamie Reid's iconic graphics for the Sex Pistols). In the pages of the society journal *Harpers and Queen*, York described the Sloane Ranger Man, an upper-middle-class, philistine conservative whose real-life counterparts frequented the pubs and wine bars of Chelsea and Fulham. His observations of their sartorial habits were heavy with prescient detail:

> I am in the San Martino in Walton Street with a woman dress designer. Opposite us is a table of eight very big boys. They all wear pin-striped navy-blue suits, the trousers with turn-ups, narrow at the ankle but loose around the seat, and Bengal-striped red or blue and white shirts. Two of the striped shirts have detachable white collars. The plumper, blander four wear black Oxfords. These have specs and look like lawyers. The other four wear Gucci loafers – the plain kind, without the red and green ribbon. They march across the floor, snap to attention, slap each other, horse around.[1]

York acknowledged the debt that his stereotype paid to earlier incarnations of 'Hooray Henrydom', citing the inter-war caricatures of Osbert Lancaster and the Sandhurst-educated buffoons of post-war British cinema as direct antecedents. Indeed, the figure of the braying pseudo-aristocrat in his finest 'clobber' enjoys an illustrious genealogy in the history of London's popular culture, stretching further back to late Victorian music hall presentations of Champagne Charlie and Burlington Bertie, and beyond to the carousing hearties of Pierce Egan's and George Cruikshank's Regency burlesques. All are identifiable through the military tenor of their bearing, their scrupulous attention to the details of the wardrobe and their devotion to prankish horseplay. In each case, their obtrusive performances were closely linked to fundamental changes in London's socio-political landscape, and their precise get-up drew attention to divided allegiances. These were tautly strung between a sentimental patriotism and mercenary self-interest: a divided attachment to a rural idyll of England and to the more cosmopolitan attractions of the city. Such dialectical relationships underpinned the ongoing development of the London suit as a synonym for London style: a cloth carapace finely tuned to the shifting rhythms of urban life. This chapter aims to draw out the meanings held in the surfaces of the London suit in the final decades of the twentieth century. Tracing their origins in the seismic changes that overturned established hierarchies in London's social and economic infrastructure during the period and observing the manner in which the menswear industry responded to such challenges, the story is one of rupture and containment – its implications visible to all who frequent London's streets, particularly those in the vicinity of the Square Mile.

It should be stated at the outset that the London suit has always been a costume whose function is dedicated to the making and management of fortunes. Monetarism and deregulation, the neo-liberal dogma that defined the acquisitive tenor of political and fiscal debate in the 1980s, were a barely audible whisper in the mid-1970s, years when the United Kingdom was rocked by successive financial crises. But York's Sloane Rangers, natural Tories and 'shiremen' who would instinctively take against the impertinence of the 'yuppies' when they later tried to purchase elements of their style, seemed acutely aware of the coming debacle. Although men of the Sloane Ranger class had long enjoyed a comfortable existence, the ease of which was reflected in their glossy Jermyn Street self-presentation, Thatcherism's advance guard was already threatening their traditional rights. As York suggests:

> [Sloane Ranger Men] talk about money all the time (but call other people who do vulgar). It's an orgasmic macho subject with them. However, they're shy of taking jobs in commerce . . . or in

> Industry . . . They go, above all into the City. The magic words are Lloyds, or a merchant bank, and failing those, a chartered accountant or stockbrokers. But the City is that much more competitive now than when their fathers went into it – full of outsiders. Rangers now have problems with the job market. Their style works against them.[2]

It would be another eight years before 'Big Bang' (the deregulation of the Stock Exchange) opened up the City to all-comers, but already its complacent inhabitants were beginning to feel the chill winds of competition. Family connections and membership of the 'right' club or regiment were no longer enough to guarantee a place on the board, never mind a foothold on the trading floor. One historian of the City, David Kynaston, notes the shocked reactions of the banker Peter Spira who returned to his job at Warburg's in 1983 after an eight-year absence. His colleagues were now more broadly representative of a globalizing impetus and a growing knowledge economy where information technology skills and strategic brilliance were at a premium, rather than the correct accent. This emphasis on talent at the expense of 'background' held significant implications for the survival of the City's famous gentlemanly rules of conduct and appearance: 'it was no bar to success that a young trader, when entertaining a client to lunch, might stick his half-masticated chewing-gum under the dining room table.'[3] Beyond changes in personnel, the physical environment of the City also offered its own premonition of change. The faceless corporate boxes of the 1970s were gradually rejected for schemes that displayed both the monstrous egos of their architects and the desire of financial institutions to project individual character and competitive spirit. From the Lloyd's building to the overwhelming Minster Court development, respect for custom and tradition seemed no longer to be uppermost in the minds of the planners.

On the human scale, sartorial architecture took a little longer to adapt to this paradigm shift, and the classic black, grey or navy-blue pinstriped lounge suit, which had dominated the City workplace since its introduction in the 1910s, remained the uniform of choice, despite its rapidly shifting setting. What did perhaps change was the old-fashioned 'Rangerish' attitude that suggested that a gentleman kept the name of his tailor and the price of his suit to himself whilst quietly revelling in its tastefully superior qualities. Recalling the first phase of conspicuous consumption that preceded Big Bang and the so-called Lawson Boom of 1988, the new-wave British designer Georgina Godley described how the fashion retail business that she set up with her partner Scott Crolla in 1981 combined elements from London's tailoring heritage, Britain's imperial past and the recent tendency towards masquerade that marked the contemporary nightclub scene.[4] This heady mix was offered to a new generation of entrepreneurs working in the creative and financial sectors whose spending power encouraged a hitherto unheard-of level of extravagance. Godley deftly justified any qualms she might have had about the moral implications of this trend:

> The early eighties were the beginning of the yuppie era – not that we called them that at first – the kids of east or south London making it big in the city; and their greed made us hugely successful. We appeased the guilt about their ferocious ambition and gluttony by providing clothes from a more pop, more democratic culture. It was the rebirth of the dandy allied to the more formal trappings of the City, and that combination was very indicative.[5]

From October 1986, the process that Godley had anticipated was heightened by the democratizing effects of Big Bang. On the eve of its implementation, the *Daily Express* expected a rout whereby the vested interests of the Square Mile would struggle to retain their primacy: 'There will soon be a lively market in second-hand sports cars. And bespoke tailors will be sending their bills to skid row.'[6] The shift in power was perhaps not so extreme as some commentators were expecting. In a *Spectator* article of March 1986, the social commentator Nicholas Coleridge recognized that the high-spending young talent now dominating the action in the City still hailed from upper-middle-class backgrounds, the only difference being that this generation was now in possession of university degrees rather than letters of recommendation from public school headmasters.[7] Nevertheless, an apparent influx of working-class 'Essex boys', especially at City institutions such as the LIFFE, provided potent symbolism for those who detected a new meritocracy at work on the trading floors. Their brightly striped work blazers, raucous shouting and waving, and propensity for after-hours pleasure injected a colourful accent into the greyness of City life, which recalled the impact made by female stenographers when they first penetrated the City ramparts in the 1890s. The propensity both of Oxbridge and Uxbridge incomers to generate wealth also undermined the older symbols of privilege. Kynaston quotes one City headhunter who claimed in the mid-1980s that: 'I'm not recruiting people who've merely got the taste to buy the right sort of stripey suit. They've got to be able to make money – a lot of money.'[8]

This apparent relaxation of class barriers was accompanied by an increasing internationalization in the outlook of employer and employee. The influence of a growing number of American and Japanese concerns in the City ushered in working practices and cultural attitudes that rendered the traditional British way of doing business archaic and even unprofessional. Kynaston cites the reminiscences of an American bond salesman, Michael Lewis, who, on visiting the senior partner of an established stockbroking firm that was ripe for takeover in the mid-1980s, found 'a portly middle-aged figure in an ill-fitted suit, scuffed black shoes, and the sort of sagging thin black socks I came to recognise as a symbol of Britain's long economic decline'.[9] As the London suit came close to representing failure and despondency, the revival of a deliberately nostalgic look during this period, by a constituency not so wedded to the Sloane Ranger haunts of Fulham and Chelsea, is not surprising. It can perhaps be read as a rearguard action, for the suit's fresh incarnation carried with it all the signifiers of Empire whilst conforming to a new corporate insistence on smartness. It is significant that Chancellor of the Exchequer Nigel Lawson's short-lived boom of 1988 was also followed by a succession of events that further undermined confidence. The ERM debacle of September 1992, the Barings scandal of 1994 (which seemed to spell the beginning of the end both for the *arriviste* Essex boy and the aristocratic merchant banker) and the closure of the LIFFE ushered in an unaccustomed sense of seriousness. Interviewed in the *Financial Times* in March 1993, the 43-year-old British director of the Banco del Progreso conveyed the manner in which the prevailing spirit of caution informed his own consumption patterns. Here is a new self-consciousness and a keen attention to 'form', which was transforming the sartorial tenor of London's streets:

> On the whole, as I seem to be a standard size and I don't like spending a lot of money on what are, after all, my working overalls (I am keen on off-the-peg suits). I travel a lot and generally buy my suits at Brooks Brothers in New York where I pay somewhere between £300 and £350 a time. But I do own a couple of Hackett's ones which cost rather more but which I particularly like to wear when I want to look very English. I'm more particular about my shirts and ties. I buy my shirts from Crichton in Elizabeth Street

– their shirts are very like pukka Jermyn Street ones. I like the colours and the fabrics and they're just £25. Some of my ties come from Crichton, some, inevitably from Hermes, and if I want to look colourful [I wear] my Garrick Club tie. My shoes are from Church's . . . We have to be fairly sober-suited here so there isn't much room for flamboyance or innovation.[10]

The mention of Hackett suits here is significant, for it was this company more than any other that had capitalized on the desire for traditional codes of smartness, and in so doing set an innovative template for wider models of sartorial behaviour amongst various categories of London men. Jeremy Hackett, whose family background lay in the textile and antiques business and whose own interests veered towards a rather amateurish concern with theatre and sport, had received some professional training at a tailor's in his home city of Bristol before graduating to a retail job in Savile Row during the early 1980s. Throughout this period, he developed a keen knowledge of the arcana of traditional menswear and a working familiarity with the trade in second-hand bespoke goods. By 1983, a sideline in the renovation of old suits and accessories had developed into a successful business that soon extended to the production of newly manufactured items based on vintage prototypes. Partnered by Ashley Lloyd-Jennings, whose eponymous shop in the recently regenerated Neal Street in Covent Garden had been known for its stock of classic English and American footwear since the late 1970s, Hackett opened his first branch in the New King's Road. Both men were emphatic that their idiosyncratic stock met a definable social and aesthetic need. Reaching a significant American market through the pages of the *New York Herald*, Lloyd-Jennings stated quite clearly that:

No trendies are buying the clothes, it's not a fashion thing at all . . . They are basically guys who work in the City, or just people who wear traditional clothes. They are mainly public school people, it's almost like a continuation of the uniform from school. They tend to be younger, the sort of people we cater for in our second-hand department are in the 25–35 years age group . . . Our new clothes are traditionally made and traditional looking . . . Not a single one of our trousers has a zip, they all have button flies and cotton pockets not polyester. What passes in other shops as traditional English is absolute rubbish. We make the traditional three-button jacket, when most new jackets have two, and sell braces with buttons, not clips and self-tie bow ties.[11]

From the outset, this closely-defined and elitist form of sartorial address became associated with an essentialized notion of English masculinity, yet the Hackett look was open to a variety of interpretations. The *New York Herald* noted that the shop had received favourable coverage in every edition of *Harpers and Queen* published since its opening and attracted similar attention in a significant number of issues of *Tatler*. These London-centric society journals epitomized the worldview of what had become known in journalese as the Young Fogey, a more cultured successor to the Sloane Ranger, who, according to the *Herald*, 'prefers traditional clothes, meals, manners and mores to anything today's world offers'.[12] Jeremy Hackett and Ashley Lloyd-Jennings played with the imagery of fogeyism in the promotion of their own personas and the fittings of their shop, where 'everything from the oars from the Oxford Rowing team to the staff, smack of the old school tie'.[13] As Sean Nixon points out in his study of masculine identity and consumption in the 1980s, Hackett was not alone in this pursuance of common-room chic. Paul Smith in Floral Street and Davies in Great Newport Street also employed a wistful design vocabulary using a category of polished and battered *objets trouvés* as shop props that would not have looked out of place in a Merchant Ivory adaptation of E. M. Forster and a line in clothing informed by the flannels of *Brideshead Revisited* and the eccentricity of Bloomsbury.[14] In order to thrive, however, Hackett had to ensure that its widening market was not alienated by this gloss of learned exclusivity. By 1987, it was exporting the brand through its concession in Bergdorf Goodman's department store in New York. Five years later, by the time of the recession in the early 1990s and the original company's takeover by Dunhill Holdings (now part of the French luxury group Richemont), Hackett boasted eight London shops, twelve outlets in Japan and a business in Madrid. As the representation of a certain brand of London urbanity, the brand was ubiquitous, overshadowing more established labels such as Austin Reed and offering fruitful models to mass-market competitors such as Next.

Hackett's range of clothing was (indeed still is) premised on a supposedly timeless round of events connected to the British social season. Marketed under the catchline 'Essential British Kit', the company provided the correct items for Ascot, the Derby, Henley and Cowes, formal wardrobes for Society weddings and Royal functions, utilitarian outfits for hunting, shooting and fishing, and sportswear for polo and rugby matches. This was in addition to the City suits, shirts and shoes with which it had started out. Rather than signifying the endurance of an endemic British class system, however, its stock bore witness to the opening up of previously exclusive pastimes to a new corporate audience. The careful and didactic promotion of products designed to 'fit in' provided an invaluable service to those of the 'new rich' whose professional responsibilities now dictated that they entertain clients under the canvas of a Glyndebourne or Goodwood marquee. Furthermore, somewhat to the embarrassment of its directors and marketing department, from the mid-1990s the Hackett brand found great favour on London's football terraces. The red-on-white St George's cross of its knitwear range and the pastel colours of its polo shirts (often faked) joined Ralph Lauren, Lacoste, Reebok, Burberry, Timberland, Armani, Versace and Stone Island as a label of choice for a new generation of working-class 'casuals' whose interests and habitat were well removed from either the territory of the Square Mile or the freedom of the grouse moor.[15]

That Hackett was by now becoming more famous for its casual wear than its formal City suits was an irony paralleled by certain short-lived trends in office dressing. During the late 1990s, a supposed 'casualization' of working wardrobes in the service and financial industries caused many commentators to predict the final death of formal clothing. A second leader in *The Times* blustered about the effects of such sartorial democratization, helpfully alluding to the intended social coding of the Hackett product in the process:

> The order of the suit has been given the order of the boot. According to a survey conducted by the London Chamber of Commerce, 'dress-down Friday' has triumphed, with nearly half Britain's workers marking the day by downing suits and slipping into something more comfortable instead. The Long Island look has crossed the Atlantic and is now as familiar to accountants on the Tyne as merchant bankers near the Thames . . . Dress-down proponents contrast the freedom of casual clothes with the stuffy hierarchical reactionism of suit-wearing . . . Yet most dress-down directives offer no such licence. They carefully endorse the playing field look that is appropriate rather than the football ground attire that is not. If sartorial snobbery has really been cast aside why is it acceptable for a businessman to wear a polo shirt with the bold

> legend Hackett emblazoned across the chest but not a shiny football shirt . . . ? The only difference is that a chukka is pukka, while business and football are supposed to mix only when confined to the hospitality lounge of the 'directors' box' (where surprise, surprise, a suit is the order of the day).[16]

Informed by American management philosophy and the more laissez-faire non-hierarchical structures of the booming 'dot.com' sector, many companies did appear to be relaxing their dress codes and encouraging the adoption of 'smart–casual' outfits, chinos and open-necked blue shirts while sponsoring such infamous schemes as the 'dress-down Fridays'.[17] Whilst such innovations may have carried great weight in the world of suburban and provincial call centres, however, their influence in the capital city was more constrained. *The Times* need not have worried. Far from espousing the homogenizing uniform promoted by global chains such as The Gap, many young professional and creative London men in the early years of the twenty-first century sought new comfort from the reliability of the London suit, now subtly refreshed by more radical tailors including Richard James, Ozwald Boateng, Charlie Allen and Timothy Everest.[18] And thus the London suit endures, weathering the social and economic winds that have battered the City during the past thirty years. Peter York's wry commentary on Sloane Ranger Man still elicits a frisson of recognition in its combining of style, place and identity:

> [Sloane Ranger Man] kit has altered little in the last twenty years except for the arrival of guccis and jeans (worn with tweed jackets – 'change coats') and the departure of the bowler hat. In the country they wear Huskys (anorak art!) and flat caps from Herbert Johnson (Herbie J.). It is *le style anglais* but it is totally different from what smart French or Italians do with the same ingredients . . . What really annoys the [Sloane Ranger Man] is that with foreigners it's a look, not a badge of faith.[19]

POLITICS/ ECONOMICS

London from the late 1970s to 2003 has been a city of free market economics in the era of the general triumph of neo-liberalism. The consequences are quite obvious: the city has become much richer, grander and cleaner. It has shaken off the residues of post-war drabness. It has begun to look stylish, even sleek. London seems, if not to have forgotten its history, at least to feel less shackled by it, not least because that history has been a great commercial asset, and commercializing history objectifies it and strips it of its power. At the same time the 1980s and '90s witnessed the collapse of London's public culture. The traces of this are everywhere in the metropolitan landscape, from the boarded-up and weed-infested old hospitals to the sites of primary schools that now sport condominia to the trains that still cannot leave on time from the ever more opulent stations. The failure is even palpable on the streets and pavements, where, as opposed to Rome, say, or Tokyo, people know less and less about how to share public space.

The changes in question are reflected in the progress of the Londoner who bestrides the period like a cheeky chappie version of a political colossus, Ken Livingstone. From 1973, when he was elected to the GLC, through 1981, when he became its leader, to its abolition in 1986, Livingstone was a particular kind of radical politician and, as such, part of one of London's great political traditions. He argued for putting an end to the monarchy, asserted that the IRA was fighting for national freedom and told Londoners they were all bisexuals. The GLC that he led was socialist, anti-racist, vigorously pro-gay and lesbian and unflinchingly concerned to promote the causes of minorities. There was more than a touch of utopianism to its policies, most obviously in its slashing of fares on London Transport. After Margaret Thatcher had successfully throttled this buoyant municipal socialism, Livingstone departed for the back-benches, only in due course to reappear as Mayor. In some ways, Livingstone *redivivus* has resembled the Livingstone of old. He has declared that the current international financial system has had more devastating effects than the Second World War. He has fought the Blairites over public–private partnership in the running of the Tube. He has taken on vested interests over the congestion charge. He was in the vanguard of the demonstration against the war in Iraq, and denounced G. W. Bush as a coward whose 'completely unsupportable government' was 'venal and corrupt'. But the Mayor is also a different Livingstone. This one works closely with the City, has expressed admiration for the sometimes draconian policies of the New York mayor Rudi Giuliani and wants a London that looks more like Manhattan, a London strewn with skyscrapers like Renzo Piano's proposed 'glass shard' by Tower Bridge. 'I am proud to be an opportunist', he has said. We might not be too surprised.

It seems as though the great luminary of the London left is now rather becoming a great public London character, complete with inconsistencies; which means, of course, that he fits into another old London tradition. But his shifts and tergiversations are also indicative. From Livingstone's rise to power to the mid-1980s, as so often before, London was a stage for major political confrontations. But historically it has also been a place not only where bargains were made and deals were struck, but where politics bogged down or ran out of steam. From the late 1980s onwards, the politicians increasingly vied to be the man or woman who could most plausibly and least hypocritically reflect a range of the contradictions to London's political life. So far Livingstone has been the victor. London in 2003 is not exploding with conflicts, but trying to contain them. Its dominant culture is not political at all, but managerial.

FROM GLC TO GLA: LONDON POLITICS FROM THEN TO NOW

John Davis

THERE HAS BEEN no more turbulent period in London politics than the last quarter of the twentieth century, years that saw the emergence of radical forms of municipal socialism and municipal conservatism, clashes between local and central government leading to the abolition of the Greater London Council, and, finally, the establishment of a new, experimental, elected mayoralty. By contrast, for most of the period since 1900, London's local politics had been stable – arguably stagnant since 1945. The Royal Commission on the Government of Greater London (the 'Herbert Commission'), which reported in 1960, had attributed much of this stagnation to institutional causes: the local borough councils too often encapsulated socially homogeneous areas, with the result that they had become single-party monopolies, while the London County Council, its Victorian boundaries now encompassing little more than the inner city, had been under continuous Labour control since 1934.

The legislation of 1963, prompted by the Commission's proposals, created a Greater London Council to cover the entire metropolitan area, with 32 London Boroughs in the second tier, enlarged by amalgamation to create a greater social balance. If the legislation aimed to revive electoral vitality, it broadly succeeded with the GLC. Labour unexpectedly won the first elections in 1964, but power changed hands in four of the Council's five subsequent elections. The picture in the Boroughs was more complicated: an unprecedented Tory landslide in 1968 toppled several Labour strongholds previously thought impregnable, but this proved an extreme example of local protest against an unpopular national government, not to be emulated until the Tory disasters of 1994: a study of 1997 showed that 17 of the 32 London Boroughs had remained under single-party control between 1974 and 1994. Attempts to revive local democracy by gerrymandering ran up against public ignorance of local government: a survey of 1986 found that 75 per cent of those polled in four south London boroughs could not name their council leader, although two of those leaders – Paul Beresford in Wandsworth and Ted Knight in Lambeth – enjoyed national notoriety. But borough politics would be animated by change within the local political parties, injecting a new ideological bite into their doctrines and consequently sharpening party conflict.

This ideological revival was most marked in inner-city Labour parties in the 1970s and '80s. For most of the century, the object of local Labour politics in London had been straightforward: whatever else they might do, Labour councils existed primarily to take working-class people out of private slums and place them in council houses. Pioneering authorities such as Bermondsey had done this on a large scale between the Wars; encouraged by central government, most Labour councils in inner London built vigorously after 1945. In the process, they created a grateful tenantry of Labour voters, and several local authorities became one-party states. Labour oligarchies took an apparently unchallengeable grip upon local power and patronage. From the early 1970s this changed. The collapse of London's manufacturing economy from the late 1960s – and particularly after the oil shock of 1973 – undermined the capital's traditional working class and created new problems – unemployment, vandalism, crime – not easily addressed by local government. London's social evolution – the departure of the skilled working class, the influx of students, young professionals and ethnic minorities – generated a more complex range of local political issues than had existed before. Student groups, squatters, community activists and the leaders of the black community did not fit comfortably into 'Old Labour' politics, while newly militant public-sector unions could no longer be treated as pliable tools. In the meantime, housing reform had lost much of its power to satisfy the electorate. Many council estates, particularly those built by 'industrial' methods in the 1960s, were liabilities rather than assets. As Sue Goss puts it in her excellent study of Southwark, whereas once the electorate had aspired to become council tenants rather than private renters, now they hoped to escape from their council houses into owner-occupation. The problem was intensified by the Conservative Government's Housing Finance Act of 1972, under Edward Heath, which required councils to reduce their rent subsidies, exposing council tenants to often substantial rent rises. Arguments over whether to implement or resist the Act produced battles within London Labour authorities that foreshadowed the left–right conflicts of the 1980s. In Lambeth, the young Ken Livingstone joined others on the new left in making resistance to the Act a touchstone of political rectitude; his later henchman on the GLC and the Greater London Authority, Michael Ward, remembered the 1972 debates as the point at which new and old left began to diverge in Wandsworth.

The new left believed that local action could tackle London's pressing social problems, and attacked the party's old guard for what they saw as its complacency and inertia. In his account of the Bermondsey by-election of 1983, Peter Tatchell, the radical activist whose nomination as Labour candidate in that election marked a conspicuous new left triumph, traced his own popular socialism to that of Alfred Salter, the socialist physician who had pioneered public health and housing reform in the area in the early twentieth century. Generally marginalized by the local Labour elites, the new left aligned itself with the militant rank-and-file in the public sector unions and with a 'rainbow coalition' of community organizations, ethnic minority, women's and even gay and lesbian groups. Such alliances tended to intensify the contempt of the old Labour leadership and risked alienating the electorate, but new left progress depended more upon the capture of local political machines, often sclerotic after years of inaction. 'Just by half a dozen people joining the ward you changed the politics of the ward', the Southwark and GLC councillor George Nicholson explained, 'you couldn't help it'.[1]

The emergence of the new left distanced London Labour from the party elsewhere; John Lloyd and John Rentoul wrote in 1987 that provincial Labour MPs looked upon the London party as 'a new Sodom'. It certainly embarrassed the national Labour leadership: indeed, the Labour leader, Michael Foot, weakened his authority by promising and failing to revoke Tatchell's nomination. The Conservatives, however, radicalized themselves nationally in these years, and the emergence of the local new right caused far fewer ructions within the party. Many Conservative councillors and activists found Thatcherism congenial: indeed, the future GLC leader Horace Cutler had sold council houses on Harrow Council in the 1950s. The Thatcher revolution simply encouraged more of them to translate their ideological instincts into policy, and to challenge those older Tory leaders whose instincts were more consensual and managerial. Michael Chartres, one of the architects of the new right's 1978 triumph in Wandsworth, remembered that 'the leaders of the old school were only interested in running the Borough, not changing it for the better'.[2] Wandsworth's Tories sought to shrink the local state, scaling down the council bureaucracy, dismantling Labour's housing empire and putting local services out to tender. Similar policies were pursued in the other principal 'flagship' Thatcherite borough, the City of Westminster.

In these years of ideological turbulence, the GLC became a political weathervane. The election of Cutler and the Tories in 1977 was a harbinger of Thatcher's national success two years later. Cutler and Thatcher would later fall out over GLC abolition, but at this point he appeared an acolyte. A suburban builder and small businessman with 'no-nonsense' views on 'scroungers', homosexuals, trade unionism and socialism, Cutler diminished the white-collar army at County Hall and virtually ended the GLC's role as a housing authority, handing over its estates to the Boroughs. In place of the Council as employer and service provider, he envisaged the Council as orchestrator of urban regeneration, through *grands projets* such as the development of Docklands, the extension of the Jubilee Line and even the doomed attempt to win the 1988 Olympic Games for London. Such schemes bore little fruit during his term of office. Elected at the height of the Labour Government's unpopularity, he fell victim to the mid-term unpopularity of the first Thatcher Government when he sought re-election in 1981.

The Labour group elected to County Hall in 1981 contained a stronger new left contingent than when the party had lost office four years earlier, reflecting the changes at constituency level. This contingent mounted the celebrated post-election coup by which Andrew McIntosh, the later Blairite who had led Labour's campaign, was ousted in favour of 'Red Ken' Livingstone in a Labour group vote. Livingstone has been undoubtedly the most talented politician produced by London's local government in recent years, although not the most effective executive. More of a controversialist even than Cutler, and consequently still more prominent, he caused the GLC to be associated in the public mind with what were essentially his own political concerns, notably the removal of British troops from Northern Ireland. The substantive policies of the Livingstone GLC were, though, consistent with new left thinking over the previous decade. The Council aimed to reverse London's economic decline through large-scale municipal socialism, coordinated by a Greater London Enterprise Board; to encourage community groups and approved voluntary organizations through a liberal grant policy; and to rejuvenate public transport through fare subsidies. Of these aspirations, the grants policy would cause most friction. Like all local authorities, the GLC was empowered by the Local Government Act of 1972 to devote a given proportion of its rate income to any cause it saw fit to promote, and London's huge taxable capacity gave the Council substantial spending power. Grants to gay, lesbian, women's and black groups, and to organizations such as 'Babies against the Bomb' made headlines, distorting what was in other respects an innovative attempt to coordinate the municipal and voluntary sectors. Mencap, Help the Aged and similar conventional charities, which received most of the Council's largesse, were amongst those most concerned at the threat of GLC abolition. The Enterprise Board spent with similar liberality, at the rate of around £30 million per annum, although its work anticipated the kind of regenerative pump-priming that would later become routine in London government. The transport policy, which took the form of the 'Fares Fair' scheme for subsidized flat-rate fares on the Tube, might have been considered the least controversial element, with London Transport ensnared in a spiral of rising costs, rising fares, falling custom and rising deficits. It proved, though, to be the Council's Achilles heel, being successfully challenged in the courts by the London Borough of Bromley, a Tube-free area that resented subsidizing the travel of others through its contributions to the GLC.

The defeat of Fares Fair was followed by the removal of London Transport from GLC control in 1984. Previously, the Council had effectively ceased to be a housing authority under Cutler and had seen its ambitious Development Plan of the late 1960s, involving large-scale urban road-building, dismantled in the face of public opposition in 1972–3. This emasculation of the Council made thinkable the question of its abolition, favoured by Tory radicals almost since its inception. Little detailed thought went, though, into the Conservatives' commitment to GLC abolition in the General Election of 1983. The subsequent tortuous efforts to devise a metropolitan system without a metropolitan authority stored up trouble for years ahead, while the public battle over the GLC's future enabled Livingstone to redefine himself as a national treasure. Defeat in the House of Lords delayed abolition for a year, but the GLC eventually passed into history in 1986.

Some have seen GLC abolition as encouraging a borough renaissance, and the years after 1986 did indeed see innovation at the borough level. The 'pavement politics' advocated by the Liberals since the 1970s lay behind the experimental devolution of council functions to seven neighbourhood councils in Tower Hamlets when the Liberals took control of that authority in 1986. Liberal Richmond embarked upon a pilot decentralization scheme, while Labour Islington set up similar neighbourhood bodies, which had commissioned 300 environmental improvement schemes in the borough by 1989. It would be wrong, though, to see GLC abolition as creating a fundamentally decentralized London system. Most of the powers taken from the GLC had passed to metropolitan quangos or to joint committees of boroughs; little was done to enhance the power of individual boroughs. This was deliberate, since some London boroughs had been as offensive to the Thatcher government as the GLC itself. Administration in some of them had reached a state that could only be described as chaotic. Lambeth was the most anarchic, with a far-left council jettisoning the conventional rules of accounting to the benefit of its workforce and the detriment of the wider population. Some 1.7 million bricks went missing in 1977, owing to a 'lack of precision in the recording of receipts'; like most council scandals, this occurred in the Borough's housing department, though Brent's loss of £4.5 million of library books between 1985 and 1989 showed that housing departments were not uniquely culpable. Fear of giving left-wing London boroughs autonomous taxing powers was said to have made the idea of a local income tax unpalatable to the Thatcher Government as it considered reform of the rates, sending it instead in the direction of the poll tax. Before the Tories embarked on this fateful journey, however, they implemented a cruder but more effective curb upon 'profligate' authorities in the form of rate-capping – the imposition of statutory ceilings on the level of rates that individual authorities could impose. Like the Housing Finance Act before it, this measure succeeded by forcing Labour authorities to comply with or break the law. The new left's romantic faith in civil disobedience caused some to fall on their swords: Knight's regime in Lambeth ended for good in 1986, with the core of dissident councillors banned from office for five years for refusing to set a rate. Hackney's left-wingers went the same way. Other Labour councils sought, less quixotically, to delay the effects of rate-capping by various forms of creative accounting – energetically criticized by the Audit Commission in 1987 – until these in turn were declared illegal. Most yielded to the inevitable. As the former Labour leader of Camden later admitted: 'if you have a government that isn't going to change its mind, then there's very little point in committing suicide in front of them'.[3]

By the late 1980s, the teeth had been drawn from municipal socialism, but the result was not the unequivocal triumph of the local new right. In fact, full-blooded municipal Thatcherism hardly spread beyond Wandsworth and Westminster. These two boroughs acquired a totemic status in the eyes of the Conservative Government, which diverted substantial central subsidies into their coffers to depress their poll tax levels and avoid losing either council in the 1990 local elections. The ploy succeeded, but the need for it advertised the difficulty of sustaining the retrenchment policies necessitated by low-tax regimes. Worse, the 1990s saw the emergence of Tory local scandals to match those in Lambeth. The socially divided borough of Brent fell into Tory hands in 1991 with the defection of two African-born councillors. Their arrival was a mixed blessing for the Tory group: one immediately called for the legalization of female circumcision, not previously a rallying cry for suburban Tories, while the other was subsequently charged with sixteen charges of fraud relating to the Council's housing department. These tragicomedies provided a sobering backdrop to the implementation of policies whose time now seemed to be past: school closures, teaching redundancies and the sacking of almost a third of the Council's staff. Worse misdemeanours came to light in Westminster, where the Council under Dame Shirley Porter was shown to have engaged in illegal social engineering at taxpayers' expense, paying council tenants to leave their homes in marginal wards in order to sell the houses at a discount to likely Tory supporters.

These revelations came at a time when the Conservatives were struggling nationally, and when budgetary cuts following 'Black Wednesday' in 1992 had fallen heavily on services dependent upon central support, notably the Tube. The council elections of 1994 duly brought disaster for London's Tories, with the party retaining control of only five borough councils. This debacle foreshadowed heavy losses in London in the General Election of 1997 and has not been reversed. The 1994 council elections could be taken to mark the end of the years of ideological fundamentalism that had begun in the 1970s. In most of Labour London, the new left was displaced by 'New Labour', much as it had displaced 'Old Labour' a decade earlier. The Blairite tendency was a well-established presence in London politics, rooted ina gentrification process that had begun in the 1960s. The defining Blairite, Tony Blair himself, had begun his political career fighting the far left in Hackney after buying a house in Dalston. Islington had seen years of infighting within the dominant Labour group between the old working class, the new left and gentrifying young professionals before the last group took control of the Council under the later New Labour minister Margaret Hodge. Other Labour ministers, including Frank Dobson, Tessa Jowell, Nick Raynsford, Chris Smith and Jack Straw, had served on London councils.

They and their fellow 'municipal mormons', as Kirsty Milne called them, had trained in student politics, where they had learned to loathe the far left. They freely admitted to being 'more concerned about the council tax-payer than the council worker'. Their managerial approach to local government proved appropriate now that much discretionary power had been removed from councils: by the late 1980s, 70 per cent of London councils' spending was regulated by Whitehall. This was Thatcher's legacy, but although the screws have scarcely been loosened since 1990, central government did prescribe a more active role for urban authorities in the 1990s than was envisaged in the Thatcher years. The introduction of the City Challenge Programme and the Single Regeneration Budget in the early 1990s focused policy on urban renewal, which became a common agenda for most London councils. With policy once again largely prompted by Whitehall and oiled by central government grants, senior officers regained much of the power vis-à-vis council members that had been threatened in the 1980s, when 'the life of a Chief Executive . . . is as insecure as that of a football manager'.[4] This reinforced the retreat from fundamentalism. Sporadic ideological skirmishes continued, most obviously within the Hackney Labour group, where rows simmered in the early 1990s over attempts to tackle fraud in the housing department and the employment of a paedophile social worker, but Lambeth renounced its recent past spectacularly in 1994, the hung council resolving to appoint a troubleshooting chief executive to clean up the borough. The job advertisement disarmingly acknowledged that the Council had 'one of the worst reputations of any in the UK; poor morale, poor services and a dreadful public image'. In 1991, Lambeth's poll tax had been 77 per cent higher than the London average; by the end of the decade it had the fifth lowest council tax in London.

Regeneration is also the principal concern of the new Greater London Authority, as it seeks to define its metropolitan role. Back in 1983, *Streamlining the Cities*, the lightweight White Paper that sketched out GLC abolition, had declared the Council's strategic role to be simply otiose. This wishful thinking haunted the Tories in the early 1990s as the Government came to be blamed for every signal failure on the Tube. A Cabinet Committee for London was created in 1992, and a business-led quango called London First appointed to attract investment to the capital, but the Conservatives remained shy of reinventing an elected London authority. Labour duly filled the vacuum, committing itself to an elected authority in 1996, and the pledge was honoured in the first Blair Government's short-lived pluralist phase. The proposals were approved by referendum in May 1998 and passed into law in 1999. By then the promised Assembly had been augmented by an elected mayor – the first directly elected executive in Britain – and the first elections under the new system, in May 2000, gained added spice from the national Labour hierarchy's futile attempts to prevent the return of Ken Livingstone to metropolitan power. In fact Mayor Livingstone's policies in office – improvements in bus services, the recruitment of 1,000 new police officers, promoting affordable housing through the planning process – have been far less contentious than those of the GLC's 'Red Ken'. His most controversial proposal, the congestion charge introduced in February 2003, is not explicitly 'political', and Livingstone has lost his one major political battle – over the part-privatization of the Tube – despite, as usual, winning the public debate. The constructive potential of London's new political institutions remains, though, to be judged.

'ARMAGIDEON TIME'

Charlie Gere

ONE OF THE best portrayals of London on film is the classic British gangster movie *The Long Good Friday* (1979). It features Bob Hoskins as the East End hood Harold Shand from Stepney, who is planning a major property development in the London Docklands in collaboration with the American Mafia. Over the Easter weekend in which he is presenting his schemes to his American partners, unknown figures embark on a series of terrifying acts of violence against his organization, including murdering his oldest associate and trying to blow up his mother. As the violence gets worse, Harold finds that he is dealing with an organization more expert, better connected and more dedicated than even his own. Unbeknownst to Harold, his partner has been dealing with the IRA and, furthermore, skimming off some of the money he is helping to deliver, and now they are taking their revenge. Two decades later, *The Long Good Friday* remains as gripping as it was when it was first released. But hindsight also offers new pleasures and insights to the experience of watching. For example, the film offers a fascinating reminder of what the Docks were like just before the regeneration and rebuilding of the 1980s. The desolate rows of abandoned warehouses in the film are in marked contrast to the office and apartment blocks that now stand in their place. Hindsight also shows how much the film anticipated future developments. Released in 1980, a year after Margaret Thatcher became Prime Minister and just as the regeneration of the Docklands began, it is more than simply a gangster movie. It is an allegorical anticipation of the dislocations about to be wrought by a decade or so of capitalist deregulation, unfettered development and globalization. That it takes place in the Docklands, where these dislocations had some of their most visible effects, is especially prescient.

Perhaps the most prescient aspect of *The Long Good Friday* is its apocalyptic aspect. The film is simply an account of the relentless destruction of Harold Shand's world by more powerful forces. The final result is never in doubt, for all Harold's macho posturing and violence. The last shot shows him and his girlfriend Victoria, played by Helen Mirren, having been abducted by the IRA, staring panic-stricken out of the windows of their limousine, on the way, presumably, to be murdered. At one level this is clearly little more than efficient plotting to produce exciting entertainment. But at another, allegorical, level it can be seen to stand for the catastrophic, apocalyptic nature of late, deregulated capitalism. The dissolution of the rules that enable Harold to become a legitimate businessman is also the source of the conditions that bring him into conflict with the force that will destroy him. This is not to suggest that, in general, such capitalism operates at the level of explicit violence, such as is portrayed in the film. But rather that it is by its very nature violent, in the sense that it involves the increasing freeing up of productive energies and the concomitant abandonment of checks and safeguards, with potential and actual catastrophic consequences. Disasters such as 'Black Monday', 'Black Wednesday', as well as the Hatfield rail crash of 2000 and other results of deregulation, are not aberrations or mistakes within this system, but confirmations of its catastrophic nature. The gangs and terrorist organizations in *The Long Good Friday* externalize the violence inherent in the capitalist 'war machine', which no longer has war as its object but is intent on sustaining a peace that 'technologically frees the unlimited material processes of total war'.[1]

It is in the part of London that Harold Shand's development was intended to take place that the martial nature of contemporary business is made most evident, in particular in the anonymous buildings of Canary Wharf, the largest office development in Europe. The location and shape of these buildings are determined by the need to accommodate the technical apparatus of war, re-purposed and mobilized for the needs of deregulated capitalism. The Wharf is sited on what was once a marshy peninsula formed out of a loop in the River Thames. It was developed as part of the project to regenerate London's Docklands, which, having once employed hundreds of thousands of people, had, by the late 1970s, more or less ceased to function, leaving thousands of unemployed and more than 8 square miles of disused land. In response, the Thatcher government founded the London Docklands Development Corporation (LDDC), which was intended to encourage and facilitate development in the area. The Toronto-based firm Olympia & York took up the challenge, constructing what was at the time the tallest building in Europe, One

Canada Square, as well as much of the surrounding area. Unfortunately, a combination of strikes and recession meant that, for Olympia & York at least, the Canary Wharf project was a disaster. By the time it was finished, in 1992, Olympia & York and many other investors were bankrupted and the tower was largely empty.

With the end of the last recession and consequent demand for office space, Canary Wharf's fortunes have been revived. The building of the Docklands Light Railway has greatly helped in attracting businesses by making it more attractive to potential workers, and, as I write, more towers are being built beside the original at One Canada Square. Since the mid-1990s, a large number of banks and financial companies have moved to Canary Wharf and the surrounding area, including HSBC (who commissioned one of the new towers), Citibank (for whom the other was built), Morgan Stanley Dean Witter, BZW, Crédit Suisse First Boston, The Northern Trust Company, Clifford Chance, among many others, as well as newspapers and other kinds of business. According to the official Canary Wharf website, approximately 5.8 million net square feet of office and retail space has been constructed to date, with a further 8.1 million square feet under construction. All of the existing space is leased to accommodate 55,000 workers. Bearing in mind that these figures do not account for the other developments in the same locale, it is obvious that Canary Wharf and the surrounding area is thriving.

Seen from Poplar High Street or the East India Dock Road, the Canary Wharf development rises up to dominate its surroundings like a postmodern Emerald City from the film *The Wizard of Oz* (1939). Its appearance is all the more spectacular in relation to the comparative poverty of the surrounding area. Indeed, there is something positively unsettling about the disparity between the normal run of ramshackle East End streets, markets and squares and the pristine *città ideale* on the Isle of Dogs. But the impressive appearance it offers from outside is not evident when actually in the Wharf. Whether visiting by foot, car or on the Docklands Light Railway, it is difficult to make sense of or engage with the architecture and the space. Apart from the remains of the docks and the towers, which, while impressive when seen from afar, appear curiously stubby when seen close up, there is little to focus on. The strongest impression is that of a kind of arbitrariness, both in the look of the buildings and how they are placed in relation to each other. There is neither the sense of history and organic growth that characterizes the City of London, nor the evident sense of planning and formality that is found in a grid city such as New York. Nor is it easy to make sense of, to 'read', the appearance of the buildings themselves. They defy such understanding because of their relentless banality and anonymity, which is reinforced rather than mitigated by the plethora of eclectic styles. In this they seem to confirm Fredric Jameson's observation about the aesthetics of late capitalism lacking the capacity for representation found in previous eras. For Jameson, the paradigmatic machine of our current age is the computer 'whose outer shell has no emblematic or visual power, or even the casings of the various media themselves, as with that home appliance called television, which articulates nothing but rather implodes, carrying its flattened image surface within itself'.[2]

It is machines of reproduction rather than production that the buildings in Canary Wharf resemble. They too are imploded in on themselves, their façades giving no indication of their interiority or how they operate, like televisions or computers. This also gives them the appearance of the banal, geometric backdrops to computer games or virtual reality, especially when seen from the Docklands Light Railway, which glides, pilotless, above the streets and docks. This overdetermined set of references to digital technology is not coincidental. They are the locations where what Slavoj Zizek, referring to the World Trade Center, calls the operations of 'VIRTUAL capitalism, of financial speculations disconnected from the sphere of material production'[3] take place. Their appearance and the form they take are directly bound up with the increased computerization of finance and business in the 1980s. Sites such as Canary Wharf were developed in response to specific developments in financial markets, including deregulation and the wholesale introduction of computerized electronic trading.

On 27 October 1986 the 'Big Bang' took place in the City of London. This term referred to the series of major operational changes on the London Stock Exchange put into operation as part of a programme of deregulation intended to enable London to remain a leading financial centre in a world of increased competition and globalization. It involved a number of liberalization measures, such as merging the functions of jobber, the dealer in stocks and shares, and the broker, who mediates between the jobber and the public, introducing negotiated commission rates, and permitting foreign banks and financial companies to own British brokers/jobbers, or themselves to join the London Stock Exchange, as well as the introduction of the Stock Exchange Automated Quotation system (SEAQ) to replace the traditional trading floor of the Stock Exchange with a screen-based quotation system. It is the last of these measures that was the most important, in that it had the greatest long-term effect on stock trading, and, indeed, on international finance in general. Although systems such as Reuters' Instinet had been available since the late 1960s, the London Stock Exchange was the first institution of its sort to convert to an entirely electronic trading system, in which the traditional operations on the floor were replaced by computerized transactions. Since 1986, computerized trading and computerized databases have superseded older methods of trading on most exchanges around the world. In doing so, they have radically transformed the nature of international trading and, more generally, of the world of international finance.

They also transformed the physical environment in which they operated. In the 1980s, almost as if a bomb had hit it, much of the City of London and the surrounding area was physically dismantled and rebuilt from the ground up. Next to or in place of the medieval and classical architecture that had typified the City, new developments proliferated, including Canary Wharf and Broadgate, next to Liverpool Street Station. What is remarkable about such developments is how unassuming they are, at least in comparison to near-contemporary projects such as the NatWest tower (now Tower 42) and the Lloyd's building. Broadgate, for example, is only eight to ten storeys high and of a discrete and unmemorable appearance, lacking the NatWest tower's impressive height or the bravura of the Lloyd's building's flamboyantly postmodern exterior. What such spaces offer instead is far more appropriate for the operations of finance and trading after the Big Bang, including vast, uninterrupted floor space, to encompass the needs of electronic trading, enabling dealers to see both their computer screens and the electronic quotation boards at the same time, and supervisors to be able to see the dealers. They also offer controlled environments to extract the heat from the computers and space between floors to contain the vast amount of wiring required. Such space requirements were in marked contrast to previous demands for office space in the 1960s and '70s, in which private offices and windows were considered a priority.[4]

The demand for affordable, large-scale efficient operating environments in preference to physical proximity to other institutions also meant that location in the City was no longer a priority. The ability to locate offices away from the centre was also enhanced by the increased use of computers and computer networks. The character of these buildings is dictated by a number of different factors, principally the relaxing of planning constraints in the Docklands development zone, the openness of the site as compared to the medieval street layout of the City and the interior space demands of post-Big Bang financial businesses, in particular the need for large open trading floors combined with room for the complex high-tech equipment and wiring. In this, such spaces cease to be the traditional face-to-face trading areas of pre-Big Bang finance. Instead they are control centres, like those used to direct operations at a distance in modern computer-controlled factories or in power stations, or to enable traffic control, or satellite launches, or even to coordinate customer care in the guise of call centres. Such centres, with their ranks of operators sitting staring at computer screens, can be thought of as the paradigmatic spaces of post-industrial, postmodern society, or what Gilles Deleuze describes as the 'society of control'.[5] They are 'enclosed and insulated, containing a world represented abstractly on a screen, rendered manageable, coherent, and rational through digital calculation and control'.[6]

The last quote is in fact a description of the principal model for all such centres, the nuclear early warning facility, such as those built in the United States in the 1950s and '60s under the aegis of the Semi-Automatic Ground Environment project (SAGE). In these paradigmatic Cold War spaces all the elements that come to typify the control centre are to be found. Rooms full of monitors and operators are supported by complex arrangements of computers, communication equipment and environmental control facilities. The City and Docklands offices are direct descendants of these anonymous bunkers, in which massive amounts of communication equipment supported rooms of personnel watching computer monitors. Within the contemporary bunkers of high finance, men and women sit at their high-tech consoles, manipulating the economy with the hair-trigger sense of immediacy and speed of response inherited directly from nuclear early warning systems. In this regard, the use of the term 'Big Bang' is telling. It derives from the cosmological theory about the evolution of the universe as a process of expansion from a highly condensed and compressed primordial state. But it also alludes to a network of other meanings, including the kind of big bangs that result from detonating nuclear weapons. The Bomb is an apt image for deregulation, involving, as it does, the release of massive amounts of destructive energy through the unravelling of the atomic structure.

But connecting financial deregulation with nuclear weaponry is more than just a question of metaphor, and the London Big Bang was more than simply a liberalization of the stock market. It was the moment that the relationship between neo-liberal economic theory, digital technology and nuclear catastrophe was made clear. One of the principal theorists of the application of games theory to economics, John von Neumann, was also involved in both the Manhattan Project, which built the first atomic bombs, and in the construction of ENIAC, the world's first digital binary computer. (Von Neumann was incidentally reputed to be the model for Dr Strangelove.) The technology that enabled the Big Bang was directly descended from computerized early warning systems such as SAGE, and military-funded projects such as the ARPANET, the ancestor of the Internet. The wholesale application of nuclear-defence technology to global finance represented more than just the expedient exploitation of useful tools. It was the point at which the technical infrastructure developed as a response to the military exigencies of the Cold War took over the running of the financial system, and in doing so recast that system in terms of continuous paranoid attentiveness on a global scale and hair-trigger responsiveness to the most apparently insignificant signs. At a deeper level, the histories of post-war economics, of nuclear weapons, and of information technology are ineluctably bound together.

In a sense the deregulation of which the Big Bang was part was a substitute for the much awaited and feared dropping of the actual Bomb, in that it represented a resolution or culmination of the tensions that had built up during the post-war era of unresolved nuclear confrontation. It was the dropping of what Paul Virilio calls 'the information bomb'. As he puts it, '[T]he metaphor of nuclear catastrophe and fallout is no longer a stylistic trope, but in the end an accurate enough image of the damage to human activity caused by this sudden implosion–explosion of computerised interactivity which Albert Einstein predicted in the 1950s would constitute a second bomb, after the purpose-built atomic one.'[7] The forces of deregulation that it represented had much the same effect as an actual nuclear explosion. Three years after the Big Bang, the Berlin Wall collapsed and, a couple of years later, the Soviet Union effectively disbanded. Much of the credit for these events is given to the comparative flexibility of deregulated and technologically advanced capitalism as compared to the sclerotic and rigidified condition of state communism. Of course, as with nuclear weapons, there has been a considerable amount of fall-out, particularly within the old Soviet Union, coming to terms with gangsterism, nationalism, financial collapse, nuclear crime and internal and external conflicts. Despite these problems, the collapse of Soviet Communism was perceived as a victorious culmination, understood not just as the outcome of complex political circumstances, but as the inevitable triumph of economic and political liberalism. The collapse of the Soviet system made the equation more believable and gave extra impetus to the drive towards the global liberalization of trade, and the imposition of the neo-liberal economic policies of the West on the rest of the world. Much as Clausewitz described war as politics and diplomacy waged by other means, so contemporary virtual capitalism is war waged by economic means. The anonymous buildings of Canary Wharf and elsewhere are the bunkers in which this virtual war is waged. Should such an analysis seem far-fetched or hysterical, then it is worth remembering that one of the principal targets of the suicide bombers of 11 September 2001 was the World Trade Center in New York, and that, as an immediate response, One Canada Square, the tower at the heart of Canary Wharf, was evacuated.

STAGING ROYAL LONDON

Fiona Henderson

IN THE SUMMER of 2001, the Original London Walks Company advertised their latest itinerary through the streets of the British capital. Entitled 'Strictly Confidential – The Secret London of Princess Diana', the new tour promised the visitor an unusual and personal insight into the London life of the late princess. According to the brochure,

> This walk explores the *terra incognita* – the undiscovered country – of the Princess's life *outside the royal goldfish bowl.* She was Rapunzel, the Princess imprisoned in the tower – or 'the POW – the Prisoner of Wales' as she came to call herself. But she was also, as she put it, 'a free spirit' . . . and when she took wing from her gilded cage, it was often to this *recherché*, oh so very private, '*star-dust*' London: to her ancestral home – the flats of friends – to discreet restaurants – to exclusive clubs – to Dodi's penthouse suite. *And here's the clincher, the walk was created by – and is guided by – the fashion model Desirée Erasmus, who moved in some of the same circles!*'[1]

Amalgamating two other walks that had been based in Earl's Court and St James's, this new itinerary concentrated on the places in the West End where the former Princess of Wales had spent time in the final years of her life. The tour quite clearly reflected the continued and insatiable public desire for access to the princess, even after her death and funeral. Tourists in London, evidently, were compelled to seek out reminders of Diana, making the pilgrimage to her former homes across London and tracing her footsteps through the shops of St James's, Mayfair and Knightsbridge.[2]

The behaviour of these visitors reflected a wider trend within London's tourism at the end of the twentieth century, an attempt to penetrate the deeply traditional image of the British royal family. Visitors to the capital have long been drawn to the formal displays of monarchy in the city – queuing for the various palaces open to the public and lining the streets to witness the daily and annual rituals of the Windsors – and this traditional tourist geography has persisted, even though the institution of monarchy itself has taken something of a battering.

The increasing ambivalence towards the House of Windsor found among the British public has not been mirrored in tourist circles. As the guided tour to Diana's London shows, visitors to the capital at the turn of the twenty-first century were more than keen to know about the everyday comings and goings of the royal family. Drawing upon guidebook accounts of the city, this chapter will explore more carefully the changing tourist geographies of royal London in the years between the Queen's Silver and Golden Jubilees. The descriptions and itineraries contained in these texts not only confirm the established royal landscape in the British capital, but also reveal important insights into the changing nature of tourism in London during this period.

London for Beginners

At the beginning of the Queen's Golden Jubilee year of 2002, the American guidebook *Fodor's London* published an itinerary through the West End, taking in the many sights of Westminster, Whitehall and St James's. Identified as a tour of 'Westminster and Royal London', the route offered the visitor a concentrated view of the city's most famous landmarks, including Buckingham Palace, the Houses of Parliament, Westminster Abbey and Horse Guards Parade. The area covered by the walk was distinctly royal – bound by the main thoroughfares of pageantry and display so often associated with the British monarchy. In urging readers to take up this walk, *Fodor's London* also acknowledged that an alternative name for the tour might have been 'London for Beginners',[3] suggesting the pre-eminence of the royal narrative in London's tourist landscapes.

The pageantry associated with the House of Windsor has, of course, long been popular with London visitors, who flock daily to witness the military ceremonies at Buckingham Palace and the Tower of London. Guidebooks helped to direct this gaze throughout the twentieth century, noting the schedules and explaining the significance of performances to countless tourists. The iconic status of Royal Guards and Yeoman Warders is immediately obvious from almost every London guide published in the last thirty years, where they parade across the covers and through the pages in their distinctive uniforms. While the visual impact of these servicemen has helped to reinforce the traditional connection between London and the monarchy, their presence in the tourist landscape has become increasingly clichéd.

Tracing this link between the capital and the royal household through the ages, however, the historian Penelope Corfield has challenged the idea of a traditional royal London. With regard in particular to the tourist experience of the city, she argues against a dominant narrative of monarchy. Instead, Corfield's interpretation of the urban landscape draws attention to the variety and complexity of the city's image. Reflecting on this lack of a 'monarchical London', she writes: '. . . as modern tourists discover, the institutional glories of London are scattered rather than interlinked: it remains an accidental, rather than an ordered city; a diverse metropolis rather than a specialist capital'.[4]

This myth of a 'traditional tourist London', shaped around a collection of rituals and displays of monarchy, clearly needs to be explored more carefully. Discussions in recent years, for instance about the framing of landmarks, have revealed the complex processes involved in constructing the tourist experience. In particular, the idea of the tourist gaze has suggested that tourists have very systematic ways of seeing – shaped and controlled by the ever-changing economic, social and cultural climate.[5] For instance, the increased influence of consumer culture has produced various new ways of seeing the city. Challenging the traditional images of royal London, these new tourist geographies distract the gaze away from the palaces and structures of monarchy and instead concentrate it on the chic shopping districts and luxury restaurants of the West End.

The tourist view of the world has been severely criticized since the early days of travel. First day-trippers and then mass tourists were accused of being superficial and naive in their search for famous landmarks and national traditions.[6] Drawing on these early critiques, Dean MacCannell has examined the idea of authenticity within tourism. Indeed, his analysis of the leisure classes from the mid-1970s suggested that staging and performance played a central role in the tourist's actual experience of place.[7] Although MacCannell's research was largely based upon the tourist's interest in displays of work, these ideas about a manufactured reality are relevant in all sorts of tourist landscapes.

A consideration of staging and performance, however, especially in relation to the traditional tourist geographies of royal London, raises a number of questions about the authenticity of rituals associated with the House of Windsor. Displays such as the Changing of the Guard and the Trooping of the Colour were often described in late twentieth-century guidebooks as formal, established traditions. The *Eyewitness Travel Guide to London*, for instance, first published in the early 1990s, informed its readers: 'Much of London's rich inheritance of tradition and ceremony centres on royalty. Faithfully enacted today, some of these ceremonies date back to the Middle Ages, when the ruling monarch had absolute power and had to be protected from opponents.'[8]

Most of the royal displays on offer for the London visitor, however, were certainly not as ancient or as established as this guidebook would suggest. David Cannadine has pointed out that most of the pageantry associated with the modern British monarchy actually dates from the late nineteenth and early twentieth centuries. He argues that many of the carefully staged royal ceremonies that take place in London throughout the year are in fact 'invented traditions'.[9]

At the turn of the twenty-first century, therefore, the idea of a traditional tourist London, shaped around the pageantry and palaces of the British royal family, seems to be a little problematic. In particular, the popularity of events such as the Changing of the Guard is undermined by questions about staging and historical authenticity. In recent years also, the tourist experience has shifted and evolved with the development of new economies and cultures of consumption. Challenging the traditional narratives of royal London, guidebook accounts in the 1990s revealed new ways of seeing the British monarchy. Discarding the rather stiff and formal images from the past, these new geographies of royal London attempted both to celebrate and normalize the House of Windsor.

TV Dinners at the Palace

In the early morning of 7 August 1993, a long queue of people began to form at a side entrance to the grounds of Buckingham Palace. Dressed mostly in jeans, T-shirts and trainers, the group did not resemble the conventional guests normally admitted to the Queen's primary London residence. Instead, armed with guidebooks and cameras, they were the first group of tourists to be given access to the 'inner sanctum' of the palace itself.

The opening of Buckingham Palace to the general public marked an important shift in the tourist perception of royal London, since it offered a unique glimpse of life behind the scenes. Although the palace had always held a central position in regal geographies of the capital, the building's image had invariably been staid and two-dimensional. Earlier guidebook photographs and sketches had predominantly focused upon its unremarkable east-facing façade – the backdrop to many of the daily and annual displays of monarchy. Following the decision to open the residence to the public, however, guides began to depict the palace in a variety of new ways. Revealing information about the daily rituals inside, these accounts served to demystify the institution of monarchy and to humanize it in an unprecedented manner.

The portrayal of Buckingham Palace as a place of work was one way in which guidebooks of the 1990s began to penetrate the carefully constructed traditional image of the British royal family. A trip behind the railings at the palace in fact revealed a vast complex of offices and support staff who were responsible for running the 'headquarters of the British monarchy'.[10] Guidebooks were keen to underline this insider's perspective, suggesting to visitors that a tour of the palace was more than just a standard visit to a stately home. *Fodor's London*, for instance, declared: 'A visit to the palace's west wing is a fascinating glimpse into another world: the fabulously gilded interiors are not merely museum pieces but pomp and pageantry at work.'[11]

The ability to witness working life behind the façade at Buckingham Palace offered tourists what might be considered a more authentic insight into royal London. Certainly, official guidebooks to the palace seemed keen to promote this idea, and they also attempted to validate the monarchy itself. Drawing a comparison with the former French royal palace at Versailles, for instance, the authenticity of Buckingham Palace – and indeed its residents – was pointed out particularly clearly in one guidebook. Introducing the palace to visitors, it noted:

> Unlike Versailles today, for example, where visitors have to imagine a recreation of court life, at Buckingham Palace you can be confident that a real monarch will still appear on the balcony, that real guards are protecting a real sovereign; and that the courtiers continue to work in their offices to ensure that the duties and rituals of constitutional monarchy continue to be performed with dignity, discipline and dispatch.[12]

The validity of this claim needs to be considered carefully, however, since these back regions – places normally hidden from the tourist gaze – are often still subject to various degrees of performance and manipulation.

Indeed, as MacCannell has suggested, there can be several layers of staging involved in transforming areas behind the scenes for public viewing. These preparations, although often necessary, can continue to mask the authenticity of the tourist experience. In the case of a building like Buckingham Palace, therefore, where security and issues of royal privacy are still paramount, what the visitor really sees on a tour of the state rooms is far removed from the reality of daily life.

Of course, various attempts have been made to shed some of these staged layers and expose the more human side to the Windsors. The effect of Princess Diana on public opinion in the final years of the twentieth century seemed particularly to hasten this move. Labelled the 'People's Princess', her celebrated common touch and ability to identify with those on the margins of society marked her out from other members of the royal family, who often seemed awkward and distant. In addition, Diana's willingness to reveal insider information about royal life, and to discuss her own problems with it openly, fed an increasing public interest in the private lives of the Windsors. Following the breakdown of Diana's marriage to Prince Charles, therefore, the monarchy came under increased criticism for its reserved nature. Reconsidering the popular image of the Windsors at this time, the palace was forced to adopt new practices and attitudes in the marketing of the royal family. Central to this move were attempts to portray the institution of monarchy and the family itself in a more relaxed and transparent light.

Guidebooks to Buckingham Palace were in a particularly good position to reveal more informal insights into daily royal life. In addition to their historical and architectural accounts of the state rooms, several books tried to portray the palace as a cosy family home. One guidebook in 1993 even revealed the Queen's daily routine at the palace. Although at points this seemed far from ordinary – like the wake-up call from a bagpiping soldier – there were moments where she appeared almost normal. In describing a typical quiet night in, for instance, the book confided that the Queen could often be found watching television. Ironically – and not without due reference to the lifestyle made famous by the BBC's alternative 'Royle Family' – the guide even suggested that Her Majesty was not averse to eating her dinner on a tray. In recounting this evening schedule, though, even this simple, everyday act of dining in front of the television came with its own royal twist:

> Once a week, the Prime Minister calls at 6.30 p.m. for an audience. It is an absolutely private exchange of views. Later, if she has no official

engagements, the Queen likes to watch TV. Helped by one of the 15 footmen, a Page of the Backstairs will bring supper on a tray up to her first-floor apartment overlooking Green Park.[13]

London tourists, of course, have never been privy to these informal royal scenes – at best they have had to content themselves with rare glimpses of the Windsors on official business about town. In the closing years of the century, however, celebrity and commodity cultures further transformed the visitor's experience of royal London. Especially in the British tabloid press, the 'celebrification' of the Princess of Wales generated an enormous amount of public interest in her private life.[14] Mirroring this trend, guidebooks began to locate Diana within their mappings of the city, eventually framing her as a modern-day tourist icon of London.

Although the overwhelming public desire for the princess faded somewhat in the years after her death, guidebooks continued to mark out her place in the city. Books such as *A Walk through Princess Diana's London* served not only as a reminder of her, but also established an entirely new royal geography of London.[15] Revealing the places where Diana had lived, worked and shopped, this itinerary – and others like it – was responsible for removing another staged layer of the Windsors. In a manner not unlike that of celebrity magazines, these accounts of Diana's London were informed not only by her official engagements about town but also by stories in the gossip columns. A form of '*Hello* tourism', these new itineraries offered visitors what may have seemed like a much more intimate insight into the royal way of life.

Following Diana's footsteps into her favourite stores in St James's and Knightsbridge was certainly one way in which London tourists could get closer to the celebrity of the late princess. An implied authenticity underpinned these new geographies of consumption, as visitors were served and waited upon by assistants familiar with the needs and tastes of the royal customer. The presence of other patrons in these shops also helped to complete the royal picture for tourists. Some customers would have had lifestyles and social circles in common with the Windsors, and rubbing shoulders with them brought tourists ever closer to the mythical world of Diana.

The Original London Walks company, of course, offered visitors what seemed like the ultimate insight into the princess's private London. Although remarkably similar to other Diana tours, what made this walk stand out was the clear attempt to construct a narrative of secrecy and intrigue around the whole experience. The central character in this performance, the curiously named model Desirée Erasmus, helped to complete this picture of celebrity life. A supposed contemporary of the late princess, Ms Erasmus not only gave the tour a touch of glamour, but also seemed to add to its authenticity. This claim to an association with Diana – however implausible – marked the walk out as a more personalized account of her London life. Following the paths of other Diana tours, though, and fuelled by the same gossip and scandal, the itinerary was no different from written accounts of the princess in tourist guidebooks. In fact, Ms Erasmus's position within the tour, as both guide and 'confidante', can be seen as just another layer of staging in the complex construction of royal London.

The Tourist Prince

In a bizarre twist to the ongoing search for a more intimate and honest account of royal London, tourists in the late 1990s were given a rare opportunity to see the city through the eyes of royalty itself, since Prince Edward, Earl of Wessex, published a personal guide to the capital.[16] A spin-off from his TV series entitled *Crown and Country*, the book located – albeit in a rather mundane fashion – the buildings and monuments in London of most significance to the royal family. Recounting selected family anecdotes from the dim and distant past, though, Wessex presented a very sanitized history of royal London. Indeed, ignoring the controversial scandals that plagued the Windsors in the late twentieth century, he defined monarchical London for visitors in a very traditional and narrow way.

The publication of a guidebook to London by a member of the royal family also reflected a transformation in the institution of monarchy. Carving out his own career in the media industry, Wessex had already stepped outside the traditional role normally assigned to the Queen's immediate family. In taking on this new position of tour guide, however, he also began to challenge the familiar boundaries between tourists and the British monarchy. Indeed, judging from some of the photographs in the text – which showed the earl in very casual trousers and jackets – he was in danger of being taken for a tourist himself. In spite of his unique position, Edward Wessex's account of the capital failed to reveal any more personal insights into the House of Windsor. In contrast to other tourist accounts of the city, though, his staging of royal London seemed to centre more upon his own desire to perform the role of tourist guide.

The changing tourist geographies of royal London in the closing decades of the twentieth century clearly reflected not only the complex image of the British monarchy but also the transformation of the tourist gaze in this period. Traditionally drawn to the formal displays of pageantry in the city, London's visitors have become increasingly fascinated by more transparent accounts of the Windsors. Indeed, in an attempt to normalize the royal family, tourist guides in the 1990s began to mark out alternative regal geographies in London. Driven by emerging celebrity and consumer cultures, these accounts of royal London have become more and more intimate. The popularity of the late Princess of Wales, in particular, has had a lasting effect on the tourist image of the capital, as visitors continue to seek out remindersof her.

An exploration of these diverse images of royal London has revealed, however, a number of questions about the authenticity of tourist sights related to the monarchy. Layers of staging, it seems, have manipulated and obscured the visitor's perception of the capital and the royal household, even into the twenty-first century. Most guidebook attempts to portray the family in a more informal light still fail to avoid these problems. Indeed, tours and descriptions of royal London on the eve of the Queen's Golden Jubilee continued to use a narrative of staging in their descriptions. Ironically, royal attempts to present themselves within guidebooks to the metropolis have also been subject to issues of performance, effectively continuing to hide the family from the curious tourist gaze.

CCTV: CITY WATCH

Niran Abbas

YOU REALIZE THAT someone is watching you – or something. On a daily basis, life in London spells surveillance in constantly increasing contexts. You are standing in a bank queue, walking down Oxford Street, trying on a potential outfit in Marks and Spencer's, stopping to enjoy a drink in a wine bar, when you see the small camera, unobtrusively observing the scene, and you start to think you are on the set of *The Truman Show*. Why is the camera watching you? Are you a threat to public order? To their advocates, closed circuit television (CCTV) cameras are something approaching a cure-all for the ills of the city, cutting street crime and making people feel safer. To their critics, they are a sinister extension of state control of our lives, intruding into our privacy and generating more – not less – fear of crime. To all of us, CCTV cameras are a fact of urban life.

Britain has the largest CCTV network in the world. There are at least 2.5 million cameras across the country, and the numbers are growing. In the course of a typical day, the average city-dweller can expect to be filmed at least eight times. If they are very unlucky – or lucky, depending on your point of view – they may be filmed 300 times. In London alone, there are 150,000 cameras – used by the police as well as businesses and other private organizations – keeping a watchful eye over the capital.

Installation of CCTV began in the 1970s, although its widespread use started only in the 1990s. The idea, however, has a far older history: it was in Scotland in 1824 that, by chance, a pickpocket was captured in action by a camera obscura and was chased and arrested. In 1993 and 1994, two terrorist bombs planted by the IRA exploded in the City of London, the historic financial district of the capital. In response to widespread public anxiety about terrorism, the Government decided to install a 'ring of steel' – a network of closed circuit television cameras mounted on the eight official entry gates that control access to the City. The cameras had the capacity to read words on a cigarette packet 100 metres away. But anxiety about terrorism has not gone away, and instead of one Big Brother, the watchful face in George Orwell's *1984* (1949), there is a vast swarm of Little Brothers. Stephen Graham suggests that they will soon be a 'fifth utility', like water, gas, electricity and telephones.[1]

The promise of cameras as a magic bullet against crime and terrorism inspired one of John Major's most successful campaign slogans: 'If you've got nothing to hide, you've got nothing to fear.' The cameras were hailed as the people's technology, a 'friendly eye in the sky', not a Big Brother, but a kindly uncle or aunt. By the late 1990s, as part of its Clintonian, centre-left campaign to be tough on crime, Tony Blair's New Labour government decided to support the cameras with a vengeance. The surveillance cameras are accompanied by notices that run from the bland 'CCTV in operation' to the peppy 'CCTV: Watching for You!'. The aim is not necessarily to catch a glimpse of every actual *event* – although that remains an important goal – so much as to anticipate actions, to plan for every *eventuality*.

Every computer input device has become a potential recorder of our actions. Every digital transaction potentially leaves fingerprints somewhere in cyberspace. We have entered the era of dataveillance.[2] A striking example of the predictive powers can be seen in 'Cromatica', a subway security system that was first tested in London Underground train stations.[3] By connecting closed circuit television cameras with an 'intelligent' computer system, the prototype monitors crowd flows and warns about dangerous congestion. It also alerts to cases of deviant behaviour, such as people going where they are not authorized, and it even spots potential suicides, or so it is claimed. The changing colours and intensities of pixels are continuously analysed to detect characteristic movements. Those contemplating suicide tend to wait on a platform, missing trains, before taking their final steps.

Such systems have much to commend them for their potential to reduce risks and avert tragedies. But there are always questions to ask. 'Abnormal' and 'bad' behaviours are not unequivocal categories. Blanket coverage permits the remote tracking of individuals as they move out of the range of one camera and into another. The City of London is one such potential hazard zone. The positive and productive power of a system like 'Cromatica' could be eclipsed by unplanned, or planned risky alternative uses.

Daily activity in the city involves life as a citizen, as a worker and as a consumer. Surveillance operates in as well as between all three sectors, and although each is increasingly geared to forms of risk management, the purposes still remain relatively distinct.

The Citizen

The convergence of high-tech and 'human face' computing cameras are cited as an active deterrent to crime and a vital tool in detecting criminals. In London, the 'comparative case analysis' function permits officers to search a vast database of unsolved crimes for possible links. Success with this technique in high-profile cases, such as that of the multiple rapist and murderer John Henry Bell, lends support to the development of these systems. 'But these in turn depend upon the use by local beat officers of increasingly sophisticated mobile data terminals that allow them to enter information on crimes and on suspects, and to perform direct checks with the Police National Computer (PNC). This encourages a turn towards greater data collection by police as yet more surveillance is required as a risk communication.'[4] The technology featured in events surrounding the notorious killings of the infant James Bulger (1993) and the television presenter Jill Dando (1999).

Facial recognition technology or biometrics was developed by US academics, among them Joseph Atick. Formerly a professor of mathematics at Rockefeller University in New York, Atick decided to exploit his work commercially in 1994, when he co-founded Visionics, a company that markets the technology under various names around the world. A week after the attacks of 11 September 2001, stocks in Visionics 'more than tripled'.[5] Atick considers that his technology, which is geared up to fight terrorism, is an enlightened alternative to racial and ethnic profiling; and if the faces in the biometric database were, in fact, restricted to known terrorists, he would be on to something. This 'Wizard of Oz' technology, however, is not really intended to catch terrorists at all: it is intended to scare local hoodlums into thinking they might be setting off alarms, even when the cameras are turned off.[6]

So who is most likely to be filmed these days? One study of surveillance systems controlled by operators found that the most likely passers-by were young men, attractive women and black people of both genders. This may explain why, according to survey findings, 72 per cent of people think that the systems can easily be abused and 39 per cent think that those in charge of them cannot be trusted to use them properly.[7] The images obtained may be digitized. Once they take the form of electronic data they are subject to other uses. The soccer fan may not wish to be caught by a commercial television camera, because his wife might see him on the sports news at home and discover that he was not in fact at work or with his mother at the time. But if, in an effort to reduce hooliganism, images from a closed circuit television system are digitized, the same fan's face may be compared automatically and remotely with others known to be previous offenders. The question is not one of personal privacy from prying eyes, however this may or may not be justified. It is rather an issue of what happens to the digitized data. Who then has access to the images and for what purposes? Can individuals control or limit the uses of the data derived from their behaviours?

The Aesthetic CCTV

When Geoff Peck, a homeless man in Brentwood, Essex, slashed his wrists in a shopping centre, his life was saved after the camera operators who had witnessed his action sent for paramedics. Following his recovery, however, Peck was less than amused when Brentwood Council – which ran the surveillance system – sold the tape of the incident to television companies without consulting him. He then watched his suicide bid in a trailer for a documentary. The omnipresence of security cameras such as those in Peckham, which covered the last movements of the murdered black schoolboy Damilola Taylor in 1992, means that a visual obituary can be pieced together for any of us. But whereas spoken tributes try to honour lives that have ended, the camera has a drier, colder eye and reveals the awkward, ignorant haste with which people rush towards death or disaster. Princess Diana, hustled through a revolving door at the Paris Ritz, thought she was speeding home to bed. Jill Dando, efficiently running errands in a Hammersmith shopping mall, had office supplies to buy. James Bulger, happily teamed up with two new friends, straggled off to play down by the railway line.

All these people were smiling, like Damilola Taylor, in an abbreviated life in four frozen frames. CCTV tells a harsher truth than most elegies. Lives don't end at some appointed moment; they just stop, abruptly and unexpectedly, as if a camera had suddenly run out of tape. The footage replays itself in a perpetual present, which is the blithe tense in which we all live. But if you look more closely the tempo has something eerie and unsettling about it. Cameras do not record motion; each time they blink they freeze an instant, and there is a gap before the next exposure, so that bodies look jittery, artificially animated from outside – not so much alive as undead. Their testimony is all the crueller because, after a death, images are no consolation. You can re-run the tapes but you can't reverse time and bring back the person you have lost.

Charlie Chaplin once said that tragedy was life seen in close-up, whereas comedy represented the world in long shot. CCTV cameras need to keep watch on entire precincts, so they prefer long shots, which make room for crowds; the singularity of the close-up is not part of their brief. Inside the lift, Damilola gets closer to the camera but he remains a background figure, blurred like Jean Fautrier's *Black Nude* (1926). The foreground is monopolized by the man with the bouquet, who must have a rendezvous ahead of him.

Camcorders in the delivery room make home movies of our bleeding, screeching entry into the world, and preserve on tape a trauma we have mercifully forgotten. When a disaster occurs there is always a witness with a camera on hand: remember the footage, taken from a passing vehicle, of Concorde blazing as it crashed outside Paris in the summer of 2000? We have become used to being perpetually on set, our every movement in a public place overseen from some secret control room. Is this the fulfilment of Andy Warhol's prophecy, which promised a few minutes of stardom for all? Not everyone is happy with this visual conscription.

Casually unfocused, blandly unable to tell the difference between a man on his way to meet his girlfriend and a boy on his way to be killed, this image is already a species of Pop Art, like those bright, glossy Warhol paintings of car crashes and executions in the electric chair that acknowledge misery and pain. To the distress of his family, James Bulger became one of Pop's short-lived celebrities after his death, when the artist Jamie Wagg took newspaper reproductions of the CCTV tapes and made laminated prints from them, which he called 'cartoons for tapestry'. The pictures did not bother to commemorate the child: Wagg simply entitled them 'Shopping Mall' and 'Railway Line'.

In Phillip Noyce's film *Sliver* (1993), William Baldwin plays the owner of a New York skyscraper who oversees the lives of his tenants from his CCTV headquarters. His motives, he imagines, are benign; when the tape shows a man molesting his stepdaughter, he issues a divinely disembodied warning over the telephone. 'We should wire the whole town', he tells Sharon Stone. But his own merely human eyes are fickle, inattentive. He records a murder, but never gets round to viewing the tape that identifies the culprit. He prefers to replay footage of himself making sweaty love to Stone. Breaking into his electronic den, she demands that he hand over her cassette. 'I want my privacy,' she says. 'I want my own experiences.' She regains this autonomy, with the aid of a gun, and shoots holes in Baldwin's bank of monitors.

The television programme *The Royle Family* caters to this paranoia: it suggests that, while the Royles think they are watching television, television actually watches them, thanks to a camera secreted in the cathode tube. An eye as disenchanted as that of CCTV shows them up in all their dreary squalor. In our cities the avoidance of eye contact is a crucial, cautious protocol. As Robert de Niro demonstrates in *Taxi Driver* (1976) – when talking to his reflection in the mirror – to catch someone else's eye is to ask for trouble. But although we don't look at each other any more, we are collectively under observation. CCTV represents all that's left of the communal sense.

The Worker

But when it comes to being spied on ourselves, it is most likely to happen at work. Tabs can be kept on workers in fixed locations, using surveillance cameras that may also be hooked up to the Internet, or active badges worn by employed personnel that locate them in a building or plant. The idea of 'webcams' is to give shareholders as well as managers the opportunity to see what is happening in the office or factory at any time of day or night. 'With corporate fraud estimated to cost companies around 6 per cent of their annual turnover, the instinct to snoop is perhaps understandable, but unions are becoming worried that companies are beginning to invade people's privacy in a direct infringement of their human rights. Last month an employment tribunal ruled that an it firm was within its rights for sacking Lois Franxhi when she used office time to search for a holiday on the Internet.'[8]

The Human Rights Act will ensure that all British law is compatible with the European Convention and enshrine the right to privacy in it. The Data Protection Act will also ensure that the employee's consent is gained for the 'processing of personal data'. Eversheds, a law firm that advises businesses, has identified six different types of office 'spook', who use different secret techniques to monitor their workforce.[9]

The Listener – Monitors telephone calls.
The Watcher – Checks company emails.
The Psychic Watcher – Logs employees' key strokes.
The Rematerializer – Finds deleted computer files.

The Brooding Presence – Videoing employees.
The Poltergeist – Sifts through employees' desks.

Camera systems installed for the purposes of preventing shoplifting in stores have become a managerial tool. In some London retail shops, CCTV cameras that are intended to keep an eye on light-fingered customers are also used to check on the internal threat of theft. The same cameras pick up other details of worker performance, such as compliance with till or refund and exchange procedures, as well as emotional labour – how 'friendly' and 'helpful' staff appear.[10] This shows how surveillance may spill out of one container and into another by virtue of extending a common technological system.

The advance of technological surveillance into the workplace has raised issues not so much about the control of workers by management, but about what areas of the workplace should be deemed private. Video cameras, keystroke counting, e-mail and Internet monitoring are felt to have different effects on such privacy, and generate different kinds of response. The question has turned from an older Labour union approach to the rights of the employees. The UK Institute for Employment Rights acknowledges that, in addition to contributing to insecurity and stress, workplace surveillance may prevent workers from organizing collectively.[11]

The Consumer

Although some argue that it is 'technology' that is shifting the balance of power against the employee, the reality is more complex. 'Technologies are actively sought that will facilitate higher degrees of consumer management and these may have unanticipated consequences for workers as well as consumers. The software, developed to manage consumption, has a dual role, in that the user is monitored. Liberty's of Regent Street in London became the first shop in Britain to attempt to use such software, called Satnet, in a "burglary" case.'[12] When someone is apprehended for shoplifting, a photograph is taken that maps their face. This is then put into a database; even if no charges are brought, the shop has the right to decide that they do not want that person in the store, and can serve an exclusion notice on them. That is one advantage for the store, in that it also helps to identify people who are trying to give a false name. Sophisticated though the technology is, it is only as good as the database on which it searches for matching faces. It can also identify high-spending customers in shops. It could look down the aisle and see a frequent and valued customer, so that the shop can send a salesperson to assist them. There are a few pilot schemes doing this. Whether favoured customers would appreciate being spied on in this way is a moot point. It is one thing to build up a relationship with a shop; quite another to realize that they are watching every move you make.

Conclusion

Perhaps the reason that Britain has embraced the new technologies of surveillance, while the United States, at least before 11 September, had strenuously resisted them, is that British society is far more accepting of social classification. The desire to put people in their place is the central focus of British literature, from Dickens to Alan Bennett. It is no surprise that a society long accustomed to the idea that people should know their place should not hesitate to embrace a technology designed to ensure that they stay in their assigned places. The camera is egalitarian, as the Marquess of Blandford discovered when a security guard watching CCTV at Harvey Nichols in Knightsbridge saw him pocket two pairs of sunglasses. The Marquess was acquitted in court, but video evidence such as this turns us inside out and exposes the pitiful banality of our misdeeds. The electronic environment of CCTVs automates processes of selection, of inclusion and exclusion, thus turning it into an agency of social sorting. It ensures that people receive the right benefits and others the appropriate advertising materials, but also reinforces stereotypes, discrimination and social difference. In the future, as in the film *Gattaca* (1998), surveillance systems will consist of technology that intimately knows each and every one of us.

SEX, POWER AND MIRACLES: A SUBURBAN TRIPTYCH

David Gilbert

'Cranmore', 32 Ambleside Avenue, Streatham

ON 11 FEBRUARY 1987, Cynthia Payne was acquitted of running a brothel in suburban south London. The disorderly house in question was 'Cranmore', in Streatham. It was not the first time that Payne had been charged in connection with the parties she gave in her house: in 1980 she had been found guilty of the same offences at the same address, and sentenced to eighteen months in Holloway prison. Both court cases gave the British press almost as much pleasure as the party guests themselves. Tales of the unusual (and often highly specific) sexual desires of elderly vicars, members of the Bar and the House of Lords, bank managers and retired RAF squadron leaders, and of undercover police officers engaged in some of the least plain-clothed operations in the history of Scotland Yard (a monocle-wearing transvestite constable helped to prepare the raid in 1987) were a wet dream for the red-top tabloids. The combination of public middle-class, middle-aged virtue and private (though at most of the Payne parties not very private) vice played perfectly to the fantasies of the readers of the *Mail* and *Express,* and fitted page three of the *Daily Telegraph* like a warm glove. Even the more prim broadsheets hid behind the fig leaf (or, perhaps more appropriately, the outsize red lacy knickers) of commentaries on the chaotic and unjust state of English sex laws, before exposing their readers to the full-frontal joys of the cases. But in all sections of the media coverage, the supposed incongruity of the suburban situation of 'Cranmore' became a key element in the way the story was told. Sometimes it seemed that the most transgressive aspect of 'Madam Cyn's' parties was that they took place well outside the Circle Line in a solid suburban villa.

Cranmore is not an unusual name for a late Victorian or Edwardian London house. Cranmores are to found in a 'County Antrim' pairing with Glenmores in several London suburbs. The Cranmore at 32 Ambleside Avenue was built in the 1890s, part of the rapid expansion of Streatham in the second half of the nineteenth century. After the arrival of the suburban railways in 1855, Streatham's population increased from around 10,000 to 20,000 in 1881, and 70,000 by 1901.[1] Ambleside Avenue itself has always been a busy cut-through between the centre of Streatham and the adjoining suburb of Tooting, and it is neither as leafy nor as grand as the streets adjoining the common just to the north in what is now the Garrad's Road conservation area. Nonetheless, Cranmore was a substantial detached house, and a real step up for Cynthia Payne from her previous home, a 'poky little place' in Edencourt Road, also in Streatham: 'I was terribly excited at the thought of running a knocking shop in that posh suburban street.'[2]

Yet Cynthia Payne's brothels did not so much defy their suburban situation as adapt to fit. At her trials, Payne repeatedly asserted that she had never had any problems with the neighbours – 'not a single complaint'. Ambleside Avenue was kept spotlessly clean, mainly through the work of two of Cynthia's 'slaves', Rodney and Philip, who did 'all the housework, painting and decorating' in return for 'a little bit of caning, insulting and mild humiliation'.[3] Part of the thrill on offer was that the parties were taking place in a setting so similar to the homes of the guests themselves, many of them elderly or infirm members of the suburban and Home Counties middle class. (In the political culture of the 1980s, one common line on Cynthia Payne was that she was the epitome of a Thatcherite entrepreneuse, supplying services to fulfil a clear market demand. In retrospect, and particularly given her repeated insistence that she wanted to provide sex that could be charged to 'the National Health', she looks more like an early forerunner of the third way – and quite probably fourth, fifth and sixth ways – a fine example of the private sector doing what it can do best, saving resources for the core services provided by the state.) Payne took great care over the homeliness of Ambleside Avenue; even her famous 'luncheon vouchers', primarily a way of getting her guests to pay indirectly (and therefore legally) for sex, had, as A. N. Wilson suggested, 'lingering associations of homely fare – the old gentlemen could then exchange the vouchers for something rather more exciting than meat and two veg.'[4]

Shortly after her acquittal in 1987, Cynthia Payne invited a reporter from the *Streatham, Clapham and Dulwich Guardian* on a tour around the house. Again, Payne was ahead of the times, since the combination of sycophantic commentary and interior design was a suburbanized anticipation of the classic *Hello!* magazine article:

> Meeting Madam Cyn proved to be more like visiting a favourite aunty than a shameless sex queen. The first thing she did was put the kettle on. Then she showed me her photo-album while two well-fed cats wandered in and made themselves at home in the elegant clutter of a spacious Victorian living room. The room is furnished with red plush chairs, antiques, photographs of friends and Valentine cards from dozens of admirers.[5]

The cats got special treatment during Payne's parties, in their own bedroom with a 'do not disturb' notice on the door. Another sign asked guests not to fornicate in the bathroom, 'by order'. Payne's role during the parties was not so much as madam, as a good suburban matron; she spent much of her time in the kitchen making cups of tea, sandwiches and poached eggs on toast. As well as being house-proud, she was also fiercely loyal about her suburb. She wanted to be buried 'right at the centre in St Leonard's Church, so everyone could walk over me', and she felt that she had 'put Streatham on the map'.[6] Fifteen years after the last trial, Cynthia Payne is still the first association made by many Londoners whenever Streatham is mentioned.

In his summing up in 1987, Judge Pryor warned that the case was a criminal trial, not a form of entertainment. But by then it was far too late to restore much seriousness to the proceedings. In the Ambleside Avenue trials history repeated itself, as farce both times. The only differences were the verdicts, and that by 1987 everyone involved had learnt their lines rather better. Payne herself was quite shameless in recycling the best lines from her earlier trial. It did not help the judge that the trial coincided with the release of a film of Payne's life, *Personal Services*, which was directed by Terry Jones of Monty Python fame. Combined with the press coverage, the film helped to move Ambleside Avenue into what Andy Medhurst has described as the 'gnome zone', that imagined suburbia of British sit-coms, Benny Hill, *Carry On* films and *Confessions of a Window-Cleaner*.[7]

One of the long-established tropes of the 'gnome zone' was of promiscuity and decidedly unconventional sexual preferences (often involving the dressing-up box and 'mild humiliation') going on behind the net curtains of the Victorian villas and inter-war semis. At Ambleside Avenue, Cynthia Payne had created a place that was hyper-suburban, where the on-screen clichés were acted out in real life. The media, too, knew just what was required of them: first, the expressions of deep shock that any below-the-waist activity took place in the suburbs; then the satisfied guffaw when the net curtains were pulled back and trousers were found around ankles. This suburban simulacrum depended on a double fiction, however. It was an image that depended on a representation of suburbia as conservative, repressed and narrow-minded, despite a counter-history that was almost as old as suburbia itself. It also relied on a construction of Streatham that was a fundamental misreading both of its distinctive characteristics and of the urban geography of the city as a whole. For Streatham was not, and had never been, distant and insulated from the metropolitan world, and London has never had much similarity to the neat ecological models of Chicago School sociology. In Streatham, deep leafy suburbia is a minute's walk from the inner city. By the early 1980s, the term 'the inner city' had ceased to be a simple description of geographical location, and in the rhetoric of politicians had become an increasingly racialized marker of crime and social breakdown.[8] If Brixton, just a couple of miles up the A23, was the archetype, Streatham High Street certainly made the grade. For those who chose look to beyond the 'Carry On at Ambleside Avenue', what was striking about Streatham was the juxtaposition of different social worlds, of an increasingly run-down high street next to elite housing, of kerb crawling in conservation areas, and heroin-selling by the horse-ride on Tooting common.

260 Longfellow Road, Worcester Park

On 27 November 1990, Britain's first suburban Prime Minister moved into 10 Downing Street. Seventeen months later, John Major surprisingly retained his job, winning the general election of 1992 with the largest-ever popular vote in a British election. Other prime ministers, including his immediate predecessor, had come from the middle classes, but Major was the first from the deep heartlands of the gnome zone. He was born in 1943, at the St Helier Hospital in Carshalton, Surrey. The family home was at 260 Longfellow Road, Worcester Park. Worcester Park is in the far south-west of London, and most of its housing stock dates from the 1930s. Longfellow Road is quite close to the station (half an hour into London Waterloo). It is one of the oldest streets in the suburb, with some residual rural wooden-boarded cottages that predate the railway, and Victorian and Edwardian houses at its southern end closest to the station. No. 260 Longfellow Road was built in the 1920s, further up the road on the way to the local sewage farm.

In his autobiography, John Major remembered the family home:

> . . . a small bungalow with four rooms, a bathroom and a kitchen. Our garden was long and narrow, dotted with sheds in which my father worked. We had a lawn just large enough for ball games, and two ponds: one shallow with a few goldfish, the other a deep iron tank sunk into the ground. There were rockeries, fruit trees to plunder and larger trees to climb.[9]

John Major's early years were suffused with suburban culture. It is well known that his father had worked as a travelling trapeze artist in circuses and music halls, but he had settled down in Worcester Park long before John was born. Tom Major had some involvement in the building trade, helping to arrange the finance for the building of bungalows, but in the early 1930s he had set up his own business, making garden ornaments, including gnomes.[10] Major's Garden Ornaments prospered with the expansion of semi-detached London in the 1930s, and by 1939 had diversified into crazy paving, turfing and landscape gardening. John Major lived at Longfellow Road until he was he was aged 12. It was an unexceptional suburban childhood, of pet-keeping (mice, a white doe angora rabbit called Frisky and a bull terrier called Butch), of collecting birds' eggs from the hedgerows behind Longfellow Road, and, above all, of a developing love for cricket. Major later reflected on the ordinariness of this background: 'Everyone must have such stories from childhood. But perhaps it is worth illustrating that prime ministers are no different. From the pages of some politicians' memoirs the statesman seems to spring perfectly formed, almost from the cot, without all the trivial things that matter so much to a child.'[11] Tom Major's garden ornament business went bust in 1955 (more to do with some shaky financial arrangements than lack of demand for the accoutrements of suburban gardening), and the family moved from Worcester Park into a small rented flat in Coldharbour Lane, Brixton. John Major spent his adolescence in Brixton, and it was there that he started on his career in Conservative politics.

This childhood displacement from deep suburbia to the inner city allowed different stories to be told of Major's rise to high office. Penny Junor's biography was re-published in 1996 with the subtitle *From Brixton to Downing Street.*[12] In the early years of the Major premiership, this story was narrated publicly to some effect. It trumped some of the common Labour criticisms of Tory leaders; here was a leader not from the aristocracy or the shires, but from the inner city. It also could be used to make firm distinctions between Major and his predecessor; in place of Thatcher's provincial racism, with its fears of the 'swamping' of English culture, Major could be represented as someone at ease with an increasingly multi-cultural society. A Party election broadcast of 1992 showed Major in the back seat of a car touring through his Brixton memories. 'It's still there, it's still there', he shouted in an apparently unscripted (and certainly uncharacteristic) burst of excitement as he passed the Coldharbour Lane flat.

But there was an alternative narrative, one that emphasized Major's ordinariness, and his suburban origins. An alternative biography from the early 1990s, Edward Pearce's *The Quiet Rise of John Major*, worked within this trope, following the Prime Minister's path 'from Longfellow Road', a place 'doomed to be called suburban'.[13] The former Tory whip, Tristan Garel-Jones, described Major as the 'personification of Middle England':

> When my constituents ask what he's like, I say he's the sort of person I would expect to see with his car parked by the pavement on a Sunday, washing the car, eating some Polo mints, and listening to the cricket match on the radio. He is extraordinarily ordinary.[14]

It was a portrait with which Major himself seemed to be comfortable. Much of the rhetoric of Major's social policy looked back to a kind of idealized 1950s Worcester Park, particularly in the ill-fated 'back-to-basics' campaign (fatally undermined by the predilection of Tory MPs for brown envelopes and Ambleside antics – and subsequently made more risible by Major's own taste for late-night curries). In one of his best-remembered (and most ridiculed) speeches, he expressed his love for an England of 'long shadows on county grounds, warm beer, invincible green suburbs, dog lovers and old maids bicycling to Holy Communion through the morning mist'. Although the words were drawn from George Orwell, the sentiment came from Stanley Baldwin, who had been Prime Minister during the great 1930s boom in suburban building. Baldwin too had used the rhetoric of deep England to appeal to the conservative aspirations of the new suburbanites, just as the Metroland developments sold all mod-con houses in Pinner and Rayners Lane by eliding them with Buckinghamshire and Hertfordshire villages in the country beyond. Major tried the same trick – except that the site of Prime Ministerial experience had shifted from Baldwin's beloved Worcestershire to the slightly green and decidedly vincible suburb of Worcester Park.

There were, however, distinct limits to 'likeability'.[15] If John Major's suburban ordinariness had been seen as a significant strength in the early years of his premiership, after the debacle of Britain's ejection from the ERM, it was increasingly seized upon as evidence of his weakness and lack of leadership qualities. As the standing of his administration plummeted, becoming by 1995 the most unpopular government in the history of British opinion polling,[16] Major's lower-middle-class suburban roots and attitudes became the focus of satire and mockery. There were many variants on Prime Minister Pooter. In *Private Eye*, 'The Secret Diary of John Major aged 47¾ crossed Adrian Mole with an updated version of *Diary of a Nobody*. On television's *Spitting Image*, a totally grey Major puppet droned on at his wife, while desultorily picking at a plate of lukewarm peas. Major's wardrobe of plain grey suits and Marks and Spencer's pullovers failed to help matters, nor did the occasional stops for meals in branches of Happy Eater. His background and manner may not have been the cause of Major's political problems or his Government's unpopularity, but as his position weakened the full force of a long-established tradition of anti-suburban rhetoric was turned against him. Tristan Garel-Jones's supposedly affable description of the Polo-sucking premier betrayed underlying elitist prejudices about the suitability of suburbans in power. Commenting on the attitudes of the intellectual elite in the 1930s, John Carey argued that the term 'suburban' was 'distinctive in combining topographical with intellectual disdain'.[17] By the 1990s, the development of the 'gnome zone' meant that this prejudice had been democratized and popularized, and that in John Major's 'classless society' everyone, including suburbanites themselves, could enjoy this topographical disdain.

2 Lady Margaret Road, Southall

At about 11.00 a.m. on Thursday, 21 September 1995, a statue of Nandi, the sacred bull that Lord Shiva rides, started to drink milk in a west London suburb. This was a fact that went generally unnoticed. To be sure, the miracle itself caused quite a stir. It was part of an outbreak of divine milk-drinking across the Hindu world. A few hours earlier, the first instance had been reported at a temple on the outskirts of

Delhi. News spread rapidly across India, interrupting government work and temporarily closing stock markets in Bombay and New Delhi as thousands offered milk to their statues. In London, the Vishwa Hindu Kendra temple in Lady Margaret Road, Southall, became the focus of attention; by the time the milk-drinking ended the following Saturday, almost 10,000 people had visited the temple. There were long queues day and night outside the temple, and a milk shortage in west London (pasteurized, homogenized, gold-top, skimmed, semi-skimmed – it did not seem to matter to the god statues). As the queues stretched north up Lady Margaret Road, Anil and Asha Ruparelia opened a second holy site in the bedroom of their terraced house. Here a statue of Ganesh Ji, the elephant god of wisdom and son of Lord Shiva, drank milk up its trunk. As Mr Ruparelia said, 'We were shocked. We've lived here for 18 years and nothing like this has ever happened before.'[18]

What went relatively unnoticed was that all this was taking place in suburbia – if not quite the classic imagined suburbia of the gnome zone then certainly somewhere that was suburban in location (fifteen minutes from Paddington, six trains an hour during morning peak) and appearance (much of Southall's housing stock is semi-detached of the 1930s and '50s, around a core of Edwardian terraces). One Sunday newspaper, exploring the theory that the milk miracles were caused by capillary action, repeated the effect with a garden gnome and Guinness, which was not quite as incongruous as intended.[19] Southall developed in the nineteenth century, its growth spurred first by the opening of the Grand Union Canal, then by the arrival of the Great Western Railway. In the early twentieth century, Southall saw itself as a cut above neighbouring suburbs such as Greenford and Hanwell.[20] It was transformed by post-war developments. The expanding industries in the area – food-processing, plastics, textiles – experienced severe labour shortages in the late 1940s and '50s. These shortages were met by migrant workers from the Indian subcontinent. Woolf's Rubber Company had a branch plant in the Punjab, and many workers moved to their Southall factory after Partition. Many of the early migrants to Southall were Sikhs, and they remain the largest religious group in the suburb, followed by Hindus. By the late 1990s, nearly 70 per cent of Southall's population could trace south Asian origins.

The Vishwa temple itself reflects Southall's history. It was originally built in 1903 as the parish hall for the church of Holy Trinity, Southall, a Victorian pile round the corner on the Uxbridge Road.[21] Later on part of the hall was converted into a men's social club. In 1976, a bad case of dry rot put the cost of repair beyond the parish and the hall was sold and converted to a temple. The local paper reported that those most affected by the closure were the Holy Trinity Players, an amateur dramatic group who had used the hall for 53 years.[22] At the spot where Nandi drank his milk, twenty years earlier the Players were performing *Hay Fever*. In 1986 the temple was enlarged to hold 500 people, with the help of one the GLC's final community grants. Five large effigies of major gods and goddesses, costing more than £7,000, were imported from India. Reports at the time failed to comment on the absorbency of the white marble used.[23]

One common reading of Southall is that it somehow ceased to be suburban in the late twentieth century. Southall is often described as the late twentieth-century equivalent of nineteenth-century Whitechapel, the place of first settlement for thousands of migrants, but with Heathrow substituting for the London docks. In 2002, the mayor, Ken Livingstone, suggested that 'Southall now has all the problems that one would associate with inner-city stress, rather than the suburbs'.[24] Just as the term inner city has become loaded with racial overtones, so the expectation of the outer city has tended to be of invincible white suburbs.[25] In Northolt, just north of Southall, local white objections to the construction of the Mohammedi Park Mosque were expressed in just these terms: 'Northolt is a "garden suburb" and should not become another Southall. This is an alien development – an Islamic ghetto – and will lead to racial imbalance.'[26] There are other localized examples of racist nimby-ism, but what is equally significant is that much of London's suburbia has quietly become marked by a high degree of ethnic, religious and cultural diversity. The new religious buildings of suburban London – the temples, mosques and gurdwaras – are perhaps the most visible expression of these changes. The massive Swaminarayan Hindu Mandir, close to the North Circular Road in Neasden, rising above semi-detached housing and trading estates, is the most spectacular and emblematic statement of the vibrancy and permanence of south Asian culture in London.[27]

It is fitting that the Swaminarayan Hindu Mandir looks out over both (the currently derelict) Wembley stadium and the Ikea furniture superstore. Wembley was constructed as the centrepiece of the British Empire Exhibition (BEE) of 1924. The exhibition serves as a reminder that suburban culture in London always had connections with a wider world. The growth of the suburbs before the First World War and in the inter-war period depended in part on the success of the imperial metropolis, while events such as the BEE and the annual Empire Day wove a sense of London's world position into everyday culture.[28] Many Edwardian or inter-war suburbanites had a rather familiar and domesticated relationship to the Empire, seeing it as much as an extension of 'home' as a distant exotic 'other'.[29] Southall itself was once best known for the Palace cinema, a late-1920s kitsch masterpiece of commercial orientalism, stuffed full of chinoiserie. As Anthony King reminds us, the suburban bungalow, once the favoured home of retired civil servants or military officers who had served in India or Kenya, is a transcultural architectural form, with its origins on the Subcontinent.[30] Seen from this perspective, the post-war changes in the population of suburbia are a new phase in a continuing story of the global connections that have shaped London.

The Ikea store highlights a different dimension of the suburban landscape and culture. London's suburbs have always been rooted in consumer culture, and have been constantly made and remade, through millions of small decisions about DIY, interior decoration and home improvements. The usual clichés see this as part of the tyranny of suburban culture, with suburbanites duped or coerced into endless rounds of competitive consumption. Yet it may be precisely this kind of endless transformation that has made suburbia so flexible. Far from the stereotypes of a monotonous, bland sprawl, much of London's suburbia has been able to adapt to social and cultural change remarkably effectively. There are and have been some significant social problems in Southall, but it is not the modern equivalent of nineteenth-century Whitechapel. The physical landscape and forms of tenure of suburban west London have made a real difference. For many, immigration into Southall was into a world of homes and gardens, neighbours and cars. A recent report from the Joseph Rowntree Foundation highlighted the relative neglect of suburbia, warning that policy makers and planners were overlooking the suburbs, to concentrate on creating an 'urban renaissance'.[31] The report pointed to stresses in some parts of suburbia, but also to their continuing capacity to adapt (albeit quietly and without too much fuss or financial outlay). The suburban world is a place where the extraordinary can be made out of the ordinary – perhaps even from luncheon vouchers, Polo mints and pasteurized milk.

THE TRANSFORMATION OF POLITICAL AND CULTURAL SPACE

Hilda Kean

TIME TRAVELLERS FROM the 1970s would still easily find their way around central London thoroughfares even with one-way systems or pedestrianisation, the framework of the roads, streets and pavements remains largely the same. A socialist or radical activist, however, would have far more difficulty mapping out a former terrain, revisiting places of meetings, political gatherings and cultural dissent. What exists within the streets and along the roads has changed significantly.

In the 1970s, meeting places in rooms over Victorian pubs, trade union halls, community and alternative cultural venues were widespread. Since many political venues were in buildings of an earlier period, they seemed to emit an aura of permanence. The age of the physical fabric created the illusion that the events conducted within their walls would also endure. The materiality of the structure and the political debates within them seemed complementary. However, these informal venues were more transitory than was realized at the time. The tradition of political meetings in pubs – dating back to the nineteenth-century days of the London Corresponding Society or the Chartists – has now withered. Fierce debate amongst the Left in pubs such as the Roebuck in Tottenham Court Road and the Cock tavern in Phoenix Place is no more. Venues like the General Picton in King's Cross, where socialist teachers thrashed out tactics of unofficial strike action in the 1970s, remain, but the radical clientele has long gone. In many cases, the system of pubs 'hosted' locally by a landlord has been replaced by chains run by managers with centralized procedures and policies.

The Roebuck no longer exists, but one can view the minutes of the All London Squatters that took place there on a squatting archive website (http://alt.venus.co.uk/weed/squatting/welcome.htm). Political dissent of a particular time and place has now been transformed into a historical record in cyberspace.

Many of the smaller buildings where activists met have closed: the NUFTO meeting place in Holborn's Jockey's Fields (together with the furniture workers' union itself), has gone. Cromer Street women's centre, the GLC-supported women's centre in Kingsway, and Labour Party, trade union and tenants centres across the capital have closed down and the premises sold off to private buyers. No material traces exist of the political moments enacted in these former structures.

Some of the larger premises used for political gatherings, however, still exist. These include the Methodist Central Hall in Westminster, which continues to be a focus for gathering after parliamentary lobbying, and the Friends' Meeting House on the Euston Road, host in October 2001 to a massive anti-war meeting. Conway Hall in Red Lion Square, the meeting space established by the South Place Ethical Society, still hosts oppositional events, such as the annual Anarchist book fair and the Christmas Third World gift fair, but its usage has also changed with the times. In recent years those who used to attend Saturday conferences on revolutionary politics in the 1970s and '80s are more likely to enter the building to attend a memorial event to a dead socialist.

The subversive use of public space itself has in turn been subverted by the State in different ways. Laws against picketing or spontaneous demonstrations have helped to create a climate in which dissidents are treated as law-breakers. Demonstrators partying at Speakers Corner, a supposed place of dissent and free speech, in opposition to the Criminal Justice Act in October 1994 were met by riot police challenging this use of public space. In different vein, the local state in Islington has recently attempted to undermine Clerkenwell Green as a locus of radical political dissent. The Green has existed in London as a site of political opposition dating back to Wat Tyler and the anti-poll tax campaigns of 1381. From the nineteenth century onwards it has been a regular starting-point for marches – of Chartists, Fenians, socialists. From the 1970s it has been a regular starting point for demonstrations about Ireland or in support of May Day. Watched over by the Marx Memorial Library and the Crown pub, where printers from the *Morning Star* used to gather, the Liberal-led Council has tried to replace the space in the centre of the square, a space for people to congregate in order to protest, with one of consumption. The Council proposed the building of yet another café, which would have undermined the Green in subtle ways, changing it into a place contextualized by individual consumption rather than political, public production. In this instance protesters who responded to the consultation exercise won a small victory on this occasion, rejecting this proposal by a ratio of 2 to 1.

But it is too simple just to cite the transformation of places used for political activity defined as demonstrating, lobbying or socialist or trade union meetings. The form of politics in London has itself changed, particularly through the lack of places for the development of cultural practice. Left-wing life in 1970s and '80s London was characterized by a flourishing of the inter-relationship and inter-dependence of cultural production and far left politics. A good example of this relationship was found in the progressive and too short-lived weekly London listings magazine *City Limits*. The magazine, which first started publication in October 1981, was itself a product of a particular political moment, breaking away from *Time Out* magazine when changes to collective working practices were imposed. However, taking pride of place as the regular first feature in the new left-wing magazine was not 'politics' but film. Film-making, studying as well as viewing and debating, was prominently covered. Cinemas themselves became configured as political spaces for the showing of radical films and discussion: these included the Roxie and Scala Cinema clubs, the Four Corners in Bethnal Green Road and the Last Chance film club in Notting Hill. As the same magazine also reminds us, even in the Thatcher years there was space for resistance: weekends were filled with alternative opportunities for debate, discussion and organization. To cite one example from the second issue of *City Limits*, for 16–22 October 1981, at the same weekend one could attend a conference sponsored by the Conference of Socialist Economists and Beyond the Fragments, or a day school on the Latin American Revolution at the Greenwich Labour Party rooms, or a conference organized by the Eastern European Solidarity Campaign on trade unions and self management, the Polish experience, or attend an Irish Freedom Festival at Caxton House in Archway. Listings of campaigns spilled over two pages of 'Agitation', from fighting council-house sales, sexism in crèches, closure of beds in St Mary's Hospital on the Harrow Road through to a workshop against ageism in the gay community to opposing a British Movement march in Marble Arch or picketing Casper Weinberger, the US Secretary of State for Defence. There were a range of 'benefits' for good causes – 'Rock for Workers' defence' in New Merlin's Cave in Margery Street, or for London play workers at the Battersea Arts Centre, or for gay workshops at the Red Lion in Essex Road. The plethora of concurrently organized events indicated not only the range of political interests but also that the constituency for such gatherings was large enough not to overlap, a clashing of events would not lead to small numbers of participants. There was a range of possibilities to learn about issues that mattered and to educate oneself: sessions to learn how to defend yourself in court, a WEA (Workers' Educational Association) forum on the nature of psychiatric units, 'workshops' or 'day schools'.

This mixture of culture and politics was found too in the old Irish pubs: the George Robey in Finsbury Park, Mooney's in the Strand, the Victoria off the Holloway Road, the Crown and Castle at Dalston Junction or the Favourite in Hornsey Road. In pubs like the Favourite, work, politics and leisure would combine: collections for Republican prisoners' families, live music and men seeking information of where work could be found on building sites. These were not pubs adorned outside with Gaelic calligraphy, or faux window displays of a sentimental past, but places where people themselves could create alternatives to the establishment. Changes have also taken place in fringe theatre. The Cunning Stunts and Common Stock Theatre companies no longer tour community halls and pubs; both the Half Moon theatres in Tower Hamlets have closed down. But some of these sites of political and cultural opposition still exist, albeit in different forms. The Cockpit Theatre remains off Lisson Grove (although no longer a focus of the Socialist Labour League), but now based, as a local Labour councillor describes, on productions about local women's experiences, which include those from the Bangladeshi community.

The London Bubble Theatre company still manages to survive and with its ideals intact, as recently seen in the productions of Jonathan Petherbridge and Farhana Sheikh subverting Swift, Kipling and the Gilgamesh epic for new audiences. In the past the theatre was recognized by its large performance tent. This sense of quasi-permanence has also changed, being replaced by outdoor promenade theatre in London parks in the summer months, subject to the vagaries of the weather. This sense of snatching theatrical moments from an outside hostile environment is also reflected in the work of Adrian Jackson and the Cardboard Citizens, a theatre company of homeless people. His 2001 production of *Mincemeat* (itself about a homeless, nameless man of the 1940s) could be shown only for a few days in the summer in a place of flux. In the semi-derelict Hartley's jam factory in Bermondsey, with builders' scaffolding already in place to change it into up-market lofts, the audience saw a play of transitional life on the margins in a building that would soon itself be altered ineradicably.

Autodidactism flourished in a number of ways in this political–cultural milieu. An emphasis on self-educated and independent learning was possible when there was a range of cheap publications that encouraged further reading and engagement with key socialist texts. The production and sale of pamphlets were possible whilst there was a range of radical independent bookshops throughout London to sell them. Bookshops linked to political groups were widespread: the Other bookshop of the International Marxist Group in Upper Street in Islington, the Workers' Revolutionary Party bookshop in Charlotte Street, the Communist Central Books in Gray's Inn Road or the Socialist Workers' Party Bookmarks, now relocated from its Finsbury Park premises to Gower Street. The education-based Corner House, or Writers and Readers, and the wonderful Compendium in Camden Town have shut. The chain of Collets Communist bookshops, which dominated Charing Cross Road and its environs, closed long ago. The main bookshop, which sported a *Soviet Weekly* stand outside, from which the Euro-Communist staff filched money for cakes, could no more survive in the changing climate than its successor on the site, the women' s bookshop, Silver Moon, now bizarrely relocating itself to an enclave within the conservative Foyles.

Although one might argue that the demise of premises selling radical books was a logical extension of the defeat of left-wing ideas, this rationale cannot be employed to explain the widespread closure across London of public libraries started in the 1980s by a range of Labour councils. Public (and free) access to books and to spaces for reading and engaging with books has been severely curtailed. When cuts were first implemented in the late 1980s, these met with fierce resistance. In February 1988 'The St Pancras Nine' occupied the Camden Reference Library in Euston Road, exercising – they told the press – 'reader power', and had food delivered to them by a basket on a rope by well-wishers. Unfortunately, they were unable to persuade Camden Council to save one of the biggest and best-stocked reference libraries in London, and this was the first of many closures of libraries and of the subsequent dumping or wholesale selling of books. Now on the site of the library is the Shaw Plaza Hotel, with rooms (minus breakfast) at £155 per night.

At the time a Council spokesperson declared that 'it is better to make cuts there, than in housing, welfare and education'. Such crude economism might have been more convincing if other services had indeed been preserved without any cuts. At a later meeting organized in March 1993 to oppose cuts in branch libraries, Fay Weldon, the novelist and

Camden resident, declared: 'If you close branch libraries you lessen people's dignity; you give in to the instant culture; you add to the general tragedy of unemployment and squalor.' Unsurprisingly cuts – and squalor and unemployment – continued in successive years, unrelieved by moments of learning or leisure in local libraries, which continued to be closed, despite opposition. There was a similar story in Hackney, where the majority of the Labour council set a budget for the financial year of 1988–9 that included the closures of several branch libraries throughout the borough and of the reference library in Stoke Newington. The chair of the Leisure Services committee resigned her position in protest, as did other left-wing members, and helped to occupy the branch libraries, including Somerford Grove in Stoke Newington, a favourite venue for pensioners who enjoyed reading. Although the occupations continued for months, they – together with the books – were wrecked by private contractors employed by the Council at 3.00 a.m. on the night of 22 September 1988. The contractors smashed bookcases and fittings and destroyed and damaged thousands of books, still being used during the occupations, as they hurled them into piles for removal and destruction. As the poster used during the campaign stated: 'Something stalked the corridors of Mare Street . . . And It Wasn't Socialism'. In Hackney the Edwardian central library was sold off in recent years to become a commercial music venue. For several years in Mare Street, squalid shacks with few shelves and even fewer books acted as vestiges of the public library provision; ironically, the shacks are erected on the former site of premises used by Council unions, which were, in turn, destroyed. The Rose Lipman library on the Hackney–Shoreditch borders has been shut and the premises rented out commercially to IT 'providers'. The new anonymous grey block – or 'learning and technology centre' – next to the town hall now contains the vestiges of former provision in its single room.

Across London we have a diminution of public places – libraries – where people might read real books or study, where books are not seen as a commodity to be owned but to be used or enjoyed by the whole community, including those without money. As a substitute, Londoners are offered in Further Education colleges and the remains of adult education institutes the Government's mantra of lifelong 'learning' and 'access'. In practice, this has meant low-grade IT skills, with students learning word processing, spreadsheets and databases or 'communication' skills. 'Communicating' in virtual space has become a substitute for using books, engaging, discussing and learning in real space. Throughout the capital, the skills of English as a Second Language, computers or customer-care skills have become widely available; the provision of courses in politics, history, philosophy, literature or even the clichéd evening classes of tap and ballroom dancing are increasingly impossible to find locally for a nominal fee at evening classes. At the City Lit off Drury Lane, courses advertised under the rubric of 'Personal Growth' mean T'ai Chi, Transactional Analysis or taster sessions in Psychodrama rather than trying out new ways of understanding and changing the world.

It is insufficient to explain the depressing state of affairs simply by reference to cuts by Conservative governments and the imposition of legislation privatizing public provision. It is the way in which the cuts were implemented that has so changed London life and changed everyday experience. The impact of the erasure of the GLC has usually been seen in the context of funding and knock-on effects for local councils in London, but in many ways the consequences have been much further reaching, undermining the concept of London itself as an entity with a positive self-activating identity. In the 1980s, the GLC promoted a particular definition of being a Londoner as someone who interacted with others culturally, socially and politically. The Council became a facilitator of such an identity in different ways – initiating political debate, providing space literally and metaphorically for Londoners to bring about change in their own lives. A perusal of the councillors' discussions recorded in the GLC minutes for 1984, and now deposited in the London Metropolitan Archives, suggests a vibrant time. Topics included policy for gay men and lesbians, International Women's Day of 1985, North Paddington Women's Centre, the Rockingham Estate Play Association, and petitions about bus routes and sexist advertisements on London Transport. These were concerns based on actually existing places in which people engaged with their locality and developed this experience within a framework of a London-wide elected council. The GLC also redesigned city space. Parks became venues for free festivals, the South Bank a place of music or open-air chess; the Festival Hall became a public space with free foyer exhibitions; County Hall itself became a venue for Londoners' meetings: ideas of public and private became blurred.

Increasingly, since the mid-1980s, London no longer flourishes as a place where 'people make history'; instead it has been repackaged as a place where people are required to fit into a history made *for* them, both in the non-statutory education sector and in the museum and heritage industry. Patrick Wright's book *On Living in an Old Country*, written in 1985, is still illuminating. As he argues, oblivion was seen by the Conservatives as the rightful abode of all those anachronistic forces that resisted the rationalization of social relations around market forces and new technology. The Thatcher alternative presented a 'respectful' but commercially minded reanimation in a new world of theme parks and mass tourism. It was within this context that English Heritage was established by the National Heritage Act in 1983. Its initial remit, like that of the nineteenth-century Society for the Preservation of Ancient Buildings (spab), was to save buildings from destruction. In London, as the annual reports confirm, it expressed concern about plans to demolish Spitalfields market, the impact of Canary Wharf and the pace of construction in Docklands and King's Cross. As the annual report for 1987–8 declared in respect of King's Cross and St Pancras, 'Nowhere in London, nor indeed in the country as a whole, better illustrates the architectural achievements of the first railway age. The problem for English Heritage is how to protect the grandeur of that age.' The problem was never adequately resolved. By the late 1990s, the organization's priorities had changed. As I write, one of the magnificent gasometers in Goods Way has been demolished, an act carried out away from the prying eyes of motorists, whilst the road was closed during the winter of 2001–2. Part of the old Spitalfields market has already been refashioned, and stallholders are fearful of what will now happen to the remaining part of the nineteenth-century market and whether they have any further role in its future.

Museums, too, were incorporated into the heritage industry. No longer is it sufficient – even with the abolition of charges – merely to look at a few exhibits; the emphasis now is on the whole heritage experience. While the Natural History Museum continues to attract families across the class divide, the Victoria and Albert Museum has defined who is a valued customer. The 'nice caff' – and 'nice' designer-goods shop – has defined its target audience. Similarly, the Great Court at the British Museum has been changed from a place of reading and studying in the British Library into a shopping and café experience. Here tourists can buy authentic 'English' drinks such as ginger beer to sip amidst the inauthentic Portland stone. Other heritage experiences are also less inclusive than they first appear. The popular Open House weekend, established as London's contribution to the European Heritage Days initiative, has allowed Londoners on the third weekend in September to see inside approximately 600 buildings free of charge. Popular though this event is – 360,000 visits were made in September 2001 – this is not about opening up space permanently to Londoners. Rather, it is a way of incorporating Londoners into giving their consent to their own exclusion from premises often built with public money for the other 363 days of the year.

Certainly, some radical and imaginative events have taken place to challenge ownership of space. Groups such as Reclaim the Streets (RTS) and the anti-globalization movement have, in turn, focused their dissent on particular places in urban London. There have been moments to seize space, albeit in transitory ways, and transform the immediate environment: planting flowers in Parliament Square in May 2000; digging up the Edgware Road flyover with pneumatic drills and planting it with trees in July 1996. In turn, the State has continued to try to restrict such community events. The police imprisonment of demonstrators and party-goers at Oxford Circus on May Day in 2001 was a recent example. The moment created by currents like RTS – even though they are just moments – recall earlier times, particularly of the squatting movement when houses were reclaimed in Elgin Avenue and Tolmers Square, and pre-figurative communities were established for many, many years. Cyberspace sites such as urban75 or indymedia do help to organize resistance and attempt to create new political parameters. But this needs to be set against the daily experience of the difficulty of imaginative engagement in a city where wages levels have polarized and opportunities for creating positive change have been restricted.

When the GLC existed at its purpose-built headquarters of County Hall in the 1980s, there was no need for large letters on the side to explain what it was. The figures of the numbers of Londoners unemployed displayed on the side of the building that faced Parliament gave an explicit message. Today, now that County Hall no longer exists as a political location for Londoners, the sign is needed to explain what it once was. On sale in the riverside environs of County Hall there is junk food, including Weston's, 'Britain's number one hot dog'. In the basement of the building itself there are a McDonald's, noisy, dark games arcades and fish are confined in an aquarium.

There are still moments in which cultural and political alternatives can be created, but the material space for this has shrunk. Perhaps more problematically, a popular knowledge of former political–cultural practices is threatened with amnesia. The transfiguration (or destruction) of buildings embodying an earlier political–cultural practice has meant that a particular sort of knowledge about the possibilities for change does not exist. Blue plaques cannot provide such connections: but a vibrant political culture connecting with the past and imagining the future may create possibilities. As the cultural historian and activist Walter Benjamin warned us in his 'Theses on the Philosophy of History', 'Every image of the past that is not recognized by the present as one of its own concerns threatens to disappear irretrievably.'

THE STATE OF LONDON

Mike Phillips

LONDON IS A city that contemporary film-makers can't seem to get right; over the past thirty years there's been a long list of directors who have used London as a location and managed to render it unrecognizable or grotesque. Antonioni shot a big chunk of *Blow Up* in a street where I lived for a while, but the outcome had so little to do with the London I knew that it might just as well have been made in Prague. In *Absolute Beginners* Julian Temple sets out to capture the same period with frankly embarrassing results. A few days ago I found myself watching *The Crying Game* with a growing sense of incredulity at the fact that the director seemed to be going out of his way to furnish his London background with the wrong accents, the wrong clothes and the wrong atmosphere. In recent times only Mike Leigh has come close to re-creating a recognizable portrait of the city, but his best work is a miniature which doesn't depict much more than a specific period in the history of lower-middle-class life in North London. And that's how it goes. England has no movie equivalent to Fellini's Rome, Altman's LA, or Allen's New York; and London is a city whose repeated exposure renders it invisible, like a series of dots which somehow refuse to coalesce into a whole picture.

I suspect that part of the reason why images of London present such a problem is to do with the resentment and hostility which forms a consistent undercurrent to British attitudes about the city. This shows up in odd ways; for instance, the use of the word *London* as a term of abuse – 'trendy London', 'London cliques'. In comparison, terms like the Great Wen and the Big Smoke are affectionate, but they indicate the sense in which London is a metaphor which encapsulates the kind of modernity that the English have traditionally viewed with fear and distaste. The politics of the capital have been plagued by a hostile interaction with central government, which compounded the material problems migrants faced, as well as frustrating and delaying black entry into the political process.

From 1964 on, London was run by the Greater London Council (GLC), which took over from the old London County Council (LCC). The GLC had an expanded catchment area which covered the outer London boroughs, but, in comparison with the LCC, its powers over local services had been enfeebled. Before 1981 few GLC politicians made much impact even on Londoners. Given that its first decade saw the massive inflow to the city of migrants from the Caribbean and Asia, a migrant presence was largely absent, apart from the chairmanship of Dr David Pitt, later Lord Pitt, in 1974. Pitt symbolized, however, the weakness of the migrants in electoral politics throughout this era. A doctor who had studied before the war in Edinburgh, and whose career spanned the entire period of post-war immigration, Pitt had established his surgery in North London during the early 1950s and then was selected to fight Hampstead for Labour in 1959. He lost, but was elected to the LCC a couple of years later. In 1970, while Powellism was still a potent force in British elections, he was selected to fight Clapham in South London, and lost again in one of the biggest swings against a candidate in the country. The message was clear. As chairman of the relatively powerless GLC, Pitt disturbed no one, but the London electorate was not prepared to allow him into the nation's seat of power. In any case, the relationship of the GLC with the ethnic minorities until the end of the decade was ineffectual and tangential. It had failed at the end of the 1960s to produce a strategy for overall planning in the city. It failed over the next twenty years to do more than tinker with London's housing problems, and it had failed to offer Londoners a political vision which could accommodate the changes which were transforming the city. In London, where about one-third of Caribbean and Asian migrants lived, our involvement in the electoral process was no more than a defensive strategy against Powellite politics.

All this changed after the local authority elections in 1981. The Labour Party, cashing in on Mrs Thatcher's pre-Falklands unpopularity, swept into power in all of England's metropolitan councils. London Labour had been led for a year by Andrew McIntosh, but a few hours after the election results were declared, a meeting of the new members replaced him with an obscure left-winger called Ken Livingstone. In the years following, from 1981 to the abolition of the GLC in 1987, the ethnic minorities were to play a prominent part in the structure of London politics. Part of the reason for this was the fact that the GLC's powers were relatively circumscribed. Unlike the old LCC it left no physical monuments to its beliefs, and the one policy for which it was remembered,

'Fares Fair', in which it set out to hold down fares on London Transport by using local taxation, was scuppered by the courts before it had properly got under way. The GLC had opportunities, however, determined by the shape of the electoral coalition which its new leader called into being to support and defend his policies.

I sat for a couple of years, not long before its abolition, on one of the GLC committees. Its function was to oversee the 'ethnic arts' in London, which seemed to mean disbursing various sums to various kinds of projects loosely concerned with 'the arts'. It was a curious, dislocating experience, partly because I never felt that I had anything to do with the policy or the purpose of the committee. All such matters had been decided long before I came along. The composition of the committee, for instance, was a sort of pick-and-mix sample of every minority in the city, each of them operating from a background of very different requirements and intentions. In any case, understanding contexts or consequences was never the issue. The slogan I heard repeatedly was 'Get the money out of the building,' and I was never present at any discussion about what we were doing, or why, and what effect it would have on the communities we were supposed to be serving.

I still feel the same sense of dislocation, largely because, in the interval since the GLC folded, its activities have been wrapped in the mists of legend, and part of the legend says that the ethnic minorities flourished under the GLC and furnished the city with a new burst of vigour and gaiety. This was the characteristic colour-supplement view which was the front line of the GLC's defence against Thatcher's attacks. In response, the tabloids' treatment of the entire issue consistently fuelled the myth that the 'loony Left' in County Hall were throwing money hand over fist at gays, blacks and nutters. In fact there was only a tiny budget allocated to anti-racist campaigning and grant aid to groups or projects in the ethnic minority communities (in 1984, the GLC's 'anti-racist year', the total budget of the Ethnic Minorities Committee, which was charged with all these tasks, amounted to £2.9 million), and the budget had to be shared out between every minority which could be bothered to make a phone call to County Hall.

But whatever was happening to the city, or to the other ethnic minorities, it's also true that the effect of the GLC on the Afro-Caribbean minority as a whole was largely meaningless, and at its worst, a disaster. Of course, the experience of the other 'minorities' across the board had similar overtones, but for the Caribbeans the intervention of the GLC played a crucial part in shaping the disadvantages the community would suffer in the future. The importance of the arts in this process was also crucial, because the approach defined by the GLC's 'ethnic minority' arts policy was to have a wide-ranging role in the re-invention of 'black culture' as the signature of the Afro-Caribbean community.

So the ethnic arts committee was a good place from which to view what was happening. There'd usually be between a dozen and twenty people present, sitting around a long, beautifully polished table, littered with the lists of projects and application forms. One of the first meetings I attended featured an application for around £10,000 from a 'community project' in North London. It was for 'research', to enable the applicant to create a range of 'multiracial T-shirts'.

On my way to the meeting I half-expected this application to be interrogated exhaustively. Here was part of a small cottage industry, already in existence. I'd been buying such T-shirts for years. If the grant achieved anything, it would simply inflate the business in an already crowded market with no assurance of success or survival. The reactions around the table to my intervention ranged from polite indifference to outright irritation. It was a small sum, someone else commented, and the point was to get the money out of the building. The grant was approved, and I still think of that experience as a template for the GLC grant aid machine and the effect it had on the Afro-Caribbean community.

The problem was that the movers and shakers within the GLC had very little understanding or sympathy for the ethnic minority communities as they were then organized. Before the emergence in the early 1980s of 'municipal anti-racism', ethnic minorities had struggled with varying degrees of creativity to meet the problems they encountered. For example, the 'suss law', the provision within the Vagrancy Act that allowed police to stop and search on no more than a 'suspicion' of some unspecified misdeed, had been used to harass and criminalize a large swathe of the black community, particularly in South London. Throughout the 1970s the black community had mounted a long running campaign against 'suss' which was assembled on a piecemeal and *ad hoc* basis, drawing on all the energies within the community. Similarly, in the aftermath of the Deptford fire in January 1981, when a fire started in a house where a party was in full swing, leaving thirteen black teenagers dead, a previously unsuspected capacity for large-scale organization emerged and climaxed in a mass demonstration – the Black People's Day of Action, which had refreshed and invigorated political activism within the black population.

At another level, various groups had begun to organize themselves around their professional interests or around common political ground. From 1981 onwards, municipal anti-racism altered the entire picture. The energies which had been directed towards political and social self-discovery were rechannelled into raising money from the GLC. It was clear that the GLC politicians were sincerely committed to fighting discrimination, but under their particular rubric, Caribbeans, Africans, Asians of various kinds and Old Uncle Tom Cobley all became 'ethnic minorities'. This meant that, no matter who you were, or where you came from, within the culture of the GLC your identity had to be determined by your relationship to white racism.

The GLC wasn't unique in this. Powellism had created race and colour as the central political fact of migrants' existence, and any issue to do with us had become a dialogue between Right and Left. The ethnic minorities were a central issue in the argument, but who they were and what they wanted remained largely unheard. Afro-Caribbeans were worst affected, if only because the shape of the infrastructure which had developed out of our migration and settlement in Britain was unsympathetic or unrecognizable to the white Left. We had no Martin Luther King, no Malcolm X, no national organization; and the rampant individualism of Caribbean attitudes was anathema. For the Afro-Caribbeans the business of material advancement was still paramount. On the surface we were working-class people who didn't behave as working-class people should.

The anti-racist agenda of the white Left, in comparison, shaped itself around opposition to apartheid, around the post-Civil Rights relationship to government programmes in the United States and around the new black nationalism in the Caribbean and Africa. The radicals in County Hall tended to assemble their view of 'blackness' from these elements, so when it came to the Caribbeans the consensus was that we had to be re-educated along these lines, and a brisk trade in black authority figures from the USA and Africa began. Whatever the issue happened to be, County Hall looked abroad for models and policies, a lesson which the Caribbean community wasn't slow to learn.

Throughout much of the 1980s the developments in the structure of black politics and organization began to slow down and freeze, as every new group and most of the old reshaped their agenda towards winning support from the GLC Ethnic Minorities Unit. If black organization had a radical bent it now became completely rhetorical. By the time Thatcher abolished the GLC, the political and social infrastructure which had begun to be erected in the black communities had been destroyed, and black activists had changed course to become clients of white Left ideology. Black radicalism had been recreated as style, re-inventing itself in the shape of a white fantasy. 'Black culture' had become a branch of a diaspora dominated and controlled by American fashions. Various individuals had acquired techniques for engaging in large-scale corruption based on 'getting the money out of the building', opening the door to a strategy in which the black communities would be ripped off in places such as Hackney and Lambeth under the guise of municipalanti-racism.

After the party ended, the nature of the damage was more or less apparent. During the period of the 1980s when the municipal socialists ruled, a number of figures and enterprises previously unknown within their respective communities had appeared and been hailed as the cutting edge of the 'black arts'. After the GLC they disappeared. Who knows what happened to the grandiose plans for a black arts centre in the Round House at Camden Town? Or the plethora of black 'collectives', 'cooperatives' and 'workshops' which mushroomed throughout that period? Most of them had few or no roots within the black communities, the only reason for their existence being their ability to raise finances from the GLC. Cut off from the stream of funds, they promptly began to die. What they achieved before they left the scene was a recasting of black identity. 'Black culture' ceased to be part of the dynamic process of black immigrant life and, instead, became a commodity owned and directed from outside. A raft of ambitious mobile young people adopted the style of a commercialized diaspora in which the important references were largely American. When the film collectives began making documentaries, their models were American icons and gurus, and most of the artefacts of post-GLC black art could have emerged from anywhere except the British neighbourhoods in which the makers lived. At the other end of the scale black people at the grass roots, both old and young, were further alienated and estranged from the dynamics of their own lives. After the GLC there were no senior black arts administrators anywhere in the system, no spaces which blacks controlled, no avenues by which black artists could challenge the insights of their white contemporaries. The major arts complexes, theatres, concert halls, state enterprises and corporations had no significant black presence, but at the other end of the scale all kinds of organizations and enterprises were channelling their efforts into constructing 'black' orthodoxies. Ironically this atmosphere promoted a marginalization which successfully enfeebled or undermined the developing identities of the ethnic minorities in the city; and for a decade the influence of the municipality helped to trap and isolate their political energies within the boundaries of race and racism. If there had been a multiracial coalition, it had been the sort of coalition a horse has with its rider.

In London, none of the conditions which might have delivered a workable coalition were present, and after the abolition of the GLC even the hope faded. The rhetoric had made much of the voting strength of the ethnic minorities, but in practice they tended to vote in pointedly smaller proportions than whites. The political culture had changed to a degree, however. A number of individuals from the ethnic minorities had been drawn into the centre of political organization, and at the other end of the scale, the London electorate were now convinced that the ethnic minorities were due some kind of role in the political process. The Labour Party leadership had strenuously discouraged the emergence of a black political agenda within its ranks, but, faced with nominally acceptable candidates, it lacked the political will to resist. A year after abolition, in the election of 1987, three black politicians were voted into Parliament in London seats.

Their success, however, held few implications for the politics of the city. They had no common agenda and no perceptible ideological base within the interests of the ethnic minorities. There were a number of issues which might have furnished the basis of a coherent programme for black politicians. The lives of the ethnic minorities in the city were bounded and determined by discrimination in jobs, housing, education and the system of justice. They had an important stake in such matters as the development of small businesses or the flight of major corporations from the inner city. They were deeply affected by movements in high street banking, by the state of the National Health Service and the implications of urban planning. Anyone could have produced their own list of priorities. The black Parliamentarians pronounced from time to time on these issues, but their judgements tended to be piecemeal and their statements often contradictory, while, as party members representing an electorate and a machine which demanded conformity, they were exiled from the possibility of assembling a common agenda which might have led opinion. In the absence of a consistent direction, the politics of the ethnic minorities throughout the last decade of the twentieth century were preoccupied with miscarriages of justice and police accountability. There were obvious successes, notably the judicial report on police mishandling of the enquiry into the killing of Stephen Lawrence, a young student who was stabbed at a bus-stop in South London. The report condemned the police for their 'institutional racism' and the term was broadened to challenge the practices of a wide variety of other institutions. At the same time this was a process which firmly entrenched minority activism behind the boundaries of race and racial confrontation, and steered around the prospect of their engagement in overall structures of decision and control in the city.

Tony Blair's new government in 1997 brought with it the promise of a new dispensation, and the prospect of the return of a London-wide authority excited speculation about the potential of a new electoral coalition. In the event there was no serious black rival for the post of Mayor, and the electorate voted overwhelmingly for Ken Livingstone, the man who had last offered the vision of a multiracial coalition. The Assembly which supports the Mayor's office featured only two black candidates, one of whom resigned almost immediately to fight the seat left vacant by the death of its MP, black Londoner Bernie Grant.

On the face of it the structure of multiracial politics in London as yet offers no avenue out of an incestuous and internecine obsession with race and ethnicity. But the Greater London Assembly might be an authentic stage in the process of change. Black occupancy of high-profile posts is limited to the Chair of the Assembly and the deputy of the board which runs the Metropolitan Police, but the Assembly has also brought in more than a couple of dozen professionals from the ethnic minorities to serve as decision-makers or advisers under the aegis of the Mayor's office. This may be the tiniest possible indicator of change, but it also fulfils the necessary criteria for progress towards the assembly of a multiracial agenda together with the personnel to pursue it. There is one prediction which can be made with absolute certainty. London's long-term health and prosperity will depend on its ability to re-invent a politics which reflects the identity and interests of its multiracial population. In the meantime, it is equally certain that the vigour and energy of its cultural and ethnic collisions will produce more frustration than opportunity. In this sense the city is tied to the prospects of the ethnic minorities, and the key to its future is the success or failure of its political will.

FROM *London Crossings* (2001)

INFRASTRUCTURE

Logic would surely dictate that an efficient, functional infrastructure is an essential prerequisite for any modern city to thrive. But then London is rarely governed by logic, or else how could the city have allowed its systems and services to end up in the state in which we find them today? For what is extraordinary about London's recent history is the way in which its economy and its infrastructure have seemingly undergone diametrically opposed changes in fortune. Twenty-five years ago, nothing to do with the city seemed to work very well. Its traditional industries were in terminal decline; its venerable and hidebound financial institutions were struggling to compete with younger and more vibrant economies to East and West; its old and outdated public transport systems seemed on the verge of capitulating to the private motor car; and its Victorian sewers and water mains had developed an unfortunate habit of collapsing underneath the capital's traffic-clogged streets.

Within a decade, however, Margaret Thatcher's radical agenda of wholesale deregulation and privatization had effected a complete and permanent transformation in the way that London went about its business. Having survived a roller-coaster cycle of boom and bust, its economy has emerged as one of the most powerful in the world. Many of its public utilities – water, telecommunications, gas – have thrived under private ownership and the aggressively competitive pricing strategies that the ending of state monopolies has brought – or so at least its many ideological and commercial supporters would confidently claim. But what about London's public transport systems, once so innovative that they were admired and copied by other cities around the world? For anyone familiar with contemporary London, there is no need to provide an answer to such a question. For anyone who is not, it would be hard to convey in words exactly how awful it can be to attempt to travel across the capital by bus, Tube or railway.

Even the most ardent apologists for the public service sell-off would be hard put to persuade London's long-suffering and increasingly cynical commuters that the current woeful performance of the city's trains and buses represents any kind of improvement on the services formerly provided by the public transport authorities. In the case of London's overburdened commuter railways, a clumsily organized commercial separation of the previously unified public system into a complex mosaic of competing companies, combined with a generally lacklustre effort from many of those new railway companies and a series of fatal accidents for which blame never seems to be apportioned adequately, has achieved something unimaginable in the bad old days of the nationalized network – a growing feeling of nostalgia for British Rail, the once universally derided State railway company. In the near future the Underground network is due to be carved up along similar lines, much to the dismay of its many millions of dissatisfied users.

Above ground, London's privately operated bus network still maintains a strong resemblance to the old London Transport system. Most double-decker buses are still painted in the familiar pillar-box red, albeit with a variety of new commercial logos painted on their sides. Indeed, many of the buses now operating on London streets are the very ones that had been designed and built by London's former transport authority decades ago. The much-loved but increasingly ancient Routemaster bus is perhaps the most eloquent symbol of a transport system that has suffered years of under-investment and lack of forward planning. Originally designed in the 1950s for a seventeen-year working life, and built in their thousands up to 1968, there are still as many as 800 of them putting in daily service on the capital's streets. And although plans are now in place finally to phase them out, it is likely that a good number will still be in service to celebrate their 50th birthday in the summer of 2004. Developed by London Transport to serve the capital's specific needs, and once the flagship of a thoroughly modern and well-planned transport system, the 'RM' is now just a quaint anachronism. Needless to say, none of the various off-the-shelf vehicles that have replaced them has managed to capture the trust or affections of Londoners in the way that these wheezing, rattling old workhorses from a former era have done. So what does that say about the next fifty years of London's transport?

BLOWDOWN: THE RISE AND FALL OF LONDON'S TOWER BLOCKS

Joe Kerr

AS A GENERAL rule one should be cautious about treating the physical landscape of architecture as a literal representation of the social, political or economic landscapes of the city. The often excessive amount of time it takes to acquire land, to generate a design, to gain the necessary planning consents and then actually to build means that architecture responds only slowly and clumsily to the rapid and subtle transformations of policy and of circumstance that daily influence and shape urban life. However, while the cityscape might prove a very unreliable barometer of short-term trends, it can often present an eloquent image of the broad sweep of historical change.

This is particularly true of the metropolitan skyline, for it is there that the vertical scale of the city's buildings can be read. To view the silhouette of the city is to see shifting relations of power and influence mapped out over long swathes of time, for in architecture height is intimately associated with the expression of power. Rarely do economics or logic alone dictate that buildings should be built tall.

In the late 1970s, when this book begins, London was emphatically at the end of the most sustained campaign of high-rise building in its history. The demise of high-rise social living had been heralded by the disastrous partial collapse in 1967 of Ronan Point, a systems-built housing block in the East End. This event is etched in the memory of all Londoners over a certain age. Although the suitability of high-rise living had been contested by social commentators and architects from at least the early 1960s, Ronan Point sounded the final death-knell for all new commissions of tall blocks, although they continued to be built into the 1970s, such was the slowness of the process of municipal housing construction. One of the first acts of the Thatcher Government elected in 1979 was to legislate against the building of social housing altogether, thus ending a chapter in London history that stretched back to the foundation of the London County Council 90 years earlier.

By the end of the 1970s it also seemed that London had seen the last of that other form of high-rise architecture, the office tower. Tall offices had had an even shorter life cycle than social housing. In the late 1950s Nikolaus Pevsner could still observe that St Paul's Cathedral was the tallest building on the London skyline, but when the National Westminster Tower (now Tower 42) on Bishopsgate was completed in 1981, not only was it the tallest of a succession of towers built in the City in the intervening twenty years, it was also the last – or so it seemed at the time. The evangelists of conservation, who in 1984 had famously defeated the proposal to build an office slab opposite the Mansion House in the heart of the City designed by the long-dead architect Mies van der Rohe, believed they had ensured that London would no longer reach for the skies. Indeed, English Heritage later proposed that the worst 'offending' towers, for instance the Euston Tower and the Shell Centre, might even be reduced in height in order to diminish their impact on the skyline.

From the mid-1980s, however, the deregulation of the money markets popularly known as 'Big Bang' ushered in a new and feverish round of high-rise construction. Today across the City of London – and even more dramatically at Canary Wharf on the Isle of Dogs – a whole new generation of towers is transforming the London skyline. But the revival in fortunes of the commercial office tower has not led to a similar renaissance in high-rise living, at least not in the public sector. Indeed, the very opposite is true, for the vast stock of brutal concrete towers in which so many Londoners were rehoused during the post-war housing programme is now actually diminishing at an extremely rapid rate. According to Government figures, more than 12,000 high rise flats were destroyed nationwide in the period between 1991 and 1997, but it is in London that the demolitions have occurred in the greatest numbers.[1] Tower blocks, as outdated and unwanted as the ideals that originally spawned them, are now being torn down as rapidly as they were once thrown up during the heyday of the Welfare State.

The contrasting fortunes of London's two most important types of high-rise architecture, the social housing block and the commercial office tower, were vividly illustrated recently by a startling architectural tableau, visible only for a very short time to passengers travelling on the capital's oldest railway line from London Bridge to Greenwich. Any one of them who had bothered to glance up at the right moment and peer through the streaked and stained windows of their decrepit train at the equally dirty and dishevelled landscape of Bermondsey could have glimpsed the now familiar spectacle of a 1950s social housing estate under demolition. Parallel to the railway line an eleven-storey point-block stood empty and forlorn, awaiting final destruction. Its outer walls had been stripped off to expose a concrete honeycomb of former flats, their walls still bearing the contrasting colours with which the former tenants had attempted to assert their individuality within this collective environment. From a safe distance this stripped-down structure looked for all the world like some obscene and over-scaled parody of a child's doll's house. It would be an arresting view under any circumstances, but what gave this particular panorama an especial poignancy was that, viewed from the height of the railway line, one could see right through the skeletal remains of the housing block to the distant cluster of shimmering new-built towers at Canary Wharf. Thus the final humiliation for this former bastion of social architecture was that its downfall took place in the shadow of structures that were emblematic of the very free-enterprise culture that had hastened its destruction.

Naturally, there are logical reasons why this type of housing deserved to meet a premature end. Widely disliked both by tenants and neighbours, many high-rise housing blocks had fallen into such a parlous social and structural condition that action had to be taken. While some blocks have been successfully refurbished, in many cases there has been an overwhelming economic argument for demolition and replacement. For instance, one recent Government study of twelve different schemes involving demolition of council housing concluded that, in at least 50 per cent of cases, redevelopment was demonstrably the cheapest option.[2]

It is abundantly clear, however, that the impulse to destroy these hugely unpopular structures is predicated on far more than a simple economic equation. One has only to be there and to witness demolition to appreciate this, for the manner of their destruction provides a highly revealing clue as to the motives of those local authorities that have become keen advocates for actively destroying large swathes of their own housing stock. Unlike the south London estate described above, which was slowly taken down piece by piece, the preferred method of demolition in most instances is to dynamite them in a single, instantaneous act of destruction.

Having acquired the highly filmic name of 'blowdown',[3] these violent spectacles now regularly punctuate the social calendar of London's poorest boroughs. Indeed, Hackney Council now proudly holds the

European record for demolitions by a local authority, having recently, in February 2002, blown up its seventeenth tower block.[4] Widely advertised by the local authorities responsible, in recognition of the enormous publicity value to be derived from these acts of architectural 'cleansing', demolitions draw large crowds in the manner of public executions of centuries past. Every opportunity to maximize the publicity value of the event is eagerly grasped, and often involves the participation of celebrities alongside local luminaries. Hackney is particularly adept at capitalizing on the highly photogenic moment when the plunger is pushed to detonate the explosion, an act variously performed by Mother Goose from the local panto, the actress Patsy Palmer of *EastEnders* fame, assorted local schoolchildren and any number of dignitaries keen to associate themselves with such a populist gesture. So institutionalized are these happenings that, on the last blowdown I witnessed, the crowd was marshalled together after the event itself for a group photograph by a local artist, as if to emphasize that this explosive intervention had been made on behalf of the whole community.

One cannot help but suspect that the prime reason for using this spectacular means of disposal for unwanted housing stock is to deflect attention from the reality of local deprivation and poverty, and from the general inadequacy of the local authority's attempts to ameliorate these problems. Taking the longer view, one can only marvel at the opportunism with which councils such as Hackney take credit for ridding the world of these despised objects, when they were often responsible for building them in the first place as little as 30 years ago. Moreover, the money that it was necessary to borrow initially to build these highly expensive structures has in most case not even been repaid yet, with the repayment schedule making a significant contribution to the worsening financial situation in which such London Boroughs as Hackney (which recently went bankrupt) now find themselves.

No wonder that they proudly advertise blowdowns as forthcoming attractions on their official website, not least because they can be reasonably sure that, unlike some of their more serious local policy initiatives, at least they will work. For given all the practice that the various parties involved (demolition contractors, the local authority, the press) have now had, these events are more or less guaranteed to pass off without a hitch, unlike Hackney's first disastrous attempt at detonating a tower block in the mid-1980s. On this occasion a vast crowd assembled on Hackney Marshes to witness what was then an unprecedented event. Forced to stand at some considerable distance from the condemned object (in this case a typically grim 1960s prefabricated concrete point block, an unwanted architectural orphan inherited from the recently abolished Greater London Council), we saw the tell-tale plumes of smoke issuing from the building as the charges ignited a second or so before the boom of the explosion rolled out across the marshes. The site was rapidly enveloped in a dense white cloud of dust and smoke. As that dispersed, all eyes strained to see the expected void where for a generation that ugly and unloved Goliath had stood as a blemish on the landscape. But we were in for a shock, for, as the air slowly cleared, a strange object loomed out of the mist where there should have been only sky visible. It quickly became apparent that the explosion had merely blown out the bottom four or five storeys of the tower, leaving a battered stump tottering at a precarious angle, to the great embarrassment of both the Council and their contractors, whose banners were still proudly displayed on the now inaccessible façade of the leaning tower of Hackney. The authorities responsible had clearly succumbed to all the negative propaganda surrounding high-rise blocks, believing them to be less soundly constructed than they unfortunately proved to be. One can only imagine the private glee of all those architects who had pursued the modernist dream of decent housing for all, only to see their work later scorned and rejected, at this proof of the strength of their ideas.

But that was then, and today, after nearly two decades of successful blowdowns, the contractors Controlled Demolition Group are the acknowledged leaders in the field. To give some sense of the scale of such an operation, Hackney's seventeenth high-rise demolition, the twenty-storey Sandridge Court on the Kings Crescent Estate, required 50 kilograms of explosives and 1,700 detonating charges. It was estimated to have yielded a 15,000-tonne mound of rubble. One can actually view videos of this dramatic event on the company's website,[5] since they are justly proud of their unique expertise. As Darren Palin, Managing Director of the Controlled Demolition Group, was quoted as saying shortly before their recent record-breaking achievement: 'We have blown down over 500 structures worldwide and have worked with just about every authority in the UK – but Hackney Borough Council must be our most loyal customer.'[6]

One might have expected that the calamitous destruction of the World Trade Center in New York on 11 September 2001 would have changed public attitudes to the destruction of tall structures, but it seems that the enthusiasm of London's municipal authorities for blowdown has not diminished one iota. Thus it was that on one damp and blustery Sunday morning early in 2002 I joined an expectant throng in Victoria Park in the East End to witness an ambitious demolition attempt. Following a long blast on a piercing siren, itself reminiscent of other destructive events in London's recent history, and the deafening screech of a warning rocket, two huge 1960s slab blocks were detonated with high explosives, and rapidly sank to the ground amidst the regulation cloud of dense white dust. In a matter of a couple of seconds, these vast structures, which for three decades had been home to a shifting community of hundreds of people, had disappeared forever, leaving only a surprisingly small mound of debris to mark the site of this failed experiment in modern living.

As the exhilarated crowd was marshalled together for the post-blowdown portrait, I wondered if I was the only person who felt vaguely troubled at witnessing the spectacle of two closely adjacent towers being blown to smithereens a mere six months or so after 9/11. I must confess always to feeling a sense of loss at the sight of buildings being destroyed, not only because it shakes one's innate belief in the stability and permanence of architecture – and these were after all homes, the building type we most need to invest with a particular sense of security – but because demolition is always predicated on failure. In the particular case of social housing, it is a set of political ideas about equality and opportunity that have been so readily discarded and physically erased, and as I trudged back across Victoria Park I remained unconvinced that this aggressive intervention in the physical fabric of the city was quite as positive and progressive as its promoters would have us believe.

The landscape of this tatty and depressed enclave of the East End is a collage of social experiments, a physical representation of 150 years or more of attempts to ameliorate – or control – the dismal living conditions of London's poorest communities. The park itself was donated by the Victorian banking heiress and philanthropist Baroness Burdett-Coutts (1814–1906), the largest and most enduring of the many interventions that she paid for in the social landscape of the inner East End. Between the many various high-rise blocks visible from the park are the scattered remnants of speculative terraced housing and austere canal-side warehouses, which were the typical urban formations of the East End prior to wartime bombing and post-war redevelopment.

Those terraces, once home to the upper echelons of the working classes, and the adjacent warehouses that in living memory sustained a local light industrial economy, are now both in the hands of affluent gentrifiers, who have in the last twenty years transformed the demographic

profile of the more attractive neighbourhoods of east London. But within this newly smart, spruced-up landscape, the vast concentrations of poorly built and badly maintained social housing seem increasingly out of place on the skyline. The older but revitalized fabric of the city seems to have rendered these still comparatively recent visions of inner-city community life redundant, and they now seem inevitably doomed to extinction. And in their place will appear new terraces of pitched-roof family houses, built in conscious imitation of the dwellings that were once condemned as unsuitable for decent family life, and which they temporarily replaced. It as if the older skin of the city is re-growing to cover the scars left by the removal of these tumourous growths on the social body of London. In Patrick Wright's memorable phrase, the tower blocks had become the 'tombstones of the Welfare State',[7] although it now seems as if the corpse of democratic socialism is destined to lie in an unmarked grave.

The dream of living in the air was originally promoted by middle-class technocrats not for their own occupation but for the working-class tenants of their client authorities. This has meant that in Britain high-rise living has traditionally carried the opposite social connotations that it does, say, in America, where height denotes wealth. Despite the undiminished enthusiasm for blowdown in some quarters, however, the signs are that high-rise housing is facing a resurgence in popularity, although this time around it is not as part of a social housing programme but as a new addition to the portfolio of private, speculative properties being offered for sale to affluent Londoners.

The trend was started by Margaret Thatcher's flagship local authority of Wandsworth, who in the 1980s sold a public housing block into private hands. After a comprehensive refurbishment and the addition of a secure concierge entry system, various leisure facilities and carpets and potted plants for common areas, the flats were successfully marketed to young professionals, notwithstanding the tomato ketchup bottles periodically hurled at their expensive cars from the unmodernized council block next door. More recently, a decaying East End tower block designed by the renowned architect Denys Lasdun was listed as a historic monument, spared demolition by Tower Hamlets Council and transformed into a spectacularly expensive, luxurious, gated apartment complex.

Poverty-stricken Inner London boroughs now have an unprecedented opportunity to cash in on their proximity to the Square Mile through the recycling of previously undesirable high-density estates, and even Hackney has eventually cottoned on to the commercial potential of its crumbling housing stock. Having dynamited three cockroach-infested towers on the Clapton Park Estate, the last surviving high-rise block once called Sudbury Court has been sold off by the council and transformed into the highly desirable Landmark Heights. As *The Observer* newspaper's property pages recently commented in an article on the joys of tall flats: 'With the right mix of people and good management, the high life is a great way of escaping the city without leaving it.'[8] It is hard to disagree. And it proves that the problem all along with the great welfarist vision of homes in the sky was not that high-rise living was inherently alien and abhorrent to Londoners as many detractors once claimed, but that it involved the wrong people and the wrong management. Given that the new, independent inhabitants of Landmark Heights and the many blocks like it are unlikely to be marshalling young children into piss-smelling lifts (or up twenty flights of stairs if the lifts have broken down), they have every chance of enjoying their expensive but well-maintained eyries. It is perhaps the most curious consequence of London's social transformation over the last two decades, that rich and poor have now changed places in the sky.

END OF THE LINE

Rod Mengham, with photos by Marc Atkins

UNDERGROUND RAILWAYS EXIST as alternative spheres to the cities they serve; they take on a character of their own, which we tend to think of in terms of rationalized space and time, as places where the unexpected is not meant to happen. The Tube map with its symmetries, its rows of diagonals, its repetition of angles, is an excessive rationalization of something that in reality is much more irregular. An accurate map would look worryingly chaotic, its proliferation of unrepeatable patterns would make the city look out of control. Where the Tube ends is where the pattern most obviously unravels; it is where the dream of symmetry gives up. Most people never reach the end of the line, where the idea of the city no longer obtains. Almost no one has travelled to the end of all the lines. That would mean being exposed to a degree of variety that the blueprint could never absorb. At every Underground stop, people climb to the surface, emerge into the light of day, but the train goes on, the circulation continues, the Circle Line providing a visual and conceptual magnet for the way that the city stays alive by pumping flows of energy around the system. At the end of the line this fiction dissolves; it is not only people but the place itself that releases its grip on the idea of the city as a closed system. Our project is an enquiry into what relates these different places, apart from their entry into and exit from a system they are so iconically related to. Perhaps the termini are all portals into something other than the idea of the city we automatically link them with.

Of course, the Circle Line offers resistance, and is in many ways in absolute contrast with the suburban tangents. There is no emergence, no aperture, except for those created during the Blitz, when bombs would come through the road above, or even bounce down the escalators, skip along the hallways and explode on the platforms. These violent incisions would not dispel the secrets of the entombed – the

Northern line
Balham
Tooting Broadway
South Wimbledon
Clapham South
Tooting Bec
Colliers Wood
Morden
Ammo City
Zone 3
Zone 4
No smoking
Morden.

Morden

myth-making potential of all those repressed corridors – but would foster anew the sense of an alien habitat. This is caught most obviously by the film *Quatermass and the Pit* (1967), where the breach into a deserted station uncovers the race-memory of another planet altogether. It is in the city's centre that the largest number of abandoned stations remains: there are 40 altogether, repositories of gloom, amplifying the distant vibrations, allaying the slight breezes that pulse through the labyrinth, to decelerate as they get further and further away from the rushing air of tunnels where the trains still run. The lost stations comprise one extreme; the other consists of termini on the Central, Northern, District, Metropolitan and Jubilee lines: the ones that burrow furthest into another time, or into an entirely different organization of space. And yet the tide line of the city's history is indelible precisely here.

Morden has been in pole-position as the southern end of the Northern Line only since 1924, the year when Charles Holden crafted seven stations reaching out into the fields of Surrey. Now the terminus is under siege, filled up from within by a creeping lattice of iron scaffold poles, an infestation of plasterboard and yellow and black tape, which forces a savage geometry into the calm and carefully legislated spaces of Northern Line house style, the endless adaptations of white, green and black porcelain tiles. The platform indicators are bronze-edged lanterns, redolent of BBC Heritage, the reassurance of a 'Dixon of Dock Green' opening credit. But the lettering is both older and more modern than that post-Second World War community survivalism. The Johnston Sans typeface was first introduced in 1916, year of catastrophes, and yet seems to hold the clue to an ordered existence as economically and inevitably as a Bauhaus doctor's prescription. The real reason for journeying here is to visit the octagonal booking hall; and to leave here for any other destination is to unsettle a rare composure. People come and go looking down and straight ahead; but the space beckons upwards with a series of gestures, past the broad horizontal fluting of the gently pitched ceiling to a pinnacled skylight, whose glass panes are leaded in the form of a giant snowflake, a symmetry that has formed on its own. The entrance hall is made ceremonial by a startling, immensely simple, chandelier: a great brass circlet suspended by 20-foot chains. The façade of Portland stone hints subtly at the ritual importance of setting forth, the commencement of a journey to the Underworld. Its two bas-relief columns share facets of Doric and Egyptian styles; but they are only allusions, not direct quotations like the stage-set pastiche down the road. The station came first, the rest of Morden curved away from it, but never quite matched up to the dignified arc of its approach road. Direct competition came from above – Holden's design was totally crushed by three hideous storeys added in the 1960s – and from the corner of the road opposite, where the Portland stone was echoed, or rather amplified, in 1936, when a futuristic bulwark of a building was incised defiantly with a series of fasces; like the Party badge of a local financier dreamily hedging his bets.

Epping is not so much the end of the Central Line as the beginning of The Essex Way, that bucolic footpath winding a course as far as Harwich. The station wall sports a plaque celebrating the twenty-first birthday of this simulated ancient track. It has never been easy to decide where the Central Line should yield to the Forest. The Great Eastern Line (land-grabbed in the New Works Programme of 1935–40) had beached up in Ongar – three stops further out from Epping – in 1865; the first retrenchment came after the Second World War, when passengers for the Ongar outpost had to slip a loop in time, walking from one Epping platform to another to exchange their electric Tube trains for steam. This concession vanished in 1970, when the last trails of coal smoke disappeared with the surgical removal of Ongar, Blake Hall and North Weald – names redolent of the Squire's Last Stand and the primeval impasse. Epping represented a compromise between these

Epping

feral sidings and an unidentifiable point nearer to Liverpool Street and the urban climax. Modernity was at the top of its bent with Gants Hill, whose concourse was modelled directly on the stations of the Moscow Metro – but Epping is already on the compost heap. It is a rural halt: convolvulus on wire netting, heavy laburnum, climbing roses, hanging baskets, blackberries. Local boys help old ladies with their suitcases. The old red-brick Victorian overland station is flanked by horse chestnuts, greenhouses and an allotment garden with runner beans and cabbages. It does not do to stand still for very long in Epping: spiders wander over my hands as I write on the parapet; a ladybird alights on my mobile phone. The line is closed off, but there is nothing to stop the trains from plunging forward in a re-run of Edward Upward's story of 1928, 'The Railway Accident' (Upward grew up in nearby Romford), except four red lamps planted – everything here is planted – on spindly metal poles in the middle of the tracks. One hundred yards further on, tall ragwort forms a screen as the rails begin to curve out of sight. The waiting room is different. It is the antechamber to a system that classifies everything in its vicinity. The suburbs as Mending Apparatus. The room possesses a single bench that faces a passport photo booth. Which is what the passengers wait for: their criminal typology; their Lombroso credentials. In Epping, the inhabitants conspire against the Greenwich Meridian.

At the western extremity lies Uxbridge, entombed in a future remembered by all those who were teenagers in the 1960s. The old market town, centred on a neo-Classical colonnade, flagpole and clock tower, was falsified forever, rendered permanently asymmetrical, by the imposition of a concrete pavilion, the railway's version of South Bank brutalism. Inside the station, however, are the carefully antiqued remnants of a more homely brand of utilitarianism that was always more subtly disturbing. The wooden benches conjure up the era of Harry Palmer, the Michael Caine character for whom the most familiar objects turn suddenly very strange, and vice versa. In *The Ipcress File* (1965) Palmer believes that he is being held captive in Albania, but makes his escape onto the streets of London. Uxbridge is the Albanian version: all the artefacts are so convincing, so precisely evocative, they have to be stage copies. There is the original wooden refreshments kiosk, advertising the alternatives of 'A Mars a Day' or 'Cigars'. The clock and platform indicator have a concatenating rhythm beyond the reach of the original design. It was an age of gadgetry, but the Uxbridge streamlining looks homemade. Pride of place goes to the four stainless-steel cigarette machines,

UXBRIDGE

Tobacconists
DAY & NIGHT SERVICE
CIGARETTES
CIGARETTES
PLEASE
LET COIN DROP
PLEASE
LET COIN DROP
PLEASE
LET COIN DROP

Uxbridge

boasting their provision of 'Day and Night Service'. The one going concern here is Frank's Coffee Shop, which still operates with the original sandwich board. Frank's message includes a prehistoric telephone number, consisting of a two-letter prefix and five digits: UX 35489. Anyone phoning that number and expecting ringback will have one hell of a wait. Nowadays, the Underground itself is art; in the 1960s, art and the railways had to be formally introduced – via civic heraldry and stained-glass windows, job lots from the new Coventry Cathedral. But the most obdurate features of the design, the most aesthetically ambitious, are two extraordinary, *couchant* abstractions of wheel and carriage, midway between rolling stock and Halley's Comet: these historical projectiles, coursing through the masonry like Hittite chariots, belong in a corridor of the Pergamon Museum in Berlin, in the passage leading towards the monumental film sets of the Cold War period. The interior of the station is Portmeirion English: one of the lesser known studios of the British film industry. The props were all leased out from Shepperton in 1965.

Stanmore is way beyond the end of the line. The station is marooned, tipped into a gully, by the constant backwash from a busy traffic artery. Its status is announced by a traffic island, covered by rampaging weeds that almost hide the entrance. There is an immensely long, incredibly steep, staircase down to the platforms at the bottom of the hill. Pensioners can be seen puffing and pausing on every landing. This place was never anything but peripheral, a hill station that might be abandoned. The construction was only half serious. Even the grandeur of the woodwork is wafer-thin. The station is surmounted by a loft conversion, with three dormer windows dressed with net curtains. But no one has ever moved into these corporate bedrooms, and further varieties of weed sprout from the chimney tops. At best, Stanmore is a depot for rolling stock, rather than a concourse for passengers. The vast shunting yards are empty, and the ten pairs of railway tracks are garnished with a thick rust. At the stroke of a pen, bureaucracy's finest decommissioned the plans before they were ever realized. All over the network are these tokens of aporia; behind the schedules and the signalling routines are strategic exceptions: the superfluous platform, the silent stairwell. Stanmore is the annexe of uncertainty, the shrine of second thoughts. It was never made redundant, but paralysed at a fixed point in the history of the Tube's development. Passengers climbing up and down the hill traverse the strata of transport archaeology, with the platform level classified as the prehistory of railway heritage. No wonder the landings carry advertisements for

Stanmore

The National Trust – history is no more difficult of access than boarding the train, and less of a nuisance.

Nevertheless, that illusion of the British past we consent to is counterpointed by police notices seeking help in the investigation of crimes of rape. The edifice begins to crack under the weight of these posters, blue plaques of unwillingness and immediate harm.

And so to Upminster, in the utter east. A spaghetti junction of moving points, its visual clamour put to shame by the self-possession of a row of drainpipe boxes. Each is embossed with the date of their manufacture, 1931. This is the home of the so-called Underground Signal Box, an operations centre that oversees the migrations of millions of passengers, planning the flux and reflux of a daily cycle whose echoes reach as far as the station car park. There is a tide line of rubbish that ebbs and flows in the turning space before the main entrance. The Signal Box is a hot property, caged in, fenced off. Marc and I peer at its darkened windows, where shadows move close to the venetian blinds. These must be the shapes of the controllers, eyeing us up, shifting uneasily backwards and forwards, away from and towards the light. I avert my glance to the thick cast iron of the bridge, which absorbs the last scraps of sunlight and is surprisingly warm to the touch. But Marc is pointing his camera at the tower and producing a small commotion. We do a quick march down the platform and out through the Victorian station building with its pointed brick arches and patched roof.

We go past the end cottage with backdoor rowan tree and size up the shopfronts. Upminster has a fetish for accuracy, for exact calibration: even the barber shop is called 'Martino's *Precision* Hairdressing for Men'. The first shop in the High Street proper is a joiner's and woodturner's, the 'Essex Centre' of woodcraft, from which the technology of modern transport sprang (from the work of wheelwrights, not from Essex). Britain had a radial system of carriers to London from the mid-seventeenth century, unique in Europe, and the prototype of the centrifugal/centripetal Underground network. A pristine culture of capitalism. The end of the line is always the next staging post; the culture of termini is always transitional, the organization of space provisional. The western range of buildings on the High Street is conceived on a monumental scale, with pillars and capitals, and Egyptian details reminiscent of Morden in the south. An approach road to the metropolis, but only half of one, already half-cannibalized by thriving family businesses, just off-camera. Wealth has spilled out of the old moulds of class and profession, already a frozen memory when the architectural cousins of Howard Carter, discoverer of the tomb of Tutankhamun, came metal-detecting in Upminster and put their finds in a living museum, evoking the earliest known urban planning tradition.

Stanmore

Upminster

We skirt a row of tethered German shepherds as each one stands up, sensing the approach of suspicious characters. There is no sanctuary in the church – the closed circuit television surveillance reaches as far as the high altar, and outside, in the churchyard elms, is a chorus of paranoid birdsong, several choruses, a veritable spaghetti junction of alarm calls. Upminster is on guard; even the wildlife is recruited. The project is to stop the migration of meanings, arrest the flow of defining characteristics, to anticipate and prevent outsiders from rearranging the buffers, one cold rainy night.

Upminster

Richmond wins the competition in property prices. In Richmond, you have arrived. The concourse houses the Richmond and Surrey Auction Rooms; you jump off the train and invest, before you even get to the street. But something peculiar happens as you walk down the platform: there is a strange little overgrown patch of ground between the train and the station end of the railway tracks, where the line peters out. This small deposit of neglect, with its little pockets of chalk and different-sized gravels, has accumulated indifference at specific moments of alteration and redefinition: it is a transport midden, a municipal burnt mound; by-product of energies that were focused elsewhere. Like time-lines in the Thames foreshore, the overlapping of materials is constantly revised, realigned by the superimposing of new layers: the addition of elements reorganizes the entire existing order of monuments. But the evidence of powerplay is not enshrined in the canonical details of a metal-framed clerestory, or an abstracted Egyptian façade; it is preserved in a pile of detritus. Its obsolescent mass, un-designed and unamenable to design, is conspicuously ignored. It is meant to be invisible, but its formlessness is reflected, magnified and distorted by the huge mirrors at the other end of the platform, convex and enveloping like an end-of-the-pier amusement. Richmond has seven platforms. The central two, with cast-iron pillars, capitals and trefoils, are original, while the rest, with forged steel

Richmond

equivalents, repeat the blue and grey colour scheme, but shift the tones and textures. The most dramatic recension is not only recent, it is still in process. South West Trains are installing a 'Real Time' Customer Information System. But the Tube journey is never in real time; it is subject to dilation, a time exposure, as Marc's photographic activities constantly remind me. As the motion of the body through space accelerates, the mind dwells on its captivity, lapsing into the same condition between different stations. The first Underground railway carriages were called 'padded cells': there were no windows, because it was judged that there was nothing to see. Not even the staging posts. The mind was confined within itself.

On the front of Richmond station, the sharply angled fluting above Egyptian-style pilasters completes the web of allusions, north, south, east and west, to Middle Kingdom architecture. But this grandiosity, although heavily suggestive, is less structural, less integral, to the Tube than the hieroglyph, the graffito awaiting its Rosetta Stone. The carriages are full of cartouches that preserve a code of silence about the true names for all the destinations. Morden is really 'Ammo City', but there is no knowing why. The Underground is a place where we read, unceasingly, a series of mottoes impacted with meanings that do not belong there. Surreptitious, sidling, they appear with the force of revelation, but reveal only the banal, like the scribbled communiqués of the Duke of Portland in Mick Jackson's novel *The Underground Man* (1997). The duke, who has constructed a system of tunnels beneath his estate, enabling him to travel by coach and horses for miles underground, slips an assortment of notes under the doors of his manservants and maidservants: conundrums, such as 'What is that state of mind we call "consciousness" if not the constant emerging from a tunnel?' In the tunnels of the Victoria Line, nearly all the current advertisements are rudimentary and without entertainment value. Their most important message is the website address you can click on to see the real advertisement. The only perspective here is a cyberspace perspective. When we emerge from the tunnel at the end of the line, we walk from terminus to terminal, enter a tunnel much longer than any we have just left. The Underground from which we emerge into consciousness is unbearably private: without the freedom of the street, it fosters an intimacy with strangers that was the paradoxical ground of wartime myths of community. Travelling blind in this short space has an imagined scope unimagined in the endless suburbs of the Net. Digitized fantasy always needs to be fleshed out by actors; holograms stalk the Green Belt, the Garden Cities and country parks. Each padded cell is its own world, its own itinerary of symptoms: read your ticket for the precise aetiology,

Richmond

the carved channel you have travelled in secret, the time-signature of the gradients. Hold your breath until the journey ends, and your name is off the critical list.

RATS WITH WINGS: LONDON'S BATTLE WITH ANIMALS

Gargi Bhattacharyya

IN THE SPRING OF 2000, the New Labour government of Tony Blair unleashed the theatrical spectacle of the mayoral election. After the much-loved, much-hated, berated and debated Greater London Council had fallen to the hand of a Tory government that feared this alternative power base for left-leaning disaffection with national government, the city of London lacked a unified form of local representation. The proposal to elect a mayor for London, to administer the local governmental business of the city through leadership of an elected assembly of representatives, was a plan that acknowledged the political might and aspirations of this significant block of votes. For New Labour, there was a hope that this would begin the process of inserting strong party personalities into the terrain of regional particularities – a way of integrating local and national layers of government and further hegemonizing the New Labour vision.

Instead, the battle to be mayor became another famous New Labour nightmare. Ken Livingstone left the party, ran as an independent and then beat the official Labour candidate, Frank Dobson. Once again, Londoners have used their local power to unsettle the project of national government.

Wanting to be mayor became the most primal of desires and battles. The desire represented the clash of old and new – a test of all our powers. In the process, new ways to manage this fresh colonization emerged. The bogeymen of New Labour – controlling, controlled, without the blood and guts and bellies of our belligerent resistance – washed around thecity like waste. And no one wanted to live like that. Victory was a foregone conclusion.

Being mayor, of course, is another matter altogether. After the euphoria of the win, the new world must still be built. Time to look clearly at what lies ahead.

The London mayor has a limited but significant jurisdiction. To this elected post and the assembly that surrounds it fall the tasks of local regeneration and environmental maintenance, traffic and transport, culture and leisure. Although the high-jinx of local elections made the city feel autonomous, the Big Brother controls of central government remained dominant, if now just out of sight.

In the film *Passport to Pimlico* (1949), the residents of this London neighbourhood elect to declare their independence. They erect check-points and immigration barriers, and demand the respect of any other independent nation. In an anticipation of the fragmenting national spaces of the later twentieth century, the film raises the question of what is required in order for sustainable government to be possible. The London that votes against privatized public transport and for a greater autonomy for the city also raises this question. What does it take to sustain self-government?

The limited remit of the mayor permits jurisdiction over the local economy – in one conception, at least. This is the world of regeneration projects and local business, the version of economy that regards the wonders and enticements of London as something apart from the rest of the country. As part of this responsibility, a pledge is made to remake the public life of London's streets, most especially the famous streets and squares that have come to characterize the city.

Plan one – the plan that links and gives birth to all other plans – is the scheme to transform London into an arena of economically beneficial and socially cohering public spaces. This is the plan that wishes to reclaim public space as the most comfortable of homes, the space in which we once and for all work out our strange relation to each other. Some spaces, such as Trafalgar Square, come in for special scrutiny in this process. As one newspaper put it, 'Like Times Square and the other great squares, what Trafalgar Square looks like is representative of the city as a whole. It is a public space for the enjoyment of Londoners and visitors alike.'[1]

As is so often the case, culture appears as the key term in the project. A revisited attention to the public heritage spaces of London will provide an opportunity to recreate the public arenas of the civic myth. In the process, new cultural industries emerge that can take advantage of the processes of this reinvigorated public life. Now, we hope, citizen can mingle with tourist, civic participation can combine with entertainment, commerce and community can at last find themselves in step. This is the moment when everyday life, the happy camaraderie that is the city's greatest asset and tourist attraction, can once again embrace public spaces. After the years of clampdown and criminalization, now city streets value crowds – including the crowds of actual city-dwellers necessary to render authenticity to any tourist excursion. Re-peopling is the plan for leisure and service growth – in order to provide both backdrop and custom for the regenerated city. In a return to the most foundational of urban questions, however, this project requires a strategy to manage and accommodate the forces of nature. London must still learn to manage its animality.

An earlier incarnation of urban economic boom fell foul of the tricky relationship with animals. The city of London has imploded once before through the attacks of plague and fire. London in the 150 years before the Great Plague of 1665 grew from 'a middle-ranking European town of about 50,000 or 60,0000 people, smaller than Paris, Rome, Naples, Venice, Antwerp and several others, into a monster of over 500,000, the greatest city in Christendom'.[2] Too successful a concentration of humans and their complex of wealth-generating activities enable the spread of the parasitic vermin that can destroy the system from which they feed. So rats flourish in the crevices of urban intensification, then carry the contaminant that will destroy the whole happy arrangement.

The human achievement of the city – a concentrated network of interdependent social relations that serves to enhance the capacity of human endeavour – reveals a constant vulnerability to the incursion of the natural. Without warning, these parallel forces may derail or even destroy every gain of this experiment in the expansion of human culture.

Of course, the cities of today are more resilient – fortified on many fronts, no longer vulnerable to the unexpected freak of nature. London will never become Pompeii or Atlantis – we have had our brush with dangerous nature and survived.

But somehow the fear of vermin lingers.

Pigeons have been shown to constitute a health hazard in a number of regards. These include the production of chlamydia psittaci, which causes an irritation in the lungs, and the spread of tuberculosis, encephalitis and, perhaps, even e-coli. More recent research suggests that pigeon droppings dry to create an airborne dust that carries disease into the respiratory and digestive systems of hapless humans. In the manner of other successful vermin, pigeons flourish on the waste products of human society, adapting to live most happily and voraciously at the edges of our attempts to transcend nature. Contemporary vermin are an indication of nature's smarts – because these creatures relish the dirty excesses of human cultures, they feed on what is made in the flight from nature.

Unlike other urban birdlife – including the lamented sparrow, former familiar of the city – pigeons have not been banished by the acceleration of urban processes. Seemingly undeterred by such factors as poor air quality and a contraction of urban greenery, pigeons have learnt to survive in precisely the habitat that emerges. Squatting in offices and businesses, invading the rafters and airshoots of an increasingly and overly built environment – pigeons show that they can survive anywhere. Quickly rearranging their numbers to optimize access to available food, pigeons learn to live and grow fat from the discarded food debris of city life.[3] While people find the accelerating pace and cost of the city more difficult to live with, pigeons arrive to occupy every available scrap of sustenance. The estimate is that there is one pigeon for every human Londoner – but who doubts that the pigeons will soon come to win the numbers game?

When the mayor chooses to do battle with the pigeons, on their home turf in Trafalgar Square, he is taking on this age-old tension between humanity and our vermin. We may escape nature and forget agriculture, become so enclosed in the machinery of human activity that we no longer recall any other force in the universe, but somehow the tricky innovation of verminous life forms will shadow any development that enhances human life. No progress without new vermin.

As well as the newly resilient pigeons, other creatures are learning to benefit from the cast-offs of a deindustrializing, leisure-everywhere, urban landscape. The infamous rat, king of vermin, is also growing in number.

> Mild winters and cutbacks in pest control expenditure have also been blamed for the increased problems. So have the consequences of privatising council services and water provision, although there is a national protocol that is meant to overcome ambiguities about where the rat control responsibilities lie. Defects in underground drainage are said to be responsible for much of the infestation. Private water companies are accused of reducing rat baiting in sewers and there is a widespread belief that rats are becoming resistant to the most widely used baits.[4]

Rats also flourish on the debris of half-finished fast food – also reproduce at a frightening speed and scale, also carry all manner of disease. In addition, rats are well adapted to the unexpected infrastructural changes of cities that are no longer industrial centres. Part of the long move away from the centralizing master plans of high modernity can be seen in the fragmentation of deregulation, privatization and the piecemeal marketization of the most mundane of public services. The slow erosion of drains that are not quite anyone's business creates an ideal terrain for these super-rats who have learned to flourish on our poisons. Our decline is their gain.

Perhaps because of this, the battle with these most human of animals, those that arrange their lives around the business and rhythm of the human world, reveals an extra-rational intensity. Beyond the need to avoid disease, the push to eradicate shows the frenzy of another motive.

> The notion of an animal stands for the unhuman, the anti-human. It is a symbol for the forces which we fear in our own nature, and do not regard as a true part of it. It displays those forces as continuous with ones which we fear in the world around us – with floods, earthquakes and volcanoes – and thereby dramatizes their power.[5]

Animal stands in as the boundary of the human here, what is beyond us is the realm of the animal. Yet there is also the grudging acknowledgement that the trace of the animal remains within us, bursting out at unexpected moments, creeping into the business of civilization. This double role of alien otherness and internal disruption makes the animal twice as dangerous – a threat from both without and within. All of the dangers that resist containment by the powers of human intervention, the resilient materiality of a world that is not amenable to reason, all of that burdonsome weight becomes concentrated in the figure of the animal. Do battle with these forces and you decide the destiny of humanity.

Despite the continuing fears of the animal, a fresh concern about the consequences of ecological erosion tempers our impulse to destroy this otherness.

The mayor has a statutory duty to publish a biodiversity strategy, the first ever statutory duty in this area at a regional level. So the ascension to local/regional government includes this requirement to accommodate the natural, to come to some peace with the animal.

The commitment to biodiversity is a conservationist role – the aim is 'to protect and enhance the natural habitats of London together with their variety of species'.[6] The come-lately vermin who emerge in response to city development fall out of this account of city nature – because they have no natural habitat in this rendition.

Of course, the balance between human and animal, culture and nature, is not so tidy. 'London also supports a wealth of wildlife in . . . "unofficial countryside", where nature has reclaimed vacant land'.[7] What nature reclaims, humanity has lost. The acknowledgement that there could be some movement in the boundary between city and countryside, that instead of urban spread being a one-way process that countryside could creep back unannounced, this is an acknowledgement also that the battle between human and animal is never over and decided. Culture must mark and guard its territory zealously, because the slow push of nature is always waiting in the shadows. Again, with reference to our resilient vermin, the question is the version of nature that awaits us.

> The loss of London's ponds threatens the great crested newt, which is now extinct in many London boroughs. On the positive side, many water birds, including the beautiful kingfisher, are colonising new areas, and the magnificent peregrine falcon has recently nested in London for the first time.[8]

The regretful story of loss is already familiar – poor and greedy management of resources reduces the range of species in our local environments. The parallel narrative is less familiar – that some animals may find new habitats or learn to live in new places. This is the animal of beauty and magnificence – an incarnation sufficiently rare to elicit wonderment rather than disgust. The ability to adapt to new environments and to survive the landscapes of human intervention does not in itself raise verminous fears. On the contrary, in other spaces the chance for city-dwellers to brush up against the spectacles of a non-threatening nature is regarded as a therapeutic boon.

> The health benefits of the Biodiversity Strategy stem both from the psychological effects of the natural environment on people's feeling of wellbeing, and from locally accessible interesting green spaces acting as an inducement to take exercise.[9]

Managing animality requires this search for an instrumental pay-off, a human benefit from the accommodation of another force. The quest to sustain biodiversity, even in the seemingly uninviting terrain of the city, marshalls the double argument of environmental good – both a good in itself and, handily, also good for us. In the era of popular ecology, in aspiration if not quite in practice, this argument is easy to make. We have all learned the benefits of nature, in its place. Even the baby-biting urban fox, whose numbers have risen, allegedly, to 25 per square mile in London, compared to no more than 7 per square mile in the countryside, has its animal-loving defenders: 'Experts also point out that many people welcome the creatures as a slice of rural wildlife that brightens up city life.'[10]

But aren't vermin another issue altogether? A symptom of a fast disappearing biodiversity being overtaken by the more opportunistic survival strategies of urban vermin?

A parasite is a being that lives through the life-support system of another. Lacking the ability to sustain its own life without access to this external support, parasites feed off the energy reserves collected by their host. Rather than rely on the vagaries of trying to gather food, this is 'an animal or plant which lives in or upon another organism . . . and draws its nutriment directly from it'.[11] Although the relationship between parasite and host describes a connection in which one benefits at the expense of the other, usually without killing it, the whiff of death hangs around the arrangement. The parasite sucks the life from the host – slowly but surely, a little energy at a time. Vermin, 'animals of a noxious or objectionable kind',[12] employ the strategy of parasiticism among their opportunistic repertoire of survival techniques.

If animality represents an unpleasant reminder of a world beyond the scope of human control, then vermin and parasites are more unsettling still. These are the creatures that will not keep to their own space, the ones who creep into the crevices of our lives without ever becoming domesticated. Without the grand otherness of nature proper, vermin threaten to overcome our humanity with the most debased versions of animality.

The pigeons invade the spaces of public life and make them uninhabitable for humans. Or if not uninhabitable, unpalatable – not appealing to the new citizens who may eat, drink, play and debate and buy all manner of assorted entertainments in the freedoms of the regenerated city. As such, they threaten the project of sustainable local governance. How can London regenerate through the leisurely pursuits of public places if these places belong already to animal others?

There is another cartoon-friendly version of the Londoner, the one shown in *Mary Poppins* (1964), as the friend and feeder of pigeons. The battle to de-pigeon Trafalgar Square encounters opposition from precisely this alternative version of performing London – the London that feeds the birds for 'tuppence a bag'. Defenders of pigeon-feed, attendant droppings, disease and all, argue that they are the keepers of heritage integrity. As Tony Banks, Minister for Sport, commented, 'The birds date back as far as Roman times. Ken Livingstone has only been in power for two terms. Some Londoners love the pigeons, some call them rats on wings. I happen to love them and suspect I am not alone.'[13]

When playing the role of populist prince, the mayor must appeal to the sense of loss and intrusion – loss of autonomy, intrusion of concerns that do not benefit Londoners themselves. Pigeons occupy an uneasy halfway, not an invasion, but not quite native, part of the landscape but not quite indigenous. In the classical manner of vermin, pigeons make spaces their own through the process of parasiticism. By becoming an omnipresent accompanier to city life, pigeons become indistinguishable from the life of the city. The vermin invade London life to the extent that their presence becomes a characteristic of London-ness. Are the real Londoners those who defend their space against the corrosion of pigeons, or those who learn to accommodate pigeons in a version of the city that balances inhabitants and vermin, carrier and parasite? Cleansed of the contamination of pigeons, does Trafalgar Square lose some of its essence of tourist London-ness?

It would be all too easy to present the pigeons as a verminous figure of New Labour – adapting opportunistically to whatever terrain becomes available, feeding randomly on the scraps of larger beings, parasitically creeping into the vulnerable spots of contemporary life. Banish the pigeons and these spectres of modern living can be defeated. But events rarely fit so tidily into the characterizations of political cartoons.

The battle between mayor and pigeons continues a far longer struggle to establish and safeguard human ascendancy in urban spaces. This reaches beyond the detail of any immediate political skirmish, back to the ongoing struggle to become human and defeat animality. Of course, this is a never-ending endeavour, something that is acknowledged in the mayor's modest proposal to redistribute the pigeon population, not decimate or banish it. The city may be made through an accumulation of human culture, but there is no fortification against the intrusion of vermin. Every outdoors moment threatens to revert to artificial countryside, every attempt to perfect the vision of the human city opens some new opportunity for contamination.

The Great Plague of 1665 was the culmination of many plague-ridden years. Yet after this horror, plague disappeared from Britain, overtaken by new diseases and scourges. This tardy victory over vermin does not seem to have resulted from any human intervention. Instead, some uncharted shift in the parasite economy of disease and urban wildlife dethroned the coupling of black rat and bubonic plague, and new complexes emerged to feed off humanity's hapless endeavours.

What chance of containment now the rats have grown wings?

ABANDONED BUILDINGS

Nicholas Royle

IF WE ASK the question how many abandoned buildings are there in London, the strictly correct, absolutely literal answer must be, of course, none. In a city where property values and the cost of land continue to manifest no fear of heights, no individual or other body owning a piece of it can afford to follow a policy of complete abandonment. And yet the evidence to the contrary is all around us. Take a walk down any inner – or outer – London street in an area where either commerce or industry has squeezed out residential land use and there behind the garish plastic and the razor wire is the truth of the matter: we are living in a ghost town.

People tend not to abandon dwellings unless ordered so to do. The Government may compulsorily purchase homes alongside a road to be widened, or it may condemn an area of slums or dynamite a tower block. But businesses vacate buildings every day of the week, in many cases leaving them to rot, in others permitting them to stand empty for as long as it takes before either a sale or redevelopment becomes viable. Most of London's abandoned buildings are to be found in interstitial locations or unstable areas, where social and economic conditions fluctuate according to fashion and markets. Despite the premium on land value in central areas, the proportion of abandoned buildings to buildings in use in, say, W1 is much the same as it is in W12. In a city where overcrowding is so bad that many of the poorest families have to sleep five or more to a room, where the numbers of homeless on the streets continue to rise despite the Government's official figures, where even people with reasonably well-paid jobs and no dependants cannot afford to get a foot on the property ladder within Zone 2, staggering numbers of old buildings are permitted to stand empty and remain unused. This has been the case for the last thirty years and will persist for the next three decades unless there is a radical shift in policy and control. While, on the one hand, there is a clear moral argument that more space should be freed up and made available to help tackle homelessness, on the other hand it is also possible to argue that London's abandoned buildings add a particular, very special dimension to the city that, were they all suddenly to be either demolished or refurbished and filled with shiny new workstations, we would miss them in ways that may not seem immediately evident.

I have been exploring London's abandoned buildings since 1985, when I was working in a pizza restaurant next door to the then-deserted St George's Hospital at Hyde Park Corner. A Croatian kitchen-hand showed me a way into the hospital that involved jumping down from the enclosed triangle of roof space at the rear of the restaurant where the staff ate their pizzas and then leaping across a short gap (over a long drop) before climbing in through an open window. You lowered yourself down from the window ledge on to a fallen metal sign – and that was it, you were in. Signs announced that the hospital was patrolled by security guards who would deal with any intruders as if they were terrorists. We wondered why. Perhaps because just the other side of the Wellington Arch and behind the high wall lay the gardens of Buckingham Palace. There seemed no other reason to adopt strong-arm tactics with harmless urban explorers caught wandering through the long-empty labs and patrolling corridors strewn with broken glass and crumbling masonry. In fact, the labs were far from empty. They were filled with cupboards and cabinets, which in turn were filled with the standard paraphernalia of hospital labs, as well as boxes and boxes of slides, both 35 mm colour transparencies and three-inch-square glass plates bearing black-and-white images of diseased organs removed from deceased patients. It was possible to roam all over the hospital, from the anxiety-producing darkness of the basement via the still-peaceful chapel with its beautiful stained-glass windows to the eerily empty rooms on the third floor overlooking Hyde Park Corner. Deserted, St George's had an atmosphere of poignant mystery quite distinct from the feelings it would have generated in patients, staff and visitors during its years as a functioning hospital. Left to rot for several years, it had become a twentieth-century ruin.

One detail that was, in retrospect at least, conspicuously absent from St George's – and which would be a feature of the abandoned buildings I would explore a few years later – was graffiti. The rear of the former West London Hospital on Hammersmith Road, when I visited it in October 1998, had been tagged by graffiti writers, among them one whose signature I had come to be familiar with over the previous couple of years. Up to the point when my casual interest in London's abandoned buildings developed into something approaching an obsession, graffiti was just white noise to me. Largely illegible, for the most part graphically indecipherable, neither an irritation nor something I found particularly interesting, it was just there. But as I explored more and more abandoned buildings and spent more time studying the interstitial landscape defined by the Westway and London Underground's Hammersmith and City line, one name did eventually stand out: Fume.

Fume is everywhere. His tags, dubs, throw-ups and pieces are hard to avoid in west London. He is not confined to the west, by any means, but that is where he appears to have been most active, bombing trains, tagging the very parapet of the Westway where it crosses Ladbroke Grove, and breaking into abandoned buildings. It was his tag I saw on what was left of the rear of the West London Hospital in 1998. If he went inside the old hospital, he left no mark. Entering via a gaping door leading to the basement, I quickly accessed the upper storeys, where I found deserted wards drenched in autumn sunlight, store cupboards stuffed with drips and drugs, vacant corridors whose acoustics made you take a passer-by on the street outside for a security guard approaching the next corner. The building was demolished in the summer of 2000; an office block now stands in its place.

Built in 1908 and intended to take all of five years worth of whatever stresses and strains early twentieth-century London and its visitors could throw at them, the Franco-British Exhibition Halls in Shepherd's Bush are still standing today. Or they were at the time of writing, having already outlived numerous death sentences. The halls, which face demolition to make way for the new White City shopping and leisure development, were a clever way to get exhibition-goers from Uxbridge Road across to Wood Lane and the entrance proper to the vast purpose-built exhibition space that was White City. Nothing remains of the White City, apart from the name itself – the ground on which it stood is now home to the White City Estate, the BBC's new White City building and Hammersmith Park, where a recently recreated Japanese Garden seeks to bring the past back to life. But the Franco-British Exhibition Halls clung on throughout the remainder of the last century and on into the new.

After the Franco-British Exhibition itself in 1908, the halls – basically long sheds on stilts – were used for the Coronation Exhibition in 1911 and the British Industries Fair ten years later; then they remained in use once or twice a year until the exhibitions moved to Earl's Court. They were then used as hangars or construction space for gliders; parachutes were made there during the Second World War; the City Display Organisation used them for many years to manufacture sets for film and television; more recently an American insurance firm converted the Uxbridge Road entrance and the first two halls for use as office space. Several of the halls further back from Uxbridge Road became home to the exclusive Vanderbilt Raquet Club; Diana, Princess of Wales was among those who played there.

Just beyond the locked doors of the white, arched entrance on Uxbridge Road, close to the Holland Park roundabout, the intermittently collapsed false ceilings and severed tubes of what had once been an air-conditioning system testify to the building's relatively recent incarnation as offices. Security guards apart, however, the only people who have been working hard within – indeed, on – these walls in the last few years are graffiti writers. 'Fume', 'Niggaz', 'w7' and 'THE' crop up regularly, but most prolific by far is Fume. In the graffiti writers' argot, Fume is 'up'.

To understand what drives graffiti writers is to understand part of the appeal of abandoned buildings. The graffiti writer wants his work (most, although not all, writers are male) to be seen by the general public. Indeed, it is his very intrusion into the public sphere, usually by illegal means, that is the essence of the activity: getting into the train yard and leaving his mark on the side of a carriage, scaling a wall and signing his name in the most inaccessible spot possible. But writers do, in fact, have a narrower, bipolar audience in mind, made up of other writers and the authorities they are continually trying to outwit.

When Fume breaks into the Franco-British Exhibition Halls to tag the walls in red and leave a memorable 'piece' (short for masterpiece) on one wall directly underneath a break in the ceiling, which admits light to show off his work to the best advantage, he's aiming to gain the respect of his peers and to get one over on the police and security guards whose job it is to keep him out.

It's their job to keep me out, too, and they do it so well that I am unable to find an illegal way in and have to resort to an above-board approach to Chesfield plc, the company responsible for the development of the site. A representative kindly takes me round, but the atmosphere is inevitably dampened by the mere fact of my being accompanied. These places are best explored alone. I sneak in briefly towards the end of 2002, while contractors are busy ripping the guts out of the building prior to its becoming a paintball venue for the remaining months of its life.

The Grade II-listed former Paddington Maintenance Depot, sandwiched between the Westway and the canals of Little Venice, stood empty for more than a decade, its curving lines and unusual appearance earning it the nickname 'the Battleship'. Access to both the lowest level of the maintenance depot and the adjoining Roundhouse building was simple. Leaving Paddington Station by the back entrance, you passed under Bishop's Bridge Road and entered the former Paddington goods yard. This vast triangular space was bordered by the Westway, the railway line out of Paddington and an aqueduct connecting Paddington Basin to Little Venice. Vacant for years, it represented an irresistible temptation to all those who take pleasure in empty spaces at the heart of big cities. The Westway at this point is blessed with neither one, nor two, but three levels, the lowest of which gave access to the bowels of the maintenance depot. In 2000, however, the goods yard became Paddington Central, a building site, and enormous office blocks sprang out of the earth seemingly overnight. Like robotic ivy, scaffolding crept up the sides of the maintenance depot, and the graffiti writers Known and Fume took advantage to adorn the tiled exterior with their tags and dubs.

On the building's north side, a window was left open. Inside, writers had clearly been enjoying the run of the place for some time: Tube, Demo, NIG and, most of all, Fume. I seemed to be following him, or was he somehow anticipating my next move? The truth is that we were both drawn to the same kind of spaces. Abandoned, the former maintenance depot is charged with a potent melancholy. Stripped of its furniture and fittings, it's a blank canvas. It could have been anything; it could *be* anything; it could *yet* be anything (but for the knowledge that it was soon to become the headquarters of a high-street fashion chain). It and other disused buildings are part of the imaginative life of the city. Accretions of narrative gather like dust on the windows; fictional spores spread from the walls to the floors and out into the streets. Collapse all those empty rooms and it would be like taking the silences out from between the notes. In terms of contrast, there would be no more black and white, only shades of grey. You'd lose not only vital parts of London's history, but also myriad variations on its possible futures.

HIGHER AND HIGHER: HOW LONDON FELL FOR THE LOFT

Tom Dyckhoff

THERE IT WAS, the ad, staring up at me from the Homes and Property section of the *Evening Standard*: 'newly built loft-style apartments'. Andy Warhol would have been proud. Here was the mass production not of art, but of architecture – not screen prints on the production line, but the Factory itself, drained of life, but packaged and pumped full of profit. In Crouch End, too.

The loft, along with feng shui, skinny lattes and Cool Britannia, was what London was all about in the 1990s. Or rather, that's what it was supposed to be about. That's what *Wallpaper** magazine told us. And before we can do anything about it, this fact has already been immortalized as history, the loft's style and symbols preserved beside the 'Regency home' as the '1990s home' at the Geffrye Museum of English domestic interiors in the East End. Every detail is in place: the double-height 'space' (never a room), the wooden floor, the white walls (the odd section picked out in canary yellow); the mezzanine for sleeping; the Matthew Hilton Balzac armchair (displaying the owner's modish, and mandatory, interest in young British design); the casually placed copy of *Wallpaper**; the designer kitchen – olive oils, *River Café Cookbook 2*, Smeg oven – for impromptu dinner parties with creative friends; the suitably urbane reading material on the Conran shelves – *Captain Corelli*, Rem Koolhaas. And all – so neatly – on the edge of the loft's natural habitat, that swathe of inner London that now sings with the capital's highest property prices: Clerkenwell, Hoxton, Shoreditch, Spitalfields, Borough, Soho, SoBo, NoHo, SoSho, Cityside, Aldgate Triangle, South Central and every other neighbourhood that property developers try, in vain, to Manhattan-ize.

Yes, every detail is in place. This is, indeed, the image of the London loft, 1990s style. High gloss, high price, and we all bought it – at least some of it.

The Pure Source

It was never meant to be like this, of course. Lofts were meant to be cheap (or, even better, squatted), for people who chose not to live a 2.4 kids and a Volvo existence. They were the latest in a line of artists' hangouts, like garrets or studios, where creative types with time on their hands got up to wacky antics or fabulous parties, to which you were not invited. Think of Robert Rauschenberg's 1950s loft, or Warhol's Factory. Their style was no style, 'spontaneous' or just as found, which, since they were usually former industrial spaces, meant exposed pipes, acres of rough brick walls and huge steel windows. They were cold, not cosy, anti-domestic spaces, or, rather, spaces reformulated for an alternative domesticity.

The 1990s London loft took these bohemian ideals and turned them into profit. It is one more story of international capitalism assimilating a counter-culture and selling it back, tamed and controlled. You'll have heard the story before, repeated in every gentrifying Western city from an almost identical template: Sharon Zukin's ground-breaking 1982 study of the 1960s and '70s New York loft, which gave the phenomenon its now hackneyed name: *Loft Living: Culture and Capital in Urban Change*. The story sprung from Zukin's Greenwich Village block, which metamorphosed in just a few years from industrial sweatshop, through squat, mixed-use home for artists, to 'developed' luxury home of lawyers and accountants. To Zukin, loft living was nothing to do with interior design or 'lifestyle' choices. It was another symptom of the lurch of the Western city from one form of capitalism – manufacturing – to another – based on service industries and consumerism – and encouraged by a city eager to kill several birds with one stone (such as to gentrify 'declining' neighbourhoods) at little cost to itself.

In fact, this same tale is told, quite openly, by those who seek to profit by loft development – the developers, the media, those with power over the built environment. They miss out the politics, of course. They just need the bohemian myth part. Whenever a developed loft space is sold – in London, New York, Berlin, wherever – it is marketed with just enough association with the 'original' 'authentic' artists' lofts to be attractive, but not enough to be dangerous to core consumerist values. You are buying a fragment of the freedom achieved by the 'original' artist loft livers by opting out of mainstream society, only without the inconvenience of opting out of mainstream society (no transport, no heating, no Starbucks). You are buying back the freedom that was yours at birth, only, like a drug, it is controlled, diluted, padded out to increase the return.

Zukin's history begins in the late 1960s, with New York's pre-eminence in the art world and its economic shift towards cultural production and consumption. Thanks, in part, to the initial spark of Andy Warhol's Factory, the lifestyle of what were once eccentric artists living in decrepit industrial spaces became fashionable and, eventually, sellable. Likewise, the story of the London loft started when it became, in turn, the centre of the art and design world in the late 1980s. True, there had been London artists 'doing a Warhol' in disused industrial spaces before. Apeing their New York colleagues, artists in the 1960s and '70s settled in declining industrial pockets, such as Covent Garden, Wapping, Limehouse and Rotherhithe. Bridget Riley even joined a young collective in Hoxton (very prescient) to help fellow artists find cheap studio space.[1] Like their New York counterparts, such pioneers had their own little pyhrric victories against developers' bulldozers, most famously saving Covent Garden, albeit for a future as a heritage shopping mall. But, as yet, London's loft movement lacked the critical mass of that in New York. And artists' lives certainly weren't the stuff of popular mass aspiration – not yet.

Not until 'Britart'. When Damien Hirst set the Goldsmiths College art show 'Freeze' in a disused industrial space in Bermondsey, in 1988, he unwittingly kick-started the loft movement as well as Britain's artistic revival. Initially, the two were closely connected. Charles Saatchi, the most prominent collector of Britart, had already imported the industrial, SoHo loft aesthetic to his gallery in Boundary Road, St John's Wood, in 1985. There were practical reasons: the work he collected – installations, Abstract Expressionism and, now, Britart – was physically large, and disused industrial spaces were big and cheap. But the Young British Artists that Saatchi was to court were to make the practical aesthetic, and to make the aesthetic desirable. Almost within a matter of days after 'Freeze', the YBAs were cool, 'regarded as social assets rather than bohemians', as Zukin says of their New York counterparts of the late 1960s.[2] Or, rather, their lifestyle was cool – a decadent, SoHo lifestyle aping the 1950s Colony Room crowd, doing what they want and getting paid from it. And, it followed, the spaces in which they hung out were cool. It didn't matter whether or not the Britartists themselves actually lived in lofts. Some did – like Gary Hume in Hoxton Square – some didn't. What mattered was that the right people – wealthy collectors, pop stars – were seen in loft-style spaces, and that the glamorous package was paraded in the media. It didn't matter, either, that Britartists were hardly counter-cultural. What mattered was that they were perceived as counter-cultural, free, individuals – things to be envied from our office desks. The disused industrial space became the landscape of decadence in the late 1980s, where Britart was shown, where illegal raves took place. It was dangerous, and therefore attractive, and therefore profitable.

The Dealers

The 1990s loft rose from the ashes of the yuppie's Wapping warehouse conversion after the financial crash of 1987 and its high-profile property collapses. Residential developers learned from the mistakes. 'We were more cautious, more discriminating', says Harry Handelsman, chairman of the Manhattan Loft Corporation, the most prominent of the 1990s loft moghuls.[3] Instead of the anything goes, pile 'em high speculation of the Docklands apartment market, loft developers sold small – spacious lofts but small developments, such as Handelsman's first, a former 1920s printers in Summers Street, Clerkenwell, launched in 1992, the day after Black Wednesday. And instead of relying on a reluctant central state to create entire neighbourhoods, as in the Docklands, developers invested in more central and sellable areas, where there was an existing, if shabby, infrastructure, and, crucially, where attractive artistic 'pioneers' had already settled: still edgy and urbane, but not too far from a Tube station. The crucial difference between the warehouse yuppie and the loft liver, however, was in their uniform. Both are essentially similar beasts: aspirational, conformist, about fulfilment through mass consumption, about a 'liberating' form of class structure based on what you earned and what you could buy. For the yuppie, this meant a cool hi-fi and a Porsche: bog-standard aspirational stuff. But for the loft liver it was about conforming through being nonconformist, a kind of mass individualism. You had to have quirkiness, culture. Your interiors had to mimic the interiors of those artists who had enough free time and creative latitude to rifle through skips for old dentists' chairs and 1930s office furniture. Matched with some classic modern furniture, true, and a spot of Britart – you didn't want your home to look like a jumble sale. A yuppie wouldn't have been seen dead with odd furniture and loser artists. But for the loft liver, a dusting of cultural credibility was vital. The developers sold this creative individualism through the glossiest, funkiest brochures and marketing campaigns (they were selling, after all, to a highly design-literate community, many of whom owed much of their income to designing developers' marketing brochures). Take the marketing literature for the Beaux Arts building in Islington (really in Holloway . . . perception is what counts with selling lofts): 'Freedom of expression', runs the headline: 'You are in control . . . You can do whatever you like . . . You end up with more personality', as if personality was for sale next to sun-dried tomatoes.[4]

One way that the loft liver could demonstrate his or her individuality was through the quality of the loft's architecture. This had to be interesting, un-suburban. 'Our business is essentially taking architecturally attractive buildings and enhancing them', says Handelsman.[5] 'I would not consider buying a building I would not live in myself.' The literature for Summers Street, for instance, trumpets the quality of the original building, designed by Captain Stanley C. Peach, designer of the Centre Court at Wimbledon. 'Authentic' period detail, especially iron columns and other reminders of past uses, attracted a premium, as did 'authentic' history, especially if associated in some way with liberal political causes. Literature for the Beaux Arts building highlights Islington's history of nonconformism, as a 'bastion of free-thinking eclecticism', equating the purchaser's choice with radical politics.[6] Despite, of course, the building not being in Islington itself.

The locale was part of the package too. Like a game of cat and mouse, developers followed loft-living pioneers, the new bars and clubs, the warehouse parties (sometimes mimicked in launch parties for developments), places colonized by new media industries, the places to be seen, and pounced on buildings when the time was right. Summers Street was ideally placed, according to Handelsman. 'Clerkenwell was not an obvious residential area. But there were the seeds: the growing design, graphics and media industry; we had the Eagle [a gastropub], the Quality Chop House [a 'progressive working-class caterer', in its own words, which sells classic British and European food at non-working-class prices], and Viaduct [a modernist furniture store]. There was a slight infrastructure that we could sell to our punters.'[7]

The final marketing ingredient was the implied, somehow attractive element of risk, for both you and the developer. These neighbourhoods and buildings were perceived as physically and socially run-down, dangerous, far from the conventional centre of things: you both took a risk in buying. Yet you were tantalized by this, by being where illegal warehouse raves were taking place, the edge yet the centre of things. So you weighed these perceived dangers against the potential profit you might make should gentrification take hold. And, to sugar the pill, you were portrayed, and portrayed yourself, as an urban pioneer, frontiersman, doing good in a lawless country, saving the city from dereliction and polishing it up with brushed stainless steel and, fingers crossed, one day, a branch of Starbucks.

Handelsman was the most adept at packaging all this as a lifestyle brand. As the design writer Caroline Roux noted, 'his activities have generated more column inches than any other developer this decade. Harry didn't invent "loft living", but he did put the quote marks round it.'[8] Just look at the company name, for a start. No matter that Handelsman was born in Munich, and grew up in Belgium and France, his company, in iconography, design and name, was New York loft. By buying from him, you were close, but not threateningly close, to the decadence of Britartists, to 1970s SoHo, to Andy Warhol. You were practically invited to the party.

It was hard to convince anyone to invest in lofts in the late 1980s and early '90s: government, banks, local councils, they were all cautious, says Handelsman, following the Docklands property collapses. They certainly failed to understand this new product, the London loft. When Handelsman approached Camden Council for permission to convert the building on Summers Street, 'they were shocked. Planners thought we were mad. It was more because of the small numbers of flats we were developing. They were used to the 1980s excesses. In the end we got planning in ten weeks, which was unheard of, perhaps because they were still in shock.'[9]

By the mid-1990s, though, lofts had taken off commercially. Once people could see that there was money to be made, everybody wanted a piece. By this time, as in mid-1970s New York, lofts had become crucial to London's shift towards a consumer, rather than a manufacturing, economy. London's planners and the Conservative and New Labour governments of the 1990s essentially gave up on manufacturing, and did all they could to encourage the notion of London as a consumerist playground, through policies such as the lottery projects and, says Handelsman, a more relaxed attitude to property development. Local boroughs, starved of public subsidy and city-level direction after the abolition of the GLC in 1986, were only too eager for developers' interest. Loft living effectively became urban regeneration policy. The key was to invest in, say, a lottery project or environmental improvements where there were existing loft pioneers, and watch and wait as developers crept in. (You can see the package working in Southwark, where lottery projects like Tate Modern, pioneer developments such as the Globe Theatre, and Southwark Council's environmental improvements – new trees, new pavements, etc., often in collaboration with cool young designers – have reeled in speculative developers. Handelsman's Bankside Lofts sit right beside the Tate.) Finally the whole London playground could be packaged up as national marketing. By the mid-1990s, Britart, Britpop, Blairism and lofts = Cool Britannia. It was old-fashioned boosterism, yet on a scale and with such a rush that Zukin could not have imagined, touted through magazine articles, music and blockbuster exhibitions, such as 'Brilliant: New Art from London', held in 1995 in Minneapolis, a roadshow of coolness.

Yet, the noisiest promoter of lofts was neither developers nor government. Sharon Zukin and Andy Warhol could not have imagined the proliferation of lifestyle media by the 1990s, the sheer number of magazines, TV programmes and column inches selling endless dreams of consumption: from the loft-living king and queen, *Elle Deco* and *Wallpaper**, through endless segmentation (*Feng Shui for Modern Living*, now sadly passed away) to bottom-shelf DIY handbooks. This proliferation marked, for the self-appointed style guru Peter York, the shift in mass-market style from the country to the city: 'thus a range of English Country Dreams titles (*Country Living*, *Country Homes* and *Interiors*, etc.) is now fiercely opposed by the Chuck Out The Chintz brigade – *Elle Deco*, *Wallpaper**, etc.'[10] Industrial style, stripped wood floors and Eames chairs were now the norm, in fashion terms, the final, if debased, triumph of international modernist style. This media iconography of the loft fuelled a great cycle of production and consumption: it was about selling print, interior design and furniture, selling advertising as much as selling property.

I doubt whether there was any building type more written about in the 1990s than the loft (except, perhaps, the Millennium Dome). It was as if the loft existed only to be written about. Of course the articles were utterly predictable. That was the point. It was like religion, reaffirming what you already knew and secretly hoped for. Magazine articles were sometimes literally indistinguishable from marketing brochures in their gushing enthusiasm. Usually, without a hint of irony, the article chronicled the heroic 'pioneering' struggles of the advertising executive/startup entrepreneur, etc., attempting to fulfil that archetypal human need, shelter, by making a loft shell habitable. It was a journey of self-discovery through DIY. The tears! The sandblasting! The builders! The quest to find somewhere to buy a pint of milk! The text would go on at length about the loft's exquisite details, authentic of course, and about its limitless 'space and light', without which a loft simply wasn't a loft. It would also mention the essential idiosyncrasies of the loft's interior design, the little collector's items found in a local skip, the stark modern furniture bought from the local style store – the loft uniform. The new residents might also have succumbed to the charms of feng shui, that snake oil for the interiors industry. The article would be liberally sprinkled with words and phrases such as: 'urban', 'cool', 'east London', 'texture', 'arty, bohemian chic', 'hip and happening', 'funky', 'industrial', 'exposed', 'space', 'flexibility', 'it was a blank canvas', 'raw', 'sandblasted', 'eclectic taste', 'mezzanine', 'zen', 'liberating'. Here's a good one: a 29-year-old stockbroker, Johann Gulotti, in 1993 on his 1,313-square-foot loft in Clerkenwell: he loves 'the potential for imposing myself on the space. It's like a clean canvas . . . Johann considers himself a typical loft living convert because he has strong opinions about the kind of space he wants to live in.'[11] Unlike everyone else, of course.

Johann was not alone. The loft reached the penultimate, decadent stage in its development with the boutique loft, where, essentially you now no longer had to face the bother of decorating a shell yourself. Instead, you could buy it ready individualized for you. In 2000, the supremely well-connected PR it-boy, Matthew Freud, and John Hitchcox, once a colleague of Harry Handelsman in the Manhattan Loft Corporation, launched the yoo apartments (no capitals) in Maida Vale. Now even the neighbourhood didn't have to be 'challenging'. The building was a former telephone exchange – not, strictly speaking, industrial. Each apartment was kitted out in bespoke style by the loft designer par excellence, Philippe Starck: you could choose your identity before signing on the dotted line. Other boutique lofts followed: the Piper Building in Fulham; the Jam Factory in Borough, where you can get your apartment fitted out by a groovy young designer of your choice (Robert de Niro bought a loft there, apparently – rumour of a celebrity resident is vital for sales). At the Glass Building in Camden, the entire building was new, designed by the ironic court architect of loft living, CZWG. Dressed top to bottom in plate glass, it did not even pretend to be an industrial building, although it was still called a loft. Likewise, loft livers were no longer loft livers, but yuppies, investment bankers like Yuen-Wei Chew: 'I agreed to keep spending the money because it was working, so there was no point in stopping. And . . . I employed five people for a month, so I don't think that was money ill spent.'[12] Unlike those distant, 'original' loft-living artists, new loft livers found their personal freedom not through time and fulfilling activity, but through spending money.

Cold Turkey

By the time that Tony Blair entered 10 Downing Street, in 1997, however, the loft was dead. The first cries came in magazine articles lamenting the loss of the original 'authentic' loft. 'Aficionados of loft living must act, before it is too late', worried *The Times* in 1997, before hunting for the endangered species.[13] Then came the backlash: lofts were impractical for families – all those sharp edges and hard wooden floors – lacked privacy, were expensive to fit out, were in areas that simply refused to gentrify, and, the greatest domestic crime of all, were not even cosy. The more radical noted the obvious failure of loft living and the 1990s consumerist urbanism to solve fundamental problems of urban poverty, that it had had little physical impact on urban landscapes outside a relatively tiny area of inner London and that an economy based on coffee and furniture might not be very robust. But there was a more superficial, and therefore more fundamental problem with the late-'90s loft: it had become suburban. The final stage of its development was the mass-produced, newly built loft-style apartment. Yet the whole point of a loft was that it was meant to endow the owner with easily displayed difference and individuality: now you could buy this individuality at B&Q for £19.99 a square metre. *Wallpaper** magazine had become the global pattern book for the international modern style, whose components you could buy anywhere. As far as the manufacturers of these components were concerned, the loft had triumphed. They had simply switched their production from one style, one uniform – florals and flying ducks – to another – pebbles and fake parquet. Yet the essential attraction of lofts – difference and space, individuality, rawness, flexibility of lifestyle – had disappeared. Now the dealers were selling nothing but padding.

Loft living as a style has become a joke, says the design writer Stephen Bayley: 'slick and uncontroversial, easy-listening modernity . . . an original, and once daring, architectural language has been adapted, compromised, packaged and diffused – rather as Arts & Crafts became the suburban joke-oak semi.'[14] In 1997, Britart and design glitterati, from Gavin Turk to Tomato, held a show, called 'Aspirational Living', in London. One exhibit, by the artist James Dean and the men's fashion designer Charlie Allen, created 'the world's smallest loft', a garden shed from B&Q. It satirized the ever-shrinking size of lofts, as developers sought to increase profits from their square footage. Worse, lofts have become unfashionable. As I write, the anti-loft look fills the lifestyle magazines:

opulence, florals, flock wallpaper, hippy chic, even walls and rooms. Once the elitist driving force of a trend is removed – the ridiculous, indefinable fashionability among those that make the rules on such things – its death knell is sounded. True, lofts are spreading from Crouch End to Aberdeen: developers rely only on finding new territory where the gospel according to *Wallpaper** has yet to be heard. This movement, like a ripple on a pond, is powered by a source that has long since disappeared. According to *The Daily Express* of 3 September 2001, 'the humble suburbs are where most British homeowners would like to live'.

DOWN IN THE DIRT

Patrick Wright

ANTHROPOLOGISTS HAVE PRODUCED elegant theories about dirt. Mary Douglas has described dirt as an idea that defines the outside of a culture, a conceptual domain in which all differences disappear and only the threat of defilement remains: as dirt, so the argument goes, everything is the same.[1]

We know about defilement on Dalston Lane too, but here the filth in the streets is far from undifferentiated. Indeed, it calls for discrimination of the closest kind. Children know better than to play in the autumn leaves without at first poking about in them with a stick to see what exotic content they might mask. The freakish winds that have, in recent years, torn up so many ancient trees in the shires and filled our leading novelists with a sense of impending doom, are recognized around here as Nature's way of cleaning the streets. One gust and the sky is filled with a marvellous diversity of things. A million plastic bags drift aloft. Tons of newsprint, hamburger wrappers, and umbrella silk from the City flutter overhead. The 'Great Wind' of 1989 even managed to pick up thousands of brand-new, black plastic rubbish bags from a council depot and distribute them evenly over this borough and the next. Here was the solution once again becoming part of the problem, but not quite in the manner Sir Alfred Sherman envisaged.

If dirt is where all differentiation finally stops, then litter must be the domain of its last feverish efflorescence. East London has long been full of scavengers and rag-pickers who eke out a living by sorting through the rubbish. A few totters still work the streets with horse, cart, and bell, and the street markets are going strong. Down in Whitechapel, Hogarthian characters sit on the wintry pavements offering up fragments of salvaged rubbish for a pittance: glass, bones, and a hank of weeds. Dalston Lane is also defined by this circulation. The street is really a clogged river of junk flowing through the city, eddying here, forming deep and stagnant pools there. There's an unexpected wealth of charity shops in the area: the British Red Cross Society's modest establishment has been joined more recently by Age Concern, the Family Welfare Association, and, just around the corner, a true hypermarket run by Oxfam. It's not quite clear whether these agencies are competing here for the sake of opportunity or froma sense of mission.

A whole collection of junk merchants work the same street, some of them as specialized as anyone's idea of niche marketing could demand. 'Mirror TV' revives exhausted television sets, while Ossie turns over already much-recycled kitchen equipment for canteens and restaurants. Further along stands the more generalist outfit of Collins & McCabe ('DHSS welcome – Enquire within'). You would have to be pretty desperate to find much of value among the exhausted household furniture on display here, and there's not a great deal to be said for the old technical manuals either: *Halsbury's Statutes of England*, *Accounting in the Foreign Exchange Market*, *Property Tax in Singapore* . . . Indeed, the whole operation seems to be held together by the hard currency of a smelter behind the scenes. As the sign says, 'Spot cash for scrap metals'.

Collins & McCabe operate out of a battered old corner shop, but Mr Hewison across the road gets by without even this modest concession to the idea of permanent structure. He has learnt that, with the help of a ferocious dog or two, it is possible to run a demolition and salvage business without wasting time on bricks and mortar of your own. All that is necessary is to rent a derelict bomb-site, and then fence it off with huge advertising hoardings, which have the advantage of providing a handy little income while also bringing constant variation to the area. One week it's Moroccan holidays and rats courtesy of NALGO ('One family that's better off with the poll tax'); the next it's the new Volvo ('Where the Pursuit of Excellence Inevitably Leads You'), and an apparently stark-naked girl draped, like a bleached shrimp, over purple velvet to demonstrate 'the ultimate leg experience' of 'Voilance de Le Bourget'.

Inside this kaleidoscopic compound is a hastily improvised shanty of temporary structures, each one filled with different categories of upwardly mobile debris. Mr Hewison knows how to pull a likely proposition from its original setting, but he's no master when it comes to reassembly. So his collection mounts up like a great pile of quotations that won't resolve into a coherent statement, and customers are left to make whatever connections they can. He's got an old, red telephone box, an Ardizzone-style petrol pump, pub signs from some distant hostelry called the Chigwell Arms, a couple of red ticket kiosks for anyone who wants to open their home to the public, a huge chimney pot from a house on Piccadilly, garden seats, wagon wheels that still have the tinsel of some forgotten Christmas hanging from them, sash windows, wrought iron, a couple of fake Doric columns retrieved from a redundant theatre or restaurant design, and, of course, lots of stripped pine. I went by recently to find a lady from Islington trying to buy the collapsing wooden shed in which the caustic-soda bath is kept. Old Mr Hewison was having trouble containing his laughter, but he was certainly entertaining the offer.

This incessant scavenging has also achieved a cultural dimension. The used-book dealers are here, picking over the flow and finding new areas of sale in a dwindling market. Even the British Red Cross Society is advertising for books. Driffield confines his notices to *The Daily Telegraph*. He specializes in finding back-titles for aged authors who have forgotten what they have written or, in some cases, for their widows. Iain Sinclair, who knows exactly which upmarket dealer was involved in levering up the reputation of which Faber or Chatto poet, runs his own experiments to see how far a literary reputation can be made from a heap of valueless old books. As the literary culture disintegrates into mutual backscratching in the Sunday reviews, jobs teaching 'theory' in North America, and the whimsical tipsterism of the literary prize, a mutant canon of English literature – quite distinct from the official one now under the management of American academics – emerges along the edges of Dalston Lane. John Lodwick, a novelist of the Forties and Fifties, is the latest addition. A few months ago, his books could hardly be given away, but a few carefully sown references have already cracked him up to £30 for a fine copy with dust-wrapper. Lodwick has been picked up by a pivotal mid-level dealer in Cambridge, and the critical profiles are bound to follow.

In the Sixties, members of the Exploding Galaxy (hailed and reviled as 'London's love-anarchist dance group') lived communally in a house a few hundred yards west of Dalston Junction. These performers, whose repertoire included such works as the 'Kinetapocalypsoidal Bumping Bodies Ballet' ('Never have so many been so nude so early and for such good reasons', as an appreciative reviewer wrote in *International Times*), had a kinetic relationship with clutter, but they also had their own domestic problems with household filth. Indeed, in the autumn of 1967, their house at No. 99 Balls Pond Road was so infested with lice and the excretions of five or six untrained cats that a couple of residents became worried about the possible outbreak of disease, and decided that something must be done. After pondering the situation, they came up with a ploy designed to raise their fellow communards' consciousness of this hygiene problem without imposing anything so crude as a hierarchical decision on them. The answer, they decided, lay in cannabis resin. The 'increased awareness' brought by the drug would make the 'ugly aspects' of the house more noticeable. Some people might find such a revelation 'absolutely unbearable' and respond by getting 'withdrawn and cut off from the environment', but the members of the Exploding Galaxy were creative and artistic types who, so the advocates of the hashish solution calculated, would push through this initial sense of abjection to 'create works which act as a sort of "social antidote"'. The cannabis was given to the 'Exploders' as they woke up one morning, and it seems to have worked admirably: in fact, 'the entire house was cleaned, disinfected, and actions taken to ensure the restoration of hygienic conditions'.[2]

Through 1990 another marginal collective was finding a different kind of art in the rubbish, this time in a squat rather closer to Dalston Junction at No. 147 Balls Pond Road, which happens to be another of Hackney's derelict listed buildings. The Maberly Chapel was taken over as a 'carcass' in 1825 by a certain Mr Ashley from Charles Square in Hoxton, who fitted it out with galleries and created a chapel capable of accommodating 'a congregation of Independents' of up to 800 souls. When I first noticed it a few years ago, this building had returned to its original state as a carcass. Still bearing the signs of discontinued industrial endeavour (the 'Regolux Venetian Blind Company', etc.), it was in use as a junk shop and crammed to the ceiling with knackered furniture. There were signs of a sporadic sifting process, for the objects that were finally deemed to have become unsaleable were hurled out of the door onto the few yards of ground (once a small graveyard) between the chapel and the street, where they lay rotting in an undifferentiated heap. 'Quite a mess', I once remarked to an elderly woman at the bus stop. She was in no doubt that there were better ways of keeping the rubbish off the streets: further, she told me that when she had been young, just before the war, the Maberly Chapel had been headquarters for Oswald Mosley and the blackshirted 'biff boys' of his British Union of Fascists. The young men who came here used to be given 'a free shirt and a pair of boots' – an offer that, as my interlocuter snarled before boarding her bus, was 'not to be scoffed at in those days'.

Since that fleeting encounter, the junk dealers have moved on too, and the Maberly Chapel, which is owned by the Sikh Society and, like too many other listed buildings in Hackney, well on the way to eventual demolition as a 'dangerous structure', has been squatted by a group of artists going (at least on the day I asked them) by the name of Dene Cholmeley. The corrugated iron along the street front has been turned into a collage, with cut-out fragments of bodies, holiday images, men in camouflage, and highlighted snatches of text ('He ended up making history', 'London Calling', 'How far will you be able to push the boat out?'). Behind this weirdly ornamented barricade, the forgotten graveyard has been turned into an installation. The junk that got left behind as worthless has been picked over yet again, differentiated and displayed according to the precepts of a renegade art. A straw man, made out of woven palm leaves, is leaping out of the window, and selected fragments have been stuck up all over the outside of the building: hub caps, dried flowers over the door, a typewriter, old romantic novels opened at gnomic places and nailed to the wall, paint pots, bits of a smashed-up cash register. As for the cavernous interior of this scorched and disintegrating edifice, it is filled by a huge ship made up from the ruined chapel's own timbers with translucent oiled paper stretched out between them and ornamented with diverse insignia and strange found objects. In 1840 this was the Maberly Sabbath School, an institution run for the children of the 'very poor' where, thanks to a recent alteration in Rule 27, corporal punishment was forbidden.[3] One hundred and fifty years later, the biblical apocalypse is back: Noah's Ark sailing out on a rising tide of filth, a fervid if not strictly dissenting cult of the Last Days of London.

This tacky sense of an ending has come to hang over the whole city in recent years. An interest in debris and human fallout is part of the New Baroque sensibility, shared by young Apocalyptics and played-out Marxists alike. The range runs from *Absolute Beginners* (the film) to a commentator like Elizabeth Wilson who, quick to adjust her dogmatic heart to the fashions of post-modernism, eulogizes the spastic movements of the dancer in Covent Garden who has turned himself into a broken object or 'living doll'.[4] All over London young photographers have been reviving the black-and-white imagery of the rat-catcher, the old paraffin heater, the disused and cluttered-up church interior, the peeling walls of the unimproved slum tenement, the fragmentary but exotic combinations of the restaged bomb-site.[5]

London has been through something like this before: picking over the debris, finding surprising new meaning in the ruins. But the first blitz came with a greater sense of reality. Neo-romantic artists, such as John Minton and Graham Sutherland, found strange figures in the debris. The engraver, John Farleigh, wandered through the blitzed streets in 1941, recording that there was 'a loveliness about the whole atmosphere', and that bombing had cleansed Tottenham Court Road of its vulgarity and enabled it to achieve 'beauty and humility'.[6] He celebrated the fact that the signposts had gone, saying that they had really only been 'symbols of our suburbanity', and preferring to wander wide-eyed into the deeper meanings of a city reduced to rubble. He even found a consoling lesson in the fact that the fake Corinthian columns of an Oxford Street department store had outlasted the rest of the building: evidently, it was important not to cast tawdry design in such permanent form. But for many people, at least, the desperate aesthetics of the blitz were based on a commitment to something greater than the momentary and startling effect. In a commentary written to accompany a series of watercolours by the Polish artist, Wanda Ostrowska, Viola Garvin described the ruins of the city as 'pediments of solidity' on which the newly steeled spirit of the nation could rest.[7]

Fifty years later, the revived styles of the blitz find no such 'pediments of solidity' on which to base themselves. People who lived through the bombing talk of the palpable silence that came between the raids. The new cult of the blitz comes wrapped in the different silence, more like the one that follows an arrested bulldozer than an exploded bomb, that is to be found to the end of planning, the end of reform, the end of State responsibility. It is in this less palpable silence that the debris has started to glow again. The first blitz produced a spirit of solidarity and common interest that was built into the foundations of the Welfare State; the second is an aesthetic effect found in the ruins of that reforming endeavour.

Hackney Council doesn't need to trouble itself with the morbid aesthetics of the second blitz, but there's a lot at stake in its ongoing battle to keep the streets clean. On 9 February 1990, 67-year-old pensioner, Stephen McGrath, fell over and drowned at the junction of Dalston Lane and Pembury Road. His misfortune was to have landed in 'a grassy hollow', which had been flooded for a week.[8] In a subsequent hearing the council admitted that the drains had been blocked with rubbish, claiming that the fault lay with an 'untrained' street sweeper who had apparently not understood that rubbish should be swept from the pavement out into the road. A week or two after Mr McGrath's accident, the body of a younger man named Mr Pat O'Reilly was found in the pond on nearby Clapton Common. He was estimated to have been floating there for a good three weeks. How does a body float unnoticed for so long in a large but much-visited ornamental pond? The police explained their own failure to find it by pointing out that 'the pond is so dirty, even though it is five feet deep you can't see down more than five inches'. As for the old-age pensioners who came to feed the geese and the children who fished there, they had been aware of something bulky in the water, but they hadn't bothered to distinguish it from all the other debris. As one local said: 'I'd seen it, but I thought it was a bag of rubbish. That was at least three weeks ago.' The police explained further: 'The man's clothes had filled with air . . . making the body look like a plastic dustbin bag of rubbish.' This gruesome story shocked many hard-bitten people into silence, but some were rightly moved to speak out. As leading members of the Hackney Irish Association, Councillors Lawless and Eustace (themselves subject to unjust ridicule as 'legless and useless' in some of Hackney's remaining public bars) issued an uncompromising statement claiming that the man had not been found sooner because he was Irish. They were reported to have slammed police suggestions that Mr O'Reilly had probably 'turned to the life of a vagrant'. This was 'a classic case of stereotyping' in which a 'perfectly respectable man was linked with vagrants simply because he was Irish, liked a drink and was missing'.[9] They were almost certainly right about the police; but so, apparently, was Mary Douglas with her idea of dirt as the domain in which all such differences are lost.

FROM *A Journey through Ruins* (1992)

SLOW FLOW: THIRTY YEARS OF TRANSPORT IN LONDON

Helen Caroline Evenden

IF A WEEK is a long time in politics, thirty years is a short time in transport. In 2000, at the launch of *Moving London*, a pioneering digitized map of London's integrated transport network developed by The Architecture Foundation, Mayor Ken Livingstone attributed to Margaret Thatcher the statement: 'any man travelling on a bus over the age of thirty is a failure'. Whatever the truth of that attribution, it is quite certain that during the next thirty years many more men and women of all ages will certainly find themselves travelling on buses. Any other course of action will lead to the celebrated total gridlock that has only narrowly been averted since the 1970s.

Changes to the way in which transport services are run and maintained can be immediate, from repairing broken-down escalators at Tube stations, to increasing the price of train tickets or removing bus conductors. Changes to the moving vehicles themselves are also relatively quick and easy to implement, such as the livery of buses or the TX1 reinvention of the design of London's world-famous black cabs. Changes to transport infrastructure – the roads, tunnels, bridges and piers on which the moving vehicles depend – are slow, expensive and highly politicized. Since the 1970s significant changes to London's transport have been few and far between. Residents of London and the South-East who travel within the capital on a daily basis will recognize little evidence of progress. Indeed, one could be forgiven for thinking that changes to London Transport (or Transport for London as we are learning to call the capital's newest transport body, created by Mayor Livingstone in 2000) have all been for the worse. Our once admired, clean, modern and reliable public transport system has become an unloved, unkempt, out-of-date and unpredictable service. While expensive advertising campaigns at many of the privately owned bus stops around the city tell us of improvements to services, we are expected to appreciate crawling across London in Tube carriages and on buses of which the best were designed in the 1950s. Those who are lucky enough to get into a carriage or on to a bus during the seemingly constant rush hour travel at the same speed as the Victorians and pay some of the highest fares in Europe for the privilege. To make matters worse, it seems that the honourable English tradition of queuing has not survived into the new millennium.

Private transport fares little better. Motorists here are held to ransom with some of the highest taxes for petrol and road use in the world – and that's before we even start to think about parking fees and congestion charging. The millions of pounds collected from motorists seem in the main to be spent on smarter parking tickets, smarter uniforms for parking wardens and very smart solar-powered pay-and-display machines and other cosmetic arrangements that do not provide fundamental changes for the better. Driving in central London has become for many a passport to 'road rage' – a condition that I'm sure existed long before the media coined a term to describe it. Yet there are thousands of Londoners and commuters who still love getting into their cars and cruising the tarmac of the capital. Our streets are a carnival of aesthetic pleasure, from the stylish classic cars and clever low-emission vehicles that are road-tax exempt to the amazingly sophisticated new vehicles laden with gadgets, from Global Positioning Systems to boom-boom state-of-the-art sound systems. For me, driving in London remains one of life's pleasures. My idea of driving heaven includes crossing any bridge over the Thames, refuelling under the pagoda canopy at the Chinese Garage petrol station, and sitting at the Whitehall traffic lights with a Routemaster on my left, the Treasury building on my right and Big Ben in my windscreen.

Ever since the car was invented opinion has been polarized between those who loathe the polluting and dangerous vehicles and those who love the machine that revolutionized personal transport. The public transport enthusiast and architect Brian Richards is a member of the former group. Richards has long been lobbying for alternative, intelligent transport solutions. In 1976 he presented an international selection of proposals for 'Moving in Cities', including low-tech fold-up bikes and high-tech moving pavements capable of carrying 10,000 people an hour. Many of his suggestions, from digital bus information displays to computerized vehicle-tracking systems, have since become commonplace in London. For the daily commuter, however, convenient, comfortable journeys remain the stuff of fiction. So the die-hard car enthusiasts remain just that, but the fashion for transport changes as frequently as clothes on the high street, big cars, small cars, no cars.

Ensuring that the infrastructure of the city can accommodate fashionable transport solutions is problematic. Take the pedestrianization of Trafalgar Square for example. The scheme to change the role of London's most famous traffic island has been an on–off planning decision for decades. Lord Rogers sensibly proposed altering the configuration of the square, among other innovations using underground access, but his vision was lost to political wrangling. One could be forgiven for thinking that the realization of Norman Foster's World Squares for All scheme, which includes the closure of a single street in front of the National Gallery, would stop everyone in Greater London getting to work. The fact is that small changes to infrastructure make a big impact on the patterns of movement that traffic planners refer to as 'flows'. London's flows have been mapped, categorized and re-plotted countless times. The integrated transport jigsaw is now so complex that the closure of one road can indeed influence driving conditions for miles around.

During my lifetime the major change in transport has quite simply been expansion, both in terms of quantity and size. There has been an expansion of both public and private transport. Public transport in the form of more Tube lines, more buses, more trains and more aeroplanes. Private transport in the form of more cars, more motorcycles and more pedal cycles than ever before and, with the exception of the not-so-smart Smart car (which has a footprint bigger than my much-loved Fiat 500 and yet only two seats), most vehicles are bigger than before. At 3.15 pm, the narrow, double-parked streets are filled with mums driving SUVS (sports utility vehicles) on the school run.

We have a proliferation of options for mode of transport – car, bus, bike, Tube, black cab, mini cab, Karma Kab, motorbike, scooter, micro-scooter, skateboard, rollerblade. The privilege of extended movement via public, private and hybrid public–private vehicles (taxis to you and I) is still expanding, fuelled by an increasing standard of living. Indeed, almost everyone who really wants to travel is able to do so with far less inconvenience than in previous times. The story may be one of expansion in all forms, but the crucial questions are these: Has this expansion led to more pleasurable journeys in and across the city? And is there greater satisfaction with the greater freedom of movement? The simple answer is NO. Unless, that is, you enjoy pushing past fellow travellers to secure a seat, or you like smelling your neighbours' armpits and reading other people's papers, the experience of public transport in London is typically miserable.

A crucial factor for our miserable journeys is that investment in transport has failed to maintain the necessary pace to cope with the expectations for greater freedom of movement for ever greater numbers of people. Transport infrastructure is particularly difficult and expensive to change in a city as varied and dense as London. The most impressive investment in infrastructure has been made below ground, where the difficulties of altering the Underground reflect the original decisions made when the system was installed. Unlike Paris, where in the nineteenth century Baron Haussmann boldly solved congestion by creating now-familiar patterns of boulevards and squares, London's Underground system was installed under a policy of minimum surface disruption, tunnelling below poorer districts to avoid property demolition and related payments to landowners in a city largely formed of private estates. Now London Underground (read Transport for London) has more than 100 miles of tunnelling with which any new addition to the system clearly has to integrate. During the 1970s and '80s Underground architecture was limited to re-patching the existing system via the refurbishment and restyling of historic stations. London Underground searched for a new identity, experimenting with graphics and signage, while the bigger issues were crumbling beneath thin new veneers of improvement, like Sir Eduardo Paolozzi's mosaics installed at Tottenham Court Road station in 1979.

Undoubtedly, the most significant and impressive project to contribute to London's transport began in 1990 with the process of finding architects and engineers for the Jubilee Line Extension (JLE). Following on from his success with Hong Kong's Metro, Roland Paoletti, chief architect of the JLE, set out to create public transport environments that demonstrate a return to the superior architectural content pioneered by Charles Holden's Piccadilly Line stations of the 1920s and '30s, one of the golden ages of London's transport. Paoletti employed an interesting design strategy for the stations, commissioning different architects for each of the eleven sites, from world-class architects to younger architectural practices. His strategy was rewarded with some much-appreciated generous public spaces, including the masterpiece, cathedral-like Underground at Canary Wharf. Canary Wharf Station by Foster and Partners was awarded the best transport infrastructure project in the world by *World Architecture Magazine* in 2001. Further west, Westminster's Blade-Runner-like complex of escalators and exposed structure saved Michael

Hopkins's reputation after his architectural disaster above ground with the notorious MPs' office building, Portcullis House.

The JLE achievement was not without difficulty and sacrifice, however, and met the bureaucratic problems typical of public sector projects. Rules had to be bent in order to achieve excellence, and the only way of achieving that was to create a break-away team from London Underground's obstructive and ill-informed old guard. For example, the ingenious and reflective glass wall by the artist Alexander Beleschenko for MacCormac Jamieson Prichard's Southwark Station is a delightful surprise as one reaches the top of the escalator. Yet it was made possible only by Richard MacCormac's specification that listed the artwork as internal cladding – site-specific artworks were beyond the engineer's brief for a functioning station. Despite the celebrated JLE architecture, things did not get off to a good start. Tony Blair's journey on the line left a rather embarrassed Prime Minister trying to strike up conversation with a Walkman-wearing young lady who was clearly a far more experienced Tube traveller, equipped with the tools necessary to secure some personal space on the usually crowded environment. Of course, Tony's PR trip was in optimum conditions and he was able to get a seat.

Mainline railway stations across the capital have also seen the hand of distinguished architects – with varying degrees of success. In 1990 Terry Farrell and Company completed their revamp of Charing Cross Station. The postmodern achievement not only encased the riverside face of the station with fake Doric columns, but also managed to squeeze 37,000 square metres of office space in the air right above the tracks. The American model of utilizing the free areas above spaces for transport, such as railway tracks and roads, was also exploited by Farrell at London Wall in the City. Shortly afterwards, Nicholas Grimshaw's office created one of the longest railway stations in the world for the Eurostar Terminal at Waterloo. The blue skeletal roof welcomes Europeans to London, only to subject them to taxi queues, traffic jams and the still-to-be redeveloped South Bank. Liverpool Street and Paddington stations have also benefited from facelifts and a welcome return to the chic-hotel-with-station-attached scenario advocated by the master engineer Isambard Kingdom Brunel. Despite the overhaul, Paddington Station is now more confusing and just as dirty as it ever was, due to the continuing use of diesel-powered locomotives. The most important railway redevelopment – indeed currently the largest infrastructure project in Europe – is the reconfiguration of the old rivals, St Pancras and King's Cross stations, who together will receive thousands of passengers from Eurostar trains.

Unfortunately, London's roads have failed to benefit from the attention of world-class architects. Only the once-neglected spaces beneath London's elevated road sections are seeing something of a renaissance and are being used to house everything from indoor climbing walls and skateboard parks to subterranean night-clubs. Rex Wilkinson (CZWG architects) even proposed Radio City, a flamboyant B-movie-inspired office development proposed for the area adjacent to the Westway that included transforming the motorway structure into elegant, cartoon-like caryatids. Unfortunately, because of the economic downturn of the late 1980s, the developer, Roger Zogolovitch, failed to realize the scheme.

The M25 orbital motorway was the last significant contribution to our through-flow problem. Since its debut in the late 1980s, the M25 has held a regular feature on morning and evening rush-hour radio as the number one traffic jam in London, and the 'London Orbital' has provided much contemplation for journalists and authors, including Iain Sinclair's book of the same name. The story of London's roads over the past thirty years is one of continual small-scale adaptations rather than radical progress, such as could be achieved only by major north–south, east–west tunnelling beneath the city.

Central London streets are being carved up in an attempt to segregate two-wheeled from four-wheeled streams of traffic. The cycle lane – so successful in flat European cities and provincial university towns – simply cannot be fitted into London streets that are already too slim for buses. The stitching together of cycle routes across London's boroughs has resulted in dead-end routes that frequently spit cyclists out on to busy roads at borough boundaries. Even worse, bus lanes and red routes are seen as just another potential source of income for the Local Authorities and the Treasury. The only progress appears to have been in the monitoring and penalizing of individual drivers, a poor substitute for assisting the already hard-pressed motorist to transit from A to B more effectively. Even when the harassed motorist does manage to reach his or her destination, the parking rates are more than the minimum wage. It appears obvious that the situation will grow even worse, even closer to gridlock, before the public force effective action on the politicians.

Some braver souls have looked to the River Thames for at least part of the solution to the movement of people and cargo. In the river itself, a recent series of new piers now enable some river services, albeit largely for the enjoyment of tourists, since commercial commuter services start up and flounder at an alarming rate. As long ago as 1796, the architect and engineer Willey Reverley thought he had the answer when he proposed to a House of Commons' Committee a 'novel, grand and captivating' scheme to straighten out the Thames. Needless to say, the radical scheme came to nothing, but significant changes in the use of the river have taken place since the 1970s. The process of moving industry further down river (if not to other parts altogether) began in the 1960s and has steadily accelerated. Office, residential and leisure facilities have replaced the old heavy industries, while the Jubilee Line Extension and the Docklands Light Railway (DLR) have improved transport links to the east. The ten new DLR stations funded by the developer Olympia and York to promote Canary Wharf were initially designed for tiny passenger flows estimated at 16,000 passengers per week. The underestimate of use is staggering, when one notes that ten years later Canary Wharf was opened with a capacity to accommodate more than 100,000 passengers during the peak hours. Fortunately, unlike the DLR planners, Paoletti and his team of architects foresaw the demand for public transport in the area, and since opening the passenger flows at Canary Wharf have been proved to be correct and are still rising.

The biggest change in access to new travel and increased distance of journeys has been the staggering rise in domestic and foreign air travel since the 1970s, obvious to everyone and manifested in the expansion of Heathrow, Gatwick and Stansted airports and the establishment of London City Airport. Political and planning procedures to expand these airports take many years and cost many billions of pounds. Unlike the fanciful scheme to put a circular runway on top of King's Cross Station, proposed by Charles Glover in 1931, modern-day airports continue to grow – with Terminal 5 at Heathrow the most current example of the airport as city, shopping mall and international hub. The changes to airport design during the period have sought to change the travel experience from one of enclosure, that is, sitting in dark, air-conditioned halls, to one of exposure to natural elements, that is, sitting in sunlight-filled glass sheds from which one can see the planes take off and land. Picking up on the successful Asian model of Changi Airport in Singapore, Richard Rogers has even proposed outdoor spaces for the new Terminal 5 scheme.

Since the 1970s, the British Airports Authority (BAA) has made major investment in air traffic infrastructure as a catalyst to reduce journey times from the airport to the city centre, creating the Heathrow Express and the M4 express taxi lane. Private investment by property developers, such as the £400-million contribution to the JLE by Canary Wharf Limited, has improved transport south of the river for thousands of commuters. Perhaps now some of the money falling into Ken Livingstone's coffers will lead to some much-needed public sector investment in what is, after all, a vital public sector industry, not a private playground for those with vested interests. To date, much of the investment in transport has been a reaction against the pressure caused by increasing numbers of vehicles and desire to travel; there has been little or no evidence of radical thinking and application to plan an integrated transport policy for the future.

Despite the massive costs of transport infrastructure, it is easier to identify change in transport in London by considering the static environments rather than the moving objects – the vehicles or modes of transport themselves. Very little has changed with the moving objects: cars are still in the main four-wheeled vehicles powered by internal combustion engines; motorbikes are still two-wheeled, petrol-powered vehicles prone to accidents; trains are still restricted to running on tracks laid by the Victorians; the best buses on London streets are still Routemasters developed in the 1950s; bikes still fight with larger traffic and frequently get stolen. The only new inventions apart from rollerblades (the snazzy update of roller-skates) are concertina, low-floor buses and the hope of two hydrogen buses in the pipeline (courtesy of an EU experiment). We may have a handful of electric- and gas-powered vehicles, but the dominant expression of increased wealth is still larger vehicles than are necessary for urban transport purposes.

How many commuters under the age of 40 can remember the sight of vehicles queuing for petrol or diesel in 1974 when the OPEC nations quadrupled the price of oil? In 2000 people were again forced to queue as panic spread when tanker drivers refused to deliver fuel to stations and city dwellers feared that bread would once again fail to make it to the supermarket shelves. The strike was relatively short-lived, but again served to demonstrate our total dependence on the car. Monies from private vehicles have not provided the sums necessary for genuine change – some Londoners may drive Aston Martin cars, but the Aston Martin bus I so want to see to democratize the luxury of stylish transport still seems a long way off. If the heavy taxation of private motor cars (through both Vehicle Excise Duties and the taxation of petrol and diesel) were to be used for the development of public transport and roads to the same extent as in countries like the USA, we could have first-class buses whizzing down golden bus lanes! At present the money is simply taken for general taxation purposes.

Livingstone's Congestion Charge is the most significant change to private transport in London to take place during the thirty years now under consideration. It was introduced on 17 February 2003, with all the administrative problems that such a new impost inevitably brings in its train. The long-term consequences of the charge for the Mayor and his American transport gurus are significant. A successful congestion charge in one of the world's major cities would greatly assist Transport for London in managing traffic flows and should net millions of pounds a year. If the ticket machines work, if people pay the £5 daily charge for entering central London and do not attempt evasion, via deliberately dirtied number plates, foreign plates and the use of unregistered vehicles, then the congestion charge may be the biggest success of Livingstone's mayorship. Interesting unknowns remain concerning the effects of congestion charging on within-zone and out-of-zone property values and the business, leisure and social life of the city centre.

Camera-controlled congestion charging is very likely to show the flaws in the use of already obsolete technology employed to manage traffic flows in a major world city. London's system relies upon cameras recording every plate entering the zone. The plates are then checked against a database of payment and, if the vehicle has not been paid for, penalty notices are issued to the registered owner – courtesy of access to Driver and Vehicle Licensing Agency (DVLA) records. London's only rival in the congestion-zone approach is Singapore, one of the most law-abiding places in the world. There, a far more sophisticated system is in place, in which a monitor in every car registers entry and deducts the appropriate fees. In other words, London is simply struggling to keep pace with more advanced technologies already employed elsewhere.

Surely we must all realize that congestion charging is merely a short-term political response to long-term under-investment in infrastructure. The Greater London Assembly has replaced the Greater London Council during our period, with some of the same individuals involved in both bodies. Neither body has been permitted the finance-raising powers necessary really to improve transport in London. Even the potential fees from congestion charging represent a small portion of the sums required to start talking about improving Tube stations or fleets of trains. The investment decisions necessary to reduce traffic congestion in London take more than the terms of office of many local councillors and national politicians, who move from department to department far too quickly to have any effect on such long-term, expensive and controversial decisions. Perhaps the indecision and slowness of the political process reflect the slowness and indecision of the population of London itself – who do not want to give up their cars even if they are able to travel only at the same speed as horse-drawn carriages.

There will never be a shortage of suggestions for moving other people into and across London. There will, however, always be a shortage of solutions acceptable to those affected by any of them and those who ultimately have to pay for them. The success or failure of more ambitious schemes is a roller-coaster – on the up are the success stories of the JLE, Heathrow Express and the Croydon Tramlink; on the down is the much-delayed CrossRail link between Paddington and the City at Liverpool Street via the West End. Any further major schemes are likely to rely on yet further taxation on private cars or outright bans, or the public–private partnerships initiated under the Thatcher regime.

London's transport is so complex and affects the interests of so many differing parties that it seems likely that the period 2000–2030 will largely reflect the inertia of the past thirty years, that is, no overall strategy but a continual muddling through to the next crises caused by a long-term, if uneven, increase in the standard of living and the expectations of London's citizens. As long as there are thousands of jobs in UK-based car factories – and I acknowledge that the numbers of jobs are decreasing as plants like Dagenham shut up shop – the motor vehicle will always be available, if not affordable. It may be, however, that environmental circumstances and justified safety concerns force a redesign and a reprioritization of public transport sooner than many of us think. It should also be the case that much greater efforts will have to be made to innovate the environment surrounding the moving vehicles to reflect the priorities of the pedestrian.

Radical and rapid change to transport is about as likely as a regular service from the No. 37 bus. Planning decisions and the organization of vast sums of money necessary to alter (whether for better or worse) the transport systems and their concurrent environments take so long to implement under the politico/economic system in place in Britain that London's flow shows little indication of acceleration.

ARCHITECTURE'S URBAN SHINE AND BRUTAL REALITY

Murray Fraser

THE STORY OF the architecture of London since the late 1970s can be read as the story of two contrasting architectures: one of surface and polish, the other of solidity and ordinariness. Saturday night versus the weekday grind. While varying in degree in buildings that range from the extreme to the barely noticeable, they have offered in effect two dialectical visions of what London ought to look like as a major city. In design terms, they represent perhaps a pair of feuding twins that would prefer not to acknowledge each other's presence.

Both approaches have stemmed from a very different view of the inherited urban environment of London as it stood in the late 1970s. For anyone who arrived in the city at the time and took a look around at its architecture, the overwhelming sense was of a city that had simply lost the will to care about itself. In parts it remained light-heartedly Georgian, but in the main it appeared Victorian in its dullness and earnestness, with some livelier areas of more recent sprawl in the outer fringes, including the ubiquitous Dunroamin' semi-detached homes of the inter-war era. In the city centre there was by the late 1970s a scattering of totem poles that aped the values of American corporate modernism, but far more commonplace were pockets of worthy modernist buildings in areas that had been bombed in the war, and which were largely given over to feeding the spatial needs of the Welfare State. Such was the torpor that dismal mass-housing estates built of bricks were by now being lauded just for not being overtly made from concrete, even if in fact the bricks served only to conceal hidden concrete cores. Overly praised brick estates such as Marquess Road in Islington subsequently proved themselves to be equally inadequate housing solutions, and many have since been pulled down or remodelled alongside the derided tower blocks of the city. The question for architects in London at the end of the 1970s was how to inject something that might cut against the overriding sense of stasis. Ought the city to be transformed into a glittering showcase that stood up to international comparison, or were there intrinsic values in the everyday, stolid urban environment that should be developed and enhanced?

As one side of this dialectic, there have been numerous attempts since the early 1980s to add a smooth and glittering veneer to what was obviously becoming a more complex and multicultural city. This is the architecture of skin – a few centimetres thick at the most, and entirely dependent on artificial environmental servicing to keep it working – and what it wishes to offer is a skim-coat of affluence. Such buildings are as crisp as newly ironed shirts, at least for the first few years after completion, but their unspoken fear is of looking cheap and shoddy, or, worst of all, old. We can see this approach in the architecture of the Lloyds Building (1978–86), the first building in the capital to use stainless steel as its primary sheathing material. It was also a building so intolerant of the ageing City of London landscape around it that it dare not even let its occupants look out of windows. Deciding that there was nothing of worth in the area, Richard Rogers and his team frosted the glazing on the external walls and encouraged the occupants instead to draw their daylight and views from a tall vertical atrium that rose through the centre of the building. This, combined with the famous device of placing all the servicing and escape stairs on the outside of the structure, produced an unhealthy detachment from the rest of London that did little to enhance the public reputation of the insurance business going on inside. A similar tendency to create a clean hermetic world, one that prefers to build upwards and seal itself off from the decaying cityscape, can also be found in the teeming office cities that have sprouted up at Broadgate or Canary Wharf, force-fed by the slick underground stations built for the Jubilee Line Extension during the 1990s.[1] Now the approach has spread to even newer replicants on the western side of the city, such as the field of corporate high-rises sprouting up at almost-Shanghai pace at Paddington Basin.[2] Based on totally identical structural and servicing systems, these buildings then simply choose to wrap themselves in skins in styles that range from thin-stone cladding to even skinnier glazing solutions.

Cultural and landmark buildings in London have also sought to borrow the impossible glamour of urban shine. In the Sainsbury Wing extension to the National Gallery, the Philadelphia-based practice of Venturi Scott-Brown indulged in a knowing game of architectural allusions and visual puns, all played out by using a sequence of smooth skins made out of rich materials that mimicked those of surrounding buildings in chameleon fashion. Then there have been the truly grandiose cultural projects, such as the redevelopment of Covent Garden Opera House into the ultimate up-market shopping mall, at a cost of around £200 million, and the Great Court in the British Museum by Norman Foster, the offices for politicians at Portcullis House, the comical smile of the Media Stand at Lord's cricket ground, the Millennium Dome and, the best-loved of all, the Millennium Wheel, aka the London Eye.[3]

More often than not, the architecture of polished surface is the product of the globalization of high finance, linked as it has been in London to the eastward push of the capital, and to a consumerist desire for a readily identifiable lifestyle that the city's residents can buy into. The blurb for a recent survey of new buildings in London, written by the critic Ken Powell, boasts:

> London today is vibrantly reinventing itself, and the quality of its new buildings is putting the city at the forefront of world architectural innovation. Through a wealth of stunning new projects and bold revisions of its older buildings, architects from all quarters are reimagining London's cityscape.[4]

The photographs of the new buildings to be found inside Powell's book are indeed reassuringly free of dirt and people. The book taps into a mentality of cultural boosterism, with an attempt to portray a glossy and clean-cut image of London, as if all it could possibly aspire to was to be looked at in the same way as one might view the Central Business District of Chicago. Yet this is also a vision that to most inhabitants of London seems grossly at odds with anything that they experience day by day in a cityscape of delayed Tube trains, dog shit on the pavements, pushy squeegee merchants and casual crime.

So we can also find, at the opposite end, the continuation of a tradition of humdrum and gritty architecture of mess, overlap and seeming chaos. As opposed to the architecture of skin, this is the architecture of weight – very often of solid, literal weight – sure of its own authenticity, and pointedly refusing to offer any easy answers or visual solace to those who crave quick-fix economic solutions. It is the ethos of the social housing estates, as well as a host of consciously grungy and roughly finished architectural interventions, and an intellectual fascination with the banal and the everyday. In this regard, we can look back to seminal examples such as Alexandra Road Estate, completed by the London Borough of Camden in the late 1970s, and representing the pinnacle of those moderately high, stepped linear ziggurats that were so admired at the time. Whenever socially inclined architects from Italy or wherever have since come over to London, many have made a beeline to meet Neave Brown, the designer of Alexandra Road, and he has dutifully continued to show the connoisseurs of hard-core housing architecture around his masterwork. Rather than conforming to the accepted existing street arrangements, with its crisp divisions between road, pavement and building frontage, the architects who designed the urban megastructures of the 1970s preferred to create their own hill-like landscapes, as if they had been asked to reinvent the very terrain of the city in order to assert the architecture of weight. On to these concrete hillsides could then be distributed the particular activities required for the project, which in most cases meant housing, but which also might take in other collectivized visions of social improvement, such as museums or theatres or libraries. Thus, from the world of entertainment, another touchstone for London was the hewn landscape of the National Theatre as part of the South Bank complex, which although in spirit and conception a project of the 1960s did not open its three auditoria to the public until 1976–7. This was the same time that, elsewhere in the city, the Sex Pistols and The Clash were playing their first gigs and putting out their first singles. Denys Lasdun's design for the National Theatre, for all of its aspirations to 'high culture', was in architectural terms another carefully designed exercise in the sombre and muted manipulation of concrete. It even sought to reinforce the allusion to a series of sedimentary rock layers by patterning its concrete surfaces with bark-like timber effects, suggesting an atavistic and weighty civilization that was in irreversible decline and sinking imperceptibly into the mud. Even more worthy and historically dated by the time of its completion was the new British Library at St Pancras, finally opened in the mid-1990s, yet another of the multi-layered megastructures of London culture, disguised by a brick mask, as well as a terrifying warning of what too much time can do to architects' imaginations.

Instead, it has been the smaller and more reticent examples of the architecture of ordinariness and grit that have tended to garner the greatest plaudits in this approach, whether it is the muted simplicity of the Lisson Gallery (1990) or, more recently, the Thames Barrier Park by Patel Taylor Architects in Silvertown in the eastern Docklands

(1995–2000), the only public park to be built in the city for decades, or the Clissold Leisure Centre in Stoke Newington by Hodder Associates (1996–2001). It can be found in the low-cost feel of the Peabody Trust Housing in Murray Grove (1998–2000), made out of bog-standard prefabricated steel units piled on top of each other, but glazed and tiled beautifully, or in the sublime, no-nonsense scale of the 'super-shed' designed by Wilkinson Eyre for Stratford Station, way out in the eastern margins (1997). London is becoming a city of restaurants, and here the joy of the quotidian can be seen in the numerous restaurants that have been built into converted abattoirs, garages, pumping stations and such like. At the closer level of the individual domestic realm, there is an innocent pleasure in the reuse of ordinary pavement lights in the highly compressed flats of Doris's Place by Peter Barber Architects (2001), located in Shepherdess Walk in Hackney. Barber is now designing an innovative housing estate in Bow that seeks to reassert the idea of the street as the only authentic and viable place for children to play in and for people to talk in. The street, a collectivized spatial format that was devised millennia ago as the primary organization pattern for the very first cities, is once again seen as the bearer of progress.

And when the tendency is amplified and taken to its logical extreme, the recent Straw Bale and Quilted House by Wigglesworth and Till (1999–2001) acts as an even more polemical piece of architecture by those who want to express the essentially ad hoc, messy and contingent reality that one finds daily on the streets of London. With their sandbag or straw-filled walls and their soft quilted façades facing on to a prosaic Islington street and an adjacent railway cutting, Wigglesworth and Till are seeking an architecture that openly welcomes age, decay and dissolution. It is a statement against the exquisite or the exotic, and a belief in the values of *The Everyday and Architecture*, itself the title of a volume of a journal that Wigglesworth and Till put together in the mid-1990s and which harked back to the earlier French theorists of quotidian life, such as Henri Lefebvre and Michel de Certeau.[5] Similar ideas have also played host to what has become by now a generation of dark and dirty student design projects for various sites in London, as created in the capital's schools of architecture. This pattern probably started with the NATO group at the Architectural Association back in the early 1980s, which led in turn to Nigel Coates's eroticized vision of *Ecstacity*, the nearest parallel in the architectural world to the sexually heightened, emotionally distanced city of cruising and scoring that was captured so memorably in the songs of the Pet Shop Boys.[6]

It is easy to see where the current crop of anti-heroic architects draw inspiration for their mind set. In a tradition that harks back to William Hogarth or Charles Dickens, the dominant strain of cultural analysts of London have preferred the gloomy and weighty and sardonic to the bright and light and shiny, the incomplete and unsatisfactory to the smooth and finished, the gritty and the multicultural to the happy and homogenous. In recent years, we have watched the *longeurs* of Patrick Keiller's film, *London*, a razor-sharp view of the city's urban condition in the early 1990s that hit a chord with so many of the city's inhabitants in terms of how they felt about their surroundings.[7] In Keiller's vision, the fictional protagonists set off in hopeful search for traces of their poetic heroes, but instead stumble upon a series of unsettling events, including lines of police preparing to confront a demonstration against the social fall-out of Thatcherism. It is a kind of worldview echoed by writers such as Iain Sinclair and Patrick Wright, who prefer to look at the arteries of communication that also happen to leave swathes of redundant and despoiled land in their wake, whether it is the River Thames, the Lea Valley or the M25 Orbital motorway. Just as the prints of Gustave Doré (1832–83), or the descriptions given by Dickens in *Dombey and Son* (1848), once recorded the decimation of Victorian London by the railways, here again we find an analysis that regards the architecture and engineering produced by a desire to control circulation as the unspoken danger to the cultural fabric. We are told, for instance, that the Thames Barrier flood defence has sanitized and gentrified the whole swathe of the River Thames that lies upriver, leaving only the mouth of the Thames Estuary as still true to the wild and anarchic undercurrent that has long epitomized London. In another vein, there is the photographic artist Richard Wentworth and his collections of determinedly mundane photographs of cracked pavements and grubby shopfronts along the Caledonian Road in north London, a street that would seem to want to defy glamourization above all others.[8] From a psychoanalytical standpoint, Adrian Rifkin goes so far as to suggest that it has always been this positive refusal of London to conform to an image of benign plenitude – combined with its belligerent refusal ever to reveal itself as a stable or recognizable whole – that are the factors that continue to sustain it over its history.[9]

At root, it is these two rival visions of what London ought to become – one the result of boosterist economic projection, the other an attempt to reflect the gritty realities of everyday life – that have underlain architectural debate over the last few decades. It was never really about any of those tedious style wars of the 1980s and early 1990s. After all, who really gave a stuff about the arguments of modernism versus postmodernism, high-tech versus classicism, conservation versus redevelopment. They were only the fripperies. It was the impetus behind the desire of London to change that was up for grabs; or, to put it another way, how could re-growth be combined, or at least intercut, with the seemingly necessary and continuing image of social and spatial fragmentation? For this reason, the most telling filmic portrait of London's architectural development in the last few decades remains John Mackenzie's *The Long Good Friday* (1979). Here a London underworld gang rooted in violence and corruption attempts to grab a part of the influx of American capital that was beginning at the turn of the 1980s to pour into the unregulated redevelopment of the huge empty tracts of Docklands, in the wake of Thatcherite free-market policy. This film could have been made only in the poisonous and transitional atmosphere that existed in London at the time, with Britain apparently being forced to choose between a future with Europe or with the USA, between a yearning for tradition and heartless progress. Bob Hoskins, who played the role of Harold Shand, the London crime godfather, has since noted:

> What was extraordinary about it at that time was that we were just on the verge of Thatcherism. It was bang up to date. It hit the nail so firmly on the head, of where the Eighties were gonna go.[10]

As the film opens, Shand is on the point of cementing a deal to unite the English and American underworld in a massive waterfront development. With the local politicians and police force firmly in his pocket, he wants to convince the 'investors' from New Jersey that the scheme will be a cash-cow. But at the moment of apparent triumph, his sordid world falls apart as a result of development greed. It is the recurring theme of the film that the old is being dispassionately sold off to cater for the new and the globalized, simply for the sake of profit and affluence. And it proves to be the most negative and mundane consequence of the same globalization process, the surfacing of retaliatory violence from subjugated peoples within the fragmenting British Empire – in this instance, Shand's gang is brought down by the IRA – that threatens to destroy the emerging order. With the subsequent and very real IRA bombings of the City of London, and the counter-measures of the 'ring-of-steel' and the virtual imposition of military controls within the financial quarter, we came to see this battle being fought out on the actual streets of the capital in the early 1990s. The means to deter further Republican violence was to throw up a barricade ring around the City of London, introduce police controls at a reduced number of entry points to restrict traffic and to stop and search large vehicles, and put in place a permanent CCTV surveillance network through the area.[11] The IRA responded by bombing Canary Wharf on the Isle of Dogs instead, leading to the introduction of increased security there. Irrespective of the actual location of redevelopment, what *The Long Good Friday* attacks is the emergence of a ruthless mercantile class that aims at building itself the ultimate glamorous lifestyle, but, this being London, it is really the seediness that seeps through in the film. The search for profit invites only destruction, setting off a further round of growth and decay, like two ferrets fighting endlessly in a bag. Real life seems to enjoy nothing better than imitating art, and so today we have the most distinctive recent addition to the skyline of the City of London, the Swiss-Re tower by Foster & Partners (1997–2004) – already nicknamed the 'gherkin' due to its pointed silhouette. It is being completed on the site of the former Baltic Exchange, which was blown up by a massive IRA van-bomb in April 1992 that killed three people.

The principal struggle for the most imaginative architects in London since the early 1990s has been to find a way to mediate between the two extremes of the smooth skin and the striated lump, between the aesthetics of super-lightness and super-heaviness. The best projects have striven to collage the two contrasting approaches, by playing on the values of the old and contingent and gritty, while still imparting a sense of dreamy gloss to what is otherwise in the main a dull and unchanging urban continuum. Possibly the first sustained impetus came in the form of the importation of loft-living from New York City in the early 1990s by the Manhattan Loft Company and its many emulators. But more recently it has tended to be in arts buildings that the true marriage of grime and glitter has prospered best. Peckham Library by Alsop Architects (1998–2000) was made ubiquitous on the television news because of replays of CCTV footage of the last movements of a murdered schoolboy, Damilola Taylor, and it remains that practice's best work, largely because of its ambitious struggle with a tight budget and a studiously un-heroic task of placing a local library in an area of intense social deprivation. In an attempt at grand civic gesture on the cheap, the building flashes electric blue by night and is raised up on raking stilts to create a covered public arcade for passers-by to walk through. The cladding materials are suitably tough and slick, and yet it is in the ingenious interior arrangements, and particular in the bustle of the interior pods located on the upper level, packed with jostling children by day and covered with timber fish-scales, that provide the building's defining image.

Yet in the style-meets-grunge stakes, leading the pack in London architecture at the moment is the Swiss practice of Herzog de Meuron, first through their much-hyped conversion of the derelict Bankside Power Station into the Tate Modern (1994–2000), and most recently in the Laban Dance Centre (1997–2002). The latter is an iridescent, high-concept jewel that has been built for an experimental dance academy on a decidedly unglamorous industrial estate in Deptford in south-east London. Here an exquisite architectural skin is meshed into a prosaic workaday plan that is livened only by some gentle curved walls and a series of circulation ramps that are wrapped around a central 'egg-in-a-box' auditorium. The design manner seems to be borrowed from Rem Koolhaas, the contemporary Dutch guru whose fascination is with fusing avant-garde sensibility with engineering. Into this knowing mix, the Laban Centre also introduces a direct sense of worthiness. It has the first 'brown' roof ever built in London, finished off with a topping of crushed concrete drawn from the demolished buildings on the site, and acting as a vast elevated breeding reserve for black redstarts, which for some reason need our help. The Laban Centre is also a project that received partial funding from the state's National Lottery good-causes pot, and thus is expected to bring a sense of gloss that can be seen as helping to regenerate a run-down area. The external façade consists of high-performance polycarbonate sheets from Germany, which dazzle green, blue, red or yellow depending on how the daylight strikes the building, like the effect on a dragonfly's wings. Set irregularly among them are flat, clean window panes that reflect the sky with the surreal image of a Magritte painting. The Laban Centre manages both to respond unflinchingly to the surrounding urban grime, as well as placing a dreamy and milky veil over the exquisite and ephemeral movements that are happening constantly within the dance studios. The artist Michel Craig-Martin was brought in to develop in the interior a striking palette of vibrant greens and pinks and yellows, which add a microscopic layer of sumptuousness for relatively little expense; elsewhere in the building, the walls and surfaces are left as rough-finished concrete or similarly blunt materials.

In projects such as the Laban Centre, we can uncover the dialectic of the smooth and the grungy in built form at its most highly developed level. It has become the motif for all aspects of the design. And there have been numerous wider cultural consequences of the efforts of architects and others to assimilate the rougher side of the urban fabric in London. Two extreme examples from either end of our time-span can be used to point to an intervening change in cultural attitudes. First came the album and singles covers of The Clash, the self-proclaimed radical heroes of early Punk, back in the late 1970s, which gloried in the grime of graffiti, driving on motorway flyovers, dangerous housing estates and imminent riots. Posing against squalid urban backdrops for photographs, in *London's Burning* the band sang deliriously of driving fast at high level across town:

> I'm up and down the Westway, in an' out the lights
> What a great traffic system – it's so bright
> I can't think of a better way to spend the night
> Than speeding around underneath the yellow lights.[12]

Recently, with the publication of *Jamie's Kitchen*, featuring the annoying yet hugely successful celebrity chef Jamie Oliver, the tale has turned full circle.[13] He too is again pictured against what seems to be every tagged and crumbling or rusting wall in London, but this time it is done in glorious and soft-focus Technicolor. Any visiting alien who happened to pick up this book would get the impression that London is in a worse state of physical decay than Havana. But it is of course intended only as a deliberate and highly marketable fusion between the grim and the fashionable; it is the social and economic forces of areas like Hoxton made explicit in print. What once might have been taken as signs of social decline are now fine for fashion statements. Elsewhere in the city, overlooking the Westway, the Trellick Tower by Erno Goldfinger has mutated from sink estate to desirable domestic icon. It is little surprise that a recent unscreened film by Patrick Keiller about the condition of British housing came to be titled *The Dilapidated Dwelling*, for despite the profusion of lofts and the endless glamorous retrofits of Victorian terraced houses, this is the self-image that the inhabitants of London are most at home with. In what might be interpreted as a desire to assert a reciprocal relationship with the climate, and despite the new influxes of wealth, London at the start of the twenty-first century remains defiantly a city of leaking roofs, cold window panes and gently crumbling bricks. Teams of not-very-good builders set up scaffolding as part of an endless game of micro-surgery that keeps the capital's houses and flats alive, for a short while at least, and reminiscent of those circus performers whose act was to keep dozens of plates spinning or else they fell. If we were honest, would we really want it any other way?

It is, however, equally true that the Jamie Oliver image of *rapprochement* with grunge is just as much of a misrepresentation as the super-slick erasure of tat that has been essayed in Canary Wharf or elsewhere. London, possibly now the premier centre of international finance and certainly one of the wealthiest and most expensive cities on the planet, is going through a process of seemingly unstoppable gentrification and displacement, threatening our notions of social cohesion as it sweeps back and forwards across the inner city and suburbs.[14] It is perhaps the collective guilt about this social upheaval – a kind of Haussmannization by cash – that is fuelling a renewed cultural taste for what Tom Wolfe long ago termed 'boho chic',[15] referring to an affectation towards poverty that serves to conceal real wealth. Now with the advent on the Sony PlayStation 2 of *The Getaway* (Team Soho; London, 2002), this being the first instance of a computer game that fully exploits a highly believable 'real-time' environment of central London, a kind of virtual apotheosis has been achieved. Players of all ages can drive around their city recklessly in the guise of a criminal, causing death and mayhem without fear of punishment. They even get a chance to get out of their car and go into the glitziest of West End restaurants, and shoot the place up.

METEOMEDIA; OR, WHY LONDON'S WEATHER IS IN THE MIDDLE OF EVERYTHING

Tom McCarthy

I LIVE IN a twelfth-floor central London flat. The flat has long, tall windows facing west and north. Talking to people on the phone, I stare across the city and the sky. The vista usually provides a backdrop to the conversation. Often, though, it's the conversation's subject: I tell friends what weather they will have in 20 minutes, warning those in Hackney that long, vertical walls of rain are gliding towards them over Islington and Dalston, or assuring those caught in a West End shower that the broad shafts of sunlight I can see sweeping northwards from Big Ben will hit them soon. During public events – Jubilee fly-pasts, test matches, May Day demonstrations – the television becomes a shared chart or crib sheet: I can reference the blimp or helicopter that I know is on my interlocutor's screen as well as mine and tell him or her that 200 feet to its east the cloud that is worrying the umpire's light meter gives over to blue skies in St John's Wood, or that the rioters and police we're watching battling it out in Oxford Street will shortly be united by a drenching.

Weather and communication: that is the two-fold promise that modern London's airspace makes. Aerials and phone masts pick up, decode, encode and transmit again through clouds that swallow and regurgitate them or slide by above them, scanning roofs and streets like bar codes. When viewed from high up, London invites commentary, interpretation and prognosis – more so than other cities due to its ever-changing climate. Weather and communication, weather and telecommunication: the tallest (and hence most weather-enveloped) building visible from my flat is the British Telecom Tower. Although built a decade and a half before 1979 (and named the Post Office Tower), the building owes its present name and status to that year's election and its aftermath. In 1981 Margaret Thatcher's Government separated BT from the Post Office; in 1984 they floated BT as a plc, selling 50.2 per cent of its shares to the public. Throughout the 1980s, though, and to the present day, the tower has remained closed to the same public who own it. Technically, it is what is known as a Pulse Code Modulation (PCM) Switching Centre – one of the world's very first. Staring at it day in and day out, month after month as it lights up, looms out of fog, bounces sunlight, dodges lightning and gets drubbed by hail, I like to fantasize that in its upper floors sit gods, or at least priests, who modulate all of the city's sky flows, who set its pulse-rate, write its code and flip its switches. When London is studied centuries from now by alien Terrologists, this building and not St Paul's will be identified as its religious heart, its spire.

Weather, communication, code, interpretation, influence: these things have always gone together. For both Seneca and Aristotle, the airy region was one of conveyance, of transferral and translation, in which 'meteors' or atmospheric phenomena (*meteor* means 'elevated', 'lofty' or 'sublime') were produced by the influence of the celestial sphere on the sublunary one. For Virgil, too, weather told a coded tale of influence, of cause and effect, and hence was decryptable: his *Georgics* describes a world of signs in which the movement of ants, swallows, frogs and ravens can be read and interpreted, as can the appearance of the clouds, sun and moon. Seventeenth-century English Puritans treated the sky as a switchboard connecting them to God, divining portents in its storms and light shows. The anonymous author of *A Strange Wonder; or, The Cities Amazement* of 1641 (subtitled *News from Heaven*) describes exceptional meteorological events as God's 'signes and Tokens', 'prodigious ensignes', 'ominous harbingers', 'Cyphers', 'notable Messengers'. Londoners were so addicted to such Cyphers that, according to Daniel Defoe, in *Journal of the Plague Year* of 1721, during plague years they scoured the clouds constantly for 'shapes and figures, representations and appearances'. It is standard to think of the atmosphere as a medium, a 'pervading or enveloping substance' (indeed, the terms 'air', 'ether' and 'environment' all appear in the *Oxford English Dictionary* definition of the word *medium*), but we should go further. Weather is, and always has been, more than just a medium: it is also *media*.

Shakespeare understood this. In *The Tempest*, his great play about the weather, Caliban tells Trinculo and Stephano that the island's atmosphere is 'full of noises, sounds and sweet airs', the humming of 'a thousand twanging instruments' and 'voices'. He could be describing radio. Caliban is not so much consuming and decoding these transmissions as feeling them billow around him, finding form and losing it again, like clouds. The weather is a teaser. 'Weather writes, erases and rewrites itself upon the sky with the endless fluidity of language; and it is with language that we have sought throughout history to apprehend it', writes Richard Hamblyn in *The Invention of Clouds* (2001). Easier said than done, though. Aristotle knew that *epagoge*, or linguistic reasoning, would never yield meteorological certainty; the best it offers us is speculation. Vladimir Jankovic, author of *Reading the Skies: A Cultural History of the English Weather, 1650–1820* (2000), points out that since *meteoros*, 'rising', can refer to rising wind within the stomach, *meteoro-logeo* means not only 'talk of high things' but also 'windy speech', 'high talk', 'empty musings'. Shakespeare understood this too, as testified by Hamlet's ability to make the verbose Polonius see in the same cloud a whale, a weasel and a camel. Hamlet's deliberate mobilization of language's powers of indeterminacy is linked to weather throughout: 'when the wind is southerly I know a hawk from a handsaw', he claims – an utterance that Claudius's spies and twenty-first century critics alike will busy themselves trying, and failing, to decipher.

When language grapples with the weather there is slippage and there is displacement. Samuel Johnson's quip that 'when two Englishmen meet, their first talk is of the weather' is an easy one to make; Gwendolen's intuition (in Oscar Wilde's play *The Importance of Being Earnest* of 1895) that 'whenever people talk about the weather, I always feel quite certain that they mean something else' is much more astute. For centuries manuals and charts have tried to map meteorological phenomena on to social ones, from *The English Chapmans and Travellers Almanack for the Year of Christ 1697* (which aligns the ten-week frost with the Gunpowder Plot, the time when 'the whole heaven seemed to burn with fire' with the invention of the art of printing) to Election Weather Tables compiled by today's Met Office (Labour only wins in fair weather, apparently; that fateful day in 1979 was foul) or the Weather-to-Stock Market Correspondence Graphs studied by the more esoteric among our economists. The weather unfolds endlessly across non-meteorological discourses, across Other Stuff. It is an index both of truth and of all that is random, meaningless. Like all media, it bears a plethora of messages – perhaps even *the* message – while simultaneously supplying no more than conversational neutral, white noise.

Lying almost exactly on the line that runs between my windows and the British Telecom Tower is the London Weather Centre. It has been there, on Clerkenwell Road, since 1992. In 1996, one year before the weather change that would reverse/consolidate (delete as you deem appropriate) the political winds blowing since 1979, its parent institution, the Met Office, went down the same road as BT had twelve years previously and became a trading fund. A digital and free-market analogue to the Mount Pleasant postal depot round the corner, the London Weather Centre acts as a big sorting office, receiving, separating, ordering and redirecting meteorological information that has come in from all around the country and the world, tailoring it to suit various clients' needs. So football stadia in Sunderland and Portsmouth, aerodromes in Glasgow, electricity and gas stations in Anglesey and Norfolk all receive prognostic bulletins from the London Weather Centre – even if the source data behind those bulletins was gathered not two miles from the stadium, aerodrome or station. It is only official weather data if it has passed through London.

This pattern stretches back 400 years. With the explosion in the seventeenth century of a new, popular, cheap-to-produce media form, the pamphlet, people started sending in to London endless weather reports. They had great titles: *A Report from Abbingdon towne in Berkshire, being a relation of what harme Thunder and Lightning did on Thursday last upon the body of Humphrey Richardson, a rich miserable farmer: With Exhortation for England to repent*; or *A Full and True Relation of the Strange and Wonderful Apparitions which were Seen in the Clouds upon Tuesday Evening at Seven of the Clock*. Why did their authors send them here? Because they craved inclusion in the next issue of *Philosophical Transactions*, the journal of the London-based Royal Society. Being reprinted there made the texts 'official' and 'legitimate', conferring what Jankovic calls 'visibility within the national republic of letters'.

Initially, these reports were event-based, for the good reason that weather was conceived not as a system but rather as a set of discrete occurrences. By the mid-seventeenth century word had reached London of the Italian stage designer Giacomo Torelli's magnificent, multi-canopied cloud-sets, in which rolls of painted cumulus were lowered and raised by ropes and pulleys: the real weather, too, was thought of in spectacular, theatrical terms. Edward Ward describes in *British Wonders* (1717) the 'scene' in which 'strange coruscations in the skies' appeared 'whilst crowds and mortals stood below beholding the tremendous show'. When the Thames froze, the weather show was augmented by human spectacles: archery contests, skating, games of football, acrobatics. In the late eighteenth century, when hygrometry, barometry and electrochemical research took over, lecturers would show off their gizmos to audiences who cheered in admiration as these new Torellis reproduced clouds, lightning and tides inside glass boxes. By the nineteenth century, *Philosophical Transactions* carried titles such as 'On the Late Extraordinary Depression of the Barometer', and provincial correspondents gave over to London-based professionals, who processed readings telegraphed to them by armies of data gatherers.

A more fundamental shift than that from the anecdotal to the scientific, though, was the shift from an event-logic to an event-*space* one in the thinking of weather. This, too, occurred in London – and it happened as a media event, when London's *Daily News* adopted the meteorological approach pioneered by Heinrich Wilhelm Brandes, the first person to suspect that weather might be a spatial issue. In 1816 Brandes had translated weather data for each day of 1783 into graphic symbols on map bases, then laid them out in series, and discovered that low pressure over Switzerland, a south-easterly storm in Italy and north-westerly winds in France were all connected, part of one and the same system. On 31 August 1846 the *Daily News* established Brandesian logic firmly in the public consciousness when it published the world's first weather map. Nothing would be the same again: local weather readings became parts of a jigsaw that depicted globally evolving systems. As Jankovic writes: 'the meaning of locality changed from its status as an exclusive end of investigation to a specimen in a larger entity, a point on a grid'.

The rest is history: we are all Brandesians now. Now rings of satellites from five networked programmes – GOES-E and GOES-W (both American), EUMETSAT (European), INSAT (Indian) and GMS (Japanese) – constantly map the entire planet's climate, sensing Earth's atmosphere and surface at infrared wavelengths, measuring its radiance with broad, spectral-channelled radiometers and high resolution spectrometers and interferometers, inferring its parameters of temperature and water vapour. Data assimilation software generates computer models of cloud and water movement that have names such as FOAM (Forecast Ocean Assimilation Model). This all takes place at the Met Office's HQ in Bracknell, one of only two forecasting centres in the world (the other is in Washington). There, a Cray T3E MPP (Massively Parallel Processor) computer subdivides the modelled area into a number of rectangular sub-domains, each of which has a 'halo' of data around its perimeter, an MPI (Message Passing Interface) enabling it to communicate with each other sub-domain of the UM (Unified Model). Bracknell then relays its information to London, to Clerkenwell Road.

I've visited the London Weather Centre. It's beautiful. Alex Hill, the Centre's chief, spent two hours immersing me in waves of data billowing from screen to networked screen: the meso-charts that generate the dramas of connectedness we see on TV forecasts every day; the tephigrams that chart atmospheric temperature and humidity vertically; the SFLOCS – images that sense and plot every single lightning bolt's electric impulse. I can't remember what SFLOCS stands for and I don't care: it's another figure in a poetry of acronyms, a vague, ambiguous and seductive series of transmissions flowing from a neo-Rilkean realm of haloed techno-angels down to us. *Data est*: it is given. Data is what centres us inside the universe, its gift.

Hill took me to the London Weather Centre's roof. He took me there to show me the Stevenson Screen, rain gauge and Campbell-Stokes sunshine recorder (a crystal ball with a metal ellipse around it) – but most of all he took me there to see the view. I've never had such a strong sense of being in the middle of everything. You could see St Paul's, the London Eye, the Telecom Tower, King's Cross, my flat. You could see Hampstead Heath. You could see all the way to the Crystal Palace and the Alexandra Palace pylons, London's city gates. Contemporary London does have gates: the edges of its broadcast zones and weather zones. Just as London has its own television and radio, it has its own weather. Snow on the roof of a car driving through town on a cold-but-not-arctic winter's day designates a hick, or at least one of those semi-hicks, 0208-ers. The city's buildings generate their own heat and redirect the wind, creating gale-filled corridors and doldrums within metres of one another. Peter Ackroyd describes how London's smog was so bad in the 1950s that theatre audiences were unable to see the actors. It's Torelli all over again – but this time with the city playing the role of the creative genius. London can make rain fall upwards. It pulls off remarkable, stupendous atmospheric tricks thanks to its energy, its density, its lovely, lovely pollution. On some evenings I'll phone or be phoned by one of two or three friends who also live high up, my fellow meta-metropolitans, and we'll watch cloud strips and vapour trails alike light up and glow, hit from below by a sun drowning in haze behind the Telecom Tower. The colours are unnatural – blood-orange, purple, RGB (RedGreenBlue) – and constantly changing, often making us quite literally shout out in amazement, sometimes even moving us to tears.

The dramatic atmosphere, or atmospheric drama, of contemporary London is like that of Troy: it is the drama of a city under siege. London has always thought of itself as besieged – by the Black Death, by the Dutch fleet, by foreign speculators. And these phantoms have always ridden with the weather. Winds carried plague-spoors and bore Dutch ships towards us ('Catholic Winds', as they were known). The great stock-market crash of 1987, in which BT's shares crashed to earth alongside the free-market promises of 1979, coincided (as those esoteric graph-compiling economists will point out) with a hurricane. This was exceptional, though: London's weather, generally, is what climate statisticians call 'median': middling, not extreme. The city does not get tornadoes or typhoons.

London does, however, face one major meteorological threat: flood. Strong tides racing up the Thames have caused disastrous inundation several times, even sweeping London Bridge away in 1090. These floods continued well into the twentieth century, but were put on hold with the completion, in 1984, of the Thames Barrier just below Greenwich. I grew up in Greenwich while the Barrier was being built. On our classroom walls in the late 1970s were posters showing a child's doll floating over a submerged street; from time to time slow wails would fill the air as flood sirens were tested; in the night I'd picture the doll's eyes as I drifted into sleep to the sound of pile-drivers hammering steel beams into the river-bed, a constant Morse-code pulse that spelled out 'danger'. Now, less than two decades after its completion, the Thames Barrier faces imminent obsolescence due to rising global water levels and the increasing downward tilting of south-east England. According to Alex Hill, the Hadley Centre's most extreme end prediction (modern science, like Classical poetry or Puritan theology, has its own narratives of disaster: ozone depletion, global warming, acid rain) is for Cambridge to have a beach by 2050. The night after Hill told me that, I had another vision as I fell asleep: a small Dutch boy with Johnny Rotten's face pulling his finger from a dam and smiling as he flashed his maniacal eyes, two gleaming white chrysanthemums made of ivory or marble. As Rainer Maria Rilke said, every angel is terrifying.

London is a great city and, like all great cities, it is haunted by the spectre of its ruin. An apocalyptic atmosphere broods over it, one registered in the work of the great writers who have taken London on, from Samuel Pepys to Thomas Pynchon – and nowhere more so than in T. S. Eliot's *The Waste Land*. Published in 1922, the year that the Met Office broadcast its first Radio forecast on the BBC, the poem is one long weather report: it rains in April, snows in winter, rains in summer too; the wind blows towards the Heimat; there is fog on London Bridge; the Thames flows out past Greenwich (where the sirens go 'Weialala leia'); there's a drought, but black clouds are massing over

Himavant; the thunder speaks; *Datta*. In *The Waste Land*, all cities become London; London becomes all cities, cracking and bursting in the violet air as their towers tumble to the ground. The poem's privileged tense is the gerundive, the ongoing present: breeding, mixing, stirring, covering. This is a feature common to all weather reports. Listen out for it next time you hear the Shipping Forecast or watch the weather section of the news. They never use an active verb, never say 'it will rain', 'winds will blow': it is always 'becoming windier', 'clearing up', 'moving westward', 'growing brighter'. I asked Alex Hill why this was. 'Simple,' he said. 'You can only describe weather as being in transition from a point *A* to a point *B*. In transition *between* – never *at*.' In dramatic terms, it is called *in medias res*: in the middle of things.

Since 2001, as the global climate heats up in more ways than one, London, caught at the confluence of systems moving over from the United States and from the Middle East, finds itself even more *in medias res*. When storm clouds groan and rumble people scour the sky for aeroplanes flying too low. I track them from my windows, waiting for the day when one of them will hurtle like a meteor into the Telecom Tower, painting the sky a new blood-orange. If it happens it will be spectacular. Until then, we'll continue talking about the weather.

CULTURE/ SUBCULTURE

To start with punk is to begin with an ending. John Lydon's raucous, throaty, demonic cackle at the beginning of 'Anarchy in the UK' was the last great expression of the ferociously confrontational spirit of rock music as 'white riot'. It was the culmination of a process that went back at least as far as Mick Jagger's first simian pout into the TV cameras in the mid-1960s or Pete Townshend's first guitar-thrashing. It was the sound *par excellence* of a London subculture, of a culture thrusting up from under. Long before reality television made it possible in principle for everyone, this was the sound of the kids from Dartford or Charlton or Hackney howling to be noticed, insisting on what they were. It was the sound of those whom Labour as much as Tory governments had left chronically disenfranchised. Punk was violent, nasty, filthily offensive. It spawned dark, mordant geniuses like Lydon. Suddenly London was full of Mohicans snarling vengefully at the opera- and ballet-goers. Now, of course, the Home Secretary David Blunkett would want them fined for 'yobbish behaviour'. But then there were sides to take, if not in culture wars, in culture scuffles at least.

Of course, crossovers had already started. By the mid-1960s Jagger was already proclaiming that the rich girls were 'getting their kicks in Stepney, not in Knightsbridge any more'. By the late 1970s he himself was hobnobbing with the aristocracy. Punk was the last major explosion of a truly uncompromising London subculture, indomitable, irrepressible and in your face. The story since then, in all the cultural spheres, has been one of multiplication, proliferation and mixture. Culture and subcultures no longer eyeball each other across a no man's land. They blend or reverse into each other, copy, parody and steal from each other. At the same time, as with designer drugs, the smorgasbord spreads ever more temptingly, widely and variously before the user. What do you want to enjoy right now, the pre-Impressionist exhibition at the Wallace Collection, lesbian cabaret in the upstairs room of an Islington pub, a recherché nineteenth-century French version of *Hamlet* at the Royal Opera House, *A Comedy of Errors* done into Bronx-speak, Mis-teeq, Heather Small or (a quaint bit of retro) Shed Seven at the Monarch in Chalk Farm? Get out your diary, pick-'n'-mix. Think of what has happened to London's universities between Punk and Blair. The old federal University of London has now become a ghostly remnant. Its member institutions are briskly thriving, but more and more on their own. The old distinction between the University and the polytechnics is long gone, to be replaced by what – in theory at least – is an expanding range of choices between increasingly specialized institutions. Other, sometimes more dubious 'universities' are springing up. Can you tell the real ones from the fakes? Is that even an appropriate question? Can we know any longer exactly what it means to spot a fraud? In Blair's *soi-disant* egalitarian Britain, culture is properly democratic. The cultural elites are learning their place, which is no grander than anyone else's. London in 2003 is a city hugely saturated in tastes (or, the current word, cultural 'opinions') and profoundly chary of judgments. After all, who wants to be called 'judgemental?' Thus the very concept of a hierarchy implicit in the 'sub' of subculture is under threat. Or is it? There remain countless Londoners who are neither seen nor heard, who have no cultural presence or representation, who have never *got as far* as culture or subculture. Beneath all the cultures and subcultures, there is still, as ever, anonymous London too.

ALTERING IMAGES

Andrew Gibson

THE PERIOD THAT runs from Punk to Blair has seen boom-time for – not to say the fetishization of – the London writer. In the 1990s Iain Sinclair remarked that contemporary *littérateurs* divided London up between them like feral beasts – Carter in the south, Ballard in the western suburbs, Moorcock in west central, Ackroyd in Clerkenwell, himself in Hackney and the east (to which can be added, most recently, Smith in north-west London). If such figures had become fiercely territorial, however, that was an index of just how significant representing a sector of the metropolis had become. London writers were staking claims. No one was going to be able to claim to encompass London itself, as Charles Dickens seemed to have done. In any case, the older Dickens's claim to encompass London seems much less assured than that of the younger Dickens: compare *Our Mutual Friend* with *Martin Chuzzlewit*. Nonetheless, the representation of London seriously mattered. Who wrote about London, how and why, and about what part of London, had become a crucial issue, perhaps as never before. Take for example the Ackroyd–Sinclair face-off – and it is a face-off, however courteous and even appreciative they sometimes seem to be about one another. Their territories overlap, most obviously in the case of Hawksmoor – or Blake. (Peter Ackroyd may hope to be the contemporary representative of London's greatest radical genius, but it is Sinclair who really pitches for authentic connection with the visionary London tradition. Compare the timid piety of the staid 'William Blake' exhibition at Tate Britain in 2000, to which Ackroyd contributed, with the story of the 'wetbrain' in Sinclair's *Downriver*.) Yet however often similar in focus, the two novelists write very differently. Ackroyd may reject the label 'postmodernist', but he is scarcely a 'late modernist' either, as Sinclair claims to be. They also appeal to widely differing constituencies. Ackroyd's tends to be conservative, establishment and to some extent religious. By contrast, Sinclair's tends to be radical or marginal or at least convinced of its own marginality, although it is also becoming increasingly trendy. If the two writers have been conducting a turf war, it is because they recognize that they are playing for a particular set of stakes, and those stakes are high.

For both Ackroyd and Sinclair are bidding to be memorialists of a London that, in many respects, seems to be on the wane, a London that is vanishing. In this respect, what is remarkable about so much contemporary London literature is how quickly it can look like an exercise in archaeology. It may be partly for this reason that Angela Carter's London novel *Wise Children* (1991) is so consciously an exercise in fantasy or 'magic realism'. Carter knows that, like the white Brixton in which the novel is set, the world of the kind of theatres and music-halls that capture her imagination is definitively on the other side of a historical divide and only to be glimpsed in a distorting mirror. Similarly, the power of Michael Moorcock's scrupulous effort, in *Mother London* (1988), to preserve a sense of London as a traumatized, post-Blitz city on into 1980s culture and beyond now seems directly proportional to its futility. If historians and geographers of London are currently not only unusually thick on the ground but unusually busy and unusually conspicuous, it is surely for the same reason. London is at a historical watershed. The mythologies of what English culture has taken to be 'the capital' are being transformed and in many instances disintegrating. We are obsessed with stories about 'historic London' because the London about which the stories are composed is a London that is rapidly being superseded.

There is no simple or unambiguous way of describing or accounting for the shifts in question. But one obviously significant date is 1979, the year that marked the beginning of the 'Thatcherization' of London. This may be a significant date, but it is also partly an arbitrary one, in that it suggests a single major cause of changes that were already partly taking place. The process of memorialization started well before 1979, not least in the work of Ackroyd and Sinclair themselves, though it was arguably only in the 1980s that either writer became fully conscious of the meaning of what he was doing. Yet, in one way or another, Thatcher's rise to power and the increasing dominance of Thatcherite economics in London seemed to reflect transformations even when they did not directly bring them about. It is a precise awareness of this that powers Sinclair's savage attack on Thatcherism in *Downriver* (1991), that great novel of 1980s London that spans the decade as no other. (Sinclair was well aware of the point: the text closes with the words 'November 1989, London'.) When, in 1994, in *London: A Social History*, Roy Porter anathematized Thatcherite policies (and Thatcherite indifference) for the devastation that they had wrought on London, he also separated the last two decades of the twentieth century off as a quite distinctive phase in the capital's development.

This phase has a number of different features. First, since the 1970s, in a reversal of the vector common to most if not all capital cities and apparently the product of prevailing winds, the city's centre of gravity has been moving steadily eastwards. Wealth and power have been accumulating along a stretch of London that runs from the City to Silvertown. (This is surely directly related to the widespread conviction that there is currently a haemorrhage of power at Westminster: in this respect, at least, Blair's genuflections are eastward-directed.) Initially, the shift was halting. To walk through Canary Wharf in the early 1990s was to encounter a postmodern ghost town, a stately, busted, futuristic cityscape done in de Chirico style, with eerily empty, echoing streets and occasional solitary figures standing idly at street corners. In Patrick Keiller's film *London* (1994), Robinson suggested that he adopt Canary Wharf and dedicate it as a monument to the French nineteenth-century poet Arthur Rimbaud, which would at least have made it a little more useful than it seemed to be at the time. In a curious historical irony, the past that Canary Wharf had never had seemed already to have died. Now, however, like the miles of condominia that line the banks of the Thames downriver from St Katharine's Dock, the towers upon towers of the Isle of Dogs are confident and eloquent. Canary Wharf believes that it is here to stay. Not only that: as its own publication (*The Wharf*) bears witness, it is starting to feel that it is definitively part of the show, even more central to it than others may be noticing. In this respect, the historical vertigo induced by a walk through Wapping ('Was that a real or a simulation warehouse?') seems testimony to the very spirit of an emergent new London. It will certainly tell you more about present-day life along the river than *Last Orders* (1996), Graham Swift's charming but strictly mythical evocation of an old-fashioned, white, working-class community in Bermondsey.

Secondly: after 1979 London definitively ceased to be a city that had faith in any form of collective endeavour. As Keiller's film beautifully, elegiacally and melancholically testifies, this was at best a precarious and patchy faith. It is most authentically identified with the LCC, perhaps in particular with Herbert Morrison and the pre-war years. The city is still littered with the dilapidated ruins of social hope, like Arnold Circus. Keiller's film contains a brief, poignant sequence about the old Shoreditch development of 1897. Light plays amongst the trees. Children dawdle happily. The only sound is of their laughter. Keiller conjures up a brief and faded image of a paradisal garden, although he is also shrewd enough to wonder whether, by this point in historical time, he is not merely indulging one of what the film calls the various 'nostalgias of London's electronic age'. In reality, in 2003, the traces of the faith at Arnold Circus are now even fainter than Keiller's film suggests. Flats are boarded up. Estate agents' signs poke from crumbling mortar. Compare Sinclair's recent evocation, in *London Orbital*, of the ruins of hospitals and asylums scattered along the route of the M25, and what they say about the meaning of current health 'provision'. Alas, Arnold Circus seems ripe for colonization by Whitechapel's *nouveau riche* (including the artists).

Of course, in the late 1970s and early 1980s, Ken Livingstone's GLC kept the faith in vigorous pockets – Lambeth, Camden, Hackney, Brent – and by energetically pursuing specifically focused or specific interest policies: the promotion of gay, disabled and minority rights, the slashing of prices on London Transport under the 'Fares Fair' rubric. Thatcherism swiftly put an end to this 'loony leftism', and Mayor Livingstone has apparently no plans to resuscitate it. Part of the problem is no doubt that in some ways at least – bizarrely in the age of global capital – London has now suffered from more than twenty years of what, alluding to the John Major years, Keiller calls suburban national government. It has been suburban in the sense that, for more than twenty years, middle England has been doing its best to dictate its unimaginative terms to the metropolis. It remains suburban partly because, as Keiller again points out, to such a large extent the city's human resources are pumped from the suburbs in the morning, and pumped back to the suburbs at night. Do people still care for civic space? Are they even still aware that they share it, as they obviously are in Stockholm or Tokyo? Too few, it seems, or too little: Keiller's film describes a world in which the concept of the public *amenity* has definitively come under threat. On the roads, on the pavements, in the markets, shops and pubs, London knows and approves itself to be a rugged free-for-all, the very image of a neo-liberal metropolis in the twenty-first century. Whether it is a question of your health, your children's education or your seat on the bus or Tube, London tells you that the city is ruthless, cruelly unjust and unremittingly sharp-edged; that, unless you are the beneficiary of casual charity, you must scrap for what you want, that that is the very condition of metropolitan survival. It's almost tempting, after all, to assert a principle of historical continuity or, better, recurrence: contemporary London partly reverts to Defoe's or Smollett's city. The brutality of early twenty-first century London life certainly seems Smollett-like. Of course, for much if not most of its history, London has been a remarkably violent capital city, with its own specific and developed traditions of metropolitan violence. But random, indifferent, ferocious violence is currently becoming steadily more visible. Watch the rumbles come swirling out of the pubs on Friday and Saturday nights.

It may be that, as Conrad and Eliot long ago advised it to, London is finally giving up any pretensions that it once had to being a civilized city, as Paris and Rome can claim to be. (Berlin, of course, has been caught in the same dilemma as London, although for very different historical reasons.) The issue, however, has been precisely and particularly fraught over the past two decades, because the question of whether or not London is to be a European capital has become so important. This is my third point: the sense that the identity of London depends on a relationship with Europe in new, specific and different ways is crucial to what has become of the capital since the 1970s. Of course, the notion that London was somehow not a European capital like the others was always delusive and purely mythological. Recent geographers have shown just how far imperial, Victorian London was shaped, not just by the many connections with the Empire, but by rivalry with Rome, Paris and Vienna. This rivalry meant emulation, which in turn meant imitation. The more the capitals competed with each other, the more they looked like one another. Hence the appearance, for example, around 1900, of London's Parisian boulevards. Hence the Continental inspiration and European theatricality of that great national monument, the Victoria Memorial.

But the contemporary Europeanization of London is historically quite distinctive: the return to London from Paris by Eurostar, for instance, offers a specific experience of arrival, an experience quite particular to contemporary culture. On the one hand, as the train surges to the surface from the tunnel, then slows to a crawl, clatters awkwardly over uneven points and drags its way through featureless stretches of Kent and the suburbs, the traveller certainly knows that he or she is back in a dysfunctional, stubbornly small-scale England. It is easy enough to imagine that, not many miles away, people go to bed in chronic fear and loathing of the asylum seeker. On the other hand, disembarkation at the great terminal at Waterloo is an encounter with an opulent space whose openness and generosity is reflected in the cosmopolitanism of the commercial culture that surrounds it. The Eurostar terminal is quite unlike Gatwick or Heathrow, not a bland, anonymous 'international' space, but a European space in an English city. In this respect, it is the journey to London that represents England, not the English capital itself. If, between 1939 and 1945, London appeared to embody the very spirit of England, now you have to go to the Wye Valley, where white refugees from the Midlands complain about 'wogs' and 'the Common Market', or a frontier town like Rye, which seems forever draped in bunting and on permanent alert, ready to repel the invader. But the European invaders have no need of Rye: they have skipped it, got behind enemy lines and made their presence felt in the capital. Their brasseries have spread from Camden to Clapham to Notting Hill. You see their papers at the newsagents on the corner and hear their languages in the shops and bars, where they may as likely be serving as shopping or drinking. It may be they who give you directions in a part of London that they know better than you. London's Europeans are no longer just tourists. Nor are they refugees or small-time entrepreneurs, beginning in enclaves, then struggling slowly towards integration. More and more, they are just ordinary Londoners like the rest of us.

But the issue is not as simple as this suggests. It might be more accurate to say that London is now a city where England and Europe do battle with one another on specific patches of terrain. This conflict was at stake in the war for the symbolic heart of nation and Empire that took place in the struggle over the redevelopment of Bank Junction in the 1980s. Jane M. Jacobs has been very clear about the relevant collision of identities and agendas. On the one hand, the Corporation was committed to an idea of 'townscape' that stressed the importance of seeing the city (and the City) in pictorial and compositional terms. These conservative terms derived from English traditions in painting and were anti-modernist. The idea of townscape emerged in contradistinction to Continental models in planning. In the context of the 1980s, it served to express a kind of domesticated nostalgia for Empire produced in opposition to a feared and demonized Europe. This was partly because European modernist planning was identified as a 1930s phenomenon and could therefore be associated with fascism.

Thus when developer Peter Palumbo's vision finally gained Law Lord approval in the early 1990s, he chose not to continue with his first scheme, for an eighteen-storey modernist tower designed by Ludwig

Mies van der Rohe, but opted instead for No. 1 Poultry, a five-storey postmodern development that was the brainchild of James Stirling. Ironically, however, Stirling's scheme was itself thought of as suspiciously European. It was described as 'aggressive' and 'militaristic' and, most significantly, likened to 'a German defence works'. The fact that Stirling had previously been responsible for the Neue Staatsgalerie in Stuttgart was taken to be equally revealing. There was a widespread perception that Stirling had actually Germanized the heart of the City itself. This was linked to a narrative of growing German economic ascendancy over Britain. Yet it was precisely German and European among other international businesses that, at the same time, were more and more forming the foundation of the contemporary City. In fifteen years, for example, its Euro-currency market rose from US $11 billion to US $661 billion. A booming new Euro-bond market had brought European banks hurrying to the City, their ranks continuing to swell throughout the 1980s. Like others, they were not interested in questions of townscape, but in new kinds of architecture that would accommodate new conditions (like the growing importance of the new technology, which itself dictated the production of a certain kind of space). However offensive to conservatives and conservationists, No. 1 Poultry was symbolic of a process of Europeanization that the City itself was actually undergoing, and on which its more conservative forces were themselves partly dependent.

If Stirling's scheme is postmodern, then, fourthly, the term might also be used of another remarkable transformation of London that has happened since the early 1980s. At the weekend, the paths along the banks of the Thames are crammed with people. The space of the river has been opened up. Not very long ago, it was still crowded with traffic, its prospects blocked, or at least curtailed, by throngs of funnels and masts. Now it is a place of vistas. We go to the Thames to scan it, to contemplate the views. So, too, London as a whole is becoming a great repository of items on display. Since the 1990s, the city has paid an extraordinary amount of attention to its museums: the Tate Modern is flourishing, Somerset House and the Wallace Collection have been refurbished. But museums are sprucing up their image because the competition has grown so intense. For they have to do battle with the metropolis itself, which is rapidly becoming its own museum. This is nowhere more evident than in the fate of the British Museum, which in its turn has been partly 'museumized', becoming an exhibit in its own right.

The drama of exhibition and spectator is everywhere in London, from the street theatricals of Covent Garden to the ever more common limousines and customized number plates on the roads. Contemporary London seems persuaded of the truth of George Berkeley's dictum that *esse est percipi*, being is being seen. Or, to put matters differently, London life is more and more an objective demonstration of Debord's conviction that we live in 'a society of the spectacle'. Scrutiny is the condition of urban life: we are all scrutinizers, but also all under scrutiny, most notably by CCTV. The extreme version of this is Sinclair's idea of walking the city: the walker is no longer a stroller or *flâneur*, but a stalker, a man with a thesis. With Sinclair, walking the city becomes a research activity – and indeed, London is currently becoming a prolific breeding-ground for researchers into London. The observation and description of the city now form a central part of what constitutes city life. We are all potentially each other's specimens. If London space is increasingly a space of the spectacle, this may even be connected with the collapse of socially-minded London: Martin Heidegger, at least, thought that a life lived predominantly in terms of viewing and views was a life that correspondingly tended to diminish the sense of *Mitsein*, companionship, mutuality, fellow-feeling.

Fifthly and most dramatically: within the next decade or two, London will no longer be a predominantly white capital. Sinclair, Ackroyd, Ballard, Moorcock, even Keiller still imagine London as substantially a white city. Its prospects or its fate are still in the hands of those traditionally thought of as English. But, before very long, what these novelists call London will no longer be London at all. In this respect, if the London in the making has a founding text, it is not by Sinclair, still less by Dickens. It is Sam Selvon's novel about first-generation Caribbean immigrants, *The Lonely Londoners* (1979). Selvon's melancholy figures stare at the cityscape – its wintry sun, 'like a force-ripe orange', its curious, edgy, parochial, defensive inhabitants – as though London were 'some strange place on another planet'. Tolroy, an immigrant who always carries his guitar with him and plays it on the pavements and in the Tube, is a forlorn figure. As such, he is indicative both of the isolation of Selvon's characters and their regret for a life that seems to be definitively missing from the host culture. The 'lonely Londoners' are more human than those by whom they feel excluded. They tend to share a relaxed attitude to difference. They respond to 'prejudice' with patience, incomprehension, even compassion.

Yet significantly, at the same time, some of them are also quietly making their way in London, buying up property, letting out rooms, studying, struggling to gain a first foothold in the professions. Selvon is absorbed by the ways in which his characters gradually find their way around London or work out their own accommodation with London life. But as they explore and adapt – and this is a crucial part of what Selvon is saying – so too the city around them changes, almost imperceptibly at first, more decisively later, and with huge implications for a London to come. Selvon understands that immigration must transform London. This is precisely what it does in his novel, and in more than one way. On the one hand, white London culture is modified in contact with Caribbean culture. Saltfish, pepper sauce, breadfruit, ochra and dasheen start appearing in shops. Selvon even makes us wonder whether it was Caribbean immigrants rather than the white middle classes who were the first to popularize garlic in London. More predictably, immigration has consequences – carefully documented by Selvon – for sex in the city, and therefore for the future make-up of its population. On the other hand, *The Lonely Londoners* transforms London itself, providing a vision that effectively turns it inside out – 'The people who living in London', writes Selvon, 'don't really know how behind them railway station does be so desolate and discouraging' – freeing the imagination of the city from all prior solidifications. It's the vision of those for whom London has still to be a proper home, still to be *theirs*. It's a London whose characteristic feature, to use a word that appears in Selvon's first sentence, is 'unrealness'. But Selvon also anticipates London as it exists at the beginning of the twenty-first century, a London in which 'unrealness' is being superseded, where there is no possibility that the city will be 'unreal' in quite that way again.

The Lonely Londoners is about a culture that, had it but known, in Bayswater and Notting Hill, looked forward to a London of which Carnival itself is not so much an embodiment as a prophecy. London, of course, had long been a haven for refugees fleeing oppression abroad: but they were always absorbed into the dominant culture. Now the question of what constitutes 'the dominant culture' is itself being steadily transformed. London is multiracial, 'multicultural'. In so far as the concept of 'multiculturalism' has become part of New Labour mythology, it has been infected with the usual triviality: your culture can be included in the 'multicultural society' so long as it knows itself to be part of the postmodern smorgasbord and therefore subject to a law of ready exchangeability. Your culture is acceptable as part of 'multiculturalism' so long as it doesn't assume that it matters too much, so long as it doesn't take itself very seriously. (To think otherwise about your culture is to risk demonization: in mid-2003 the significant view of 'multicultural London' would come from London's Muslims.) But from another angle, before it is turned into any kind of value, the term 'multiculturalism' alludes to a new historical development. For all the fantasies of the extreme right (and some Tories), this development is irreversible. Multiculturalism is, quite simply, increasingly self-evident. Zadie Smith puts the point more vividly:

> It is only this late in the day that you can walk into a playground and find Isaac Leung by the fish pond, Danny Rahman in the football cage, Quang O'Rourke bouncing a basketball, and Irie Jones humming a tune. Children with first and last names on a direct collision course. Names that secrete within them mass exodus, cramped boats and planes, cold arrivals, medical checks.

It is multiculturalism in Smith's understanding of it, above all, that means that contemporary London can now disconnect from its former past and leave it to the care of historians and novelists. This is the case, not least, because the city is being invaded by a plethora of other histories. For immigrants drag their histories with them, says Smith, and these histories make imperious demands; they are not to be denied.

Whatever the distortions in perspective produced by the hype surrounding Smith – and it has obviously been damaging for Smith herself – *White Teeth* (2000) is a novel of the new London. It buzzes with voices, accents, idioms, languages unimaginable to Dickens or Thackeray. This, says Smith, is contemporary London, and if you cannot hear it, you do not know, or no longer know, your capital city. Her characters live at a host of different speeds, in many different complexes of times. Smith evokes contemporary London – most specifically, Willesden – as a world of intricate criss-crossings, entanglements, mixtures, networks upon networks of coincidences, myriad causes and effects. In this respect, her London is precisely opposed to a nationalist conception of the metropolis founded on a fear of infection, penetration, adulteration, miscegenation, complication, devastation. As Alsana brusquely asserts, remembering Enoch Powell, 'Rivers of blood silly-billy nonsense'. In Smith's London, O'Connell's Pool House is owned by an Iraqi family and has an Irish flag and a map of the Arab Emirates knotted together and hung from wall to wall. White Archie asserts that 'being married to a Jamaican has done wonders for my arthritis'. It is Bengal-born Samad who turns out to have 'the English goldfish-memory for history'. When Millat turns Islamic fundamentalist, he suffers unresolved agonies of conscience over his infatuation with Martin Scorsese movies ('Was it his fault if Channel 4 ran a de Niro season?'). Incongruity has the force of rule rather than exception, the unlikely becomes the norm: when the earnest schoolteacher, intent on her charges 'learning about each other through each others' culture', asks Samad's son Magid to tell them about his favourite music, he starts singing Bruce Springsteen's 'Born to Run' and Michael Jackson's 'Thriller'. Samad is destined to a similar disappointment, finally lamenting, of his two good, well-trained Muslim boys: 'You show them the road and they take the bloody path to the Inns of Court. You guide them and they run from your grasp to a Chester sports centre. You try to plan everything and nothing happens in the way you expected.'

For Smith, the significant experience of contemporary London is precisely the frustration or refutation of single-minded or monolithic plans, expectations, frames of understanding. Contemporary London encourages us to 'give up the very idea of belonging'. Yet Smith also repeatedly insists that her characters are *from* somewhere, that they have roots, that their pasts in general and their histories as Londoners in particular are extremely specific. If the old historical narratives of London are definitively at an end and now sit in the archives, awaiting the researcher, out in the city itself the surface of life can always crack to reveal the sobering power of another, different historical narrative. London life is even partly defined by the possibility of the encounter with an alien history. Thus Alsana, Cara and Neena, referring casually to 'the murder of innocents' in conversation with ex-central European ex-park-keeper Sol Josefowicz, are suddenly brought up short as it strikes them, 'the way history will, embarrassingly, without warning, like a blush', what the ex-park-keeper's historical experience might have been. The twenty-first century metropolis is characterized by its irreducible plurality of historical worlds. Alsana senses the difference between a London used to living 'on solid ground, underneath safe skies' and the vivid Bangladeshi awareness of the precariousness and contingency of life, always 'under the finger of random disaster', but which now becomes part of the city's consciousness of itself; just as well, perhaps, in a London that is starting to live, not only with floods, but with overheating skies, hurricanes, even earth tremors.

As Millat stands schizophrenically, one foot in Bengal and the other in Willesden, so, equally, Smith's is a world where the local and the global are everywhere tangled up together, where patches of London have a closer connection with patches of other lands than they do with other parts of the city. Smith evokes Willesden as Doreen Massey evokes

Kilburn, as, in Massey's phrase, 'absolutely not a seamless, coherent identity', with 'a single sense of place which everyone shares'. Massey walks from the sari shop to a Muslim newsagent 'silently chafing at having to sell the *Sun*' because of its anti-Islamic bias. As she struggles with her shopping, overhead 'planes are beginning their long glide down to Heathrow'. It is no longer possible to imagine Kilburn in isolation from its links with the world. Kilburn is global and local at once: 'it is (or ought to be) impossible even to begin thinking about Kilburn High Road without bringing into play half the world'. Places in London are always places of connection, meeting places, extroverted, looking elsewhere. Place is insistently displaced.

But this does not mean that London's places are getting absorbed into the blandness of an internationalized or 'globalized' world, a blandness only reinforced by the sentimental and sanitized nationalisms that it spawns as 'heritages'. (The great irony of the heritage industry is that it makes all heritages look the same, and therefore not like heritages at all.) London's places are now great meshes of local and global together, palimpsests where the global overwrites the local, and then is overwritten in its turn. But the maze of interrelation itself is never abstract. It is irreducible to the contemporary fashion for abstraction, for being nothing much in particular (except more or less rich, more or less poor). It is always material and specific to specific locations. This extraordinary new complexity to 'metropolitan particularity' is what London asks us to think, right now. But metropolitan particulars are never distinct from the great system of linkages that also constitutes the city. Its atomization into privatized domains is always finally a delusion, though a delusion that currently wields a seemingly mesmeric power.

PUNK

Michael Bracewell

and the Serpentine will look just the same
and the gulls be as neat on the pond
and the sunken garden unchanged
and God knows what else is left of our London
my London, your London

Ezra Pound, from Canto LXXX

THE HOUSE WAS semi-detached, with three bedrooms, a pleasant, cottage-style garden and a grey wooden fence overhung at one end by a lilac tree. Built of Dorking brick in 1922 – the year that T. S. Eliot had published his poem *The Waste Land* – it stood on a road of similar houses, deep into London's furthest suburbia. Like many of its neighbours, the house had received enemy fire during the Second World War, in the form of incendiary bullets. Across the bay of the French windows, you could still see a neat, diagonal row of scorch-marks in the parquet flooring; in time they had become as much a feature of the house as the inherited piano stool and the kitchen dresser, the oval gilt-framed mirror and the crystal cockerel.

This was London's southern commuter belt; a landscape created in the 1920s around the rural gentility of Edwardian estates, common fields and Victorian cottages. A land, noted by the novelist E. M. Forster, 'of amenities, where success was indistinguishable from failure'.[1] But that seems harsh. By the time that this essay opens in the middle of the 1970s, the house and its suburban road – mellowed by fifty years of soft April evenings and amber autumn Sundays – still appeared a place of unbroken respectability, of order and routine, held in place by codes so rigid that they were barely spoken or referred to. An outpost of Eliot's Waste Land? Perhaps; but only in those threadbare places where an old, underlying sadness showed through the neatness and modest prosperity; more of a desperate tiredness, in fact – Hugh Kenner writes of Eliot: '. . . Mrs Eliot reported to Pound that her husband had done no work of the kind that augments vortices, not for weeks. He returned daily from the bank and fell into a leaden slumber until bedtime.'

In the 1930s, in a comfortable villa off the Brighton Road, just ten minutes walk from the Dorking brick semi, a young man called Denis was seen to preen himself – aloof, unspeakably contrary, at times obnoxious. The same young man took to wearing make-up in the streets; when asked what he intended to do with his life, he answered, 'breathe'. He made friends with a disabled girl who later became a nun. In damp suburban parks they took the air, one hobbling, the other mincing – in his own words, 'as though my legs were bound at the knee'.

In the late spring of 1977, in the bedroom at the front of the semi, a boy of 18 was reading a book called *The Naked Civil Servant*, which had just been published by Fontana. This was the first volume of Denis's autobiography, written when he had 'dyed' his name, as he said, and called himself Quentin Crisp. Although Crisp described himself as 'an effeminate and self-evident homosexual', the book was about being queer in a much broader sense: punks, like Crisp, could lay claim to being what the latter termed (as a self-portrait): 'I am an auto-fact – self created.' On a cheap stereo in one corner, to a jagged little drum line, a football terrace voice leered out: 'I wanna be a field day for the Sundays / so they can fuck up my life.'

This bedroom in the London suburbs was both dressing room and theatre; when he got ready to go out, the 18-year-old was wearing a charity shop suit, its lapels burned and ripped, safety-pinned up one side, and a faded T-shirt badly printed with the face of a serial killer. His hair looked as though it had been cut with the bread knife and then dyed with the dregs of school ink; his lower eyelids were crudely lined with black pencil. Crisp had written:

> As my appearance progressed from the effeminate to the bizarre, the reaction of strangers passed from startled contempt to outraged hatred. They began to take action. If I was compelled to stand still in the street in order to wait for a bus or on the platform of an Underground station, people would turn without a word and slap my face. If I was wearing sandals, passers-by took care to stamp on my toes; and once a crowd had started to follow me, it grew and grew until no traffic could pass down the road . . .

At the old East Croydon station, back in 1977, the spring evening smelt of flowers and petrol. Croydon, the celebrated Bavarian Anglophile architectural historian Nikolaus Pevsner had decreed, 'resembled down-town Johannesburg from the air'.[2] Seen from the flyover at dusk, the modernist office blocks – built during the Space Race in the late 1960s, and named accordingly, 'Zodiac House', 'Apollo House', 'Lunar House' – had a paradoxically Soviet air, their featureless windows, concrete and glass, like punk itself, timelessly modern, expressing modernity reaching critical mass – the modern as a worn-out thoroughfare.

The Greyhound pub, where Siouxsie and The Banshees were playing that night, was separated from these towers by an underpass; evening traffic slid into the tunnel, its dark entrance marked with dirty planks of cold white light. Brake lights gleamed scarlet in the dusk. Our boy walked with his arms folded tightly across his chest, head lowered, hopelessly self-conscious yet oddly defiant. Commuters gaped or laughed; some were openly hostile. Clearly, many of the audience for the evening's performance had considered their appearance; travelling alone, they had each become Quentin Crisp, attempting not to make eye contact with anyone; en masse they seemed to move like pantomime dames, or walked with their shoulders hunched, as though trying to become invisible: fey boys and chunky girls, graduates from their twin obsessions with Roxy Music's dandified time travel ('we wanted to look like members of the Inter-galactic parliament', Brian Eno would recall) and David Bowie's glamorous alien on a dying planet – 'stuck on your eyes'.

Amongst what Liz Naylor would memorably describe as 'the regular knob-heads wearing straight-leg Lee Coopers'[3] this scattering of suburban punk poseurs sourced their look from Weimar Germany, science fiction, Andy Warhol, pornography and the Sex Pistols – bondage trousers that forced you to mince and hobble, skirts made of black PVC, diamante, plastic macs, winkle-picker boots . . .

Today, 25 years later, punk rock and all its works have become a new Bloomsbury Group – the personnel and venues, artefacts and anecdotes, are the stuff of university conferences, coffee-table survey volumes and museum collections. How ironic that Malcolm McLaren had announced: 'History is for pissing on.' And yet punk's articulation of modernity, its ability to mint 'newness', has yet to be updated; the components of punk retain the blank, pristine modernity of machine parts. The names of first wave punk groups expressed this modernity – sharp, functional, with an industrial sheen: Wire, Magazine, Adverts, Buzzcocks, Television.

This sense of the modern, by coincidence or that biblical, portentous something-in-the-air that led Culture to record 'When Two Sevens Clash', was apparent when the Banshees fan took the train into central London to see an exhibition by the artists Gilbert and George: their 'Dirty Words Pictures, 1977'. The monochromatic and blood-red panels of these monolithic photographs showed a London our suburban outsider recognized as the theatre of his auto-faction: a place of timeless modernity, like the towers of East Croydon, yet concentrated, intense, never-ending. (Crisp had said that Style was to know what you were and to do it like mad.)

Gilbert and George showed London in 1977 as a montage of office towers, railinged city streets, night buses, lowering skies, faces in the crowd, derelicts, broken glass, sun-bursts off the NatWest Tower, the blank windows of the offices at London Wall. From the suburbs to the City, for the young punk, was the journey from – that leering football-terrace voice, again, speeded up: 'an evening of fun in the metropolis of your dreams . . . '; or Bowie's instrumental soundscapes on 'Low', that Jon Savage called 'post-everything music'.

Here was punk London shown in art: London at a time when rubbish was piled in the streets because of the strikes, and corrugated iron seemed to stretch from Chelsea to Covent Garden. He looked at the pictures, with their titles like punk novellas: 'Are You Angry or Are You Boring', 'Cunt Scum', 'Fucked Up'; they looked to him like maps of a secret geography – a London that he would always recognize, for years to come, as *his* London, as much a consciousness as a place: a territory deep inside himself, for ever.

This London had its own arcane topography – by 1977, in fact, too much of the network had been exposed to the light of day. (One sunny afternoon along Ladbroke Grove a middle-aged freak sold him a second-hand copy of Nico's 'Marble Index', 'Now this is the last time I want this record to see daylight' came the instructions from the tribal elder, whose frail hands trembled in a dust-filled sunbeam.) Punk shops were soon to be stops on a tourist map: 'Boy' ('The strength of the country lies in its youth' read a brass plaque by the door, but the shop was looked down on by first wave punk purists) and 'Sex', along the King's Road; the suburban boy outsider went next to PX near Floral Street in Covent Garden (gaining access through the low door set into the iron shutters), and bought himself a silver earring off a blonde woman wearing tank goggles in Detail, on Endell Street.

When it opened, he felt that he'd been waiting for the changing room from the twenty-first century that was Anthony Price's shop, Plaza, at the top of the King's Road, below 20th Century Box and facing Beaufort Market. When Plaza finally opened – some time around 1978 – punk had fragmented into an eclectic array of sub-sections, from gobbing spike-tops to futurist industrial; Plaza was a minimalistic quartermaster store for the youth modern(e) who urged punk to renew itself from the instant cliché of a two-chord rant; fabric samples and garment samples were fastened to perspex sheets on the racks and then the human mannequin behind the mirrored counter handed you your chosen items. The changing rooms were totally mirrored, like a sex voyeur's dream or the nightmare of the insecure. Price was the genius behind Roxy Music's styling, and he caught an early post-punk sub-strand by creating clothes like fetishized sci-fi uniforms – girls in military shirts, with purple lurex and black crêpe epaulettes. Perhaps these were the clothes to be worn in the landscape of Gilbert and George's 'Dirty Words Pictures'?

By 1978, the cartoon anarchy of early punk was a wretched funfair, shabby and boring, its point worn out. The future lay in new audacities, authorized by punk's proactive approach to rule-breaking: Public Image Ltd's 'Metal Box' became a new soundtrack for suburban London in the grip of mid-winter – the string synthesizer of the closing track 'Radio Four' sounding like the music for punk's final credits. Odd new groups from provincial Northern cities had also picked up the challenge of newness; on Sunday nights at the old Lyceum Ballroom on Wellington Street, there would be quadruple bills of these groups: Mekons, Gang of Four, The Human League and Stiff Little Fingers; Delta 5, Cabaret Voltaire, Ludus, The Fall. Each brought with them to punk London's mix of brutalist concrete and Dickensian side streets their own sense of place: ruined industrial cities in the North, where science and technology were framed by the Gothic.

But Covent Garden, then, was also mostly derelict; violin menders and esoteric bookshops kept their air of the 1930s, undisturbed by any sense of change. For years the ceremonial entrance to the Empire mansion block opposite the Lyceum had rusted railings drawn across its porch, a withered bouquet laced through its chains. On the benighted, poorly lit streets of Covent Garden in the late 1970s, the theatrical melodrama of New Romanticism – punk's major successor – was first identified: dusty and deserted districts of central London – Holborn, Gray's Inn Road, Fitzrovia – were co-opted as moodily-lit stage sets for young people dressed as Humphrey Bogart or Lord Byron.

It is perhaps a common experience – for every generation – that their defining period (an enlargement of what Virginia Woolf described as 'a moment of being', when one's consciousness seems fully engaged in the present) makes a single sensation of memory and geography. Walking through London, in this sense, becomes like walking through the chapters of your autobiography, with sites and routes doing the work of written chapters. For those who found their way on to the arcane geography of punk in London, many of the movement's venues and passes now seem possessed of a somewhat poeticized obscurity – the old Electric Ballroom where Wire taunted an audience largely composed of drunk skinheads with a three-hour piece of performance art; the furthest reaches of the Portobello Road, where you could buy import bootlegs by The Residents, Devo and Pere Ubu; West Kensington Underground Station, a room full of Polaroids in a tall house in Notting Hill Gate, the Notre Dame Hall in Leicester Square . . .

The most indelibly etched of these sites were the ones that you had to track down – drawn as though by a need from a far-flung bedroom in a Dorking brick semi; charmed by a 7-inch single in a weird sleeve that seemed to promise the entrance to a secret London which would change your life forever.

TALES FROM TRASH CITY

Paul Davies

I WAS FIRST there in Browns at the top of Shoreditch High Street when it was still a suburban-looking pub with a big window on to the street. It was the mid-1980s. The strippers would perform, somewhat precariously, before a screen that would roll down to conceal them from passers-by. Now it has a solid, grey façade featuring large metal torches, all the motifs of a castle, and you don't expect to get in wearing trainers. One hundred yards up Hackney Road, Ye Old Axe, once a crumbling dump that the strippers loved, has sprung an 'art gallery' over the cast-iron skylight that used to drip rainwater into sodden patches across its ornate Victorian interior. A stainless-steel ventilation duct now skips across the moulded ceiling, and private dancing cubicles have been hastily built across the back room. Now, by regulation, the girls no longer dance around the interior columns, but stick to the stage before hunting for table dances. In Ye Old Axe's sister pub, The Spread Eagle, office workers may find themselves being table-danced on abandoned office furniture. Not exactly 'American Style', not quite, yet.

There used to be a pool table in all the strip pubs that ran in a unique line from Liverpool Street to Cambridge Heath Road. In the Crown and Shuttle, the girls used to dance on it. Sometimes it was the only space they could dance on. Improvisation was crucial. That little place, just up from Liverpool Street on the left, closed in 2000 in a real estate deal, but it still stands empty. Tiny, the congestion of bodies, smoke and stale beer made it vaguely intimate. The girls remember it fondly too; they held a party there when it closed. Further up, in The Norfolk Village, striptease has reappeared (it closed in 2000, then tried its luck as a gay bar). Here hastily requisitioned easy chairs sit where the pool table used to be, for not very private dances. Three years ago it felt like this:

The girl strolls in, all 'Home Counties', with hair in a bun and floral dress. Later, at 2.15 on a Saturday afternoon, she will be waggling her arse for the six of us here in The Norfolk Village, and seem to be enjoying it. She could, of course, be acting. She checks her rings, and talks to a regular customer, from Hackney Environmental Services. Her name is 'Sally' in The Norfolk Village and something else in Browns, and something else everywhere else; and with 'Natasha' (who is reading a left-over copy of *The Sun*, and wants to work as a fashion cutter) she nibbles a triple-decker ham and tomato sandwich at the end of the bar. Wearing their opening skimpy outfits, their hands rise to mouth almost in unison. There are just three of us customers.

'Sally', flashing pin-black irises from their deep sockets, fishes *Health: A Nutritional Companion* from her backpack in the Ladies, struts back, and sits down to concentrate, sipping from a slowly cooling mug of coffee.

It's a slow, peaceful, Saturday afternoon, in this room with so little of a Norfolk village about it. The girls are resigned to their slow shift; unbothered, they raise an eye in the direction of the door when an occasional, sheepish customer creeps on to this empty stage, in hope of some impromptu show, or embarrassed, just to turn around and leave, or staying just for a half. The dancers need a minimum of six to raise their jugs and do the rounds, and that can't count the two bouncers joking at the end of the bar.

'Sally' begins a pool game with the barman, which she loses because her high heels make her totter and her silver mini dress rides up if she moves her knees anything but six inches apart.

On stage, her routine is smooth and detached. Those piercing eyes staring straight ahead, she confronts the meagre audience. Over time, the same identical moves, so practised and smooth, they belie the effort. This is a profession. You have to learn how to do it; a lot of it bends you backwards in pain. And you have to balance. You have to be a good conversationalist all the time. From Sunday tea with mother, you have to tower high on six-inch heels and do gymnastic rolls across the stage, always staring straight ahead at those punters unselfconscious enough to be found transfixed at the edge of the stage.

Now only The White Horse still maintains a pool table, even a pool room. Resisting change, John and Pauline and their daughter have been behind the bar since 1976. They first tried jazz entertainment, but by 1984 realized that striptease sold more beer. The White Horse is well run. Along with Browns, they have publicly criticized Hackney Council's 'tax on morality' (the 'Sex Encounter Licence'), and openly challenge the hypocrisies of political pressure groups. They even hold an all-day charity Stripathon every November in aid of a community of elderly publicans. But there are still redevelopment pressures, as the Square Mile looks north to eye up the seven-storey warehouse they stand within.

Shoreditch High Street is unique. For thirty years it has peddled its own particular brand of sex entertainment. Originally a string of pubs offering traditional pub striptease, money, media, legislation and a certain roguish instinct have both transformed and sustained it. It is an underground culture symbiotic with the most monumental structures of the City of London. It is a remnant of traditional East End pub culture transformed by a globally ascendant sex industry. It's nice girls making nasty faces during fake sex. It's women asserting their power on stage, and often men treating women shoddily off it.

On 12 September 2001, round 2 o'clock in the afternoon, 'Allison' dangles her glittered shoe over the edge of the stage and half-heartedly slaps her bottom. She's not a great dancer, but it doesn't matter (what I mean is, she doesn't do much, and that can make a great dancer; she just, sort of, languishes around). Today she's chosen 'Livin' on the Edge' by Aerosmith. It's blasting out like there's no tomorrow, and she's just great, in her Stars and Stripes outfit, swinging her pigtails and slapping her arse between videos of catastrophic stunts, cats jumping into washing machines and piles of trucks in flames, while, outside, the world holds its breath.

Waving her beautiful little silver-glitter shoes and nothing else, laughing at us, at me, at the bankers in here over lunch when they should be toiling over their screens (business slackens off when the city gets nervous). Now we have, on John's personally composed videos, with some marvellous irony, gymnasts falling off beams painfully, and from the bars, and landing on their heads as they vault over the horse, all 600 yards away from the City of London.

If the free world goes up in flames, make sure you are in The White Horse. Those dancers will still be passing their jugs around, and choosing the appropriate soundtrack. 'Nice shoes', I say. 'Uuuummm', she motions, pleased, pouting and blowing an appreciative kiss. Of course they're nice shoes. Dancers are ambivalent about customers, but customers are rarely ambivalent about dancers. The records are important, 'Cheryl', who's next, only dances to 'classic rock' during the day, like BTO and Heart. Now 'Cheryl', she's a real artiste. 'Blondie', she always likes little literary allusions, like dancing to Janet Jackson's 'All For You'.

I like it, it feels just right, sitting in here, better than ever, on a bar stool with a pint of John Smith's Extra Smooth, flashing amber lights of the work crews glinting through the dark venetian blinds, with a glow in the west and fireballs on the screen, and a half-naked dancer going round with her jug. For a £1 a go, she'll get it off for you, smiling.

Back in 1986. There were no poles, no table dances and no contact, no cubicles, no 'art galleries', no clandestine table dances, no VIP or Shower Rooms, just girls getting their kit off in the pub like that. We were all reading Andrea Dworkin and it definitely wasn't respectable. Now the *Evening Standard* sends its female reporter to striptease school, and lap-dancing clubs like Spearmint Rhino are favoured venues for corporate Christmas parties, and are run by devout Christians. The *Hackney Gazette* even reports that Rhino are anxious to open a venue here in Curtain Road (much to John's disgust).

Then it was just East End strippers, 'Rippers'they called them. The venues included, at one time or other, almost all the pubs springing from Liverpool Street up to Cambridge Heath Road. It started in the 1950s as a response to flagging pub sales and television. Lorry drivers forced to park up over the Bishopsgate goods yard sustained business in the 1970s. By the '80s, the Big Bang had brought a new audience to mingle with the locals and the drivers: builders and bankers. Now with the corporations taking over, some girls are doing it for themselves.

'Olympia Moments' is a monthly private club run by 'Ulrika', 'Max' and 'Jane'. They have forsaken the pubs and the middlemen. This is girls doing it for themselves. Tonight they are underground somewhere in Aldgate.

You could cut a knife through the atmosphere, just as you could collect the spots of perspiration gathering on the brows of the mostly middle-aged male audience. Girls are welcome too, and Julie's waiting for her private dance behind the makeshift but effective screen. She wants to find out what it's like. She can't exactly tap 'Ulrika 'on the shoulder yet, for Ulrika's shoulder is covered in green Fairy Liquid, from her Frankenstein monster act. Tonight there's a Hallowe'en theme, and Olympia Moments shows are highly theatrical, harking back to the tradition of burlesque. The guys there are part of a network, now sustained via the Internet as well as the pub venues. 'Ulrika' is very smart. She has business cards.

'You know what makes me attractive?', she says, pointing at her head. 'I do my homework!' 'I read the papers before I do a shift, I read the sports news! That way I have something to talk to the guys about.'

And so 'Ulrika' became a cult, a second identity for her, and a special identity for the customers whom she contacted through the Web, met at the pubs, and for whom she'd wait in Starbucks at Liverpool Street to sell them tickets for the next show. It's a cult thing, this world, and 'Ulrika' is not the same in jeans and T-shirt as she is as 'Ulrika' on stage. What is it for her? 'It's us doing what we want to do, for pleasure', she says. It's interesting.

I have written about all this before. I curled up on the sofa with a little underground magazine called *Trash City*. It's based around this world, and the fantasies that support it: girls and guns, bad 'B' movies, even long-forgotten classic rock and the best fish 'n chips. Neither an overt red light district, nor a colony of 'titty bars' with pretensions to respectable business, the High Street is still somewhere where English boys sneak off to, behind the bike sheds. *Trash City Magazine* was written by a bunch of computer geeks in HSBC Bank. The editor, the very likeable Jim McLennan, eventually realized his fantasy for real, and left to start again, firing guns and digging for precious stones in Arizona.

Meanwhile, up in Metropolis, the first of the 'American Style' clubs to have grown out of the pubs, beneath the purple and pink lights, in her purple and pink little outfit, 'Nicky' was doing her rounds, bobbing her head and tossing her hair, big smile for the boys, a hug and 'h'llo darlin'' to an old, fat favourite, trying very hard to be the classiest thing we'd ever seen.

It was Nicky's turn to collect for her dance; her jug was already brimming. She'd paid £60 to work here for her shift and she was going to make it back and more. Her friend, after last night's shift, a Monday, had made just £60. But Nicky was a natural, she was so sweet, she was so bubbly, and she made everybody feel special, she had to. In the ultraviolet her blond hair shone like silver, and her body glistened like satin.

Soon I'd be seeing right into it, in a routine that closer resembles an acrobatic gymnastics routine around a pole than dance, up close into her gleaming snatch, into her puckered arse, up at her smiling eyes, and down once more at my thinning wallet, and my fattening waistline.

This is what *Playboy* did. Not that it's not attractive, but an image becomes uniform, and it's harder for dancers to be original or different here, when the standards get set, when a pub goes upmarket.

But sometimes, for me, it's just the sexy music; that daft pan-European beat; the waiting time before any girl gets up on stage; the absent-minded watching of German equestrian events or summer ski jumping on grass; or the waggle of the chin of the man tucking in to the home-prepared pie and chips; or the way, even, that the sandwiches are delivered to each table, with a deference you would associate with a top-class restaurant, or your first sickly sip of beer because you were pissed up at 2.30 a.m. last night; or a wink from John the landlord. Sometimes it's not the girls at all.

Sometimes its just a bash along to Tina Turner. She's singing 'When the Heartache is over . . . I can live without you!!!' – and it rumbles along, dragging us into the afternoon and another day, with German equestrian events on the big screen. Lots of heroes have been here. Cosi Fanni Tutti stripped for art, and the keyboard player from *The Fall* (1986) did too. There's 'Roxy' and 'Chelsea' of (B) movie fame and Jo King (no pun) who loved it and lost most of it and now runs The London School of Striptease.

'Almost everybody in here is not succeeding in their life', I wrote, in one dejected moment in The White Horse. But I was wrong. How fantastic this room is. It's like the end scenes of *Ally McBeal*, laden with idiosyncrasy and surreal dignity.

IMAGING BRIXTON

Allen Fisher

THERE ARE AREAS of human experience in which Brixton does not play a constitutive and recognized role. I do not know about them. I come down the old hill from the back of the Prison and the windmill to the Town Hall and Market. A visitor from San Francisco remarks, doesn't it worry you, this crush around, this crush through the night after the Tubes have stopped, doesn't it freak you this many races experience, doesn't it freak you out? This is part of a theory of creation, Brixton always in the process, hot corners, slow alleys, dirt and brilliance, have you been there? Yeah, of course you think you have, is that right? You may have been there, yeah, down the old hill in London traffic, where the culture breaks, you're clear about that, breakage, tone colours, smell of burning, exhaust fumes, cooking, exhaustion pushed in your face, the chip fry – the traffic breaks, looking ahead sudden tail lights, that's right, sudden and then swerve, sudden and that's right ahead for a mile to the rail-bridge crush over *bon marché* and its dereliction, community slop bucket. Give me a break, changes lanes into my path and birds over the rail-bridge, or its news-sheets or chocolate wrappers, seem purple.

In the early 1980s, a street sound like no other, how things came into being. Not for the first time, never that, the first taste always, but not a first time, that proposition out, well out of line, on this buzz box, re-read the liquid digits. Overlapped, out of line, of course necessary business, but not anything, not a thing at all, rather a place and action cluster, invariant, like they say, but as if eternal without return, ongoing without arrow nonsense, no stupid pictures of directions, much simpler in its pragmatic exactness, getting the business done. Buy the olives from washtubs red blue into face with coriander and tins of anchovies, boxes of salt fish, you want to keep quiet, then get lost. Not here, you dumb, this is street dice, back of a milk crate, street dealing. Davies on the hand backs and out of here, down the escalator to the sax worn, the smoothed-out tramway of a tenor where the stairs turn, sound crushed in the wringer where the tunnel funnels sparks in a rush of noise and hot exhaust burning the shine off. In his head on a bike around the garden by the Ritzy numbered roses. Counting glazed cobbles from the earth edge, burning wicker from the furniture store. Van flat from the earthly morning lager, street pies and gong smack. You think you know something? You think you've really tried gong, you bet you ain't. This is the centre of all universes, all pie shops, all record deals. This centre, the centre that moves rapidly without catch me. This is a nuclear need me, this is busker town, read the black-boards, this is fasterville.

You imagine someone inventing a patois, a local speech sink, a close to the territory held there. It is imagined, it is no starter here, it gets on my wick just as ignition hits it. Ineluctable inference from cosmological reasoning, get it, sheer voids akin to existential trammel. Innocence after this, get go for this. Essential necessity of post-experiential drive to the market, bike and all. Stand to watch the car burning outside the Prison gates. Inmates in the bar opposite choking in a smog dome. London's and there, The George. A self-fulfilling, self-emptying act, sprung high street inside railings to prevent road cross prevents skateboards, prevents generally rather than exceeds. You can make music on it, past Red Records past the rocket shop into the Tube tunnel, into the gas blast, into the sound zoom. This is Brixton, essential to the sound zone necessary business. Measurement limited, limits restricted, uncertain what to try for next. Next door, another try for this, improvised go-for-it. Now go for it, Brixton with the pane flap, flip of the flack back.

Alleys of broken-glass rubbish. Sprung-floor bounce of the dump chute, chain bike to the car park. Shop in the market east of the old road down to the pink meats, black fish and sandstones. Back to broiled chicken, old parsley and milkwood, green bananas and plantains. Salt and cheese market, anarchist pub room miked for the dub site, rigged for the Railtons, The Front Line. Burnt fence and rust railings, blue wall and damaged entrance. Dream apparency on a plastic lawn west of the sports shop, west of the mug shot. Burnt CDs and a brain test, two-pound tench on a man chest. Rush the bike to Herne Hill corner. Rush the trike to the blues deck, under the London sky-dome, watch myself burning there. City horizon a blaze in the red set, silver lifts through a cloud drench. Auburn clouds and a spent bag, smog box measure on a glass screen. Affirm the permanent presence of things, calmer and calmer before a flip cross. Betting shop ashes and a cash prize before daybreak, before the warp in the hardboard opening to the townhouse, rock sound and the house sound. Unplaced in the first abode, permanently unplaced but nowhere else. Always Brixton, down to the market, across, down to the kids' park. Watch buskers on the beak out. Now go, up the hill for a lunch bun. Case estate and their bushed hedge. Case study in the ball park. Lime trees down in the robber mall. Consumer this and waste away, never get out of here.

Continuous pressure to get the picture. Repetition of the sound waves. Repetition and the shop shutters. Graffiti and the repaint. Rubber walls and the cheap shop. Clothing twice the price undercuts the jumble sale. Then what? Yellow shoes for the hell-of-it. Laced up boots to The Fridge queue, then the crush dance, then the pogo floor, then the stage jam. In the blue smoke on the wet floor beyond the lawn flats. Ice in the beer glass, gum on the stool rim. Fried chicken and red rice, fried pickings and fluorescence. Kitsch frame around the lake scene. Peel of enamel on a lead dust. Roar of traffic at the Town Hall, block Coldharbour with a street cry, west to the Sunlight Laundry. In April 1981, dry-cleaned petrol cocktails thrown in Brixton. Black and white with common frustrations, miseries, confrontations with police and thugs. The Judge cites disorder or terrifying lawlessness of crowds, linked to police and community leader relations with ethnic groups. Poor housing, decay of facilities, corrosive unemployment, destruction of hope. Under nuclear threat, attention to a policy of direct co-ordinated attack against positive discrimination.

Imaging Brixton in 1980 and after involves participation in a number of paradigm shifts in perception, aesthetics and consciousness, many already apparent many decades before this and many new to the period. The Brixton encounter involved day and night interactions with a range of situations, from a variety of phase shifts and cusping experiences to the more recently apparent fractal complexes and crowd-outs; that is, a social interaction in the process between one state and another and hardly ever in either; a political situation forever in preparation for the next move that proved to be elusive and under-achieved; the fractal architecture of a moving street climate at multiple boundary layers, a range of entrances–exits, shuttered shop fronts, small padlocked doors, barbed wire over broken glass over syrup skinned wallings, with the sound rebounding in the alternations of old church entry way to the deadening cloak of Electric Avenue and the railway; the eventual crowd-out against some perceptions in preference to others, in favour of some racial groups (usually white) in favour over others (often black); the shifting graphic blur from torn hoardings and burnt murals to neon lettering and back-projected sex shots.

1980s Brixton under surveillance. Helicopters to check the movement of prisoners to court and back, to check the movements of others unnamed, but in any case to add to the ambience of harassment, and locked against the suss laws, the weed checks, the baseball, the back beat. The laser beam ground shot. Up and down the old road, west and east across from Acre to Harbour, a siren rush on a police weapon, a bus of armed undercover, a trolley of coshes. The push in the back promoted by a paste-up and regular sweet tooth promoting burger crime. Thatcher mob encouraged a push back up the downward escalator at the station, down the track to the White Hart and the zap band or the improvised session or the new age North Africa. Into the art studios in Acre or Stockwell, into the art bins annexed to Goldsmiths and Camberwell, into the squats and hard up against the toad jets, the drug snappers and dealing deadheads promoting rottweilers and street scum trading banners, superhype photography as posters, badges of simulated courage. A culture of terror that domesticates the expectations of the majority. In a period just before spectators displace participants in a phase shift to consumer happiness, a period of maximum pressure to mask arms sales in preference to meeting stunted children raised in poverty. Cuts in social programmes to celebrate the import of American values. Brixton orange, Brixton green, black-red Brixton chrome, blue Brixton, lilac park, Brixton pink fur. Sound of dub against Ska against soul. Sound of rubbish truck against car alarm against barking dog. Smell of old cabbage, smell of chicken curry, smell of car exhaust. Flashing car lights, flashing photobooth, flashing CCTV.

Brixton gradually shot, lost its warm social in maximized personal profits, the tripped passenger at the Tube stairs trodden on and again pushed over, defined political economy, defined neighbourhoods, defined street wisdom. Counterflows from autonomy and personal relations, live politics, you organize around your own oppression. Aesthetics as effective consciousness, affective *détournement*. Deep anxieties and fears respond to powerlessness. Intervention cut vocabulary, decision and concision. Jostle from a rut, visible momenta. Refusal of work at one level in order to create at another. Spontaneity against power. The poverty of theory exemplified in the practice of poverty. Everywhere Brixton on into its borderland, coercion, deceit and blood countered with exhilaration, refused by joy, countered by jubilation, fused by collective experience. The stone Victorian pineapple in the funeral garden, Ethiopian flags at the Reggae store, tins of food labelled in Greece and Singapore. We window shop a moving railway in which debris remains unchanged. Glitter bars, syrup lights, strobe effects. Shout out loud in the street across traffic roar, passing Walkman bass, passing market stall selling wares, and beyond a sky plane, sky scrapper, a set of sky stripes.

The web of interests theory, false promised as the striving for coherence. A crowd-out of lies and *détente*, a wound that runs through the heart of Europe, recalls the regular nuclear train running through Brixton Station, couples news of plans to manufacture neutron human death to leave property intact. The intermediate nuclear threat, arms reductions walkouts, Star Wars, three baskets of central controls beyond London that affected Brixton directly. Lions of neo-liberalism from retreats of sullen silence prepare a nemesis for those seen as nebbish. The poor borrowing in expectation of plenty on the edge of a fourth world, beyond development, calls for a global economy around local markets, calls for mindful markets, calls to subvert supermarket power, calls to grow your own in a street situation, calls to re-run the bioframe with a conscience with a community discussion of informed need, calls to subvert the subjective individualist, watches anarchist support for conservative angst, watches repeats of repeats on television high street, watches repetition of riot image of global fantasy of newsreel loops.

When William S. Burroughs came to Brixton, London turned out. Gift and sacrifice on many lips. Symbolic exchange on grounds for disruption and resistance. When Gilles Deleuze and Félix Guattari came to Brixton, they opened a tortilla bar. Hyperreal Brixton was complete, that is, always in the process of production, being produced and producer. You could mistake this for elsewhere or everywhere, the glory has departed. This Bricks down, one by one, the kids throw the bricks down, this continues to be Brixistan Hundred. The pressure to prevent Brixton proposes communities made consumers; neighbours given negative traumas, clutches of nastic moments. Target fodder necessarily alien in their own war zone, in place of the barricades human barriers confront fleets of magistration. The Justice of the Peace becomes Minister of War. All judgements are determined beforehand. You're in prison equals you're guilty. The lived immediacy of Brixton High Road and Atlantic Avenue threatens this and that, but avoids alienation, avoids the hose fight, avoids the knuckle down, avoids the sweetened cream cheese, wants the everyday, wants the get up and go, wants a cool lager, wants the massage envelope. The oracle is behind the betting shop on Coldharbour Lane, the bun house in the ground floor of the snooker hall, the rocket science is above the photo gallery. You wanna buy herbs, get a bucket of cash and call me Monday.

A lot of Brixton people believe in themselves. Brixton is contra-New York in this respect, 'anything can happen and submit to the moment' becomes 'here it is happening and we make each moment'. We have to do this. The police weapon bus moves in a rush up and down the old hill. A box of tapers falls off the back of one, it is full of dead fuses. Plastic pots of over-cultivated plants fill the shelves and windowsills. Wall paintings yell of war, community gardens, children playing, factory skylines. What is grey green at Brixton Station is blue grey in the arcades, red grey in Brixton Road, unbrushed steel in the gaming hall. Red buses punctuate silver and red greys pushing towards Streatham. The Town Hall clock says ten to two all day. It has just gone lunch break or the streets are clearing in tired reflections on damp pavements and tarmac. We live in danger, a repression made from anxiety. A child's toy calls out on the dead lawn, it is wordless.

We give our opinions outside The Prince of Wales, in the new agora, at the traffic lights, up from the bus stop, dialogue, interaction, change. In the process of inventing, in preparation for new participations. We started making street theatre when we forgot that we were making street theatre. Assault was symbolized by bottles of fire. A new anger imaged in flaming cars, smashed shopfronts, toffee-strewn pavements. The captains of industry become the pirates of industry. All that is not new form and not restraint is noise, the only possible source of new patterns. We care about our patterns. Our unit of survival is organism plus environment. The organism that destroys its environment destroys itself. Our geometry shifts to new comprehensions of gravity and gravitas, a hydraulic feeling that is vectorial, projective, tropological and thus a function of the place we are in, Brixton. We undercut dualism through immersion. This is the urban beach in a complexity of tide flows and appearances. I am a storm bath with a nervous motorboard. I have shifted away from image as catharsis to image as liberation. The mob of spectators run for more copies of the front page, more posters from blown up images of image production, labelled riots. The mob moves in from the Stock Exchange horizon, from St Paul's and from the City. Down the old marsh crossing to Kennington and Stockwell. Their absorption of images matches their need for a simulacrum. Brixton on their walls and pixelated on their screens, threaded into their fabrics.

The sound is Day-Glo, in a brightness of belling and whistling, their shouts are collage prints and assemblages, they smell of means tests. When Jean Baudrillard came to Brixton he was snookered by them. Their hyperreal was actual. Their oppression led to beggar production. Their age imaged as need plus greed. I videoed their actions and posted the box of it to Paris. 'This is South London', I wrote, 'These are images of Brixton.'

SECRET CITY: PSYCHOGEOGRAPHY AND THE END OF LONDON

Phil Baker

> The sectors of a city are, at a certain level, readable. But the meaning they have had for us personally is incommunicable, like the clandestinity of private life, of which we possess only a few pitiful documents.
>
> Guy Debord[1]

Bearings

THE WORD 'PSYCHOGEOGRAPHY' was increasingly in vogue in 1990s London, but what does it mean? It originated in the 1950s with the French avant-garde-cum-revolutionary group the Lettrists, who later became the Situationists, and it first appears in Guy Debord's 'Introduction to a Critique of Urban Geography' (1955), where a compact definition is given: it is the 'study of the effects of the geographical environment, consciously organized or not, on the emotions and behaviour of individuals'.[2]

Debord adds that the adjective 'psychogeographical' has a 'rather pleasing vagueness', and anyone reading recent usages would discover that it is about Jack the Ripper, ley lines, why tower blocks are bad, Hawksmoor churches, the places we remember from earlier in our lives, landscape gardening, Stonehenge and the Kray twins.

And it is indeed about all those things. Most uses of the word now involve three or four main ideas, separately or in combination: the emotional and behavioural effects of the environment, and its ambience; 'cognitive mapping' (the city in our heads, with the places that have special meaning for us); and what might be more prosaically called 'local history'.

Chinatowns, cemeteries and red-light districts all have their own distinct auras, and this idea of different ambiences is central to psychogeography. The zones and quarters of a city are made up of distinct psychic micro-climates; places attract and repel us, or feel psychically warmer and colder, in a way that can be mapped. This emotional effect of place can be extended to single buildings, or even rooms. In different hands it can be supernatural, tending to ideas of something like haunting, or entirely materialistic. At its most down to earth it might include this description of the Broadwater Farm Estate:

> The Hardcastle estate seemed to have no other purpose than to stage endlessly repeated dramas of public disorder. It was what it was designed for. Its labyrinth of forecourts, low-rise walkways and access balconies, blind alleys of fear and danger. Its high-rise vantage points a silhouette of menace. Its whole architecture was a solid fortress of deprivation . . .[3]

At its more esoteric it would include Iain Sinclair's argument, in *Lud Heat* (1975), that Hawksmoor churches exercise an occult malevolence that causes violent crime.

Debord's Lettrist comrade Ivan Chtcheglov pushed the idea of ambience to extremes in his 'Formulary for a New Urbanism' (1953). Chtcheglov came to the attention of the authorities after attempting to dynamite the Eiffel Tower, but before he disappeared into the psychiatric system he left this brief but inexhaustible tract. It shows his sense of zones and quarters, and his vision of a purpose-built psychogeographical city divided into distinct zones (fulfilled, in dystopian form, by Disneyland), along with his enthusiasm for the colonnades and deserted squares of Giorgio de Chirico, and an element of belated Surrealism:

> Certain *shifting* angles, certain *receding* perspectives, allow us to glimpse original conceptions of space, but this vision remains fragmentary. It must be sought in the magical locales of fairy tales and surrealist writings: castles, endless walls, little forgotten bars, mammoth caverns, casino mirrors.[4]

Chtcheglov was at the forefront of the Lettrist interest in the affective environment, and the construction of emotionally determinant ambiences by decor. There would be 'rooms more conducive to dreams than any drug, and houses where one cannot help but love'.[5] This aspect has largely fallen away from later notions of psychogeography, but Lettrist-Situationist psychogeography would include Dr Caligari film sets, Piranesi's prisons (Piranesi was 'psychogeographical in the staircase', according to Debord[6]), visionary, amateur and 'wild' architecture (Postman Cheval, Mad King Ludwig), and even interior design.

The feeling of place is inseparable from the meaning of place, often within personal cartographies that have their own landmarks.

> Her aura transfigured for me the whole upper part of Gloucester Place, so that I could not willingly go there for two or three years after I had lost her. Often, however, she would meet me at what we called The Object. The Object stood in an arcade off Baker Street, and looked something like a large bollard . . .[7]

There is a more extensive private map at the heart of Georges Perec's 'Places' (*c.* 1969–75), a description of twelve Paris locales that he associated with a former girlfriend. It turns the city into a personalized memorial, and commemorates what he called 'dead places that ought to survive'.[8]

Psychogeography is not interested in 'objective' panoptical mapping, but only in the private cognitive maps of our customized cities. Debord's cut-and-pasted collage maps of Paris, *Discours sur les Passions d'amour* (1957) and *Naked City* (1957), have become definitive examples of this 'renovated cartography',[9] but defaced Tube maps are another instance, with three southern stations on the Victoria Line labelled 'dump', 'dump' and 'dump', for example, or three stations on the District Line replaced with 'Ali's House', 'Drugs Here' and 'Sex Town'.[10]

These cognitive maps overlap with larger histories. Chris Petit's essay of 1993 on Newman Passage ('Jekyll and Hyde Alley', a sinister location that he terms the 'secret heart' of Fitzrovia) situates it in a personal cartography of film locations:

> When I first came to London twenty years ago and didn't know anyone, I haunted cheap movie-houses that were soon to vanish – the cartoon cinema in Victoria Station, the Tolmers, the Metropole, the predominantly homosexual Biograph in Wilton Road, Classics, Jaceys; these were not selective days – and, almost unconsciously, as something to do on Sundays, I started to track down London film locations: a sinister park near Charlton Athletic football ground from *Blow-Up*; a crescent house and a riverside apartment in *The Passenger*; the house on the corner of Powis Square in *Performance*; the Covent Garden pub and Coburg Hotel in *Frenzy*. I would visit these places and feel a little less anonymous, a little more specific,

> and by patiently stitching them together I made my own map of the city, a limited (and superstitious) one, albeit with more meaning than the official ones . . .[11]

Another private map uses the familiar trope of city as text:

> My own personal copy of the West End is now covered in marginal notes and amendments which have transformed its meaning for me: the street corner on Shaftesbury Avenue, a little way down from Cambridge Circus, where Edgar Manning shot three men one day in 1920, for example; or the building in Gerrard Street that is now a Chinese supermarket and restaurant, but used to be the notorious 43 Club; or the tiny dining room in Lisle Street that today offers 'The Cheapest Chinese Food in Town', but in 1918 was a shady chemist's from which Billie Carleton's circle got their cocaine.[12]

'All cities are *geological*', wrote Chtcheglov, 'you cannot take three steps without encountering ghosts bearing all the prestige of their legends'. Much of what is now called psychogeography is resonant and marginal local history, including a good deal of the material in Sinclair's middle work, such as *Downriver* (1991), Tom Vague's *Entrance to Hipp: A Psychogeographical Guide to Notting Hill* (1997), and numerous books on curious, low, dated or unknown London before the term psychogeography came into vogue; for example, *The London Nobody Knows* by Geoffrey Fletcher (1962), *Evil London* by Peter Aykroyd [sic] (1973), *London's Secret History* by Peter Bushell (1983) and *The Black Plaque Guide* by Felix Barker (1987).

Psychogeographical history often tends towards a combination of the esoteric and arcane with the deviant and sordid, or antiquarianism with crime and lowlife. Jack the Ripper and the Elizabethan magus John Dee are of psychogeographical interest (the Ripper has, for better or worse, become central to the psychogeography of Whitechapel, while Dee is part of the psychogeography of Mortlake), whereas Cromwell and Pitt the Younger are not. It is also more fully psychogeographical if there is a sense that history affects ambience, and that the character of place inheres and affects feelings and behaviour, or if it challenges the mainstream contemporary reading of a place. In that sense it can be an alienated and recalcitrant form of history, and one that resists being recuperated into 'heritage'.

Alienation was an important factor in the recent popularity of psychogeography. Even in its most basic aspect, the feel of place, 'psychogeography' is a useful shorthand for aspects of place that are not reducible to economics, and for the effect of the built environment on the quality of life, which has been the subject of unprecedented anger and dissent. As for cognitive mapping, it is universal and inescapable. But its recent fetishization has accompanied a post-consensus, post-societal sense that society as a whole (famously declared not to exist in 1987[13]) offers no salvation, only one's own routes and places. Its overlap with histories and myths of place is a further way of gaining a purchase on the inhospitable environment of the metropolis. People want to inscribe marks and find traces in the city, like the stories they used to tell about the stars and constellations, in order to feel more at home in an indifferent universe.

Landmarks

Classic urban psychogeography could almost be said to begin – retrospectively, and from a Situationist-influenced perspective – with Thomas De Quincey, and it can be traced through the Surrealists, Walter Benjamin, and the Lettrists and Situationists. But London psychogeography over the past 25 years owes less to all this and more to Iain Sinclair, whose work is inspired by a completely different tradition that surfaced during the hippy era. Take the opening of a book of 1970 on Carnaby Street: 'The girl said, "Carnaby Street is a happy place. I think it must be on dragon lines."'[14]

Sinclair's roots are not with the Situationists but with the 'Earth Mysteries' school. The 1960s saw a resurgence of interest in the countryside, and in the land's apparently ancient lore and sacred geometry; particularly ley lines, or long man-made alignments in the landscape. John Michell's *The View Over Atlantis* was published in 1969, and Michell stimulated interest in the work of Alfred Watkins. 'Ancient people everywhere placed their shrines and monuments on straight alignments across miles of country', explains Michell, 'the existence of these forgotten alignments came to [Watkins] in a flash of intuition . . .',

> [like] the sacred dragon lines of old China, secret, mystical ways across the landscape are known to exist throughout the world. There is a common principle behind them which does not yield easily to modern-minded inquiries; but if you frequent ancient

sanctuaries with an inquisitive mind, you are open to the influence of ancient mentalities.[15]

Watkins's best-known work, *The Old Straight Track* (1925), was republished in 1970 and reached the mass-market with Abacus in 1974. It was in this climate, and further influenced by books such as Elizabeth Gordon's *Prehistoric London: Its Mounds and Circles* (1914), that Sinclair wrote his seminal *Lud Heat* (1975). Complete with diagrams, this suggested that Hawksmoor churches are aligned across London in a sinister occult geometry, and that they exercise a malevolent influence by 'unacknowledged magnetism and control-power, built-in code force'.[16] Drawing on numerous sources from Thomas De Quincey to the lost pyramids of Glastonbury, Sinclair's essay is an exhilarating masterpiece of paranoia.

Lud Heat inspired Peter Ackroyd's novel *Hawksmoor* (1985), in which he developed a contrast between the worlds of Sir Christopher Wren (Enlightenment, rationality, daylight, procreation) and Nicholas Hawksmoor (secret disaffection, sooty darkness, old Gnostic and pagan beliefs, sterility). The most psychogeographical aspect of the book – behavioural determinism, albeit occult, by the built environment – was not widely remarked on by reviewers, but a species of psychogeography had now entered the London literary mainstream, and Sinclair/Ackroyd's eccentric take on Hawksmoor has since threatened to become as much a part of London as Jack the Ripper.

Disaffection had meanwhile continued to smoulder with the legacy of the Situationist International. During 1970, Malcolm McLaren (the future Sex Pistols impresario and mayoral candidate, but then an art student influenced by the Situationists) researched a documentary film on the psychogeography of Oxford Street: 'From Tyburn at the gallows to the Gordon Riots and Barnaby Rudge . . . The coming of the department store and crowd control. The politics of boredom . . . more Mars Bars are sold on Oxford Street than anywhere else.'[17]

Associated for a while with the Angry Brigade, interest in the Situationists was a minority, under-the-counter affair. As Maclaren remembered it later, you had to go into Camden's now defunct Compendium Bookshop and pass 'the eyeball test'.[18] But it flared into a higher profile at the end of the 1980s, with Greil Marcus's *Lipstick Traces: A Secret History of the Twentieth Century* (1989) and the Situationist retrospective of 1989 at the ICA and the Pompidou Centre in Paris.

The two streams of psychogeography, Situationist and Earth Mystery, fused with the founding of the London Psychogeographical

Association (LPA) in 1992. The LPA signalled its Situationist alignments by an overt use of *détournement* in the opening line of its manifesto article, 'Why Psychogeography?': 'There is a spectre haunting Europe, nay the world. The spectre of psychogeography.'[19]

Essentially a far-left post-Situationist group with a penchant for pranksterism and disinformation, the LPA claimed to believe in the wilder reaches of esoteric psychogeography, from ley lines outwards. Slippery and prickly, their stance on these things was a tongue-in-cheek strategy against 'recuperation' (compare Debord's covering his *Mémoires* in sandpaper) designed to make academia keep its distance. 'We offer no attempt to "justify" or "rationalise" the role of magic in the development of our theories; it is sufficient that it renders them completely unacceptable.'[20]

Between 1992 and 1997, the LPA's numerous publications included 'Smash the Occult Establishment', which was about Greenwich, the Royal Family and Freemasonry; and 'Open Up the Northwest Passage', the Northwest Passage being a navigational metaphor from De Quincey's urban wanderings, which Debord adopted and transformed. The LPA could argue that St Catherine's Hill is the mystical omphalos of England, relating it to planetary alignments and the possibly ritual death of William Rufus in 1100, but they could also make trenchant use of Gestalt 'figure/ground' reversal to illustrate the way in which the working-class population of the East End was relegated to a backdrop during the 1980s and '90s.[21]

The centre of London shifted eastwards during the later 1980s, initially during new excitement about the City financial district. The concomitant rediscovery of the East End – which was, to many people, exotically unknown and unmodernized territory – was a further impetus to psychogeography. Due to prevailing winds and cleaner air in the West, the eastern side of Northern Hemisphere cities tends to be the poor side, which in turn makes it the 'bad' side. East London had long been a centre of immigration, making it subject to fantastical orientalizing discourses,[22] and it was also associated with Jack the Ripper and the kind of period criminality that has long been part of London's image in France. In September 1960 the Situationist International held its Fourth Conference at a 'secret address' deep in *l'East End*, the British Sailors Society in Limehouse, *quartier célèbre par ses criminels*.[23]

Debord shared the Surrealists' ugly fascination with *Jacques L'Eventreur*, going as far as to dub him 'psychogeographical in love'.[24] Psychogeography and Jack the Ripper seem enduringly linked. Alan Moore's work was particularly notable in this period, including his Ripper graphic novel *From Hell* (1991–8; latterly filmed), which also included Hawksmoor. He extended his psychogeographical range much further with his 'Beat Seance' events of 1997, such as 'the Highbury Working', using ghostly and occult tropes for the resurrection of marginal local history.

Iain Sinclair's career had meanwhile consolidated. A small-press novel on antiquarian book dealing and the Ripper, *White Chappell Scarlet Tracings* (1987), was followed by *Downriver* (1991), full of marginal Thameside history and observation, and by the time of *Lights Out for the Territory* (1997), Sinclair was at the height of his celebrity. *Lights Out* still featured esoterica, but it was less arcane than the earlier work, and in part constituted a sociological safari into the world of satellite TV dishes and pit-bull terriers. It is only around now that the word 'psychogeography' began to appear in Sinclair's writing, usually applied to others, such as the LPA or Chris Petit.

Lights Out includes discussion of the London artist and curator Rachel Lichtenstein in terms that are applicable to Sinclair's own project: 'an artist who specialised in not-forgetting, the recovery of "discernible traces"'.[25] In 1999, Sinclair collaborated with Lichtenstein on *Rodinsky's Room*, a book about an abandoned room in Brick Lane which had, since the mid-1980s, been mythologized as a time capsule. Rodinsky also furnished Sinclair with material for *Dark Lanthorns: Rodinsky's A to Z*, which included a facsimile of an annotated London A–Z owned by Rodinsky and marked with places of personal significance. It was subtitled 'Rodinsky as psychogeographer', in a notable instance of the 'personal mapping' aspect of psychogeography.

By 2000, psychogeography was fully into the mainstream with Peter Ackroyd's *London: The Biography*. Although Ackroyd denigrates the word, his book is underpinned by an ultimately irrationalistic psychogeography, claiming that the character and atmosphere of different London districts inhere over time by an 'echoic' haunting process that controls human activity within them. It was very different from Roy Porter's *London: A Social History* (1994), which concluded that London had had its day; that the Thatcher years did it serious damage; and that it had fallen to be a tourist city and a barely regulated international zone. It is, in other words, not the Eternal City, which is exactly the opposite of Ackroyd's argument.[26]

Ackroyd's almost Platonic worship of continuity is a neo-conservative attempt to contain change, and to reinscribe a city that threatens to become illegible. 'The indigenous or native spirit which animates a particular area' ensures, for example, that 'the secret life of Clerkenwell . . . goes very deep', and that Bloomsbury remains steeped in occultism (Masonry, Theosophy, the Golden Dawn, astrology, occult bookselling). 'So here again there seems to be a congregation of aligned forces . . . remaining active within the neighbourhood of a few streets.'[27]

In the year that Ackroyd's book was published, the old British Library dome in Bloomsbury was reopened at the centre of a newly hollowed-out white space of retailing and catering. Its ghosts exorcized, it was reconsecrated as a temple to tourism, the new centrepiece of an area burned out by it.

Ruins

Guy Debord's *In girum imus nocte et consumimur igni* (1978) mourns Paris as a place entirely vanished: 'whatever others may wish to say about it, Paris no longer exists. The destruction of Paris is only one exemplary illustration of the fatal illness, which, at this moment, is carrying off all the major cities.' Back when Paris existed, it had 'a people which did not live on images' and 'the modern commodity had not yet come to show all that can be done to a street.'[28]

This idea of ruin is recurrent in psychogeographical writing, whether it is Jacques Reda's *The Ruins of Paris* (1977) or Patrick Wright's *A Journey Through Ruins: The Last Days of London* (1991, with its ironic dedication to Mrs Thatcher), or indeed the exacerbated sense of decay in Sinclair's work, as in his terminally titled *Lights Out for the Territory* of 1997.

There is an even more recurrent idea that is, I want to suggest, not unrelated. A common denominator between the esoteric and low aspects of place is that they tend to be little known, or in a sense 'secret', which is a favourite word of psychogeographers. Compare two recent books: Mark Manning writes of 'this secretive borough of Clerkenwell, that only reveals itself little by little over the years, with the poetry of its secret names, its silent courtyards, churches and hidden parts', while Bill Drummond writes of walking the outline of his name on the map:

> I was playing a private game with myself and my London A to Z. But the best thing about these walks was that they took you down streets, up alleys, across back gardens, over ditches that you would never normally have visited. You would discover things: shops,

> cafés, old saucepans, skips full of discarded treasure . . . and secret signs. The secret signs were always the best.[29]

This passion for the secret keeps psychogeographers off the tourist map. Louis Aragon writes in *Paris Peasant* (1926) of his dislike for Montparnasse and Montmartre. He preferred 'fringe' and 'equivocal' zones, where 'freedom and secrecy had the best chance of flourishing',[30] and he found his definitive site in a decayed and soon to be demolished Arcade, the Passage de l'Opéra, where he could exercise his rare talent for detecting what André Breton termed 'a sort of secret life of the city'.[31]

For the Surrealists, secrecy inevitably tended to be a form of eroticism, while in Situationist terms the idea of secrecy – as well as being congenial to Debord's paranoid grandiosity – has a more structural meaning as the opposite of the Spectacular. There is, however, a much simpler meaning of 'secret', because it has come to be a less trite and genteel synonym for 'unspoilt'.

'Unspoilt' took on its modern meaning around 1925, as a response to urban sprawl and tourism. It is a key word for understanding the twentieth century, with its assumption that places are ruined unless they are not. Bali has become something of a paradigm here. Alex Garland's bestselling novel *The Beach* (1996) featured the ruin of Thailand, with the season-by-season resortification of its beaches, and a group of people who are prepared to kill to keep a particular beach unknown. The notion of the secret has, of course, been recuperated to give guide books themselves an extra frisson, such as *City Secrets: London* and *Secret London*.[32]

The value of the urban secret changes from era to era. The great secret of the late nineteenth century was the extent of poverty and degradation, giving rise to revelatory books such as William Booth's *In Darkest London* (1880). But by the end of the hyper-transparent late twentieth century, the secret was positive, and it was desired as never before. This desire for secret places relates to perennial fantasies of places 'off the map', like De Quincey's London *terrae incognitae*, and of liminal zones and glimpsed paradises – in the fictions of Alain-Fournier, H. G. Wells and Arthur Machen, for example[33] – but it gains a new, belated urgency in over-developed, over-exposed millennial London:

> There are certain areas of London that I suspect retain their integrity and beauty only by becoming invisible. Threatened or abandoned, they fade slowly into an astral plane, an alternate universe

> where all the forgotten buildings and ruined architecture of the world still exist, still function, are still inhabited. Sometimes I think I have only to turn round suddenly at the right time to see an ectoplasmic Brookgate shimmering through all that glassy concrete Barbican stuck in its place.[34]

'Another of London's imagined nooks and corners', commented one reviewer, 'up Leather Lane and the fourth dimension on the right'.[35]

Hakim Bey has written lyrically in *Sacred Drift* of the desire for spaces off the map. 'If the modern world has been thoroughly *mapped*, nevertheless we now know that maps by definition cannot be accurate . . . because geography is *fractal* . . .'. We have to vanish into 'hidden fractal dimensions of the map of culture where the rational tyranny of Consensus and Information cannot penetrate'. For Bey, the traveller seeks 'the secret hidden spaces of real life, untouched by control and mediation, where the authentic and marvellous still flourish'.[36]

Bey's ideas of psychotopology, Temporary Autonomous Zones and nomadic drifting are recognizably built on Situationist ideas of psychogeography, 'situations' and the *dérive* (drift), pioneered by Chtcheglov and Debord as 'a technique of transient passage through varied ambiences'.[37] It has subsequently become a paradigm in French thought,[38] but on the street the *dérive* was an attempt to recover the unencompassable urban Sublime by becoming lost and disorientated, with the chance of finding unknown places.

It is harder to be lost now than it was when Walter Benjamin wrote: 'to lose one's way in a city, as one loses one's way in a forest, requires practice'.[39] Mobile phones offer 'FINDme', which will recognize your location anywhere in the country and provide information on services, leisure and tourism. And that is only option one: option two is McDonald's Locater Line: 'To find the location of your nearest McDonalds, key 1501'.

Chtcheglov wrote that 'A mental disease has swept the planet: banalization'. The relatively widespread fascination with psychogeography in the 1990s coincided with a perception of so-called dumbing down, which had its correlative in the urban landscape. Psychogeography, the gnosis of place, was the opposite of that dumbing down, and the palimpsests of secret knowledge written up by Sinclair and others were the opposite of banalization.

Virtually unchecked market forces have reduced London to a city of tourist spectacle. A few theme park sights ('What are the must-see sights in Great Britain?'[40]) are dotted through a giant service industry, which reached self-parody in the mid-1990s with the appearance of rickshaws on the West End streets.

Ambient zones of a kind not reducible to a few 'must-see sights' are particularly endangered. It would be no great loss if Shakespeare's Globe Theatre was crated up and reassembled in Austin, Texas, but the impending erasure of the second-hand book zone in Charing Cross Road, or the ambience of Pimlico Road (recently hit by its first Starbucks, and set for redevelopment) are devastating, like the loss of small Italian cafés such as Alfredo's or Boggi's. Cyber-flaneurs can find such cafés at www.classiccafes.com, a website that also offers a good resumé of psychogeography as it was up and running by 2000:

> Psycho-geography is the hidden landscape of atmospheres, histories, actions and characters which charge environments. The lost social ley-lines which make up the unconscious cultural contours of places. . . . With cafés, a sort of dowager atmosphere comes to the fore, apparently drably familiar yet full of secrets.

Time zones are a notable variety of endangered ambient zone: 'in the late Seventies the street had an air of the Forties, with an art-deco café and a non-art-deco café, a knock-down prices linen store and a bookshop which offered ear piercing'.[41]

Elusive temporal ambiences can still be found (in parts of Pimlico and Victoria, for example), but increasingly time zones survive only inside buildings. Roughly contemporary with Rodinsky's Room was Dennis Severs's celebrated time-warp house in Spitalfields – 'the secret house at 18 Folgate Street'– which has recently been the subject of an essay by Peter Ackroyd.[42]

Of course, there has always been resistance to change: as long ago as 1875 the Society for Photographing Old London was formed in response to the demolition of old buildings. Previous eras bemoaned the loss of major edifices, such as the Euston Arch in 1962, or the more widespread transition from nineteenth-century buildings to hotel and office tower blocks in the 1960s and '70s, which gave rise to books such as *Goodbye London* (1973). In contrast, the current banalization is less about great monuments or architecture than a more subtle and pervasive ecological loss of a whole texture at street level.

Plate glass, seen as a utopian possibility in the nineteenth century, was a dystopian reality by the end of the twentieth, when racking business rents favoured catering chains, bureaux de change and estate agencies.

Consider the area around the British Museum and former British Library, long associated with small oriental booksellers such as Luzac's ('with their latent mystery', says a mid-twentieth-century writer, 'as if they were the beginning of a story by Algernon Blackwood'[43]). It now features an American Express bureau de change, a TEFL college and a couple of souvenir shops. On the other side of Museum Street, opposite the museum, was an extraordinary shop selling conjuring paraphernalia. It is now a Starbucks.

Further back on New Oxford Street was a shop at no. 56 called Cuba, selling mid-century clothes – old Crombies, drape coats, silk scarves – with a wooden sign outside ('Estd 1985'). It is hard to believe anything even so modestly idiosyncratic and low-budget could ever have flourished there. No. 56 is now a bureau de change. Going eastwards, its near neighbours include a coffee chain and a sandwich chain. Crossing Coptic Street, an inoffensive restaurant is holding out on the corner, followed by a McDonalds, a plate-glass TEFL college and another plate-glass pizza house.

The Library itself has been decapitated from Bloomsbury and relocated to the relatively meaningless locale of Euston. Its Internet catalogue carries an ad from Amazon ('Buy great books at great prices: buy books NOW from our sponsors') and outside the Library is a statue of Blake's Newton – a negative figure in Blake's system, oddly enough, if anybody bothered to remember Blake – on a plinth bearing the proud legend: 'Grant aided by the Foundation for Sport and the Arts funded by subscriptions from the football pools Vernons Littlewoods Zetters'. No doubt that is what he is doing with those compass points: he is picking no-score draws.

Small flowerbeds in Islington are overshadowed by large unsightly signs announcing their sponsors. The slow death of quality public space, and the hyper-capitalized banalization of the cityscape, threatens to produce a psychic disinvestment in the street, conducive only to greater urban anomie. Nobody would walk for pleasure through a McDonald's landscape of proliferating estate agents, Kwik Foto developers, American college London programs, offices in the shells of former shops and endless plate-glass catering.

Since the 1980s there has been a concomitant rise of interest in private, controllable decors, such as interior design and city gardening. These autonomous zones are a dystopian fulfilment of Chtcheglov's vision that 'Everyone will live in his own personal cathedral, so to speak'. The aspirational magazine *World of Interiors* appeared in 1981, with 'tablescapes' and organic paint ('you can actually hear the difference'), presaging the decade that closed its doors on the outside world. The magazine's extraordinary success, unlikely a decade or two earlier, has been persuasively related to middle-class alienation.[44]

For those of us not in the market for organic paint, soundscapes – a portable and temporary ambience, not without a psychogeographical dimension[45] – were a less expensive alternative to an uncongenial environment, along with more specialized leaps into fetishism: 'All our paradises on Earth are becoming cluttered vacation centers . . . but there are still some nice labels left . . . It has come time for me to dive into this sardine can label.'[46]

Places change. But London is being razed by something more radical, in the erasure of place by 'space'. Overcrowding, property prices, cramped flats unsuited to 'clutter', and a not-unrelated fashion for minimalism all combined to make space an ascendant concept by the late 1990s ('Isn't space the ultimate luxury?'[47]). Place has meaning, but space is an interchangeable commodity.

As an assertion of history and memory, and of the value of ambience and atmosphere, the 1990s popularity of psychogeography was a last-ditch assertion of place against space. It often took refuge in interstitial zones of private meaning and esoteric knowledge, but it was at least an attempt to maintain a psychic investment in the street. It accompanied an alienation of an almost unprecedented kind from the built environment, responding to anxieties perhaps definitively expressed in Marc Augé's book *Non-places*.[48]

Augé critiques the global spread of the non-place, and suggests that contemporary life tends towards the condition of the corporate lobby, cafeteria or airport departure lounge. Three recent books, chosen almost at random, show how ambient this perception of erasure and ruin has become.

> . . . Nevsky Prospect, a street of ghosts if there ever was one. Jerome says that every city has its street of ghosts. Past the Stroganov Palace and the Kazan Cathedral. Past the Aeroflot offices, and the scrubby Armenian Café. Past the flat where I made love to my Politburo member. It's been turned into an American Express office now. All these new shops, Benetton, The Haagen-Daaz shop, Nike, Burger King, a shop that sells nothing but camera film and key-rings, another that sells Swatches and Rolexes. High streets are becoming the same all over the world, I suppose.

> I returned to Key West in 1991 . . . A high rise resort had replaced the Sands and the Half Shell [bar] had quadrupled to accommodate college kids who had made Key West a binge-drinking destination. . . . Mallory Square had become a honky-tonk of T-shirt shops and touts hawking time-shares and excursions to a dying reef. . . . At dinner, a man at the next table took a flash photograph of his entrée.
>
> . . . Six years later . . . Key West now had a Gap, Banana Republic, Planet Hollywood, and Hard Rock Café, with more mass market emporia promised, including a Hooters, with its franchised big-bosomed waitresses. . .

> . . . you've got to understand it's not just talk, we have action against all this shopping, all these yuppy bars, all that plate glass that's taking over most of Berlin right now.[49]

Of course, none of these places is London; but that, in a sense, is my point.

OCCULT LONDON

Roger Luckhurst

THE STERN MARXIST cultural critic Theodor Adorno judged the occult as 'the metaphysic of dunces'. Living in a world of alienated social relations, occultists lost themselves only in mystifications that came disguised as revelatory truths. They supernaturalized commodity fetishism – already a fairly magical thing in Marx's view. In that sense, their pursuit of arcane lore was a symptom of alienation rather than its cure: 'In pursuing yonder what they have lost, they encounter only the nothing they have.'

If Adorno was right, then the literary apprehension of contemporary London has been substantially given up to dunces. Consider: in Will Self's London, the dead spilled over from Crouch End in his early tale, 'The North London Book of the Dead' (1991), to occupy a variety of 'cystricts' in *How the Dead Live* (2000), from Dulston in the north-east to Dulburb in the south. In *Mother London* (1988), Michael Moorcock suggests that redemption for the traumatized city lies in a gaggle of telepaths, psychotically open to the lost voices of metropolitan history. Ghosts are inhumed in a Victorian terraced house in Michèle Roberts's *In the Red Kitchen* (1990). In M. John Harrison's gnostic novel, *The Course of the Heart* (1992), a seedy occultist living above the Atlantis Bookshop in Museum Street engages in elaborate rituals in anonymous north London houses, hoping for access to the plenitude of the 'pleroma'. His reluctant, psychically-damaged circle of initiates suffer punitive decades of haunting for their uncomprehending participation in these rites. The horror writers Christopher Fowler and Kim Newman have unleashed vampires, reanimated corpses, undead media executives and murderous secret societies onto the London streets. Marcello Truzzi notes that an important strand in occult belief is 'the inference of strange causalities among otherwise ordinary events'. The poet and novelist Iain Sinclair has some claim to be the laureate of London's strange causalities, unearthing hidden lines of force and conducting investigations into the marginal and the vanished through the language of occult conjuration and the seance. Sinclair intertwines his own project with a host of other psychogeographers of London's occluded meanings, from Aidan Dunn and Brian Catling to Rachel Lichtenstein and Stewart Home. And if we take the occult in a broader sense to refer to a hermeneutic whereby a hidden, esoteric meaning is extracted from an apparently banal, exoteric surface, then this list could be extended to Geoff Nicholson's *Bleeding London* (1997), Nicholas Royle's *Director's Cut* (2000) and China Miéville's *King Rat* (1998). These novels move through erotic mappings and deathly anti-mappings of the city, to significances generated from the tracing of London's disappeared cinemas, to a wholly other system of networks and rat-runs, hidden only inches away from the human dominion of the city. In Miéville's latest book, *Perdido Street Station* (2000), London is re-imagined as New Crobuzon, a metropolis of alchemy and magic populated by hybrid species living in uneasy proximity.

What is going on here? What is it about contemporary London that apparently defeats cognitive languages or proves resistant to Realist representation and thus encourages the occult imagination to flower? The most popular advocate of this occult London, Peter Ackroyd, has spent much of his career exploring the notion that the strange rhythms in London of time and space, of uncanny echo and elliptical encounter, are best articulated via tropes of the Gothic. This occult underside or disruptive inhabitant of Classical order and rational Enlightenment is schematically explored in his novel *Hawksmoor* (1985), where Wren's vision of light and order is shadowed by Dyer's hidden satanic meanings in his church designs. These playful possibilities become in *London: A Biography* (2000) a unitary method for apprehending a city resistant to History. London origins are lost in semi-mythical or visionary accounts, and historiography is further mocked by the patterns of disappearance and return that crumple linear time into repeating cycles or unpredictable arabesques. 'The nature of time in London is mysterious', Ackroyd claims, pointing to the 'territorial imperative or *genius loci*' that ensures certain zones retain their function across the centuries – not just the clusters of trades, but the homeless of St Giles, or the occultists of Seven Dials. These patterns exist 'beyond the reach of any plan or survey': we have to understand that 'the city itself remains magical; it is a mysterious, chaotic and irrational place which can be organised and controlled only by means of private ritual or public superstition'. The *spirit* of London survives the apocalyptic fires that periodically revisit it, and it will certainly outlast any of the passing political interventions dreamt up by the Westminster village. 'It does not respond to policy committees or to centralised planning. It would be easier to control the elements themselves', Ackroyd states in his conclusion, thus essentially naturalizing (or rather supernaturalizing) London 'muddle'.

One of Ackroyd's most attentive readers, Julian Wolfreys, suggests that London has invoked these tropes since the huge expansion of the metropolis in the nineteenth century. As the first megalopolis of the modern era, London becomes a sublime object that invokes awe and evades capture. The 'London-effect', for Wolfreys, is the sense that there is 'always a mysterious supplement that escapes signification'. Writers since Blake and Dickens have understood that London is not a Realist city but requires a writing that evokes 'the ineffability and lack which is always at the heart of London'. This 'crisis of representation' argument is regularly rehearsed in postmodern urban theory – although it is usually the sprawl of Los Angeles or the ribbon-developments of Phoenix that are the focus. If London is different, and conjures spectres in its 'crisis', it is because the creative destruction of its modernity is peculiarly hide-bound – haunted, one might say – by the ancient commands and ancestral inheritances that live on amidst the mirrored glass and cantilevered concrete. These traces, Wolfreys argues in *Writing London*, are 'spectral through and through: they are the marks of already retreating ghosts who disturb any certain perception we may think we have concerning the city's identity'. All this is finely evocative, but largely a commentary that repeats the tropes of these contemporary texts. Are we still amongst the dunces here?

There are two sets of resources that might give some justification for this outbreak of ghostly thought. The first appears from the work of the French philosopher Jacques Derrida, who has always been fascinated by the liminal position of the *revenant* as somewhere between life and death, presence and absence, material and ethereal existence. The *revenant* disrupts boundaries of time and space, and risks unravelling the confident demarcations of categorical thinking. Ontology, the philosophical study of being in the world, gets spooked: it becomes Hauntology. In *Spectres of Marx*, Derrida draws out the ethics of this ghostly encounter. Hamlet's father returns from the past, rendering 'time out of joint', to issue an impossible injunction to redress his wrong. For Derrida, this models our sense of obligation to bear witness to forebears, to listen out for their insistent ghostly presence rather than deny them. Some urban theorists have used Derrida's ideas to suggest that the city is similarly haunted by its previous incarnations. Indeed, the more indifferent to history the ruthless modern speculative transformation of city-space, the more likely it is, Anthony Vidler suggests, that 'the uncanny erupts in empty parking lots around abandoned or run-down shopping malls'. The uncanny or the 'unhomely', for Vidler, becomes 'a metaphor for a fundamentally unlivable modern condition' in advanced post-industrial cities. The literary fictions that conjure ghosts from contemporary London are therefore in some way seeking to revivify the pasts continually swept away in the ceaseless churning of London development and redevelopment. Only ghosts, after all, can walk through walls, breach the boundaries of the increasingly privatized zones of the city, and shimmer impossibly between past and present Londons.

A second resource derives from the long association of the metropolitan avant-garde with occult investigation. The Surrealists adopted the methods of the spiritualist trance-medium to unleash the revolutionary delirium of the unconscious. The city was explored in the same way: in André Breton's *Nadja* (1928), for instance, chance encounters and certain sites or zones of Paris become charged with occult significance. In direct descent from Surrealism, the Situationist International also reinvented the city through the *dérive*, a kind of delirious or drunken drifting that tore up the tyranny of the ordered and abstract space of the city planners. If the Surrealists or Situationists remained far too politically materialist ever to believe in the *substance* of occult belief, the avant-garde nevertheless ironically repeated certain organizational forms of the occultist world. The avant-garde promised secret or hidden knowledge to the committed adept. This knowledge, like occult beliefs, would shatter the oppressive banality of bourgeois society. And rather like secret societies, the history of the avant-garde is one of factions and expulsions, rivalries and violent arguments over possession of the 'true' road to revolution or revelation.

This helps to discern different aspects of the contemporary imagination of occult London. Ackroyd heads the list of those most invested in the idea of the city's collective memory as ghostly trace accessible to those who have become properly attuned. It is an unashamedly romantic view of the city, in the tradition of London essayists such as H. V. Morton and Arthur Machen. It was Machen, a Gothic novelist and chronicler of disappearing London, who anticipated Ackroyd by suggesting in *The*

London Adventure (1924) that the city was now the site of visionary promise – that the 'pleasant hills of Beulah' could be gleaned in Clapton or in chill, forgotten squares of down-at-heel Islington. The avant-garde mode of engagement with the city remains most evident in the work of Iain Sinclair and Stewart Home. Sinclair's *Downriver* (1991) constitutes an intensive investigation of the East End as a 'zone of disappearances, mysteries, conflicts'. Sinclair repeatedly uses the form of the seance in abandoned rooms or empty railway carriages to conjure lost voices, and his texts are fascinated by histories that have been marginalized or erased. At the same time, he is vitriolic about 'stinking heritage ghosts', myths sustained 'only to bleed the fund raisers' and mocks 'necrovestism: impersonating the dead, spook-speaking'. The ambiguity is deliberately nurtured, for if 'the occult logic of "market forces" dictated a new geography' of London, Sinclair implies his project is a necessary counter-conjuration, a protective hex against advancing armies of speculators and finance capitalists. Home's over-heated pulp fiction, *Come Before Christ and Murder Love* (1997), similarly uses images of sex magick rituals and occult mind control, but his fictions are written in the service of the Neoist avant-garde movement, which involves the mysterious activities of the London Psychogeographical Association. Occasional texts and manifestos emerge from the LPA. In one, 'Nazi Occultists Seize Omphalos', the election of a British National Party representative on the Isle of Dogs is attributed to the exercise of Enochian magic. The BNP have tapped into the ley line that runs between the Greenwich Observatory and Queen Mary College in Mile End. This line of occult force, the conspiratorial text informs us, has powered the formation of the British Empire, at least since John Dee's alchemical service to Elizabeth I. In *The House of Nine Squares* (1997), a set of letters and texts on Neoism, Home writes of his delight that the dead-pan missives of the London Psychogeographical Association have been mistaken as products of 'an occult group': 'This type of misunderstanding makes it much easier for us to realise our real aim of turning the bourgeoisie's weapons back against them', he writes. Home's use of occult tropes aims to generate confusion: it owes much, however, to the historical avant-garde's interest in the occult as a mode of resisting instrumental reason and the tyranny of planned space.

None of this really yet explains the sheer number of occult Londons in contemporary fiction, though. The metaphorics of the haunted city or the dialectics of a counter-occultism tend to use the very terms that most need interrogating. The more penetrating question is not how the discourse of the occult is used, but why it appears so amenable to so many current writers of different political and aesthetic persuasions. What might this be a symptom of? Some works offer themselves as symptomatic texts more easily than others – let's turn to two horror novels by Christopher Fowler as a means of advancing this argument.

In *Darkest Day* (1993), the ancient Whitstable family, the aristocratic 'backbone of England' and stalwarts of the Goldsmiths Guild in the City of London, begin to be killed off in elaborate ways. It transpires that the founding father of their modern wealth, James Makepeace Whitstable, had in 1888 constructed a murderous device to kill off any rivals to their financial empire. Whitstable's arcane knowledge combined the technical skill of the watchmaker with occult sciences learnt in India: his machine tracks the markets and then dispatches reanimated corpses as assassins. Age and damage have miscalibrated the machine, so turning it on its unknowing beneficiaries. When Fowler's detectives Bryant and May uncover the machine in a concealed sub-basement of the Guild, they knew 'they were looking at the cold damaged heart of the Whitstable empire, a manufactured embodiment of everything that had grown flawed and failed in imperialist England'.

Fowler's later novel *Disturbia* (1997) is similarly concerned with a murderous group operating from a privileged position in London. The language of the occult is less supernatural in this text and emphasizes rather the secrecy and growing occultation of the public sphere in London: 'Its keys are hidden because the key-holders are invisible to the public'. Fowler's plot involves a young wannabe journalist investigating the secretive right-wing League of Prometheus. Unmasked as an agitator, the League set him a challenge that pits his 'secret' knowledge of London against their networks of power and privilege. Vince's journey enables Fowler to entertain the reader with obscure and eccentric aspects of London history – a love of the local, preserved detail that ensures Vince survives the abstracted, panoptical control of London by the League.

Fowler's populist Gothic pits a young, mobile generation against the dead weight of inherited traditions. Hip, trashy and saturated with references to 1990s culture, Fowler nevertheless returns to an original impetus in earlier incarnations of the Gothic. The literary historian Chris Baldick regards the Gothic as an intrinsically modern form, a literature of nascent bourgeois democracies shivering with 'a fear of historical reversion; that is, of the nagging possibility that the despotisms buried by the modern age may yet prove to be undead'. The settings of the original Gothic were at the margins of Protestant Europe, where castles and monasteries condensed all the fears of feudal and Catholic tyranny. The Gothic imagination migrated from the wild margins to urban centres during the course of the nineteenth century – the same trajectory that brings Count Dracula from the Carpathian mountains to the populous streets of Piccadilly. This urbanization of the Gothic did not strip out anxieties of the pre-modern and the undead: it merely transposed them into an imperial centre that, although the epitome of Victorian modernity, was a place without overseeing regulative authority or political representation beyond the medieval bounds of the City of London. The scandal of corrupt vestries and the City's indifference to the poverty of the majority population drove much reformist politics and vengeful, Gothic-inflected fiction in the 1800s.

The most enduring images of Victorian Gothic London – Robert Louis Stevenson's *The Strange Case of Dr Jekyll and Mr Hyde* (1886), Oscar Wilde's *The Picture of Dorian Gray* (1891), Machen's *The Three Impostors* (1895) and Bram Stoker's *Dracula* (1897) – all relied on the horrors opened up by urban explorers into London slum land, Dante's City of Dis recreated in 'darkest England'. The same evidence contributed to the eventual formation of the London County Council in 1888 and the Fabian project of paternalistic municipal social engineering, as outlined in Sidney Webb's *London Programme* in 1891. This late Victorian Gothic, composed in the era of nascent London democracy, carried different valences. On the one hand, the heroic band of vampire-killers in *Dracula* rid London of the aristocratic Count and his decadent breed through their brisk middle-class professionalism and bureaucratic systems of recording and filing information – precisely the sort of positivistic enumeration of the city pursued by the first Progressive county council. On the other hand, Arthur Machen searched for an authentic hidden knowledge because, as he wrote in 1898, 'our age, which has vulgarised everything, has not spared the unseen world, and superstition, which was once both terrible and picturesque, is now thoroughly "democratised"'. For Machen, a decadent Gothic promised a return to mystery in a mapped, managed and demystified city.

Fowler embeds *Darkest Day* in this late Victorian moment – the fate of the Whitstables is cast in 1888 – but this is not simply homage to the golden age of the London Gothic. The Gothic, a literature reflecting on disturbances to political representation, found the conditions to prosper again in the era after the abolition of the GLC in 1986. The GLC had explicitly operated as a countermanding force against Westminster.

The executive simply wiped out a level of government associated with municipal socialism, replacing the functions of the GLC with some 270 quangos run by non-elected appointees. One historian of Thatcherism, Eric Evans, has argued that 'the absolute sovereignty of parliament had never in the twentieth century been so nakedly revealed during peacetime as during the debates over the abolition of the metropolitan authorities'. In Fowler's fiction, the Gothic basements of the medieval guilds still hold the machinery of power, and the proto-fascist League of Prometheus becomes resurgent under a government that 'provided all kinds of reciprocal benefits' between the old establishment and the new Thatcherites. This might also explain the imagery investing the most trenchant chapter in Sinclair's *Downriver*, 'The Isle of Doges (*Vat City Plc*)'. Here, Sinclair and friends attempt to penetrate the security cordon around the heart of the Docklands at Magnum Tower (Canary Wharf), a site now purchased by the Vatican, guarded by armed monks and the place of black magic rituals. Sinclair transposes the tyranny of one era onto another: the London Docklands Development Corporation – an 'enterprise zone' given freedom from all planning restrictions and any need to include social or infrastructural provision – is refracted through the eighteenth-century Gothic. The undead Widow that stalks *Downriver* may have finally been staked by her own party in 1990, but the farcical gerrymandering of London democracy by New Labour during the establishment of the Greater London Authority and the mayoral elections has surely provided sustenance for the continued popularity of the contemporary London Gothic.

Recent portrayals of occult London, I propose, are symptoms of stalled representative government. In its Gothic version, this genre imagines murderous despotism or incarnate evils still operating in the streets of London. In its more strictly magical version, it promises to uncover secret networks and avenues within the city. As the political public sphere contracts, these books trace a turn to an obsession with private rituals and hidden reserves of knowledge. They are symptomatic in this too because one might well want to read the occult as a *surrender* to the anti-democratic tenor of the times. How does the Sinclair in *Downriver* resist the invocations of the mad monks in the Magnum Tower? By a counter-conjuration that affirms a belief 'in some other reality, a place beyond this place'. How does Fowler imagine the future for Vince once he has defeated Sebastian, the head of the League of Prometheus? Only that Vince will take over the League, making it 'truly invisible again' and placing it back 'on the path to true power', 'doing pretty much what all government ministers did, only more so'. Are we so ground down by the repetitions of history that we can imagine no alternative to the occult exercise of power? Are we too ensconced in our books of *Hidden London*, *Vanishing London*, *Secret London*, *The London Nobody Knows* to notice just how easily the city has been taken from its citizens? And doesn't that make us all dunces?

GROUNDSWELL

Sarah Kent

THE AWARD CEREMONY for the Turner Prize of 2001 was hosted by Madonna. You couldn't wish for a clearer indication that, in Britain, contemporary art had attained celebrity status. Before handing over the cheque, the singer remarked that being an artist was about love rather than money. Did she mean that creativity stems from a love of one's medium or from a desire for adulation? Either way, her comment seemed naive, and, coming from a multi-millionaire business woman, somewhat disingenuous.

Perhaps she was acknowledging that, at £20,000, the prize is not financially very rewarding (other prizes are worth far more) and that its merit lies mainly in its prestige. Since 1991, Channel 4's sponsorship and coverage on prime-time television have guaranteed a large audience for the event and dramatically increased public awareness of contemporary art – so much so that, in the last few years, art has become almost a national obsession. In 1996, 56,000 people visited the Turner Prize exhibition at the Tate Gallery; three years later, when the inclusion of Tracey Emin's rumpled bed among the exhibits attracted both admiration and condemnation, the number more than doubled – to 120,000. Fine art is no longer perceived as an elitist practice, of interest only to the knowing or the moneyed few. Apparently more people now go to exhibitions than to football matches.

This represents an extraordinary reversal of public opinion. True that, for a few years in the mid-1960s, Pop and Op art enjoyed enormous popularity, and, on a small scale, the London art scene was vibrant. Attracted by David Hockney's gold lamé jacket and bleached hair – both deemed outrageous at the time – fashion magazines and colour supplements began photographing celebrities at gallery openings. In *Private View* (1965), a coffee-table portrait of the London art world by the photographer Lord Snowdon, this surge of activity prompted the critic John Russell to ask: 'Just what has turned London into one of the world's three great capitals of art?'[1]

With hindsight, his question seems to have been inspired more by optimism than actuality. The vitality encapsulated in *Private View* was short-lived; subsequent art movements such as Minimalism, Conceptualism, Performance and Installation art were soon to encounter outright hostility.

I remember in October 1976 a Sunday afternoon performance at the Serpentine Gallery by the Ting, Theatre of Mistakes. Enacted in silence, *Scenes at a Table* at first seemed like a meaningless game controlled by arbitrary rules. Started by an instigator chosen by the throw of a dice, an action was carried out on tiptoe until the discomfort became unbearable. The performer then 'swooned', only to be replaced by another. After a while, though, this mesmerizing exercise began to resemble normal social intercourse, in which people's allotted roles are performed according to agreed codes of conduct – and, therefore, to make horrible sense; but other members of the audience didn't see it that way.

Located in Hyde Park, at weekends the Serpentine attracts large numbers of casual visitors who rarely go to galleries; that Sunday the audience was impatient. The performers managed to incorporate into the show such comments as 'Silly' and 'What is it supposed to mean?'. Things were brought to an abrupt conclusion, though, by a man rushing onto the set yelling 'I'm sick of watching you, you pretentious creeps. I suppose you think this is a contribution to theatre.'[2]

Eventually, dismay at work that, to the uninitiated, seemed wilfully obscure or entirely devoid of talent resulted in what was tantamount to a declaration of war against the art establishment. Things came to a head in 1976, the year in which I became Visual Art Editor of *Time Out*.[3] National newspapers launched a series of campaigns designed to censor contemporary art by attacking the museums and galleries that supported it. When a reporter discovered that the Tate had bought a sculpture by the American Minimalist Carl Andre, consisting of fire bricks laid out on the floor in a rectangle, the media began a campaign of ridicule, demanding that no further public money be spent on contemporary art. The 'Tate bricks' soon became enshrined in the national consciousness as a symbol of the worthlessness of modern art and the gullibility of institutions that promoted it.

The consequences could have been serious and far reaching. With only a handful of dealers supporting new work, young artists were reliant for exhibitions on museums and public galleries such as the Institute of Contemporary Art (ICA), the Whitechapel and the Serpentine, but, because these venues were largely dependent on Government and Local Authority funding (business sponsorship, as yet, being almost unheard of), they were vulnerable to attack from those determined to undermine them.

In October 1976, the ICA exhibited Mary Kelly's *Post-Partum Document*, a Lacanian analysis of her relationship with her newborn son that included the infant's vests and nappies. The installation was pilloried by the press, and 'dirty nappies' soon attained the same mythic status as the 'Tate bricks'. Two months later, the ICA staged 'Prostitution', an exhibition about the sex industry by Coum Transmission (Genesis P. Orridge and Cosey Fanni Tutti), which included condoms and used Tampax alongside photographs of Cosey Fanni Tutti clad only in scanty underwear.

The Tory MP Nicholas Fairbairn seized the opportunity to demand that Government spending on the arts be stopped and that the Arts Council (the body responsible for channelling public funding) be disbanded. 'A shocked MP saw a porn-and-pop art show', wrote one newspaper, 'and demanded that the Arts Council be scrapped . . . Questions were asked in the Commons last night about why taxpayers' money was being squandered on such exhibitions.'[4] The campaign succeeded to the extent that, when the director Ted Little refused to close the exhibition, the Arts Council suspended the ICA's grant, so propelling it to the verge of bankruptcy.

'Make it a New Year resolution', I urged my readers, 'to write to your MP in support of the "Arts in Danger" campaign.'[5] ('Arts in Danger' was a national campaign formed to lobby Parliament for the appointment of a Minister without Portfolio for the Arts, an essential step towards official recognition and support for the arts.) Having been a practising artist, I was determined to bring about a change in public perception. Having run evening classes on contemporary art, I knew that even the most hardened sceptics could be won over by intelligent explanation and analysis. Firmly believing that I could achieve something comparable in print, I adopted my new role with proselytizing zeal. One of my first articles concluded with the stark observation that 'Britain is a cultural backwater. The sooner we admit it, the sooner something can be done.'[6] Three years later I added: 'we seriously under-rate our artists in this country even to the point of despising them.'[7]

'There is a standing joke in the London art world that to open a gallery here is the quickest route to bankruptcy', I wrote when, in 1977, Hester van Royen opened a small gallery in Covent Garden. 'There is money to be made in Old Masters, of course, but a gallery dealing in contemporary art can reckon on a lifespan of about five years unless they are propped up by wealthy backers.'[8]

Yet, by the early 1980s, the economic boom had temporarily swept scepticism under the carpet. A new breed of wealthy young buyers emerged, most of whom worked in the City and had cash to spare. A thriving market mainly for figurative painting developed and new galleries mushroomed. Nicola Jacobs and Anne Berthoud joined established galleries like Gimpel Fils, Marlborough and Waddington in the Bond Street area, Moira Kelly braved it alone in Islington and a cluster of young dealers including Robert Self, Anthony Stokes and Edward Totah joined Hester van Royen in Covent Garden. Over the next few years, the new galleries ensured that the commercial sector was the most vibrant aspect of London's art scene.

During the Thatcher era, money became the measure by which most things were judged, and, impressed by the prices being paid for artworks, magazines and colour supplements began to publish articles about the art market. These often emphasized the artist–gallery relationship, and were illustrated with photographs of artists posing with their dealers. Admiration was reserved for those doing well, though, and, since artworks were viewed essentially as commodities, only items commanding high prices were deemed to have value; suspicion was still aroused by any work that was not readily saleable.

As in the 1960s, though, the boom was short-lived. 'Black Monday' – 19 October 1987 – witnessed a huge fall on the stock market. Five years later, almost to the day, came 'Black Wednesday', when the pound fell to a record low. The art market was badly affected. Prices plummeted even for works by internationally renowned artists such as Julian Schnabel, Francesco Clemente and Georg Baselitz.

Only the more established commercial galleries managed to survive and, as newer and smaller galleries folded one after another, media cynicism resurfaced. Revealed to be an unstable investment, contemporary art was now accused of being a con foisted on the public by a powerful coterie of dealers, critics and curators. In reactionary quarters, the accusation still rumbles on and regularly surfaces even today.

The recession decimated the art market, but it also acted as a catalyst prompting artists to take the initiative. With the more adventurous commercial galleries closing and public spaces languishing for lack of funds, graduates had little chance of obtaining a show or finding a dealer. Empty factories, warehouses and shops were there for the asking, though; so were defunct schools, hospitals, office blocks and swimming pools, and artists seized the opportunity to organize group shows in unusual venues. This was not the first time that artists had taken matters into their own hands. In 1968, the painters Bridget Riley and Peter Sedgley had set up Space Ltd, a company dedicated to providing studio space for artists. Arranging short-term leases on disused buildings due for demolition, they were able to keep rents low. It was not long before the occupants began to open their studios to the public and set up galleries to hold group exhibitions. I remember a huge inflatable by Maurice Aegis floating on St Katharine's Dock to draw attention to the studios that were opening their doors to the public in this impressive warehouse complex a stone's throw from Tower Bridge.

Across the river was Butlers Wharf, another derelict warehouse divided into studios. The film-maker Derek Jarman shared the fifth floor with Andrew Logan; when I visited in January 1976, Logan was living there inside *The Alternative Tower of London*, a plaster castle that had once been the decor of Biba's children's department.[9] To keep warm, he sequestered himself inside a polythene enclosure heated by a paraffin stove. In the evenings, the castle yard became the venue for cabarets, discos and the annual 'Alternative Miss World Competition', compèred by Logan wearing a garment that was an evening dress and tuxedo combined. Most contestants were men dressed in costumes so flamboyant that the event soon attracted media coverage.

Having grown up during the Thatcher era, twenty years later art school graduates tended to be more worldly than their hippy forebears and, accordingly, their initiatives were more focused and more ambitious. Known as Young British Artists (YBAs), many of this generation now enjoy international recognition, but their first years out of college were characterized by hard work and a good deal of mutual support that was to prove invaluable.

'Freeze', an exhibition organized in 1988 by Damien Hirst to launch himself and fellow Goldsmiths graduates, has acquired mythic status. To finance his studies, Hirst worked three days a week at Anthony d'Offay's prestigious West End gallery, where he came into contact with work by international stars. 'Our art seemed a fuck of a lot more exciting', he recalls, but it was 'in desperate need of an audience.'[10]

Not content to wait, Hirst decided to take the initiative: 'There was no way that those students were all going to get exhibitions in London galleries when they left college. That gave me the incentive to find a building and do it.' He persuaded the Port of London Authority to lend an empty building in Docklands and raised money for a catalogue. The show opened in August when many were on holiday. Undaunted, Hirst dispatched taxis to pick up influential people and bring them to the exhibition, such as Norman Rosenthal from the Royal Academy and Nicholas Serota, Director of the Tate.

'Freeze' was just one of many exhibitions staged in industrial premises and other unusual venues. That same year, five artists turned City Racing, a disused betting shop near the Oval cricket ground, into a gallery where, over the next ten years, they established a serious following for exhibitions of themselves and their friends. BANK took its name from the former bank where the collective mounted its first show. After a nomadic period, they moved into an empty factory in Curtain Road, Hoxton, and invited others to join them in staging shows that featured bizarre elements such as a troop of cardboard horses galloping upside down across the ceiling.

Now a major venue for contemporary art, the Chisenhale Gallery in Bethnal Green was initially run by artists from the studios upstairs. Located in a studio block in Mile End, Matt's Gallery is also an established part of the east London art scene. It was the brainchild of Robin Klassnik; in 1979 he began inviting artists to show in his studio in London Fields and financed the exhibitions by teaching. Most memorable of the many impressive shows was an installation by Richard Wilson in 1987. He flooded the space with a lake of used sump oil whose black surface became a mirror that magically doubled its surroundings. *20/50* was later bought by Charles Saatchi and became a permanent installation in the gallery that he opened in a former paint factory in St John's Wood to show work from his large collection.

During the recession, raising money was especially difficult. Hirst persuaded Charles Saatchi who, at that time, was mainly collecting American art, to help fund 'Modern Medicine', a show mounted in April 1990 with the help of Carl Freedman and Billee Sellman in a derelict biscuit factory in Surrey Quays, Docklands. 'Gambler' followed in July. Hirst showed *A Thousand Years*, a sculpture consisting of two glass and steel chambers linked by holes cut in the glass divide.

'Bluebottles emerge from a box of hidden maggots', I wrote, 'and, attracted into the next space by a rotting cow's head, are randomly electrocuted by an insect-o-cutor. Corpses pile up, but many are maimed and die slowly. In warehouses and food stores such events are commonplace and unremarkable, but packaged as art and presented for contemplation, they take on sadistic overtones.'[11] Saatchi bought the sculpture and his passion for YBA art was born; over the next decade his support proved vital to the survival of this generation.

I'll never forget the sight of Karsten Schubert prancing up and down beside the glass, waiving his arms wildly and grinning each time the flies swarmed. The first dealer to exhibit 'Freeze' artists, he showed Gary Hume, Anya Gallaccio, Michael Landy and Abigail Lane in his Charlotte Street gallery. Later he was to go bankrupt when Rachel Whiteread quit his stable and moved to Anthony d'Offay.

Another key player was Jay Jopling. The friendship between the Old Etonian and Damien Hirst, the working-class lad from Liverpool, has become legendary. In 1991, Jopling persuaded Charles Saatchi to commission *The Physical Impossibility of Death in the Mind of Someone Living*, a shark suspended in a tank of formaldehyde that has since become an icon of YBA art. It formed the centrepiece of the first exhibition of 'Young British Artists' staged by Saatchi in his gallery. Attracting unprecedented media attention, the show gave the YBAS their name.

The predator also glided across the cover of *Shark Infested Waters*,[12] a book I wrote about YBA artists in the Saatchi collection. Over the next four years, six further YBA exhibitions established the importance both of this generation and of Saatchi's space, which was not only the most beautiful gallery in London, but the only venue in which YBA work was shown with a degree of commitment that put museums and public galleries to shame.

By 1993, artist-run spaces had become such an important part of the London art scene that *Time Out* introduced an 'alternative spaces' section in the listings; of the 53 galleries itemized that week, 19 were fringe venues.[13] Free from commercial constraints, the artists who ran them were limited only by their energy and imagination. As a result, they often staged the most innovative shows in London; they also changed the art-world map. Many were in the East End – around Brick Lane, Old Street, Hoxton and Bethnal Green – and foreign curators, collectors and critics were soon to be seen jetting by taxi between West End galleries and east London venues.

That same year Jay Jopling opened White Cube, a tiny gallery in Duke Street, St James's, just round the corner from the Royal Academy and from Sotheby's and Christie's. This astute move enabled him to introduce YBA art to wealthy foreign collectors and, during the next seven years, he concentrated on building an international reputation for such artists as Damien Hirst, Marc Quinn and Tracey Emin.

In April 2000, Jopling opened White Cube² in Hoxton Square, joining galleries such as the Approach, Maureen Paley, Anthony Wilkinson and Modern Art that had already established themselves alongside the alternative spaces. Victoria Miro soon followed; her move from Cork Street into a glorious warehouse near Old Street has given her the largest and most beautiful commercial gallery in London. With 25 venues listed in *East*, the east London gallery guide, the area boasts the largest concentration of galleries in the capital.

Art in London thrived in the 1990s because artists seized the initiative, sidestepped the establishment and promoted themselves. At first, they were operating in a financial vacuum and a hostile climate – in the early years, mine was often the only supportive voice. When enthusiastic young dealers and a major collector emerged to exhibit and foster the new work, however, the groundswell of excitement became so great that the cultural climate was transformed.

The unthinkable happened. No longer a provincial player overshadowed by New York, for the first time London became the internationally acknowledged art capital of the world. Public indifference and scorn gave way to grudging admiration, then to genuine respect. A nation of philistines, for whom denouncing art as a morally corrupting influence had been a favourite pastime, converted into art-world groupies. The climax came in the summer of 1997 with 'Sensation', an exhibition at the Royal Academy of Charles Saatchi's collection of YBA art. Attracting nearly 300,000 visitors, 80 per cent of whom were under 30, the show confirmed that Young British Artists had come of age and had been embraced by the establishment and the media. Tracey Emin, Damien Hirst and the Chapman brothers were among those accorded the status of pop stars; nowadays, scarcely a day goes by without a feature appearing on one of them in a magazine or national newspaper.

In January 2001, *Time Out* devoted the cover and eight feature pages to London's art scene. A few years earlier such a dedication of resources would have been unthinkable.[14] Ten months later, the *Evening Standard*, which gives two pages each week to Brian Sewell's fulminations against contemporary art, dedicated *ES* magazine to a sympathetic overview of London's art and artists.[15] How, though, had this remarkable transformation been achieved?

Although the Turner Prize undoubtedly contributed to this seismic shift in public perception, the opening of Tate Modern was a far more significant development. Given that even a small provincial town like Bilbao, in Spain, boasts a splendid art museum, the Guggenheim, it is extraordinary that, until 2000, there was no museum of modern art in London. The absence of an institution dedicated to international modernism made it easy for cynics to dismiss contemporary art as unworthy of official recognition and support.

The former Tate Gallery had had to perform a dual role – to house the national collections both of British and of twentieth-century art. When Nicholas Serota became director in 1988, finding a new home for the modern collection became his main priority. The plethora of alternative venues that had sprung up in London meant that, in the capital, industrial spaces had become almost synonymous with contemporary art, and most artists expressed a preference for converted industrial buildings over purpose-built museums.

A defunct power station on the south bank opposite St Paul's Cathedral was eventually chosen to house the new museum. Designed by Sir Giles Gilbert Scott, Bankside is a hulking brick structure dominated by a 325-foot (99 m) chimney.

The Swiss architects Herzog and de Meuron won the competition to convert the building with a plan that respected its industrial origins. Occupying nearly half the space, the former turbine hall measures an astonishing 500 feet long, 100 feet high and 75 feet wide (152 × 30 × 23 m). Light filters through the glazed roof and, with no views to the outside, there is nothing to distract one's eye from the cavernous splendour of an interior that resembles a vast, secular cathedral.

The 80,000-square-foot boiler house (7,432 sq. m) was converted into galleries occupying three floors overlooking the turbine hall. With white walls and light flooding in from windows and roof lights, these 82 rooms offer a calm setting for temporary exhibitions and the museum's collection of international modern art.

'I have to keep reminding myself that we're in England', remarked a friend at the opening in May 2000. The scale and ambition of the project felt so European that it was hard to grasp that a British institution had finally had the audacity to declare its belief in contemporary art – with such conviction.

The public responded with enormous enthusiasm. Despite the museum's location in Southwark, an impoverished borough that was hitherto a cultural backwater, during the first year more than five million visitors made their way to the refurbished power station, making it the most popular museum for contemporary art in the world. And despite the dramatic fall in visitor numbers suffered by most London museums after the terrorist attack in New York on 11 September 2001,

3,000 people a day visited the Andy Warhol retrospective, which opened the following February.

The opening of Tate Modern marked the end of an era, a decade in which most initiatives had come from below – from artists who, having lost patience with publicly funded galleries strapped for cash and with the few dealers still in business, took matters into their own hands.

The inauguration of the museum also coincided with the beginning of a new period of change. Once again, public spaces such as the Whitechapel and Serpentine Galleries are able to make an important contribution to London's cultural life. Lottery funding has enabled them to upgrade their galleries and corporate sponsorship has freed them from reliance on public funding. They can now stage first-class exhibitions of contemporary art without fear of reprisal and opprobrium.

The Royal Academy is also embarking on a new phase. It has acquired the former Museum of Mankind in Burlington Gardens and, when the refurbishment is completed in 2007, this will double their exhibition space. Despite fears of recession, the commercial sector is also thriving. London currently boasts more prestigious dealers in contemporary art than ever before.

At the same time, though, fringe venues are folding and young curators graduating from the new courses at Goldsmiths and the Royal College of Art have stolen a march on artists' initiatives. It remains to be seen whether these various factors will permit London's vitality as a centre for contemporary art to continue, or whether, inadvertently, the seeds of a new conservatism have been sewn.

The clearest indication that the end of an era had arrived was Charles Saatchi's decision to close his St John's Wood gallery, since, with the opening of Tate Modern, visitor numbers had dwindled sharply. In Spring 2003 he opened a new space in County Hall on the South Bank, halfway between Tate Modern and Tate Britain. The move is a bid to show YBA work to a much larger audience, but, since the new gallery has a largely retrospective role, it seems to be an acknowledgement that his pioneering role is no longer needed. After a decade during which the most vital initiatives emanated from alternative venues and the commercial sector, the establishment is, once again, asserting its importance.

LONDON IN THE EARLY 1990s

Patrick Keiller

IN THE AUTUMN OF 1989 I began to research an idea for a film about London, which was subsequently commissioned by the British Film Institute and photographed over a period of about ten months in 1992. The first print of the completed film, by then called *London*,[1] was delivered in January 1994, just in time for that year's Berlin Film Festival. It was well received in Berlin, and was released in the UK the following June, where it played in a succession of West End cinemas for most of the summer. For a film like this – without a visible cast, or even much of a narrative – to be even a minor box office proposition was extremely unusual, and its relative success was probably at least partly due to the possibility it offered audiences of finding aspects of their everyday experience represented in the cinema. The film opened at the Institute of Contemporary Arts, in the Mall, and departing audiences walked out of the cinema into the space of one of its sequences (the rehearsal for Trooping the Colour), which had been photographed from the ICA's balcony. The film set out to document, among other things, the 'decline' of London under the Tories, and it offered people the morale-boosting opportunity to share thoughts that had perhaps previously occurred to them only in isolation. As a portrait of the city, it was rather critical – in those days, Londoners were proud, not so much of London, but of themselves for putting up with its physical and other shortcomings. One would not be permitted to say such things today.

One of the starting points for the film was a passage from the memoirs of Alexander Herzen (1812–1870):

> There is no town in the world which is more adapted for training one away from people and training one into solitude than London. The manner of life, the distances, the climate, the very multitude of the population in which personality vanishes, all

> this together with the absence of Continental diversions conduces to the same effect. One who knows how to live alone has nothing to fear from the tedium of London. The life here, like the air here, is bad for the weak, for the frail, for one who seeks a prop outside himself, for one who seeks welcome, sympathy, attention; the moral lungs here must be as strong as the physical lungs, whose task it is to separate oxygen from the smoky fog. The masses are saved by battling for their daily bread, the commercial classes by their absorption in heaping up wealth, and all by the bustle of business; but nervous and romantic temperaments, fond of living among people, fond of intellectual sloth and of idly luxuriating in emotion, are bored to death here and fall into despair.[2]

This passage is part of Herzen's account of the period soon after his arrival in 1852, when London was physically very different from the city it is now (much more so than it was by, say, 1900), but it was easy to connect it with one's experience of London in the 1980s. Other people said similar things – I recall, for instance, Zaha Hadid's suggestion that London was a good place to work, because there were so few distractions.

The film took the form of a fictional journal (like Daniel Defoe's *Journal of the Plague Year* of 1721), an unnamed narrator's account of the project of his companion and ex-lover Robinson, a disenfranchised, would-be intellectual, petit bourgeois part-time lecturer at the 'University of Barking'. Robinson's project was a study of 'the problem of London', and the problem of London seemed to be, in essence, that it wasn't Paris. I had read up on the experiences of various nineteenth-century visitors from France, on the look out for further details of 'the absence of Continental diversions', and discovered Paul Verlaine's description of London as 'flat as a bed-bug, if bed-bugs were flat', and his suggestion that the way people drank in pubs confirmed the 'lamentable inferiority of Anglo-Saxons'.[3] Apollinaire's description of the south London suburbs, seen from the train, was of 'wounds bleeding in the fog'. Wilhelm Kostrowicki, before he became Apollinaire, had visited London twice in pursuit of a young woman called Annie Playden, whose family lived in Landor Road, SW9, and who soon afterwards emigrated to Texas, where she was discovered by academics in 1951, unaware of her rejected suitor's subsequent identity.[4] Reading Enid Starkie's biography,[5] I found that Arthur Rimbaud probably produced a good deal of his literary output in London (there are likely images of London in, for example, the *Illuminations* of 1872–3), and that his last address in England was not in Scarborough, as had been suggested, but in Reading. This became the starting point for a sequel to *London, Robinson in Space*,[6] in which Robinson is exiled to the English provinces.

Thus far, the film was a fairly Eurocentric, even Anglocentric project, which attempted to combine two strands of critical thinking. On one hand, there was what one might call the 'urban' literature of Edgar Allan Poe, Charles Baudelaire, Louis Aragon, Walter Benjamin and so on, which had become influential in architectural discourse during the 1970s and '80s, in the context of which London appeared to be a city where certain kinds of urban experience that one might see as characteristic of European cities were difficult, if not impossible, to find. On the other hand were the various 'declinist' scenarios of English capitalism, in particular the idea that England is a backward, failing economy because it has never had a successful bourgeois revolution, and that the City of London's dominance and priorities reinforce this failure. This view was fairly widespread at the time, and was attractive to people in the art and design professions since it offered an explanation (and, in the context of the political 'debate' about the UK's role in Europe, a cure) for the problematic nature of so many aspects of English visual and material culture – the UK's attitude to public space and cities, its apparent inability to produce adequately designed buildings, cars and other consumer goods; its unattractive food and problems with agriculture; the predicament of public services like education and transport; and a whole range of other features of everyday life that might be seen as consequences of laissez-faire.

Alongside these predictable concerns, however, was the awareness that Baudelaire, for instance, was just as fed up with the *quartier latin* as Robinson claimed to be with London. His problem was not really London, but 'The Great Malady, Horror of Home'.[7] Perhaps, one thought, this feeling of *restlessness*, that seemed to be so characteristic of life in London, was not really such a problem after all. Perhaps it was something to be valued. London might be uncomfortable to live in, but it avoided the more stupefying aspects of *dwelling* that a less spatially impoverished, more 'architectural' city might encourage. Perhaps London was even, despite its obvious anachronisms, rather modern. Even someone as narrow-minded as Robinson could hardly fail to notice the increasingly cosmopolitan make-up of its population.

Without ever really losing sight of its architectural and other preconceptions about London as a physical structure, and with occasional references to the life and work of Baudelaire[8] and Rimbaud, the film explored these ideas in various more or less convincing, sometimes rather touristic, ways, beginning with its narrator's introduction of himself as a returning seaman (albeit only a photographer on a cruise liner). Robinson's first fictional excursion (to Horace Walpole's Strawberry Hill in Twickenham) was provoked by the appearance of a non-fictional Portuguese driving school opposite his flat, one of several new undertakings in the neighbourhood that had accompanied the rapid expansion of the Portuguese community in south Lambeth after Portugal joined the European Union in 1987. By the river in Twickenham, near Alexander Pope's Grotto, the film's protagonists meet two Peruvian musicians, Aquiles and Carlos Justiniani, whose singing accompanied their walk downstream as far as Kew. Aquiles had been actually encountered busking with a colleague in Vauxhall Underground station, and we had arranged to include one of his recordings in the film.

Emerging from the arcades of Brixton market, where he had hoped to confirm a visit by Apollinaire in 1901, Robinson noticed a ship depicted on the sign of The Atlantic, the famous public house opposite, which enabled him to mention the arrival of post-war emigrants from Jamaica on the SS *Empire Windrush*, and the fact that they were initially housed in the deep (air raid) shelters under Clapham Common. There were similar episodes in cafés and restaurants in the neighbourhoods of Ealing Road, Wembley and Cranford, on the A4 near Heathrow, and a visit to Southall during Diwali. Amid the cultural diversity of Ridley Road market, in Dalston, Robinson 'became much happier and relaxed, and began to talk more positively about London's future' though his companion continued: 'I was not convinced by this: London has always struck me as a city full of interesting people most of whom, like Robinson, would prefer to be elsewhere.' This remark was based on the idea that the actual attainment of a cosmopolitan London was somehow restricted, despite the heterogeneity of its population, either by spatial characteristics – an emphasis on private, exclusive spaces, perhaps – or by something else. In an interview in Reece Auguiste's film *Twilight City* (Black Audio Film Collective, 1989), Paul Gilroy had spoken of 'an extraordinary change, in which people are able to inhabit the same space, to be physically proximate and yet to live in different worlds'. In the 1980s I had also become used to a characteristically London conversation in which the participants would share their longing to be somewhere else, with each party nostalgic for a different place – the Caribbean, southern Europe, or perhaps a different part of the UK – usually, though not always, somewhere the speaker might regard as *home*.

In the sequence after Ridley Road, Robinson 'discovers' Defoe's house in Stoke Newington, and London is revealed to him as a place of 'shipwreck, and the vision of Protestant isolation'. Soon after, during footage of the Notting Hill Carnival and the float of the Colombian Carnival Association, the narrator reads:

> He asked me if I found it strange that the largest street festival in Europe should take place in London, the most unsociable and reactionary of cities. I said that I didn't find it strange at all, for only in the most unsociable of cities would there be a space for it, and in any case, for many people London was not at all unsociable.[9]

The suggestion here, and elsewhere in the film, was that there is something about London, some 'absence', perhaps, that makes it easier than it might be elsewhere for incoming cultures to establish themselves, but that perhaps also limits the extent to which London's diverse cultures experience each other.

Towards the end of the film, Robinson makes his way along Fleet Street, where he has to be prevented from attacking the Lord Mayor during a parade, to the portico of the Royal Exchange, outside the Bank of England, where he declares: 'The true identity of London is in its *absence*. As a city, it no longer exists. In this alone it is truly modern: London was the first metropolis to disappear.' I had wondered if the last line of this rhetorical assertion might not exceed the terms of the character's licence, but it did seem to echo something about the state of London as an *idea*. Notions of absence, however, had been implicit in the project from its beginning, whether as 'the absence of Continental diversions', as the idea that London suffered, or benefited, from an absence of a (known) identity, or that its identity could be characterized as a sense of absence. Apart from these generalizations, there were a number of candidates for specific things that were absent – the memory of the historic centre, for instance, obscured by the increasing blandness of the spaces of the banking and finance industries, which had driven out most other forms of economic activity and were staffed to a great extent by commuters from outside London; the port, and its once-numerous shipping in the river. The absence of metropolitan government, of a credible London newspaper (the *Evening Standard* is read all over the South-East of England), even the lack of topographical logic in London's territorial subdivision into boroughs, all contributed to a sense that Londoners had only a very vague idea of what London was, or simply did not need to know. Perhaps London's economic dominance makes this unnecessary. In any case, people who have lived in London all their lives often have only a very limited knowledge of its topography. A good deal of the above can be dismissed as a feature of any large capital city, where the national often eclipses the civic, but anyone who has ever tried to buy a postcard of London will have noticed that it is a city that lacks a contemporary self-image.

Such images, in any case, have probably always been misleading. In the nineteenth century, London's population grew from about 860,000 in 1801 to 6.5 million in 1901. Although the children of Londoners stood a better chance of surviving than many elsewhere in the country, most of this increase was the result of in-migration either from the rest of the UK or abroad. Not only that, but many migrants did not stay in the city, so the actual extent of in-migration was even higher than the growth in the population suggests. A 'typical' Londoner of the nineteenth century might be imagined, not as a cab-driver or a publican, but as young, isolated, poor and newly arrived from somewhere else, probably more so than today. Even now, only in the 15–19-year age group is London's population actually increasing.[10]

Similar things can be said of other aspects of English culture. Leaving aside industrial items such as white bread, gin and sugar cubes, or niche-market regional revivals, whatever might amount to an 'English' cuisine, for instance, has been very hard to find since the decline in the agricultural workforce during the nineteenth and early twentieth centuries, or perhaps for even longer, since the establishment of national markets centred on London. Agricultural decline (which was one of the factors that drove migrants to London) was partly the result of importing cheaper food, often from Britain's colonies. At the same time, the cuisines of cultures colonized by the British and others began to find their way to Britain. The result is that the stereotype of unattractive 'British' food, which is still not difficult to find, contrasts with an enormous variety of imported and hybrid cuisines that is probably more extensive than that in other places where some kind of indigenous cuisine survives.

It is apparently an assumption of 'classical' economics that a nation, having established some comparative advantage in producing particular goods or services, should strive to import as much of the remainder of its material and other needs as possible. I came across this idea only recently and, to someone who can remember the 1960s, when there seemed to be a near-permanent balance of payments crisis, it came as something of a surprise. I had always thought that an industrial economy's success was more likely to be indicated by the volume and quality of its exports. Culturally, an unwillingness to make things might seem unattractive, but as an indicator of wealth, imports do make sense, given that, in the long run, they confirm the ability of the importing economy to generate the means to pay for them. A high level of imports might therefore be seen to indicate success, rather than failure, and certainly seems to have characterized the UK's economy for long enough for it to be regarded as traditional.

If the everyday experience of London in the early 1990s really was characterized by some more or less definable sense of *absence*, combined with an apparent comparative openness to incoming cultures, perhaps this has something to do with London's, or the UK's economy. In a recent essay,[11] the film historian Paul Dave referred to the film *London* in the context of Ellen Meiksins Wood's book *The Pristine Culture of Capitalism* (1991). In the context of the various declinist scenarios of post-war British economic history, Wood asks the question: 'Is Britain, then, a peculiar capitalism or is it peculiarly capitalist?' and argues that it is the latter. She also offers an explanation for what sounds rather like Robinson's 'problem of London':

> What American tourists today think of as the characteristically 'European' charm of the major Continental cities – the cafés, the fountains, the craftsmanship, the particular uses of public space – owes much to the legacy of burgherdom and urban patriciates . . . This kind of urban culture was overtaken very early in England by the growth of the national market centred in London . . . Today's urban landscape in Britain – the undistinguished modern architecture, the neglect of public services and amenities from the arts to transportation, the general seediness – is not an invention of Thatcherism alone but belongs to a longer pattern of capitalist development and the commodification of all social goods, just as the civic pride of Continental capitals owes as much to the traditions of burgher luxury and absolutist ostentation as to the values of modern urbanism and advanced welfare capitalism.[12]

This statement locates the origin of London's 'absence of Continental diversions' in the sixteenth and early seventeenth centuries, at the time that the English began to colonize other parts of the world, and it is not difficult to see a propensity for colonization in 'the commodification of all social goods', as Robinson Crusoe and his contemporaries in the sugar-growing business amply demonstrated. The urban landscape that Wood describes, which is particularly typical of London, can be seen as the current manifestation of a quality that has endured through pre-colonial, colonial and post-colonial periods.

What is particularly intriguing about London in 2003, rather than in 1992, is that the post-colonial, cosmopolitan make-up of its population is juxtaposed with a physical form that, while it largely remains in the dilapidated condition to which Wood alludes, is increasingly the subject of initiatives by people who might be construed as members of a previously absent 'burgherdom', whose aim is to make urban experience in London more like that of a certain kind of European city. Examples of this tendency might include Lord Rogers's Urban Task Force, various projects of the Architecture Foundation, the riba's award of its Gold Medal to the city of Barcelona in 1999, and the creation of new and successful public buildings and other spaces, such as Tate Modern, the London Eye and the central London riverside generally.

One wonders if the culture that Wood describes, which seems to be very much a characteristic of the era of colonization, might be changing. Latterday burgherdom has emerged in the context of an economy that, while it shows few signs of becoming a European-style social democracy, is now inevitably more closely linked to that of mainland Europe than for several centuries. The call for an urban revival, for example, is underpinned by the idea that, in order to maintain its appeal to the international financial sector, London needs to upgrade its amenities to the level of more civilized European cities. Generally speaking, this project is largely, though not exclusively, the province of a white, well-heeled middle or even ruling (if not exactly *upper*) class, but it does, arguably, represent a commitment to the kind of public and other spaces in which London's potential to become a genuinely cosmopolitan city might be realized.

At the same time 'regeneration' is both accompanied by and accomplished through the 'discovery' of previously overlooked value in neighbourhoods and property often occupied by the people most characteristic of this cosmopolitan city, who are usually among the first to be pushed out when 'regeneration' occurs and values rise. This point is frequently made, but a more fundamental question might be whether the cultural diversity and richness of old-fashioned, hard-faced London – the London of 'capitalist development and the commodification of all social goods', which is the economic reality from which the present-day post-colonial city has emerged – are actually opposed by the economic and cultural changes that the current attempts at quasi-European make-over arguably exemplify.

If cultural diversity and richness are synonyms for poverty, as to some extent they are, they are almost certainly threatened. In post-regeneration London, for example, the frequently ensuing sterility is perhaps not so much a question of culture as of residential densities. Wealthy, childless couples living in 300-square-metre riverside lofts are unlikely to generate anything like the street life of a community of immigrant families with children, each living in a single room. Diversity and richness, however, will survive in other neighbourhoods. In any case, it is not certain that the make-over, such as it is, is European in character. The pavement cafés of post-1994 London seem to have arrived, not from Europe, but via North America. The evolution of London's population, too, increasingly polarized between extremes of rich and poor, more closely resembles that of North American cities than anything in Europe.

London in 2003 certainly seems to be a more enjoyable place than it was in 1992, in all sorts of ways, but physically it has not changed anything like as much as its stock of recently-built public buildings might suggest. One of the more striking aspects of the cities of present-day mature economies is how, in the twentieth century, they changed, physically, much less than they might have been expected to at the beginning of the century. Cities now often evolve in ways that involve social change and subjectivity rather more than actual physical alteration. Much of London's physical fabric is older than that of many other cities in Europe, and older than that of much of the rest of the UK. New built environments are usually less socially and economically diverse than older urban fabric, so perhaps the fluidity of London's population is encouraged by this physical stasis, but at a price, since it condemns thousands, if not millions of people to live in unusually impoverished physical surroundings, both public and private. If London really is more open to new possibilities of various kinds than other cities whose urbanism is more conventionally European, its physical shortcomings soon restrict their impact on the general condition of the city. In the long run, London's economy is becoming increasingly specialized (in finance and administration). In this, as so often in the UK and presumably elsewhere, life in London seems to be characterized by predicaments in which a 'yes' is followed by a 'but'.

IMAGINARY LANDSCAPES, JUMBLED TOPOGRAPHIES: CINEMATIC LONDON

Pamela Church Gibson

AN ASSERTION THAT cinema, since its inception, 'has been constantly fascinated with the representation of the distinctive spaces, lifestyles and human conditions of the city' appears on the first page of a recent collection of essays, *Cinema and the City*.[1] Interestingly, however, the films that the editors describe as configuring 'London' belong to the past – the 1930s films of Hitchcock, the 1940s oeuvre of David Lean. Only one essay on contemporary London cinema is included, Mike Mason's consideration of Mike Leigh's *Naked* (1993), where the author describes the 'typically postmodern cliché', the 'shorthand' for urban decay, that since the 1960s has characterized social realism within British cinema and television drama – the 'non-naturalistic use of light', the smoke, distressed brickwork, burnt-out cars and 'inevitably, graffiti'.[2]

While this particular cinematic configuration of 'London' continues to appear on the screen, some of the earlier ones have been absorbed within contemporary cinema: for instance, the documentary work of Humphrey Jennings and Alberto Cavalcanti has fed into this later tradition of gritty realism, while the unproblematic, even nostalgic vision of London seen in the Ealing comedies of the 1950s appears to have resurfaced in a new form in the films discussed in the second half of this article. Other images of London seem simply to have disappeared – the triumphalist visions that characterized the 1960s, for instance.

There is, of course, one real difficulty with 'London' as a backdrop and setting, something that seems to have been overlooked: unlike Manhattan, Paris or Rome, central London has no coherent geographical centre or urban grid to provide a compact cine-location. There is yet another problem, similarly ignored: how can the many cinematic genres that originated in the traditions of different countries and cultures be relocated within the sprawling, amorphous, geography of contemporary

London? Bhabha makes it clear that any film-maker who attempts to re-create contemporary London cannot do so without noting the 'marginal, oblique gaze of its post-colonial migrant populations'.[3]

This essay will argue that, while independent film-makers or those on the margins may be mindful of this pertinent warning, and even seek to make this text explicit in their films, most directors within the cinematic mainstream – and those who meet with most commercial success – ignore it completely. Rather, they depict different fantasy Londons, which may evoke not only the 'upbeat' and highly selective representations of much earlier films, but even the London of tourist-board documentaries and Pathé Pictorials.

In the cinematic versions of 'London' constructed during the last twenty years, many films have sought to present differing types of realism. While some have received critical acclaim, many struggle to find distribution outside the metropolis – and few reap financial benefits. However, the highly popular 'heritage' films of the 1980s were reinvented as 'London' films in the very next decade. The original 'heritage' films, often literary adaptations, were characterized by lovingly-recreated period detail and lush settings, best epitomized in the work of Merchant Ivory. In the 1990s, their appeal was given a contemporary, metropolitan twist, the *mise-en-scène* and milieu reworked and modernized within a series of London-based romantic comedies. These particular films display a 'London' that is often difficult to recognize and, significantly, three of them – *Four Weddings and a Funeral* (1994), *Notting Hill* (1999) and *Bridget Jones's Diary* (2001) – are the most financially successful British films ever made. A fourth film, *Sliding Doors* (1997), while not a comedy, will be considered in conjunction with this worrying trilogy for its construction and deployment of metropolitan settings.

The opening years of the period under scrutiny in *Cinema and the City* were, of course, dominated by the aftermath of confrontation. While the Labour Government was still struggling to survive and the punk movement taking shape, Margaret Thatcher quietly took over the Tory party. In 1979, a year after the release of *Jubilee*, often described as 'the first punk movie', she became Prime Minister. So began thirteen years of radical, transformative government – Thatcher was in her own way just as nihilistic as Johnny Rotten.

Jubilee (1978) was the second feature film made by Derek Jarman – sometimes called the 'punk director' – and here he chose the capital as setting. In a near future, murderous girl gangs roam London and assassinate the Queen, while her namesake, Elizabeth I, is transported through time to see what has become of the city that became so powerful during her reign. Of the 'official' London, capital city and seat of government, we see Buckingham Palace and Westminster Cathedral, both hijacked – the first a recording studio, the second a disco. There is a shot of the Albert Hall and a close-up of the Albert Memorial; otherwise, London is presented as a vista of empty warehouses and decaying, half-empty terraced dwellings, interspersed by huge stretches of wasteland and illuminated by constant fires.

Jarman wanted to make a contemporary work that would re-create in a cinematic form his particular personal interpretation of the later allegorical poems of William Blake to whom, in an early note, he dedicated the film.[4] He wished to follow what he perceived to be the structure of Blake's later poems 'in which the hero or heroine dream themselves into a transfigured landscape, where they meet figures who embody psychic states'.[5] While the film shows us an 'imaginary landscape', there is nevertheless a real sense of 'place', provided through the nature of the location shooting. Jarman did his filming in Southwark, Rotherhithe and Deptford. The abandoned warehouses were a significant portent of the 'real' future and would be depicted, in their subsequent reconfigurations, in the cinema of the subsequent twenty years.

But it is also a 'jumbled topography' – there is no other 'London' apart from the monumental buildings and the Thames-side dereliction. Jarman's dark fantasies, however, were curiously prophetic – not always in the way he envisioned. The bonfires that he filmed were sometimes those lit by property developers, waiting to make use of the area. And, of course, in the 1980s the 'rotting estates, closed shops, and boarded windows'[6] would disappear, to be replaced by that symbol of Thatcherite Britain, the Docklands' enterprise zone.

Jubilee could be seen as an indirect inspiration for one dominant strand in the film-making of the next two decades, the depiction of London as a disintegrating, often oppressive, post-imperial capital. Jarman himself would return to the Docklands in his anti-Thatcherite allegory, *The Last of England* (1987). Other film-makers, taking more conventional narrative routes, have tried to provide a more 'realistic' portrayal of city-in-crisis.

This striving has provided a certain thematic unity within the curiously uneven collection of films that constitute the British cinema of the last twenty years. Here, at the de-romanticized end of the spectrum, there are differing depictions of 'London' where we are made aware that the more fortunate manage to make a living, others try, simply, to survive – and the dispossessed and alienated roam by night. One of the bleakest such offerings, *Nil by Mouth* (1998), is also one of the most recent: it examines domestic misery, wife-beating and heroin addiction on a relentlessly run-down south London estate. Other films within this strand are not as uncompromisingly wretched, for the carnivalesque aspects found in *Jubilee*, the polymorphous pleasures of the disco, the energy of the characters and the music itself, have influenced many subsequent 'London' films.

A handful of the films in this category are written or directed, or both, by those from ethnic minorities. In *My Beautiful Launderette* (1985), the first film written by Hanif Kureishi and directed by Stephen Frears, the central relationship is a gay liaison between a white youth who once belonged to the National Front and his English-born Pakistani friend. Their second film, *Sammy and Rosie Get Laid* (1987), is set in the less salubrious parts of Notting Hill – the northernmost areas, nearer to Kensal Rise than Kensington Gardens. It is in this area that Asian accountant Sammy and white social worker Rosie have chosen to live. To emphasize the dereliction, corruption and racism of the inner city, the film opens with a police raid that causes the accidental shooting of a 50-year-old black woman, and shows the riots that follow, while in the closing moments, bulldozers destroy a New Age encampment under the Westway. Throughout, there are establishing shots of the Trellick Tower, which, rather than Big Ben, is used for the first time as an emblem of post-imperial London. But Sammy's description of the pleasures of London life lapses into middle-class self-parody – the couple are seen visiting the Royal Court Theatre, watching alternative cabaret, and finally listening to Colin McCabe's lecture on structuralism at the ICA. *London Kills Me* (1991), Kureishi's second attempt to show the 'real' Notting Hill, with an authentically wasted young hero trying to give up 'this sick life' of dealing, doorway-sleeping and squat-dwelling, was both uneven and unpopular.

Less critically successful than early-period Kureishi, but equally determined to show London as a culturally diverse environment, was Isaac Julien's *Young Soul Rebels* (1991), set in south London in 1977, where two young black 'soulies' try to set up a radio station. Julian Henriques's film *Babymother* (1998), with an all-black cast, is also more upbeat – we see the heroine's relatively successful attempts to break out of the restrictions imposed by her life as a single mother in Harlesden. And other, better-known films – by film-makers from Mike Leigh to Michael Winterbottom – are set in geographically-specific, easily recognizable and realistically-presented areas of London. Yet this particular cinematic London – where people live, work and sleep in doorways – is not destined for significant commercial success; that is reserved for a fantasy London.

The romantic comedies sired by the heritage industry have, of course, their aberrant and powerful siblings – the dreadful fabrications that could be called 'gangsta heritage'. This tranche of films was spawned by the commercial triumph of *Lock, Stock and Two Smoking Barrels* (1998), the first feature written and directed by Guy Ritchie, which shows off a London of 'geezers' and gangsters that is – quite literally at times – sepia-tinted, that is as synthetic as a stage set. The topography here – a spit-and-sawdust pub, a porn baron's office, a large cannabis plantation housed in a disused building, the empty and picturesque East End streets – is as carefully contrived and as artificially constructed as the London of the 'contemporary heritage' comedy. This topography is gender-specific, created as a space of traditional masculinity, imbued by a nostalgic vision of unreconstructed working-class man, whom this film and the later templates wish to re-establish and celebrate. The 'lad' is the emotional epicentre of this film and its sequel, *Snatch* (2000).

The Long Good Friday (1979) – both politically hard-hitting and well made, unlike its bastard offspring – was, nevertheless, the start of the particular trajectory that culminated in this latest crop of gangster films. Made a year after *Jubilee*, it is in its own, different way equally prescient. Bob Hoskins plays a leading London 'villain', who wants to build an Olympic stadium in Docklands and heads an 'unsavoury consortium', with a corrupt councillor and a Detective-Inspector on its payroll; he hopes to persuade the American Mafia to join him, and two of their members have come to investigate. At a party on his yacht, he makes a speech welcoming his transatlantic guests. He concludes:

> No other city has in its centre such an opportunity for profitable progress . . . acre after acre and mile after mile of land for future developments. So it's important that the right people mastermind this new London.

As he begins this speech, his head and shoulders are perfectly framed by Tower Bridge, symbol of the 'old' London, in cinema and elsewhere. The sequence ends with a long shot of the huge white yacht as it sails past the deserted dockyards and idle cranes. But storm clouds are gathering behind the buildings – and the IRA begin their punishment of Hoskins with a series of explosions and murders. He is unaware of who they are or what they want; in fact, without his knowledge or consent, two of his henchmen have become involved with them and, subsequently, double-crossed them. A security guard working for his consortium is found crucified, nailed to the floor of a warehouse loft, that symbol of the coming decade, now ready for its conversion into one of the expensive dockside flats that would come to symbolize the London of the 1980s.

The IRA sabotage all Hoskins's grandiose schemes. 'It's my manor', he roars despairingly, when confronted by the evidence of their involvement. 'Not any more, it isn't', the corrupt Inspector tells him. 'They've taken it away from you.' As the Americans leave England, horrified by what they describe as a 'banana republic', the traditional London 'villain' is vanquished – he is bundled into his own car by IRA gunmen and driven away, the last shots showing us his baffled face framed in the window.

A sentimentalized desire for the 'manor' to return to local ownership was resurrected during the next two decades – a strange offshoot of the xenophobia of Thatcherism. Hoskins reprised his role as a dispossessed 'villain' bemused by rapid and inexplicable change in *Mona Lisa* (1986), while *The Krays* (Peter Medak, 1987) was a seminal part of this process. This film consciously used the mythology that had grown up around these two criminals, making of them likeable lads, local heroes. It is this particular seam of nostalgia that Ritchie has mined to such effect, and, moreover, his sentimental vision of Cockney criminal London is highly acceptable to an American audience. Indeed, his first film was so popular in the United States that Brad Pitt offered to waive his usual fees for the chance to appear in *Snatch*.

The most effortlessly exportable cinematic landscape, however, is the gentrified London of the four profitable romances. These films are specifically tailored to attract their transatlantic audience. In the opening moments of *Notting Hill*, Hugh Grant refers in his voice-over to 'the Cookie Monster' – a creature alien to Britain – and all four films star American actresses. Bob Hoskins tried to woo the Mafia with promises of the future; these film-makers are wiser. They know that all we have to peddle is our past, and that we must make the 'present' as picturesque as any period drama: sweep the streets, find photogenic houses and stylish interiors, and show the Thames and its bridges in panoramic shots. The Albert Bridge, in fact, plays a cameo role in *Sliding Doors*. The compassionate might call these films 'urban fairy tales', as does Robert Murphy in a recent article. But Murphy should not be so lenient – nor exclude Bridget Jones, a Cinderella if ever there was one.[7] These films are a part of the flourishing heritage industry, just as surely as any theme park.

Although they may ostensibly be set in 'the present', they have little to do with it.

The London shown in this cinematic quartet is a strange one. The educated middle classes predominate, and there are few people over the age of 40. Older, more humble denizens are seen in public spaces, but they are always white. In the entire cycle, there are two glimpses of Afro-Caribbean men, in crowd scenes, while a black woman is employed as a receptionist and an Asian man is seen dining in an expensive restaurant. The central characters – youngish, affluent, most of them decorative – usually know one another from school or university. Deviation from this socio-economic norm provides comedy – the working-class Welsh lodger in *Notting Hill*, for instance. Even he, with no means of support, is able to live in Grant's three-storey house in the salubrious heart of Notting Hill.

Although 'William Thacker' (Grant) owns a bookshop, he tells us that he has very few customers. But at least William has a job – the similar character that Grant plays in *Four Weddings and a Funeral* (1994) does nothing at all, except on Saturdays, when he goes to weddings. Outside the hotels, restaurants and attractively-presented houses where so much of the action takes place, everything is clean and contrived. There are red buses everywhere, just as in British films of the 1950s. The single Tube train seen in the films, needed to provide the plot device that generates the twin narratives of *Sliding Doors*, bears no resemblance whatsoever to any Tube train currently in use. Shiny and gleaming, free from graffiti and virtually empty, no Big Mac boxes or Tango cans could ever sully its seats, no copies of *The Sun* be left on its floors.

Seemingly, London exists to facilitate social life, both in the public arena and the private sphere. Some of the characters certainly have jobs and are even glimpsed at work – although they may be spectacularly inept. But social activities are far more time-consuming and important, together with the search for romantic fulfilment. Yet all the protagonists possess beautifully-furnished houses, many worthy of a double-page spread in a Sunday supplement. We even see that singularly Manhattan symbol of achievement, the multiple dog-walker, in *Notting Hill*. It is only Bridget Jones's small, cosy flat that contains elderly furniture – surely to emphasize her Cinderella status. Elsewhere in *Bridget Jones's Diary*, Hugh Grant, who now plays against type – he's not the hapless hero but the classic cad – provides a geographical link with earlier London films. This cad lives in a huge, terrifyingly stylish loft – in a converted dockside warehouse.

The profits made by *Four Weddings and a Funeral* – and its unprecedented reception in America – showed that this highly selective presentation of London and its inhabitants constituted a winning formula. Many of those associated with the first film also worked on *Notting Hill* and later *Bridget Jones's Diary*: the scriptwriter, Richard Curtis, the producer, Duncan Kenworthy, and, of course, Grant. There are other ways in which the first two films are linked. Each has at its centre a group of close friends ranged around the bumbling hero. One of his friends in the first film is Tom, the 'seventh richest man in England', while the second group includes Bernie, an incompetent stockbroker who is eventually sacked, and Tim, whose restaurant goes bankrupt. If the English have to grow up and get jobs, it seems, they don't always do them very well – in both movies, an American heroine eventually rescues the drifting hero from his own ineptitude.

But it is the settings that are the most notable feature of these two films. In *Four Weddings*, the weddings themselves are held in increasingly photogenic churches and lavish hotels. The funeral is held in a squat, ugly church in Thurrock on a rainy day – the grim surroundings, the glimpses of a council estate and the Essex mudflats could be read as reinforcing the voyeuristic visual pleasures provided by the other settings. In *Notting Hill*, the heroine, Anna (Julia Roberts), just happens to be the most famous film star in the world – so when the camera isn't gloating over the highly photogenic southern reaches of Notting Hill and a sunlit Portobello market strangely devoid of crowds, it can track around the interiors of the Savoy, the Ritz and the ultra-chic Hempel. The hero's own 'Notting Hill' is, as he explains, 'a small village in the middle of London . . . what's great is that lots of friends have ended up in this area'. Indeed they have – and enchanted by this elegant village and its locked, private gardens, Anna turns her back on Beverly Hills.

The third Kenworthy-Curtis-Grant collaboration is potentially the most interesting. *Bridget Jones's Diary* is a bestselling novel that is extremely accurate about the workplaces it depicts, the area where Bridget lives (Notting Hill, again) and her circle of friends. Alas, in the film the friends are sidelined and the workplace scenes cut back. The topography of the film is bizarre: Bridget, played by the American actress Renee Zellweger, seems at first to be living in The Borough, an area that is becoming increasingly fashionable. We see an early exterior shot of the building where she lives, while she is shown walking through Borough Market and crossing Tower Bridge on her way to work. In the last sequence of the film, however, when her own Mr Darcy, her Prince Charming, her rich saviour, leaves her flat after reading the revelations in her diary, she chases after him down the street. It is late evening – her front door now, inexplicably, opens onto the broad thoroughfares of the City, where snow is falling gently and has carpeted the pavements of the Square Mile. Explanations are forthcoming and, as they embrace, the camera pulls back to show us the closing image – snow-clad streets and brightly-lit shops. It is an image of London similar to that sometimes found on cheap Christmas cards.

Sliding Doors is not intended as a comedy. It is based on an ingenious idea – a central conceit of two possible narratives, which run concurrently. Unfortunately, the concept is more interesting than its execution. The characters are two-dimensional, the settings overly picturesque. Yet it is these qualities that made the film popular, and that link it with the trilogy created by Curtis. Helen, the heroine, is fired from her job in PR. She sets off homewards on the Underground – but the Tube doors close just as she runs on to the platform. The film then rewinds, revealing what would have happened had she managed to catch the train. The twin stories run throughout – and both resolutions take place in the emergency ward of a hospital. Yet despite accident, miscarriage, even death itself, the film functions as fantasy, as mild melodrama. There are scenes on and under the Albert Bridge, rowers on the Thames, meals in expensive restaurants. The film uses London, its inhabitants and its settings, just as selectively as the Curtis-Grant trilogy.

'Fairy tales' are harmless – but these are pernicious myths, tainted offerings. Their appeal is not that they are simple romances; it lies in their 'aspirational' qualities, their presentation of class and ambience. In the current climate, and in a damaged Britain, they are dangerous. It is as if both types of cinema reflect the seemingly irreparable fissures in the social fabric, the increasing gulf between those who have the freedom of gentrified London and those condemned to remain where they are. Maybe only an atypical documentary like Patrick Keiller's *London* (1994) can properly present this problematic city. It may open with a sighting of Tower Bridge, but there are also shots of Neasden, Heathrow and McDonald's, and mention of Rimbaud and Verlaine, Sterne and Pope. We see Bangladeshi children playing in a City square and Diwali celebrated in the hinterlands of west London. London, with what Keiller's narrator calls its 'fake traditions … its Irish war … and its secrecy', has a complexity difficult to configure in cinema.

Feature film-makers find it difficult – and it's not usually profitable to do so. Keiller's most recent film, *The Dilapidated Dwelling* (2000), has yet to be screened outside a conference circuit. Yet, oddly, one of the atypical commercial successes within British cinema has been a very different sort of comedy. It is romantic in its own way, with its heroine a Punjabi Sikh girl, living in Hounslow, whose life is dominated by her passion for football – and later, for the trainer of the Hounslow Harriers. In the cast of *Bend It Like Beckham* (2002) there are no megastars – only the footballer himself, making a one-minute cameo appearance at his own request. Gurinder Chadha, the director, shot the film on the streets of Southall, where she herself grew up. The film may be a light comedy, but the plot line is structured around the tensions between the older members of the Sikh community, their desire to preserve tradition, and their children, far more assimilated and often with differing demands. Its settings are recognizable, and many of the unknowns within the cast utterly convincing. *Sight and Sound* described it as 'a breezily unpretentious crowdpleaser', another symptom of the British film industry's 'insistence on making commercially viable, audience-friendly fare'.[8] Yet this is, nevertheless, a film by a second-generation immigrant woman film-maker – and it doesn't show us, thankfully, a group of moneyed upper-middle-class young people in pursuit of love.

However, it may be a brief blip – *Bridget Jones: The Edge of Reason* is currently being filmed. Perhaps this glimpse of multi-ethnic working-class London was just tokenism. And as for those who try to film London in different, demanding, innovative ways – from Jarman to Keiller, these directors have struggled hard for funding and for a wider screening of their films. Those who provide the money prefer to be on safe ground; they will perhaps fork out for the presentation of a grim London represented by the Trellick Tower, but they much prefer the certainty and charm of the Albert Bridge.

CRIME AND MEMORY IN THE CAPITAL

Robert Mighall

. . . know-nothings asked if the Queen Mum had snuffed it . . .
Iain Sinclair, covering Ronnie Kray's funeral[1]

I'm a businessman . . . with a sense of history. And I'm also a Londoner.
Harold Shand in *The Long Good Friday*, 1979

WHAT HAS CHARACTERIZED criminality in London in the years since 1979? Statistics imply a general pre-eminence in the number of reported crimes when compared with other parts of Great Britain, but they do not identify any crimes peculiar to the capital. Gun incidents have rocketed during this period. But most incidents (especially the more dramatic shoot-outs) are generally related to gang territory battles, and are certainly not confined to London (where gun crime currently accounts for only 0.3 per cent of its total recorded crime). Manchester, Liverpool and the West Midlands have more than their fair share of shootings, and the drug and prostitution rackets that generally fuel these incidents. Strathclyde is acknowledged as the murder capital of Britain, with a homicide rate higher than that of Greater London. Newcastle upon Tyne led the ram-raiding rage of the late 1980s and early 1990s. It is now a journalistic truism that London is more dangerous than New York, a consequence of New York cleaning up and London catching up. Whatever the truth, France has more guns in circulation than the UK, whilst to introduce a wholly subjective note, I don't think that London – or at least central London – has anything to compare with the Forum des Halles in Paris of an evening for sinister dodginess and imminent menace.

As regards sensational or notorious crimes during the period, London must concede a loss to the provinces. As if to mark the start of this shift, the arrest in 1981 of the Yorkshire Ripper Peter Sutcliffe saw him stealing the mantle from London's most notorious operator, Jack the Ripper; whilst two decades later Dr Harold Shipman re-scripted Jekyll in Hyde (Greater Manchester) by setting up shop as Britain's most prolific serial killer in this small Northern town. A rural surgery or the quiet terrace in Gloucester where Fred and Rose West tortured and murdered their victims now appear more representative venues for infamy than the crowded, CCTV-surveyed streets of the capital. The two American-style gun-massacres that took place in this period both occurred in rural idylls, Hungerford in 1987 and Dunblane in 1996. Brixton and Broadwater may loom large in the history of civic disorder, but race riots currently look set to become a Northern phenomenon. By comparison with events in Bradford, the annual May Day skirmishes in central London assume a somewhat sanctioned aspect, an alternative Lord Mayor's parade or a trooping of the anarchist colours, part of the pageantry of a city whose streets provide performative spaces for innumerable historical cycles.

What then characterizes criminality as a peculiarly London phenomenon during this period, beyond volume and a relative falling off of notoriety? The implied Orwellian lament for the capital's decline in the fine art of infamy perhaps points to an answer. For the awareness of, if not an obsession with, the annals of London criminality is in itself indicative of what perhaps best characterized the last two-and-a-half decades. Historical legacy, and the way that it structures our understanding and experience of London, has perhaps become the dominant characteristic of London criminality as a phenomenon during this period, and is perhaps at its zenith at time of writing.

I must immediately distinguish between 'reality' and representation here. The grim reality of street crime, mobile-phone theft amongst teenagers or the turf wars of Turkish or Albanian gangs in north London, or by Yardies in the west or south, have little legatary connection beyond personal, national or familial memories, or the legacy of decades of social deprivation in certain parts of the capital. The style, cultural references and affinities that accompany many of these sub-cultures are located elsewhere, in an actual or spiritual homeland, such as Kingston, Jamaica, or Compton, Los Angeles. Strictly Gangsta, with no more connection to London's home-grown gangster tradition than Ron and Reg Kray had with the cinematic Chicago hoods they styled themselves on. But much of our understanding of London criminality – or of London as a criminal space – is refracted through a historical lens, perpetuating various overlapping mythologies that inform our interaction with the modern capital. London is a criminal city less by virtue of what occurs there, than by how it is perceived, represented and experienced. Criminality as I am describing it here is not merely the counter-cultural opposite of the 'official' London of tourism or New Labour propaganda. It is an important ingredient in the idea of London, and informs our cultural maps of the capital in which we live today.

The following pages will explore this phenomenon and discuss how it has come to dominate London criminality since the late 1970s. My methodology can be loosely defined as cultural history, drawing connections between phenomena within diverse realms of experience. Emboldened by the pairing of Punk and Blair in the title of this book, I will look to cinema, literature and fashion as much as to macro-political trends to take soundings of London's criminality in this period.

London has been transformed in the decades since Margaret Thatcher came to power in 1979, with the most significant changes taking place in the East End. The Docklands experiment has opened up and transformed parts of the capital that had hitherto remained *terra incognita* for many Londoners, but which despite gentrification still retain a dark allure that inevitability encourages the epithet 'Dickensian'. And while this fits with the Tory paradox of economic modernism twinned with an advocacy of mythical 'Victorian values' and 'heritage', the supposed sophistication and apparent aesthetic modernism of the New Labour years have done nothing to diminish the role of dark heritage in defining the imaginative topography of modern London. Indeed, it is in the years since 1997, when Tony Blair became prime minister, that the process I am describing has gathered most momentum, and our obsession with London's criminal legacy has crystallized into highly visible representational forms.

One index to this process is provided by considering successive editions of the *Time Out Guide to London*, which describes itself as 'the ultimate insider's guide'. The edition of 1990 explored London by area, carving up the capital into The West End, The City, The River and Docklands, Local London and Ethnic London. 'Local London' means the 'villages' in the west and north, and ventures no further east than Islington. 'Ethnic London' mentions Clerkenwell ('Little Italy'), while Spitalfields serves for the whole East End, identified by its Bangladeshi community. It was not until 1994 that the East End became an 'area' in the *Guide*, and then for a mere two-and-a-third pages.

It may be that I am perpetuating what I purport to describe by dissecting the coverage of the East End in an essay on criminality in

London. But this insider's guide provides a useful indication of how criminal legacy – one of the dominant ideas associated with the East End – informs our 'map' of London as a whole, and how gentrification and criminal mythology are complicit phenomena. For the extension of the *Time Out* scope of interest eastwards is bound up with a preoccupation with the dark legacies of the area. In 1995 the East End got a full six pages. This included a two-page inset entitled 'Ripping Yarns', which chronicled crime in the area over the last 200 years, and some contemporary black-and-white photographs of sinister Whitechapel alleyways that appear unchanged since the Ripper stalked the manor. This piece sets the tone of much of the guide's passage east, with Jack as the *genius loci* for an area that 'For centuries has been associated with crime'.[2]

The lure of the East increases with each successive edition. Whilst in 1994 Whitechapel was 'unlovely', by 1997 the East had become a place for 'Sightseeing' (six pages), with Whitechapel 'offer[ing] extra rewards for those prepared to put in the legwork'.[3] Still a bit beyond the pale, but of interest to the truly adventurous, who might visit the Blind Beggar 'best known for its criminal connections', or venture to Wood's Buildings where Jack the Ripper 'claimed his first victim'.[4] By 2001 London appears to have doubled in size, because Mile End, Bow and Stratford get a whole section, as does Walthamstow, Leyton and even 'Further East'. Brick Lane is now 'hip', Smithfield is 'the Soho of the East', whilst Hoxton and Shoreditch are 'achingly trendy'. Crime looms ever larger, increasing in representational importance as gentrification or 'trendidom' sends it skulking to the suburbs. The edition of 2001 also includes an inset entitled 'Crime Time', carrying a famous picture of the Krays as local heroes of Bethnal Green. This mini essay purports to bemoan the glamour surrounding the Twins, reminding us that 'what these cheeky cockney chappies were getting up to wasn't really that nice. At all',[5] whilst devoting two pages to their legacy in the area. It even suggests a swift pint in the Blind Beggar, or a fully-fledged Krayland pub crawl. Other areas with criminal histories also start to complete the expanding map of London portrayed in *Time Out*. St Giles near New Oxford Street, the site of the most famous 'rookery' (or criminal colony) of all – which still boasts a thriving crack and smack fraternity to update its Gin Lane traditions – is noticed for the first time this year, despite having been *Time Out*'s neighbour for the last twenty years. The Borough, 'discovered' by Guy Ritchie's film *Lock, Stock and Two Smoking Barrels* (1998), and formerly the site of a criminal sanctuary called The Mint, provides 'a taste of London unlike any other',[6] and is given a section of its own, whereas before it had scarcely a paragraph.

Remember this is not a psychogeography, but an official guide to the London of 'now'. What I am suggesting by plotting the discovery of the East and other areas rich in criminal associations by *Time Out* is that 'hip' and dodgy, 'Dickensian' and des res are complicit phenomena, and that a spoonful of Ripper or Ronnie helps the loft price to go up. Crime affects house prices in the capital, but differently depending on whether you are in Camberwell or Clerkenwell, Green Lanes or Brick Lane. Iain Sinclair, perhaps the most perceptive archaeologist of London's mythical layerings, points to this when he observes how the publication of Peter Ackroyd's novels – which weave sinister mythologies around what have recently become the most desirable parts of London, Spitalfields (1985), Clerkenwell (1993), The Borough (1982) and Limehouse (1994) – 'have a prophetic influence on estate agents'. As he observes, following *The House of Doctor Dee* (1993), which Ackroyd re-locates in Clerkenwell, 'property values rocketed . . . Sharp developers should snap up proof copies of future Ackroyd fictions'.[7] Similarly, until 1997 Jacob's Island (near Rotherhithe) existed only in the pages of history and Charles Dickens's *Oliver Twist* (1837–9), where its extraordinary tangled and isolated geography made it the perfect spot for Fagin to hide out following Bill Sikes's murder of Nancy. This crime- and disease-infested rookery was all but eradicated from the late nineteenth century, and for almost a hundred years its memory was kept alive by Dickensians and the conductors of river tours who pointed it out as they passed by its former site. In 1997 'Jacob's Island' was resurrected as a luxury riverside development on what had once been described as 'the Venice of drains'. Luxury and luridness make perfect bedfellows in postmodern London. In 1998 a hotel where rooms currently cost up to £495 a night opened up in a small alleyway in West Smithfield very close to where Dickens had situated Fagin's first lair, and which had been a notorious criminal colony second only to St Giles since the eighteenth century. It is called 'The Rookery', and makes as much of its criminal associations in its promotional literature as it does of its handiness for the City and the vibrancy of this 'Soho of the East'. Finally, Bluegate Fields, a tiny area tucked between Cable Street and the notorious Ratcliffe Highway, was the site of London's most famous opium den, as frequented by Oscar Wilde's Dorian Gray. By the 1890s it had actually ceased to exist, but like Jacob's Island it returned in the form of a desirable development called Bluegate Mews in 1999.

What all this adds up to is the impression that London is haunted by criminal legacy. A rich seam of heritage has been increasingly mined during this period (with film, fiction, criminal biography and fashion playing a major role here), and now shows through like the reclaimed brick on a Shoreditch loft. Whilst the reality of crime changed in the last quarter of the twentieth century – with drugs and international organized crime bringing about the greatest changes in how and where crime affects the capital – more interesting still is the way that criminality has become part of the capital's heritage industry, offering selected mythologies for cultural consumption and perpetuation.

It is perhaps no accident that the decade that witnessed the accelerated gentrification of former no-go or no-interest areas also saw an avalanche of London-based gangster films and a deluge of criminal biographies. As an expert on the former observes: 'in the four years between April 1997 and April 2001 at least twenty-four British underworld films were released, more than were released in the twenty years before 1997'.[8] What became the *Lock, Stock*–in-trade of a group of directors, producers and actors was effectively the visual coalescence of a mythical version of Englishness (specifically London-ness), as coherent and distinctive as that of the Merchant Ivory stable from the previous decade. Ritchie merely gave mainstream exposure to a repertory of clichés, styles and mythologies that had been quietly thriving within cults and sub-cultures for nearly three decades: at least since the incarceration of the Krays (1969) and the release of *Performance* (1970), a film that, according to Colin MacCabe, 'standardised representation of London crime' through its assemblage of linguistic and ritualistic mannerisms that are now completely clichéd.[9]

The criminal biography industry, and the literalization of the conceit of the criminal as 'performer' in the media antics of the likes of Dave Courtney and Mad Frankie Fraser, reinforces the role that nostalgia and heritage play in informing the representation of London criminality. *Mad Frank's London* (2001) is partly an elegy for a vanished London: 'You try and find Rillington Place where Christie killed the women. The authorities got sensitive and simply changed the name'.[10] Shameful. Therefore, 'I thought I'd put down the real names and the places where me and others have been over the years and what we did there before everything is forgotten.'[11] Little chance of that at present, as Crims large and small prove that the pen is mightier or more profitable than the machete by adding to this endless stream of golden recollections.

The dominant trait in much of what I am describing is a studied anachronism. The Krays' official biographer and dissector of their *Cult of Violence* provides some useful signposts here. Pearson's book details the way in which Reg Kray invented the panoply of 'old East-End underworld' funereal observances (including horse-drawn gun carriage and Spitfire salute) that turned his twin brother's state send-off in 1995 into the 'greatest funeral seen in London since . . . the funeral of Ron's old hero, Winston Churchill';[12] and how for us now the public image of the Krays 'remained frozen in the 1960s', immortalized by David Bailey's lens. As Pearson suggests, the Krays were anachronisms even before the prison doors sealed their time capsule, styling themselves on cinematic versions of the Chicago of yesteryear, and building an empire around the cult of their violent personalities. Their fiefdom would have soon perished in the decades that followed, where international drug or people trafficking and large-scale white-collar fraud would have put their little-Englander affinities and adherence to the *ig-noblesse oblige* of a 'manor' starkly into perspective. Their legend sets the anachronistic tenor of criminal representation. Thus Iain Sinclair observes how 'youngsters aping [the Kray's] dress code and hairstyles, thought they were contemporaneous with Jack the Ripper'.[13] Guy Ritchie's London underworld, as depicted in *Lock, Stock and Two Smoking Barrels* and *Snatch* (2000), is set in a style more than any specific calendar time, but placed in London – Clerkenwell, Bethnal Green and The Borough – to be precise, locations where the frisson of heritage dodginess signals their desirability for a generation caught up in a perpetual cycle of culty retro-commodification. The latest manifestation of this tendency is a computer game. *The Getaway* (launched at Christmas 2002) features 20 miles of digitally reproduced London streetscape. Aficionados remark on its extraordinary realism – more of an interactive movie than a game – and the intense identification encouraged with the central character, who drives around London hijacking cars and arbitrarily wasting passers-by. The main Firm wear Reg-ulation geezer suits, are headed by a grotesque Mr Big, and hang out in a dodgy East End warehouse, which in reality would have been divided into luxury flats long ago. Whilst some of the narratives do at least acknowledge the existence of Yardies and Triads (who feature as baddies out to get our old-school gangster hero), this hyper 'realistic' game perpetuates the anachronistic, but now standardized, version of the metropolitan crimescape, in which players can now go on a virtual spree.

London is a big city, and my criminal walking tour has perhaps distorted the true picture of crime in Greater London, by focusing on the cobbled narrow passages and neglecting the anonymous suburbs or the corporations who commit real crimes on vast scales. But the vastness and the anonymity of much of the crime that occurs in the capital make capturing it difficult and representing it unsatisfying. So it is those cobbled passageways, where lads can re-enact their favourite Vinnie Jones's scenes, or where Ripper tours or Mad Frank himself perform their own mystery cycles on these theatrical spaces, that now best exemplify London criminality.

REFERENCES

ETHNICITY/IDENTITY

Katie Wales: 'London and Language'

Ackroyd, Peter, *London: The Biography* (London, 2000)
John, Ayto, *Twentieth Century Words* (Oxford, 1999)
Barr, Ann, and Peter York, *The Official Sloane Ranger Handbook* (London, 1982)
Coggle, Paul, *Do You Speak Estuary?* (London, 1993)
Foulkes, Paul, and Gerard Docherty, *Urban Voices: Accent Studies in the British Isles* (London, 1999)
Gould, P., and R. White, *Mental Maps* (Harmondsworth, 1974)
Humphries, Steve, and John Taylor, *The Making of Modern London, 1945–1985* (London, 1986)
Jackson, Peter, *Maps of Meaning: An Introduction to Cultural Geography* (London, 1989)
Lillo, Antonio, 'The Rhyming Slang of the Junkie', *English Today*, xvii/2 (2001), pp. 39–50
McArthur, Tom, ed., *The Oxford Companion to the English Language* (Oxford, 1992)
Rampton, Ben, *Crossing: Language and Ethnicity among Adolescents* (London, 1995)
Rosen, Harold, and Tony Burgess, *The Languages and Dialects of London Schoolchildren* (London, 1980)
Rosewarne, David, 'Estuary English – Tomorrow's RP?', *English Today*, x/1 (1994), pp. 3–8
Salverda, Reinier, 'Multilingualism in Metropolitan London', *English Today*, xviii/1 (2002), pp. 17–24
Wales, Katie, 'Royalese: The Rise and Fall of the Queen's English', *English Today*, x/3 (1994), pp. 3–10
__, 'Your Average Generalizations', in *Historical Pragmatics*, ed. A. Jucker (Amsterdam, 1996), pp. 309–28
—, 'North and South: An English Linguistic Divide?', *English Today*, xvi/1 (2000), pp. 4–15
Wells, John, *Accents of English*, vol. ii (Cambridge, 1982)

Jenny Bavidge and Andrew Gibson: 'The Metropolitan Playground: London's Children'

Ackroyd, Peter, *London: The Biography* (London, 2000)
Aitken, Stuart, *Putting Children in Their Place* (Washington, DC, 1994)
Bachelard, Gaston, *The Poetics of Space*, trans. Maria Jolas (Boston, 1969)
Benjamin, Walter, *Das Passagen-Werk* (Frankfurt am Main, 1990)
Borden, Ian, *Skateboarding, Space and the City: Architecture and the Body* (Oxford, 2001)
Certeau, Michel de, *The Practice of Everyday Life* (Berkeley, 1988)
James, Allison, Chris Jenks and Allen Prout, *Theorising Childhood* (Cambridge, 1998)
Jenkins, Henry, '"Complete Freedom of Movement": Video Games as Gendered Play Spaces', in *From Barbie to Mortal Kombat: Gender and Computer Games*, ed. Justine Cassell and Henry Jenkins (Cambridge, MA, 1998), pp. 262–97
John, Mike, 'The Power of London', *Thrasher*, VI/12 (December 1989)
Mayhew, Henry, *London Labour and the London Poor*, 4 vols, 2nd edn (London, 1861–2)
Moorcock, Michael, *Mother London* (London, 1988)
Office of the Children's Rights Commissioner for London, *Sort It Out! Children and Young People's Ideas for Building a Better London* (London, 2001)
Pullman, Philip, *Northern Lights* (London, 1995)
Rowling, J. K., *Harry Potter and the Philosopher's Stone* (London, 1997)
Smith, Tori, '"A Grand Work of Noble Conception": The Victoria Memorial and Imperial London', in *Imperial Cities: Landscape, Display and Identity*, ed. Felix Driver and David Gilbert (Manchester, 1999), pp. 21–39
Valentine, Gill, *Children's Geographies* (London, 1998)
—, 'Angels and Devils: Moral Landscapes of Childhood', *Environment and Planning D: Society and Space*, XIV (1996), pp. 581–99
Ward, Colin, *The Child in the City*, new edn (London, 1990)

Mark W. Turner: 'Gay London'

1 Michael O'Pray, *Derek Jarman: Dreams of England* (London, 1996), p. 159.
2 Derek Jarman, *At Your Own Risk: A Saint's Testament* (New York, 1993), p. 95.
3 O'Pray, *Derek Jarman*, p. 158.
4 Jarman, *At Your Own Risk*, p. 95.
5 London Gay Workshops Collective, *Building the London Gay Community* (London, 1982), p. 3.
6 Kath Weston, 'Get Thee to a Big City: Sexual Imaginary and the Great Gay Migration', *GLQ: A Journal of Lesbian and Gay Studies*, II (1995), p. 257.
7 Alay Brayne, 'The Big City Ghetto', *Gay Times*, 77 (1985), p. 37.
8 Brian Kennedy, 'The Gay Life', in *Kennedy's Gay Guide to London 1987*, ed. Brian Kennedy (London, 1987), n.p.
9 Rose Collis, 'Lesbian London', in *Kennedy's Gay Guide to London 1987*, ed. Brian Kennedy (London, 1987), n.p.
10 *Ibid.*

11 Frank Mort, *Cultures of Consumption: Masculinities and Social Space in Late Twentieth-Century Britain* (London, 1996), p. 166.
12 *Ibid.*, p. 165.
13 Chris Woods, *State of the Queer Nation: A Critique of Gay and Lesbian Politics in 1990s Britain* (London, 1995), p. 43.
14 Paul Burston, *Queens' Country: A Tour Around the Gay Ghettos, Queer Spots and Camp Sights of Britain* (London, 1998), p. 192.
15 Mort, *Cultures of Consumption*, p. 164.
16 Quoted in *Gay Times*, 249 (1999), p. 59.
17 Vicky Powell, 'Never Forget', *Gay Times*, 249 (1999), p. 8.

Panikos Panayi: 'Cosmopolis: London's Ethnic Minorities'

1 I would like to thank Mundeep Deogan for reading a first draft of this essay.
2 Panikos Panayi, *Immigration, Ethnicity and Racism in Britain, 1815–1945* (Manchester, 1994), p. 53.
3 Panikos Panayi, *German Immigrants in Britain during the Nineteenth Century* (Oxford, 1995).
4 Panayi, *Immigration*, p. 55.
5 The most significant black population emerged during the eighteenth century as a result of the Atlantic slave trade. See, for instance, Peter Fryer, *Staying Power: The History of Black People in Britain* (London, 1984), pp. 44–236.
6 Panikos Panayi, 'The Evolution of British Immigration Policy', in *Einwanderungsland Bundesrepublik Deutschland in der Europäischen Union*, ed. Albrecht Weber (Osnabrück, 1997), pp. 131–7.
7 This article went to press before the publication of the full results of the 2001 census.
8 Marian Storkey, Jackie Maguire and Rob Lewis, *Cosmopolitan London: Past, Present and Future* (London, 1997), p. 16.
9 See Tony Kusher and Katherine Knox, *Refugees in an Age of Genocide: Global, National and Local Perspectives during the Twentieth Century* (London, 1999), pp. 355–74.
10 See the maps in Storkey, Maguire and Lewis *op cit.*, pp. 23–34.
11 Richard Skellington, *'Race' in Britain Today*, 2nd edn (London, 1996), p. 58.
12 *Guardian*, 14 February 2003.
13 For basic information on the national situation, see Ceri Peach, 'Introduction', in *Ethnicity in the 1991 Census*, vol. II: *The Ethnic Minority Populations of Great Britain*, ed. Ceri Peach (London, 1996), pp. 15–18.
14 *http://www.salaam.co.uk*, UK directory of Mosques.
15 Sav Kyriacou and Zena Theodorou, 'Greek-Cypriots', in *The Peopling of London: Fifteen Thousand Years of Settlement from Overseas*, ed. Nick Merriman (London, 1993), pp. 102–4.
16 Sasha Josephides, 'Associations amongst the Greek Cypriot Population in Britain', in *Immigrant Associations in Europe*, ed. John Rex, Daniele Joly and Czarina Wilpert (Oxford, 1987), pp. 42–61.
17 See Yasmin Alibhai-Brown, *Mixed Feelings: The Complex Lives of Mixed Race*

Britons (London, 2001).

18 See Panikos Panayi, *The Impact of Immigration: A Documentary History of the Effects and Experiences of Immigrants in Britain since 1945* (Manchester, 1999), pp. 161–4.

19 See Phil Vasili, *Colouring over the White Line: The History of Black Footballers in Britain* (Edinburgh, 2000) and Pierre Lanfranchi and Matthew Taylor, *Moving with the Ball: The Migration of Professional Footballers* (Oxford, 2001).

20 See, for instance, *Time Out Eating and Drinking Guide 2001* (London, 2001), which lists 28 different categories of restaurants, the vast majority ethnic. See also *Harden's London Restaurants* (London, 1997).

21 Panikos Panayi, 'Anti-Immigrant Violence in Nineteenth and Twentieth Century Britain', in *Racial Violence in Nineteenth and Twentieth Century Britain*, ed. Panikos Panayi (London, 1996), pp. 15–16.

22 For an introduction to such issues, see Shamit Saggar, *Race and Politics in Britain* (London, 1992).

23 John Solomos, *Race and Racism in Britain*, 2nd edn (London, 1993), pp. 147–79.

24 B. Cathcart, *The Case of Stephen Lawrence* (London, 1999).

25 *The Scarman Report* (London, 1981); *The Stephen Lawrence Inquiry* (London, 1999).

26 Commission for Racial Equality, *Living in Terror: A Report on Racial Harassment in Housing* (London, 1987), p. 9.

27 *http://www.cre.gov.uk/pdfs/attac_fs.pdf*, CRE Factsheets, 'Racial Attacks and Harassment', 1991.

Caroline Cox: 'White Hair Right Now: Styling the London Man'

Acknowledgement: Thanks to Khalid Siddiqui

1 J. Stevens Cox, *Hairstyles for Men* (St Peter Port, Guernsey, 1949), p. 3.

2 Rodney Bennett England, *As Young as You Look: Male Grooming and Rejuvenation* (London, 1970), p. 104.

3 *Ibid.*, p. 106.

4 *Ibid.*

5 Dylan Jones, *Haircults: Fifty Years of Styles and Cuts* (London, 1990), p. 82.

6 Norman Bloomfield, ed., *Hair Today* (London, *c.* 1983), p. 2.

7 *Ibid.*

8 Jonathan Rutherford, 'Who's that Man', in *Male Order: Unwrapping Masculinity*, ed. R. Chapman and Jonathan Rutherford (London, 1988), pp. 23–4.

9 Steve Redhead, *The End of the Century Party: Youth and Pop Towards 2000* (Manchester, 1990), p. 4.

10 Leon Hunt, *British Low Culture: From Safari Suits to Sexploitation* (London, 1998), p. 7.

11 Michael Bracewell, *England Is Mine: Pop Life in Albion from Wilde to Goldie* (London, 1997), p. 28.

12 Interview with author, 14 July 2002.

13 Stevens Cox, *Hairstyles for Men*, p. 14.

14 Vishnoo @ *http://www.boogietown.netforums*

Christopher Breward: 'The London Suit'

1 P. York, *Style Wars* (London, 1980), p. 61.
2 *Ibid.*, p. 65.
3 D. Kynaston, *The City of London*, vol. IV: *A Club No More, 1945–2000* (London, 2001), p. 717.
4 The Blitz Club compèred by Steve Strange in the early 1980s was the focus for glamorous posing and dressing up by an art school and gay clientèle alienated by the macho nihilism of Punk.
5 Kynaston, *City of London*, p. 720.
6 *Ibid.*, p. 721.
7 *Ibid.*, p. 707.
8 *Ibid.*, p. 716.
9 *Ibid.*, p. 707.
10 *Financial Times Weekend*, 13 March 1993, p. XIX.
11 *New York Herald*, 2 September 1985, p. 18.
12 *Ibid.*
13 *Ibid.*
14 S. Nixon, *Hard Looks: Masculinities, Spectatorship & Contemporary Consumption* (London, 1996), p. 26.
15 *The Face*, 1 November 1995, p. 9.
16 *The Times*, 11 September 2000, p. 17.
17 *The Director* (July 2000), pp. 48–50.
18 *Financial Times Magazine*, 31 March 2001, pp. 36–42.
19 York, *Style Wars*, p. 68.

POLITICS/ECONOMICS

John Davis: 'From GLC to GLA: London Politics from Then to Now'

1 S. Goss, *Local Labour and Local Government* (Edinburgh, 1988), p. 95.
2 J. Lucas, *The Wandsworth Story* (London, 1992), p. 12.
3 M. Marinetto, 'The Political Dynamics of Camden, 1964–1994', *Local Government Studies*, XXIII/2 (Summer 1997), p. 36.
4 Anonymous, quoted in E. Dear, 'Leadership and Local Democracy', *Local Government Policy-Making*, XXIII/2 (October 1996), p. 3.

Arnold-Foster, J., 'Divided they Rule', *New Statesman*, 26 July 1996 [Hackney]
Atkinson, H., and S. Wilks-Heeg, *Local Government from Thatcher to Blair* (London, 2000)
Barnard, H., 'Neighbourhood Environmental Action', *Local Government Studies*, XVII (March/April 1991), pp. 8–14 [Islington]
Bayne, G., and R. Ashworth, 'Party Competition in English Local Government: An Empirical Analysis of English Councils, 1974–1994', *Policy and Politics*, XXV/2 (1997), pp. 129–42
Beckett, A., 'Sunnier Side of the Street', *The Guardian*, 9 October 1997 [Hackney]

Blackhurst, C., 'Housing Policy "Was Disgraceful Gerrymandering"', *Independent*, 10 May 1996 [Westminster]
—, 'Meet Heather, Britain's Town Hall Terminator', *Independent*, 8 July 1996 [Lambeth]
Brent Borough Recorder, 6 February 1991 [library losses]
Carvel, J., *Turn Again Livingstone* (London, 1999)
Cutler, H., *The Cutler Files* (London, 1982)
D'Arcy, M., and R. MacLean, *Nightmare: The Race to Become London's Mayor* (London, 2000)
Dear, E., 'Leadership and Local Democracy', *Local Government Policy-Making*, XXIII/2 (October 1996), pp. 3–5 [Islington]
Donegan, L., 'The Lambeth Shuffle', *The Guardian*, 8 February 1993
Forrester, A., S. Lansley and R. Pauley, *Beyond Our Ken: A Guide to the Battle for London* (London, 1985)
Garbutt, P. E., *London Transport and the Politicians* (London, 1985)
Goss, S., *Local Labour and Local Government* (Edinburgh, 1988) [Southwark]
Hebbert, M., and T. Travers, eds, *The London Government Handbook* (London 1988)
James, B., G. Hill and G. Ker, 'A Local Council, a National Concern', *The Times*, 15 December 1986 [Brent]
Katz, I., 'The A to Z of a Rotten Borough', *The Guardian*, 1 April 1994 [Brent]
Lennon, P., 'The Toughest Job in Britain', *The Guardian*, 25 October 1994 [Lambeth]
Lloyd, J., and J. Rentoul, 'The London Effect', *New Statesman*, 13 March 1987
London Daily News, 2 March 1987 [survey of Londoners' attitudes]
Lowndes, V., and G. Stoker, 'An Evaluation of Neighbourhood Decentralisation. I. Customer and Citizen Perspectives', *Policy and Politics*, XX/1 (1992), pp. 47–61; 'II. Staff and Councillor Perspectives', *ibid.*, XX/2 (1992), pp. 143–52 [Tower Hamlets]
Lucas, J., *The Wandsworth Story* (London, 1992)
Marinetto, M., 'An Examination of the Role of Chief Executive in the London Borough of Camden', *Local Government Policy-Making*, XXIII/2 (October 1996), pp. 6–17
—, 'The Political Dynamics of Camden, 1964–1994', *Local Government Studies*, XXIII/2 (Summer 1997), pp. 26–41
Milne, K., 'Municipal Mormons', *New Statesman*, 4 February 1994
O'Leary, B., 'Why was the GLC Abolished?', *International Journal of Urban and Regional Research*, XI (1987), pp. 193–217
Simmons, M., 'Separate Ways', *The Guardian*, 27 October 1993 [Decentralization]
South London Press, 2 May 1986 [Survey of awareness of councils]
Syrett, S., and R. Baldock, *Governing London: Competitiveness and Regeneration for a Global City* (London, 2001)
Tatchell, P., *The Battle for Bermondsey* (London, 1983)
Thornley, A., ed., *The Crisis of London* (London, 1992)
Travers, T., 'The Audit Commission on London Local Government', *Political Quarterly*, LVIII (1987), pp. 330–33
—, 'In Search of the Capital Idea', *The Guardian*, 25 November 1993

—, 'London's Turning', *The Guardian*, 28 May 1997
Walker, D., 'Shirley on the Scaffold', *Independent*, 7 May 1996 [Westminster]
Walker, D., and R. Smithers, 'Hackney: Borough of Hate and Hit Squads', *The Guardian*, 19 March 1999
Wintour, P., 'Judgment Day for London's Mayor', *The Guardian*, 23 July 2002
Wolmar, C., 'Creating Homes Fit for Tories'. *Independent*, 17 January 1994 [Westminster]

Charlie Gere: 'Armagideon Time'

1 Gilles Deleuze and Félix Guattari, trans. Brian Massumi, *A Thousand Plateaus* (London, 1999), p. 467.
2 Fredric Jameson, *Postmodernism; or, the Cultural Logic of Late Capitalism* (London, 1991), p. 37.
3 *http://www.nettime.org/nettime.w3archive/200109/msg00146.html*
4 For an account of Broadgate and its relation to the Big Bang, see Derek R. Diamond, 'The City, the "Big Bang" and Office Development', in *London: A New Metropolitan Geography*, ed. Keith Hoggart and David R. Green (London, 1991), pp. 79–94.
5 Gilles Deleuze, 'Postscript on the Societies of Control', OCTOBER, LIX (Winter 1992), pp. 3–7.
6 Paul N. Edwards, *The Closed World: Computers and the Politics of Discourse in Cold War America* (Cambridge, MA, 1997), p. 104.
7 Paul Virilio, *Open Sky* (London, 1997), p. 86.

Fiona Henderson: 'Staging Royal London'

Research for this essay was supported by a grant from the Economic and Social Research Council, Award Number R000429834454.

1 *The Original London Walks Brochure* (Winter 2001–2).
2 Visitor numbers to Kensington Palace, the former London home of Princess Diana, increased fourfold between 1997 and 1999. Statistics show that 60,125 people visited the palace in the year of her death, a figure that jumped to 240,685 in 1999. See *London Tourism Statistics* (London, 1999), p. 40.
3 E. Fodor, *Fodor's 2002: London* (New York, 2002), p. 38.
4 Penelope Corfield, 'London and the Modern Monarchy', *History Today*, XLIX/2 (1999), p. 12.
5 John Urry, *The Tourist Gaze: Leisure and Travel in Contemporary Societies* (London, 1990).
6 Daniel J. Boorstin, *The Image: A Guide to Pseudo-Events in America* (New York, 1972), pp. 77–117. James Buzard, *The Beaten Track: European Tourism, Literature and the Ways to Culture, 1800–1918* (Oxford, 1993), pp. 80–154.
7 Dean MacCannell, *The Tourist: A New Theory of the Leisure Class* (New York, 1976), pp. 91–107.
8 J. Shaw, ed., *Eyewitness Travel Guides: London* (London, 1997), p. 52.
9 David Cannadine, 'The Context, Performance and Meaning of Ritual: The

British Monarchy and the "Invention of Tradition", *c.* 1820–1977', in *The Invention of Tradition*, ed. E. Hobsbawm and T. Ranger (Cambridge, 1983), pp. 101–64.

10 Shaw, *Eyewitness: London*, p. 94. The official website for the British monarchy describes Buckingham Palace in similarly official terms; see *www.monarchy.gov.uk*

11 *Fodor's 2002*, p. 41.

12 Colin Amery, 'Buckingham Palace: A Tour through History', in *Buckingham Palace: A Complete Guide*, ed. R. Simon (London, 1993), pp. 2–27.

13 *Buckingham Palace: A Guide to the Splendours of Buckingham Palace* (London, 1993), p. 12.

14 In his discussion of celebrity in modern society, Chris Rojek explores the transformation of modern public figures like Princess Diana into celebrated icons, a process he calls 'celebrification'. See Chris Rojek, *Celebrity* (London, 2001), pp. 181–99.

15 *A Walk through Princess Diana's London* (London, 1998).

16 Edward Wessex, *Crown and Country: A Personal Guide to Royal London* (London, 1999).

Niran Abbas: 'CCTV: City Watch'

1 S. Graham, 'Towards a Fifth Utility? On the Extension and Normalization of Public CCTV', in *Surveillance, Closed-Circuit Television and Social Control*, ed. C. Norris, J. Moran and G. Armstrong (Aldershot, 1989).

2 Roger A. Clarke, 'Information Technology and Dataveillance', *Communications of the ACM*, XXI/5 (May 1988), pp. 498–512. See also William Mitchel, *City of Bits* website, *http://mitpress2.mit.edu/e-books/City_of_Bits/Bit_Biz/SurveillanceElectronicPanopticon.html#35*

3 D. Graham-Rowe, 'Warning! Strange Behaviour', *New Scientist*, 11 December 1999, pp. 25–8.

4 David Lyon, *Surveillance Society: Monitoring Everyday Life* (Buckingham, 2001), p. 40. See also R. Ericson and K. Haggerty, *Policing the Risk Society* (Toronto, 1997).

5 Jeffrey Rosen, 'A Watchful State', *New York Times Magazine*, 7 October 2001.

6 *Ibid.* Rosen discusses the implementation of face-recognition technology in the Borough of Newham and how it works as more of a simulation of crime prevention.

7 Helen Carter, 'Eye Spy', *The Guardian*, 1 August 2001. *http://www.guardian.co.uk/Archive/Article/0,4273,4231169,00.html* (accessed 12 January 2002).

8 'They're Watching You', *The Observer*, 29 August 1999. *http://www.guardian.co.uk/Archive/Article/0,4273,3896828,00.html* (accessed 13 January 2002).

9 *Ibid.*

10 See the detailed study by M. McCahill and C. Norris, 'Watching the Workers: Crime, CCTV and the Workplace', in *Invisible Crimes: Their Victims and Their Regulation*, ed. P. Davies, P. Francis and V. Jupp (London, 1999), pp. 208–31.

11 'Alarming Threat to Workplace Privacy', BBC News Online, 18 February 1999, *http://nes.bbc.co.uk/hi/english/uk/newsid_282000/282073.stm*

12 'London Council Praises Computer', 14 February 2000. *http://www.simon-net.com/asp/pressRelease.asp?ID=2668* (accessed 17 January 2002).

David Gilbert: 'Sex, Power and Miracles: A Suburban Triptych'

1 Ben Weinreb and Christopher Hibbert, eds, *The London Encyclopædia* (London, 1983), p. 834.

2 Cynthia Payne, quoted in Paul Bailey, *An English Madam* (London, 1982), p. 105.

3 Cynthia Payne's evidence at the trial of 1987. Reported in *The Guardian*, 12 February 1987, p. 5.

4 A. N. Wilson, *Daily Mail*, 12 February 1987, p. 6.

5 Julie Saunders, 'Three Ages of Cyn', *Streatham, Clapham and Dulwich Guardian*, 5 March 1987, p. 2.

6 *Ibid.*

7 Andy Medhurst, 'Negotiating the Gnome Zone: Visions of Suburbia in British Popular Culture', in *Visions of Suburbia*, ed. R. Silverstone (London, 1997), pp. 240–68.

8 See Michael Keith and Alisdair Rogers, eds, *Hollow Promises: Rhetoric and Reality in the Inner City* (London, 1991).

9 John Major, *John Major: The Autobiography* (London, 1999), p. 8.

10 *Ibid.*, p. 9.

11 *Ibid.*, p. 10.

12 Penny Junor, *John Major: From Brixton to Downing Street* (Harmondsworth, 1996; originally published as *The Major Enigma*, London, 1993).

13 Edward Pearce, *The Quiet Rise of John Major* (London, 1991), p. 3.

14 Quoted in Junor, *John Major*, p. 112.

15 David Broughton, 'The Limitations of Likeability: The Major Premiership and Public Opinion', in *The Major Premiership*, ed. Peter Dorey (London, 1999), pp. 199–216.

16 *Ibid.*, p. 200.

17 John Carey, *The Intellectuals and the Masses: Pride and Prejudice among the Literary Intelligentsia, 1880–1939* (London, 1992), p. 53.

18 Reported in *Southall Gazette*, 29 September 1995, p. 9.

19 *Ibid.*

20 Gerd Baumann, *Contesting Culture: Discourses of Identity in Multi-Ethnic London* (London, 1996), p. 37.

21 W. J. Green, *The Story of Holy Trinity Church, Southall*, being *Transactions of the Southall Local History Society* (1968), p. 3.

22 *Middlesex Gazette*, 13 January 1976, p. 9.

23 *Southall Gazette*, 11 March 1983, p. 7.

24 Reported in *Ealing Times*, 7 March 2002, p. 1.

25 See Les Back, '"Inside Out": Racism, Class and Masculinity in the "Inner City" and English Suburbs', *New Formations*, XXXIII (Spring 1998), pp. 59–77.

26 *Ealing Gazette*, 25 November 1988, p. 27.
27 Simon Naylor and James Ryan, 'Mosques, Temples and Gurdwaras in the Suburbs: Religion and Ethnicity in Twentieth-Century Britain', in *Geographies of British Modernity: Space and Society in the Twentieth Century*, ed. David Gilbert, David Matless and Brian Short (Oxford, 2003).
28 Felix Driver and David Gilbert, 'Heart of Empire? Landscape, Space and Performance in Imperial London', *Environment and Planning D: Society and Space*, XVI (1998), pp. 11–28.
29 Raphael Samuel, 'Empire Stories: The Imperial and the Domestic', in *Island Stories: Unravelling Britain: Theatres of Memory, Volume II* (London, 1998), p. 94.
30 Anthony King 'Excavating the Multicultural Suburb', in *Visions of Suburbia*, ed. Roger Silverstone (London, 1997), pp. 55–85.
31 Michael Gwilliam, Caroline Bourne, Corinne Swain and Anna Prat, *Sustainable Suburbs* (York, 1999).

Hilda Kean: 'The Transformation of Political and Cultural Space'

Acknowledgements. Thanks to Keren Abse, Peter Chowney, Shaun Doherty, Felicity Harvest, Ken Jones, Josephine Ohene-Djan, Paul Martin, Marjorie Mayo, Jane Shallice, Farhana Sheikh, staff at Camden Local Studies Archives and London Metropolitan Archives.

INFRASTRUCTURE

Joe Kerr: 'Blowdown: The Rise and Fall of London's Tower Blocks'

1 Office of the Deputy Prime Minister, 'Housing Research Summary: Demolition and New Building on Local Authority Estates', no. 115 (2000), p. 1. *www.housing.odpm.gov.uk*
2 *Ibid.*, p. 6.
3 I am indebted for this term, and for other relevant information, to my former student Fiona Scott.
4 BBC News, 'Tower Demolition Sets New Record', 24 February 2002. *news.bbc.co.uk*
5 *www.controlled-demolition.co.uk*
6 BBC News, 'Tower Demolition Sets New Record', 24 February 2002.
7 Patrick Wright, *A Journey through Ruins: The Last Days of London* (London, 1991), p. 89.
8 Ros Weaver, 'Sky Flats Hell Can Be Heaven', *The Observer* (Property Supplement), 16 March 2003, p. 26.

Gargi Bhattacharyya: 'Rats with Wings: London's Battle with Animals'

1 *Independent*, 24 January 2001.
2 Stephen Inwood, *A History of London* (London, 1998), p. 157).
3 Ken Livingstone, '3 Factors Influencing Feral Pigeon Abundance in Trafalgar

Square' (2001), *www.london.gov.uk*
4 James Meikle, 'Lurking in Your Litter: Horror Movie Warns of Britain's Rising Tide of Rats', *The Guardian*, 2 August 2002.
5 Mary Midgley, 'Beasts, Brutes and monsters', in *What is an Animal?*, ed. T. Ingold (London, 1988), p. 35.
6 Greater London Authority, *Biodiversity Strategy: Executive Summary* (2001), p. 3 (*www.london.gov.uk*).
7 *Ibid.*, p. 6.
8 *Ibid.*, p. 8.
9 *Ibid.*, ch. 3, 3.2.
10 Paul Harris, 'New Breed of Hunt Targets the Urban Fox', *The Guardian*, 24 March 2002.
11 *Oxford English Dictionary*.
12 *Ibid.*
13 Tony Banks, Minister for Sport, in *Independent*, 23 January 2001.

Alleyne, Richard, 'Pigeon Food Ban is Bird-Brained Idea', *Daily Telegraph*, 23 January 2001, article 27

Buncombe, Andrew, 'Livingstone Soaked in Pigeon Protest', *Independent*, 19 January 2001, article 37

Carlstrand, Vicky, 'Property-Polluting Pests Are Given the Bird: Pigeons Cause Massive Damage and Spread Disease', *Financial Times*, 16 September 2000, article 11

Gillies, Nick, 'Smell a Rat? It's Probably Dead Pigeon', *The Observer*, 28 November 1999

Greater London Authority, *Biodiversity Strategy* (2001), *www.london.gov.uk*

Inwood, Stephen, *A History of London* (London, 1998)

Harris, Paul, 'New Breed of Hunt Targets the Urban Fox', *The Guardian*, 24 March 2002

Johnson, Richard, 'Don't Shoot the Messenger', *The Guardian*, 7 July 2001

Kelso, Paul, 'Trafalgar Square Pigeons put to Flight', *The Guardian*, 8 February 2001

'Killer Ken', *The Observer*, 23 October 2000, article 6

Livingstone, Ken, '3 Factors Influencing Feral Pigeon Abundance in Trafalgar Square' (2001), *www.london.gov.uk*

Livingstone, Ken, 'Why We Must Remove the Pigeons from Trafalgar Square', *Independent*, 24 January 2001, article 33

Meikle, James, 'Lurking in Your Litter: Horror Movie Warns of Britain's Rising Tide of Rats', *The Guardian*, 2 August 2002

Midgley, Mary, 'Beasts, Brutes and Monsters', in *What is an Animal?*, ed. T. Ingold (London, 1988)

Naphy, William, and Andrew Spicer, *The Black Death and the History of Plagues, 1345–1730* (Stroud, 2000)

Porter, Stephen, *The Great Fire of London* (Stroud, 1996)

Serpell, James, *In the Company of Animals: A Study of Human–Animal Relationships* (Cambridge, 1996)

Walsh, John, 'The Birdman of Trafalgar Square Finally Loses His Perch', *Independent*, 8 February 2001, article 17

Waugh, Paul, 'Pigeon Tsar tells Mayor: Let Them Eat Seed', *Independent*, 23 January 2001, article 34

Tom Dyckhoff: 'Higher and Higher: How London Fell for the Loft'

1 Alison Roberts, 'Being Square Is Being There', *The Times*, 18 March 2000.
2 Sharon Zukin, *Loft Living: Culture and Capital in Urban Change* (Baltimore, 1982), p. 82.
3 Interview with the author.
4 Lesley Gillilan, 'Paradise Loft', *The Guardian*, 10 June 1995.
5 Interview with the author.
6 Lesley Gillilan, 'Paradise Loft', *The Guardian*, 10 June 1995.
7 Interview with the author.
8 Caroline Roux, 'A Return to the Lofty Ideal', *Independent on Sunday*, 3 November 1996.
9 Interview with the author.
10 Peter York, 'Room for Inner Improvements', *The Guardian*, 9 February 1998.
11 Lesley Gillilan, 'Time To Join the Loft Leaders', *The Guardian*, 21 August 1993.
12 Catherine Moye, 'The Bigger Picture', *Daily Telegraph*, 26 May 2001.
13 Amanda Loose, 'A Campaign for Genuine Lofts', *The Times*, 5 February 1997.
14 Stephen Bayley, 'Why I Hate Lofts', *Daily Telegraph*, 29 September 2001.

Patrick Wright: 'Down in the Dirt'

1 Mary Douglas, *Purity and Danger: An Analysis of the Concepts of Pollution and Taboo* (London, 1966).
2 'Lynn' describes how he was thrown out of No. 99 Balls Pond Road for setting up this experiment in Appendix 2, Paul Keeler, *Planted* (London, 1968), pp. 20–21. The fact that the only rule in this house was one proscribing the use of drugs did not prevent the tabloids from whipping up a storm over the 'Hippy HQ' where 'Food, clothing – even girl-friends – will be shared'; nor, as was claimed in a famous court case of the time, did it stop Detective Sergeant Rigby of Dalston Police Station from sending an infiltrator down to plant cannabis in the house ('He wore jeans, but they were very new') a few months later.
3 Maberly Sabbath School, *Minute Book, 1836–1856*, Hackney Archives.
4 Elizabeth Wilson, *Hallucinations* (London, 1988).
5 I refer to 'The Invisible City', an exhibition held at the Photographers Gallery as 'London Project II' in November 1990.
6 John Farleigh, *It Never Dies: A Collection of Notes and Essays, 1940–46* (London, 1946).
7 Wanda Ostrowska, *London's Glory: Twenty Paintings of the City's Ruins*, with text by Viola G. Garvin (London, 1945).
8 *Hackney Gazette*, 9 February 1990.
9 *Hackney Gazette*, 2 March 1990.

Murray Fraser: 'Architecture's Urban Shine and Brutal Reality'

1 Richard Rogers Partnership, Lloyds Building (1978–86); Arup Associates / Skidmore Owings & Merrill, master planners, Broadgate Development (1984–91); SOM, master planners, Canary Wharf development (1988–2000); Foster and Partners, Canary Wharf Underground Station (1990–2000), and various other architects on the Jubilee Line Extension (1993–9).

2 Sidell Gibson, master planners, Paddington Basin (ongoing).

3 Venturi & Scott-Brown, Sainsbury Wing of the National Gallery (1988–91); Dixon Jones, Covent Garden Opera Development (1984–2000); Foster and Partners, Great Court of the British Museum (1994–2003); Michael Hopkins and Partners, Portcullis House (1999–2000); Future Systems, Media Stand at Lord's Cricket Ground (1999); Richard Rogers Partnership, Millennium Dome (1996–2000); Marks Barfield, London Eye (1993–2000).

4 Kenneth Powell, *New London Architecture* (London, 2001), inside jacket notes. For another view of contemporary London architecture, see Samantha Hardingham, *London: A Guide to Recent Architecture* (5th edn, London, 2001).

5 Sarah Wigglesworth and Jeremy Till, *Architectural Design Profile: The Everyday and Architecture* (London, 1998); Jeremy Till and Sarah Wigglesworth, 'The Future is Hairy', in *Architecture: The Subject is Matter*, ed. Jonathan Hill (London, 2002), pp. 11–28; Henri Lefebvre, *Critique of Everyday Life*, 2 vols (London, 2002–3); Michel de Certeau, *The Practice of Everyday Life* (Berkeley, 2002).

6 Nigel Coates, *Ecstacity: The Revitalisation of London* (London, 1992).

7 Patrick Keiller, *London* (1993).

8 Iain Sinclair, *Lights Out for the Territory* (London, 1997); Iain Sinclair and Marc Atkins, *Liquid City* (London, 1999); Iain Sinclair, *Downriver* (London, 1991); Iain Sinclair, *London Orbital: A Walk around the M25* (London, 2002); Patrick Wright, *A Journey through Ruins: The Last Days of London* (London, 1991); Patrick Wright, *The River: The Thames in our Time* (London, 1999); Richard Wentworth, *Unknown City* (forthcoming).

9 Adrian Rifkin, 'Benjamin's Paris, Freud's Rome: Whose London?', in *The Metropolis and its Images: Constructing Identities for London, c. 1750–1950*, ed. Dana Arnold (Oxford, 1999), pp. 153–66.

10 *http://www.empireonline.co.uk/features/interviews/bobhoskins*

11 Jane M. Jacobs, *East of Empire: Postcolonialism and the City* (London and New York, 1996), pp. 64–7.

12 The Clash, *London's Burning*, CBS Records, August 1977.

13 Jamie Oliver, *Jamie's Kitchen* (London, 2002).

14 Saskia Sassen, *The Global City: New York, London, Tokyo* (2nd edn, Princeton, NJ, and Oxford, 2001), pp. 270–78; Nick Buck *et al.*, *Working Capital: Life and Labour in Contemporary London* (London, 2002).

15 This was a recurrent theme in Wolfe's critique of the radical and artistic groups in New York in the 1970s. See Tom Wolfe, *Radical Chic and Mau-Mauing the Flak Catchers* (New York, 1970); Tom Wolfe, *The Painted Word* (New York, 1975).

CULTURE/SUBCULTURE

Andrew Gibson: 'Altering Images'

Ackroyd, Peter, *Hawksmoor* (London, 1985)
—, *London: The Biography* (London, 2000)
Ballard, J. G., *Concrete Island* (London, 1974)
Carter, Angela, *Wise Children* (London, 1991)
Dickens, Charles, *The Life and Adventures of Martin Chuzzlewit*, ed. P. N. Furbank (Harmondsworth, 1968)
—, *Dombey and Son*, ed. Peter Fairclough (Harmondsworth, 1970)
Driver, Felix, and David Gilbert, eds, *Imperial Cities: Landscape, Display and Identity* (Manchester, 1999)
Jacobs, Jane M., *Edge of Empire: Postcolonialism and the City* (London, 1996)
Keiller, Patrick, *Robinson in Space* (London, 1999)
Massey, Doreen, 'A Global Sense of Place', *Marxism Today*, xxxv (June 1991), pp. 24–9
—, 'Places and their Pasts', *History Workshop Journal*, no. 39 (1995), pp. 182–92
Moorcock, Michael, *Mother London* (Harmondsworth, 1988)
—, *King of the City* (New York, 2000)
Porter, Roy, *London: A Social History* (Harmondsworth, 1994)
Selvon, Sam, *The Lonely Londoners* (London, 1979)
Sinclair, Iain, *White Chappell, Scarlet Tracings* (Uppingham, 1987)
—, *Radon Daughters* (London, 1994)
—, *Downriver* (London, 1991)
—, *Lights out for the Territory* (London, 1997)
—, *London Orbital: A Walk around the M25* (London, 2002)
Smith, Zadie, *White Teeth* (London, 2000)
Swift, Graham, *Last Orders* (London, 1996)

Michael Bracewell: 'Punk'

1 From E. M. Forster, *Maurice: A Novel* (written 1913–14; London, 1971).
2 Ian Nairn and Nikolaus Pevsner, *Surrey* (Harmondsworth, 1962).
3 Liz Naylor in *Punk Rock, So What? The Cultural Legacy of Punk*, ed. Roger Sabin (London, 1999).

Phil Baker: 'Secret City: Psychogeography and the End of London'

1 *Critique de la separation* (film of 1961), screenplay in Guy Debord, *Oeuvres cinematographiques complètes, 1952–1978* (Paris, 1978), p. 45. My translation.
2 Guy Debord, 'Introduction à une critique de la géographie urbaine', *Les Lèvres Nues*, 6 (September 1955), trans. in *Situationist International Anthology*, ed. Ken Knabb (Berkeley, 1981), pp. 5–8.
3 Jake Arnott, *He Kills Coppers* (London, 2001), p. 265.
4 Chtcheglov, 'Formulaire pour un urbanisme nouveau', *Internationale Situationniste*,

1 (June 1958), trans. in *Situationist International Anthology*, pp. 1–4.
5 *Ibid.*
6 'Exercice de la Psychogéographie', *Potlatch*, 2 (29 June 1954).
7 Robert Aickman, *The Attempted Rescue* (London, 1966), p. 127.
8 Discussed and quoted in David Bellos, *Georges Perec: A Life in Words* (London, 1995), pp. 417–18.
9 Debord, 'Introduction à une critique de la géographie urbaine'.
10 Both seen by present writer, autumn 1998.
11 Chris Petit, 'Newman Passage; or, J. Maclaren-Ross and the Case of the Vanishing Writers', in *The Time Out Book of London Short Stories*, ed. Maria Lexton (London, 1993), p. 137.
12 Marek Kohn, *Dope Girls* (London, 1992), p. 11.
13 Margaret Thatcher in *Woman's Own*, 31 October 1987. Among all the lost objects of psychogeography – De Quincey's vanishing chemist, Sinclair's rare books, Walter Benjamin's 'love at last sight' for passing women, the Lettrists' quest for the Holy Grail of the street in '36 rue des Morillons' (the address of the Paris Lost Property office) – some modified but tenable sense of society or community is by no means the least.
14 Tom Salter, *Carnaby Street* (London, 1970), p. 5.
15 John Michell, 'The Fuss About Leys', in *An Orthodox Voice* (Brentford, London, 1995), pp. 29–30
16 Iain Sinclair, *Lud Heat* (London, 1975), p. 11.
17 Cited in *Impresario: Malcolm McLaren and the British New Wave*, exh. cat., New York, The New Museum of Contemporary Art (1988), p. 73.
18 Malcolm McLaren, cited in Simon Ford, *The Realization and Suppression of the Situationist International: An Annotated Bibliography, 1972–1992* (Edinburgh, 1995), p. 111.
19 The London Psychogeographical Association, *Why Psychogeography?*, broadsheet (1996); widely disseminated and reprinted, e.g., in *Autotoxicity: Second Assault* (Sheffield, 1997).
20 London Psychogeographical Association, *The Unacceptable Face of Contemporary Psychogeography* (1996); reprinted in *Mind Invaders: A Reader in Psychic Warfare, Cultural Sabotage and Semiotic Terrorism*, ed. Stewart Home (London, 1997), pp. 151–3. The leading lights of the LPA were Fabian Tompsett and Stewart Home, who interwove his ultra-violent pulp fictions with psychogeographical references, notably in *Come Before Christ and Murder Love* (London, 1997); earlier references were sometimes little more than nods towards the Situationist legacy, but in this one they become more solid and extensive, with John Dee, Greenwich and the North-West Passage.
21 'Smash the Occult Establishment', *London Psychogeographical Association Newsletter*, 6 (Beltaine 1994); 'Open Up the Northwest Passage', *London Psychogeographical Association Newsletter*, 3 (Lughnassadh 1993); 'St Catherine's Hill etc.', in Fabian Tompsett, *The Great Conjunction* (London, 1992); 'East End Gestalt' in Fabian Tompsett, 'Dislocation on the Isle of Dogs', *Transgressions: A Journal of Urban Exploration*, 2–3 (August 1996), pp. 101–5.
22 E.g. 'The Whitechapel Road … is a sort of portal to the filth and squalor of the

East', John Francis Brewer, *The Curse Upon Mitre Square* (London, 1888), p. 66. The nature of this East is left ambiguous in this early work of Ripper psychogeography – which links the murder of Catherine Eddowes to sixteenth-century events on exactly the same spot – unlike the work of Sax Rohmer, notably *Dope* (London, 1919), which pivots on a West End–East End contrast, and Thomas Burke's Limehouse books.

23 'La quatrième conférence de l'I.S. à Londres', *Internationale Situationniste*, 5 (December 1960), p. 165.

24 'Exercice de la Psychogéographie', *Potlatch*, 2 (29 June 1954).

25 *Lights Out for the Territory* (London, 1997), p. 238.

26 Roy Porter, *London: A Social History* (London, 1994). For this aspect, see particularly the Preface and afterword, 'The London Marathon'.

27 Peter Ackroyd, *London: The Biography* (London, 2000), pp. 691, 469, 468.

28 Guy Debord, *In girum imus nocte et consumimur igni* (London, [*c.* 1991]), pp. 30–31, 28, 29. The palindromic title reads: 'We go round and round in the night and are consumed by fire'.

29 Mark Manning, *Crucify Me Again* (Hove, 2000) and Bill Drummond, *45* (London, 2000), both cited in Iain Sinclair, 'If I Turn and Run', *London Review of Books*, 1 June 2000.

30 Louis Aragon, *Paris Peasant*, trans. Simon Watson-Taylor (London, 1971), p. 149.

31 Breton, cited by Simon Watson-Taylor in his introduction to *Paris Peasant* (London, 1971), p. 10.

32 Robert Kahn, ed., *City Secrets: London* (New York, 2001) and Andrew Duncan, *Secret London* (London, 1995). Duncan is also the author of *Walking Notorious London* (London, 2001).

33 Alain-Fournier, *Le Grand Meaulnes* (Paris, 1913), as *The Lost Domain* (London, 1929); H. G. Wells, 'The Door in the Wall' (1906) in his *The Door in the Wall and Other Stories* (London, 1911); Arthur Machen, 'N', in his *The Cosy Room and Other Stories* (London, 1936).

34 Michael Moorcock, *King of the City* (London, 2000), p. 180.

35 Eric Korn on Moorcock, *Times Literary Supplement*, 26 May 2000, p. 23.

36 Hakim Bey [Peter Lamborn Wilson], *Sacred Drift: Essays on the Margins of Islam* (San Francisco, 1993), p. 157.

37 'Definitions', *Situationist International Anthology*, ed. Ken Knabb, p. 45.

38 The history of psychogeography is bound up with certain walking practices, notably *flânerie* and the *dérive*, which are not to be confused. *Flânerie* tended to be solitary, relatively leisurely, and bound up with commodities (window shopping, second-hand books, prostitutes) on familiar ground. The *dérive* ignored commodities, was often communal and could be gruelling. Chtcheglov saw the *dérive* as potentially a kind of ambulant free-association: 'The *dérive* (with its flow of acts, its gestures, its strolls, its encounters) was to the totality exactly what psychoanalysis (in the best sense) is to language. Let yourself go with the flow of words, says the analyst ...'. Chtcheglov, 'Letters from Afar', *Internationale Situationniste*, 9 (August 1964), p. 38 (fragment in *Situationist International Anthology*, ed. Ken Knabb, p. 372). Chtcheglov wrote this from an

asylum, possibly La Borde, where he is often said to have been a patient of Felix Guattari. The *dérive* has subsequently found echoes in Lyotard, *Driftworks* (*Dérive et partir de Marx et Freud*, Paris, 1973), and Deleuze and Guattari (nomadism *passim*, 'the schizo's stroll' in *Anti-Oedipus*).

39 Walter Benjamin, *A Berlin Childhood around the Turn of the Century*, cited in Susan Sontag's 'Introduction' to *One Way Street and Other Writings* (London, 1978), p. 10.

40 Salon Wanderlust internet site, *c.* 1998–2000.

41 Suzannah Clapp, *Bruce Chatwin* (London, 1997), p. l2. The street was Camden Parkway.

42 Ackroyd wrote the 'Introduction' to Dennis Severs, *18 Folgate Street: The Tale of a House in Spitalfields* (London, 2001), which began life as *Secret House at 18 Folgate Street* (announced for Ebury Press, 1999).

43 Arthur Calder-Marshall, *The Magic of My Youth* (London, 1951), p. 94.

44 'Can one postulate a relationship between the cult of a private controllable world as against a public uncontrollable one in which one is assigned no role? ... A magazine called *World of Interiors* would, for instance, never have flourished a decade ago ... in the 1960s, in contrast, it was the public face, in the form of clothes ... It will go down as an odd phenomenon of the recession that the rise in unemployment has gone hand in hand with a parallel rise in expenditure on the private interior.' Roy Strong, 'Biedermeier Revived' [*c.* 1984] reprinted in *Strong Points* (London, 1985), pp. 32–4.

45 Cf. Guy Debord, 'Psychogeographical Game of the Week', *Potlach*, 1 (22 June 1954), in which he suggests building a house from scratch, furnishing it and throwing a party with carefully chosen people, drinks and 'disques': it would be a work of calculated ambience, or proto-Situationist 'situation'.

46 Michael McMillan, 'A Sardine Sage', four-panel strip on back cover of *Arcade: The Comics Revue*, 6 (Summer 1976).

47 'Isn't Space the Ultimate Luxury?' ('Room to think. Room to breathe. Room to manoeuvre. Room to be yourself.') Renault Espace car advertisement, *c.* 1999. *The Guardian* property supplement was also called 'Space', as were at least two modish retailers.

48 Marc Augé, *Non-Places: Introduction to an Anthropology of Supermodernity* (London, 1995; as *Non-lieux*, Paris, 1992). Something of this had already been pioneered by E. Relph in *Place and Placelessness* (London, 1976), an early example of what would become increasing anxiety about (post-)modernization, tourism and 'Disneyfication', leading to superficial locations with interchangeable identities: 'placelessness'.

49 David Mitchell, *Ghostwritten* (London, 1999), p. 217; Thurston Clarke, *Searching for Crusoe* (London, 2001), pp. 9–10; Philip Hensher, *Pleasured* (London, 1998), p. 68.

Roger Luckhurst: 'Occult London'

Ackroyd, Peter, *Hawksmoor* (London, 1985)
—, *London: The Biography* (London, 2000)

Adorno, Theodor, 'Theses Against Occultism', *Minima Moralia* (London, 1974)
Baldick, Chris, *The Oxford Book of Gothic Tales* (Oxford, 1993)
Derrida, Jacques, *Spectres of Marx: The State of the Debt, the Work of Mourning and the New International* (London, 1994)
Evans, Eric J., *Thatcher and Thatcherism* (London, 1997)
Fowler, Christopher, *Darkest Day* (London, 1993)
—, *Disturbia* (London, 1997).
Home, Stewart, *Come Before Christ and Murder Love* (London, 1998)
—, *The House of Nine Squares: Letters on Neoism, Psychogeography and Epistemological Trepidation* (London, 1997)
—, *Mind Invaders: A Reader in Psychic Warfare, Cultural Sabotage and Semiotic Terrorism* (London, 1997)
Machen, Arthur, *The London Adventure* (London, 1924)
—, 'Science and the Ghost Story', *Literature*, 17 September 1898
Sinclair, Iain, *Downriver* (London, 1990)
Truzzi, Marcello, 'Definition and Dimensions of the Occult', *Journal of Popular Culture*, v/2 (1971)
Vidler, Anthony, *The Architectural Uncanny* (Cambridge, MA, 1994)
Wolfreys, Julian, *Writing London: The Trace of the Urban Text from Blake to Dickens* (Basingstoke, 1998)

Sarah Kent: 'Groundswell'

1 Quoted by Brian Sewell in 'Fifties London was Much More Thrilling than This', *Evening Standard*, 1 February 2002, p. 26.
2 See 'Mistakes', *Time Out*, 342 (8 October 1976), p. 7.
3 *Time Out* is a weekly magazine comprising listings of cultural events in London plus reviews and features.
4 Quoted by me in 'Prostitution Didn't Pay', *Time Out*, 352 (24 December 1976), p. 17.
5 *Ibid.*
6 'Pro Dip Show', a review of *British Painting '74* at the Hayward Gallery. *Time Out*, 240 (4 October 1974), p. 14.
7 'Civilisation As We Knew It', *Time Out*, 391 (30 September 1977), p. 13.
8 'The Puritan Exhibitionist', *Time Out*, 361 (18 February 1977), p. 9.
9 See 'Amidst the Alien Corn', *Time Out*, 304 (9 January 1976), p. 9. Biba was a fashionable clothing store in High Street Kensington.
10 Damien Hirst quoted by Richard Cork, 'Everyone's Story is So Different', in *The Saatchi Decade*, ed. Sarah Kent, Richard Cork and Dick Price (London, 1999), p. 14.
11 'Gambler', *Time Out*, 1040 (25 July 1990), p. 23.
12 Sarah Kent, *Shark Infested Waters: The Saatchi Collection of British Art in the '90s* (London, 1994).
13 *Time Out*, 1176 (March 1993), pp. 37–9.
14 *Time Out*, 1589 (31 January 2001), pp. 16–23.
15 *Evening Standard, ES Magazine*, 12 October 2001, pp. 12–41.

Patrick Keiller: 'London in the Early 1990s'

1 *London* (85 minutes, 35 mm, 1994, bfi films, bfi video), narrated by Paul Scofield.

2 Alexander Herzen, *Ends and Beginnings*, trans. Constance Garnett (Oxford, 1985), p. 431.

3 The visits of Mallarmé, Verlaine and others are documented in Cecily Mackworth, *English Interludes* (London, 1974).

4 The story of Apollinaire's affair and his visits to London is told in John Adlard, *One Evening of Light Mist in London* (Edinburgh, 1980), and alluded to in Apollinaire's *L'Emigrant de Landor Road* and other poems in *Alcools*. The Playdens lived at 75 Landor Road. An unofficial Blue Plaque (which I suspect was put there by John Adlard) commemorates this. Landor Road is named after the poet Walter Savage Landor, and *Landor's Cottage* is a story by Edgar Allan Poe.

5 Enid Starkie, *Arthur Rimbaud* (London, 1961).

6 *Robinson in Space* (82 mins, 35 mm, 1997, BBC and bfi films, bfi video), narrated by Paul Scofield.

7 *Journeaux intimes: mon coeur mis à nu*, XXI (1887), XXI (36).

8 Including, for example, the passage in *Paris Spleen*, trans. by Louise Varèse (New York, 1947), p. 99, XLVIII: *Anywhere out of the World*: 'Life is a hospital where every patient is obsessed by the desire of changing beds. One would like to suffer opposite the stove, another is sure he would get well beside the window. It always seems to me that I should be happy anywhere but where I am, and this question of moving is one that I am eternally discussing with my soul.'

9 This might be confirmed by this sequence's being the only part of the film with anything like direct sound. The picture was shot mute and all the sound was post-synchronized, but while I was editing the carnival footage, the film-maker Patricia Diaz, who was working in the same building, happened to walk past the open door of the cutting room and recognize the subject. She had been on the float with a video camera, and we subsequently arranged to use some of her sound. The film later developed a following among Colombians in London.

10 *The Guardian*, 24 August 2000, quoting *On the Move: Housing Consequences of Migration*, ed. Richard Bate, Richard Best and Alan Holmans (York, 2000).

11 Paul Dave, 'The Bourgeois Paradigm and Heritage Cinema', *New Left Review*, no. 224 (July–August 1997).

12 Ellen Meiksins Wood, *The Pristine Culture of Capitalism* (London, 1991), pp. 108–9.

Pamela Church Gibson:

'Imaginary Landscapes, Jumbled Topographies: Cinematic London'

1 Mark Shiel and Tony Fitzmaurice, eds, *Cinema and the City: Film and Urban Societies in a Global Context* (Oxford, 2001), p. 1.

2 Mike Mason, 'Naked: Social Realism and Urban Wasteland', in *Cinema and the City*, ed. Mark Shiel and Tony Fitzmaurice (Oxford, 2001), p. 249.

3 'The historical and cultural experience of the western metropolis cannot now be fictionalised without the marginal, oblique gaze of its postcolonial migrant populations cutting across the imaginative metropolitan geography of territory and community, city and culture.' Homi Bhabha, 'Novel Metropolis', *New Statesman and Society*, 16 February 1990, p. 23.
4 Jarman Papers, in Tony Peake, *Derek Jarman: A Biography* (London, 1999), p. 137.
5 Jarman quoted in *ibid.*
6 *Ibid.*, p. 248.
7 Robert Murphy, 'Urban Fairy Tales', in *The British Cinema Book*, ed. Robert Murphy, 2nd edn (London, 2001), p. 292.
8 Nick James, 'Editorial – Imagine Asia', *Sight and Sound*, XII/6 (June 2002), p. 3.

Bhabha, Homi, 'Novel Metropolis', *New Statesman and Society*, 16 February 1990
Clarke, David B., *The Cinematic City* (London, 1997)
Corner, John, and Sylvia Harvey, eds, *Enterprise and Heritage: Crosscurrents in National Culture* (London, 1991)
Donald, James, 'The City as Text', in *Social and Cultural Forms of Modernity*, ed. Robert Bocock and Kenneth Thompson (Oxford, 1992), pp. 417–71
James, Nick, 'Editorial – Imagine Asia', *Sight and Sound*, XII/6 (June 2002)
Mason, Mike, 'Naked: Social Realism and Urban Wasteland', in *Cinema and the City: Film and Urban Societies in a Global Context*, ed. Mark Shiel and Tony Fitzmaurice (Oxford, 2001), pp. 244–55
Murphy, Robert, 'Urban Fairy Tales', in *The British Cinema Book*, ed. Robert Murphy (London, 2002)
Peake, Tony, *Derek Jarman: A Biography* (London, 1999)
Shiel, Mark, and Tony Fitzmaurice, eds, *Cinema and the City: Film and Urban Societies in a Global Context* (Oxford, 2001)
Wollen, Peter, 'Delirious Projections', *Sight and Sound*, II/ 4 (August 1992), p. 33

Robert Mighall: 'Crime and Memory in the Capital'

1 Iain Sinclair, *Lights Out for the Territory* (London, 1997), p. 71.
2 *Time Out Guide to London* (London, 1995), p. 112. These photographs of contemporary Whitechapel deliberately invoke an urban Gothic aura. All taken at night and confined to the few remaining cobbled alleyways of the area (two of which are actually sites in the Whitechapel Murders File), they imply that Whitechapel is still Ripperland. As I will argue, anachronism is a dominant characteristic of the representation of criminal London.
3 *Time Out Guide to London* (London, 1994), p. 117; *Time Out Guide to London* (London, 1997), p. 104.
4 *Ibid.* The site of what was called Bucks Row when Jack dispatched Mary Ann Nichols on 31 August 1888 is now Durward Street, where Wood's Buildings abuts the crossing over the Hammersmith and City Underground Line.
5 *Time Out Guide to London* (London, 2001), p. 160.
6 *Ibid.*, p. 78.

7 Sinclair, in Iain Sinclair and Mark Atkins, *Liquid City* (London, 1999), p. 84.
8 Steve Chibnall, 'Travels in Ladland: The British Gangster Film Cycle, 1998–2001', in *The British Cinema Book*, ed. Robert Murphy (London, 2001), p. 282.
9 Colin MacCabe, *Performance* (London, 1998), p. 43. This observation may be somewhat overstated, since a few post-war films, the most famous being *Brighton Rock* (1947), set this process in motion.
10 Fraser with James Morton, *Mad Frank's London* (London, 2001), pp. 4 and 5.
11 *Ibid.*, p. 5.
12 John Pearson, *The Cult of Violence* (London, 2002), p. 208.
13 Sinclair, *Lights Out for the Territory*, pp. 71–2.

BIBLIOGRAPHY

General

Ackroyd, Peter, *London: The Biography* (London, 2000)
Clout, Hugh, ed., *The Times History of London* (London, 1999)
Garside, Patricia, *Capital Histories: A Bibliographical Study of London* (Aldershot, 1998)
Hibbert, Christopher, *London: A Biography* (Harmondsworth, 1980)
Inwood, Stephen, *A History of London* (London, 1998)
Porter, Roy, *London: A Social History* (London, 1994)
Sheppard, Francis, *London: A History* (Oxford, 1998)
Weinreb, Ben, and Christopher Hibbert, eds, *The London Encyclopaedia* (London, 1983)
Wilson, A. N., ed., *The Faber Book of London* (London, 1993)
White, Gerry, *London in the 20th Century: A City and its People* (Harmondsworth, 2002)

Contemporary London Literature

Ackroyd, Peter, *The Great Fire of London* (London, 1984)
—, *Hawksmoor* (London, 1985)
—, *The House of Doctor Dee* (London, 1993)
—, *Dan Leno and the Limehouse Golem* (London, 1995)
Amis, Martin, *London Fields* (London, 1990)
Ballard, J. G., *The Unlimited Dream Company* (London, 1990)
—, *Concrete Island* (London, 1994)
Carter, Angela, *Wise Children* (London, 1991)
Cartwright, Justin, *Look at it This Way* (London, 1991)
Coe, Jonathan, *What a Carve Up!* (London, 1995)
Duffy, Maureen, *Londoners: An Elegy* (London, 1983)
—, *Capital: A Fiction* (London, 1984)
Higson, Charles, *King of the Ants* (London, 1993)
—, *Happy Now* (London, 1993)
—, *Getting Rid of Mister Kitchen* (London, 1996)
—, *Full Whack* (London, 1995)

Jack, Ian, *London: Lives of the City* (London, 1999) [special edition of *Granta*]
Keiller, Patrick, *Robinson in Space* (London, 1999)
Kureishi, Hanif, *The Buddha of Suburbia* (London, 1995)
Lessing, Doris, *The Four-Gated City* (London, 1990)
—, *The Good Terrorist* (London, 1993)
—, *London Observed* (London, 1993)
Lexton, Maria, ed., *The 'Time Out' Book of London Short Stories* (London, 1993)
Lott, Tim, *The Scent of Dried Roses* (London, 1997)
—, *White City Blue* (London, 2000)
MacInnes, Colin, *Absolute Beginners* (Harmondsworth, 1986)
McGrath, Patrick, *Spider* (Harmondsworth, 1992)
Mo, Timothy, *Sour Sweet* (London, 1992)
Moorcock, Michael, *Mother London* (London, 1988)
—, *King of the City* (London, 2000)
Moore, Alan, ed., *The 'Time Out' Book of London Short Stories: It's Dark in London* (London, 1997)
Nicholson, Geoff, *Bleeding London* (London, 1997)
Rennison, Nick, ed., *Waterstone's Guide to London Writing* (London, 1999)
Self, Will, *The Quantity Theory of Insanity* (London, 1993)
—, *Grey Area* (London, 1994)
Selvon, Sam, *The Lonely Londoners* (London, 1979)
Sinclair, Iain, *Lud Heat* (London, 1975)
—, *Downriver* (London, 1991)
—, *Radon Daughters* (London, 1995)
—, *Lights Out for the Territory* (London, 1997)
—, *London Orbital: A Walk around the M25* (London, 2002)
—, and Marc Atkins, *Liquid City* (London, 1999)
—, and Rachel Lichtenstein, *Rodinsky's Room* (London, 1999)
—, and David McKean, *Slow Chocolate Autopsy* (London, 1997)
Smith, Zadie, *White Teeth* (London, 2000)
Stevenson, Jane, *London Bridges* (London, 2000)
Vansittart, Peter, *London: A Literary Companion* (London, 1992)
Wright, Patrick, *A Journey through Ruins: The Last Days of London* (London, 1991)
—, *The River: The Thames in our Times* (London, 1999)

London History

Barker, Theo, 'London: A Unique Megalopolis?', in *Megalopolis: The Giant City in History*, ed. Theo Barker and Anthony Sutcliffe (Basingstoke, 1993), pp. 43–60
Barton, Nicholas, *The Lost Rivers of London* (London, 1998)
Baumann, Gerd, *Contesting Culture: Ethnicity and Community in West London* (Cambridge, 1996)
Bermant, Chaim, *Point of Arrival: A Study of London's East End* (London, 1975)
Clayton, Antony, *Subterranean City* (London, 2000)
Clout Hugh, and Peter Wood, eds, *London: Problems of Change* (London, 1986)
Deakin, Nicholas, and John Edwards, *The Enterprise Culture and the Inner City*

(London, 1993)
Fainstein, Susan, *The City Builders: Property Development in New York and London, 1980–2000* (Lawrence, 2001)
—, Ian Gordon and Michael Harloe, *Divided Cities: London and New York in the Contemporary World* (Oxford, 1992)
Fishman, William J., *The Streets of East London* (London, 1999)
Griffiths, Paul, and Mark S. R. Jenner, *Londinopolis, c. 1500 – c. 1750: Essays in the Cultural and Social History of Early Modern London* (Manchester, 2000)
Hall, Peter G., *London 2001* (London, 1999)
Halliday, Paul, *The Greek Cypriot Community in London* (Salonika, 1988)
Hebbert, Michael, 'London Recent and Present', *London Journal*, xx/2 (1995), pp. 91–101
—, *London: More by Fortune than Design* (Chichester, 1998)
Hillman, Ellis, and Richard Trench, *London Under London: A Subterranean Guide* (London, 1993)
Hoggart, Keith, and David R. Green, eds, *London: A New Metropolitan Geography* (London, 1991)
Humphries, Steve, and John Taylor, *The Making of Modern London, 1945–1985* (London, 1986)
James, Winston, and Clive Harris, eds, *Inside Babylon: The Caribbean Diaspora in Britain* (London, 1993)
King, Anthony, *Global Cities: Post-Imperialism and the Internationalization of London* (London, 1990)
Kynaston, David, *The City of London: A Club No More, 1945–2000* (London, 2001)
—, and Richard Roberts, *City State: A Contemporary History of the City of London and How Money Triumphed* (London, 2001)
Merriman, Nick, ed., *The Peopling of London: Fifteen Thousand Years of Settlement from Overseas* (London, 1993)
Okokon, Susan, *Black Londoners, 1880–1990* (Phoenix Mill, 1998)
Owusu, Kwesi, Jacob Ross and Ian Watts, *Behind the Masquerade: The Story of the Notting Hill Carnival* (Edgware, 1988)
Panikos, Panayi, 'The Immigrant Experience in London's History', *London Journal*, XIV/1 (1989), pp. 71–5
Phillips, Mike, *London Crossings: A Biography of Black Britain* (London, 2002)
—, and Trevor Phillips, *Windrush: The Irresistible Rise of Multiracial Britain* (London, 1998)
Pilkington, Edward, *Beyond the Mother Country: West Indians and the Notting Hill White Riots* (London, 1988)
Pimlott, Ben and Nirmala Rao, *Governing London* (Oxford, 2002)
Sassen, Saskia, *The Global City: New York, London, Tokyo* (Princeton, NJ, and Oxford, 1991)
Sewell, Tony, *Keep on Moving: The Windrush Legacy: The Black Experience in Britain from 1948* (London, 1998)
Thornley, Andy, ed., *The Crisis of London* (London, 1992)
Trench, Richard, and Ellis Hillman, *London under London* (London, 1993)

Velazquez, Patria Roman, *The Making of Latin London: Salsa, Music, Place and Identity* (Aldershot, 1999)
Wambu, Onyekachi, ed., *Empire Windrush: Fifty Years of Writing about Black Britain* (London, 1998)

Geography, Theory of the City

Borden, Iain, Tim Hall and Malcolm Miles, eds, *The City Cultures Reader* (London, 2000)
Borden, Iain, Joe Kerr, and Jane Rendell, eds, *The Unknown City: Contesting Architecture and Social Space* (Cambridge, MA, 2001)
Certeau, Michel de, *The Practice of Everyday Life*, trans. Steven Randall (Berkeley, CA, 1988)
Gibson, Katherine, and Sophie Watson, eds, *Postmodern Cities and Spaces* (Oxford, 1995)
Gilroy, Paul, *'There ain't no Black in the Union Jack': The Cultural Politics of Race and Nation* (London, 1987)
—, *The Black Atlantic Modernity and Double Consciousness* (London, 1998)
Hall, Peter, *Cities of Tomorrow: An Intellectual History of Urban Planning and Design in the Twentieth Century* (Oxford, 1988)
Hannigan, John, *Fantasy City: Pleasure and Profit in the Postmodern Metropolis* (London, 1998)
Harrison, Paul, *Inside the Inner City* (London, 1992)
Jacobs, Jane M, *Edge of Empire: Postcolonialism and the City* (London, 1996)
—, and Ruth Fincher, eds, *Cities of Difference* (London, 1998)
Jameson, Fredric, and Masao Miyoshi, eds, *The Cultures of Globalization* (Durham, NC, and London, 1998)
Jarvis, Brian, *Postmodern Cartographies* (London, 1998)
King, Anthony, *Re-presenting the City: Ethnicity, Capital and Culture in the Twenty-First Century Metropolis* (London, 1995)
Lechner, Frank J., and John Boli Malden, eds, *The Globalization Reader* (Oxford, 2000)
Lefebvre, Henri, *The Production of Space* (Oxford, 1991)
LeGates, Richard T., and Frederic Stout, *The City Reader* (London, 1996)
Massey, Doreen, 'A Global Sense of Place', *Marxism Today* (June 1991), pp. 24–9
—, *Space, Place and Gender* (Cambridge, 1994)
—, 'Places and their Pasts', *History Workshop Journal* (1995), pp. 182–92
—, and Pat Jess, eds, *A Place in the World* (Oxford, 1995)
Mazzeloni, Donatella, 'The City and the Imaginary', in *Space and Place: Theories of Identity and Location*, ed. Erica Carter, James Donald and Judith Squires (London, 1993), pp. 285–301
Murray, Charles, *et al.*, *The Emerging British Underclass* (London, 1990)
—, *Underclass: The Crisis Deepens* (London, 1994)
Pile, Steve and Nigel Thrift, eds, *City A–Z* (London, 2000)
Rogers, Richard, *Cities for a Small Planet* (London, 1997)
Sadler, Simon, *The Situationist City* (Cambridge, MA, 1982)

Silverstone, Roger, ed., *Visions of Suburbia* (London, 1997)
Soja, Edward W., *Postmodern Geographies* (London, 1989)

Literary Theory and Criticism

Bhabha, Homi K, 'Novel Metropolis', *New Statesman and Society*, XVI (February 1990), pp. 5–8
——, ed., *Nation and Narration* (London, 1990)
Birbalsingh, Frank, 'Samuel Selvon and the West Indian Renaissance', *Ariel*, VIII/3 (1977), pp. 5–22
Bradbury, Malcolm, *No, Not Bloomsbury* (New York, 1988)
Day, Aidan, *Angela Carter: The Rational Glass* (Manchester, 1998)
Delville, Michel, *J. G. Ballard* (Plymouth, 1998)
Donald, James, 'Metropolis: The City as Text', in *Social and Cultural Forms of Modernity*, ed. R. Bocock and K. Thompson (Oxford, 1992), pp. 175–91
Greene, Gayle, *Doris Lessing: The Poetics of Change* (Ann Arbor, MI, 1994)
Ho, Elaine, *Timothy Mo* (Manchester, 2001)
Lehan, Richard, *The City in Literature: An Intellectual and Cultural History* (Berkeley, CA, and London, 1998)
Looker, Mark, *Atlantic Passages: History, Community and Language in the Fiction of Sam Selvon* (New York, 1996)
Luckhurst, Roger, *The Angle Between Two Walls: The Fiction of J. G. Ballard* (Liverpool, 1997)
Maslen, Elizabeth, *Doris Lessing* (Plymouth, 1994)
Nasta, Susheila, ed., *Critical Perspectives on Sam Selvon* (Washington, DC, 1988)
Onega, Susana, 'Interview with Peter Ackroyd', *Twentieth Century Literature: A Scholarly and Critical Journal*, XLII/2 (Summer 1996), pp. 208–21
Peck, John, 'The Novels of Peter Ackroyd', *English Studies*, LXXV/5 (September 1994), pp. 442–52
Perrill, Simon, 'The Work of Iain Sinclair', *Comparative Criticism*, XIX (1997), pp. 309–39
Pickering, J., *Understanding Doris Lessing* (Columbia, SC, 1990)
Potter, Rachel, 'Culture Vulture: The Testimony of Iain Sinclair's *Downriver*', *Parataxis*, V (1993–4), pp. 40–48
Sage, Lorna, ed., *Flesh and the Mirror: Essays on the Art of Angela Carter* (London, 1994)
Sizemore, Christine, *A Female Vision of The City: London in the Novels of Five British Women* (Knoxville, TN, 1984)
Squier, Susan, ed., *Women Writers and the City* (Knoxville, TN, 1984)
Stephenson, G., *Out of the Night and into the Dream: A Thematic Study of the Novels of J. G. Ballard* (New York, 1991)
Whittaker, R., *Doris Lessing* (London, 1988)
Wyke, Clement, *Sam Selvon's Dialectical Style and Fictional Strategy* (Vancouver, 1991)

Popular Culture

Bell, David, and Gill Valentine, *Consuming Geographies: We Are Where We Eat* (London, 2000)
Bruzzi, Stella, and Pamela Church Gibson, *Fashion Culture* (London, 2000)
Buckingham, David, *Public Secrets: East Enders and its Audience* (London, 1987)
Chambers, Iain, *Popular Culture: The Metropolitan Experience* (London, 1986)
Dodd, Kathryn, and Philip Dodd, 'From the East End to East Enders: Representations of the Working Class, 1890–1990', in *Come on Down? Popular Media Culture in Post-War Britain*, ed. Dominic Strinati and Stephen Wagg (London, 1992), pp. 116–32
Featherstone, Mike, *Undoing Culture: Globalization, Postmodernism and Identity* (London, 1995)
Gilbert, David, 'London in all its Glory; or, How to Enjoy London: Representations of Imperial London in its Guidebooks', *Journal of Historical Geography*, xxv (1999), pp. 279–97
Gilbert, Jeremy, and Ewan Pearson, *Discographies: Dance Music Culture and the Politics of Sound* (London, 1999)
Glancey, Jonathan, *London: New Bread, New Circuses* (London, 2001)
Hebdige, Dick, *Subculture: The Meaning of Style* (London, 1988)
Kearns, Gerry, and Chris Philo, *Selling Places: The City as Cultural Capital, Past and Present* (Oxford, 1993)
Miller, Daniel, *et al.*, *Shopping, Place and Identity* (London, 1998)
Mort, Frank, *Cultures of Consumption: Masculinities and Social Space in Late Twentieth-Century Britain* (London, 1996)
Naficy, Hamid, *Home, Exile, Homeland: Film, Media and the Politics of Place* (London, 1999)
Sorensen, Colin, *London on Film: 100 Years of Filmmaking in London* (London, 1996)
Urry, John, *The Tourist Gaze: Leisure and Travel in Contemporary Societies* (London, 1990)

Architecture / Art

Glendinning, Miles, and Stefan Muthesius, *Tower Block* (London and New Haven, 1994)
Lingwood, James, and Michael Morris, eds, *Off Limits: 40 Artangel Projects* (London, 2002)
Pevsner, Nikolaus, and Simon Bradley, *The Buildings of England: London 1: The City* (London, 2002)
—, *The Buildings of England: London 6: Westminster* (London, 2003)
Pevsner, Nikolaus, and Bridget Cherry, *The Buildings of England: London 2: South* (London, 1983)
—, *The Buildings of England: London 3: North West* (London, 2002)
—, *The Buildings of England: London 4: North* (London, 2002)
Platt, Edward, *Leadville: A Journey from White City to the Hanger Lane Gyratory*

(London, 2001)
Powell, Kenneth, *New London Architecture* (London, 2001)
Rogers, Richard, and Mark Fisher, *A New London* (Harmondsworth, 1992)
Smart, Andrew, ed., Introduction, *London Suburbs* (London, 1999)
Whiteread, Rachel, and James Lingwood, *House* (London, 1995)

Recommended Recent Titles

Ackroyd, Peter, *Thames: Sacred River* (London, 2008)
Inwood, Stephen, *City of Cities: The Birth of Modern London* (Basingstoke, 2005)
Lichtenstein, Rachel, *Diamond Street: The Hidden World of Hatton Garden* (London, 2012)
Powell, Hilary and Isaac Marrero-Guillamón, eds, *The Art of Dissent: Adventures in London's Olympic State* (London, 2012)
Sandhu, Sukhdev, *Night Haunts: A Journey through the London Night* (London, 2006)
Sinclair, Iain, *Ghost Milk: Calling Time on the Grand Project* (London, 2011)
—, *Hackney, That Rose Red Empire: A Confidential Report* (London, 2009)
—, ed., *London: City of Disappearances* (London, 2006)
Tames, Richard, *London, A Cultural History* (Oxford, 2006)

CONTRIBUTORS

NIRAN ABBAS is Senior Lecturer in the Department of Media and Cultural Studies at Kingston University, London. She has published on new technologies, theory and literature. She is the editor of *Thomas Pynchon: Reading from the Margins* (2003) and *Mapping Michel Serres* (2005) and author of *Thinking Machines: Disclosures of Artificial Intelligence* (2006).

MARC ATKINS's photography and videos are exhibited regularly across Europe and North America. His work is also published in books and magazines worldwide, including the solo photography books, *The Teratologists* (1998), *Faces of Mathematics* (2000), *Liquid City* (with text by Iain Sinclair, 1998) and *Thirteen* (with text by 13 writers, 2002), and international photography compilation books, including *Erotica* (2001) and *The Nude* (2001). See www.panoptika.net and www.marcatkins.com.

PHIL BAKER is a writer, and lives in Clerkenwell. He is the author of *The Dedalus Book of Absinthe* (2001), and he reviews for a number of papers and journals, including the *Sunday Times* and *Times Literary Supplement*. He is also author of biographies Dennis Wheatley (2009) and the artist Austin Osman Spare (2011).

JENNY BAVIDGE gained her PhD from the University of London in 2001. She is now Lecturer in English at the University of Greenwich. Her research interests include children's literature and the representation of London in literature and film. She has published widely on the subjects such as urban childhood and the work of Iain Sinclair, and she is a member of the editorial board of the *Literary London Journal*. See www.literarylondon.org/london-journal.

GARGI HATTACHARYYA teaches in the Department of Sociology at Aston University. Her publications include *Tales of Dark-skinned Women: Race, Gender and Global Culture* (1998), *Race and Power: Global Racism in the Twenty-First Century*, with John Gabriel and Stephen Small (2001), *Sexuality and Society* (2002) and *Traffick: The Illicit Movement of People and Things* (2005).

MICHAEL BRACEWELL has written six novels, including *The Conclave* (1992) and most recently *Perfect Tense* (2001). He is also the author of several works of non-fiction, including a study of Englishness in popular culture, *England is Mine* (1997), and *The Nineties* (2002), a selection of his journalistic writings. He has written catalogue essays for many contemporary artists, including Sam Taylor-Wood, Gilbert & George and Sarah Morris. He is also the author of several books about art-rock group Roxy Music.

CHRISTOPHER BREWARD is Principal of Edinburgh College of Art. His research interests range across urban studies, fashion culture and the history of design. He is a trustee of the Costume and Design History Societies. He is the author of *The Culture of Fashion* (1995), *The Hidden Consumer* (1999), *Fashion* (2003) and *Fashioning London* (2004). He co-curated the major exhibition 'British Design, 1948–2012' at the V&A.

CAROLINE COX is a cultural historian, author and broadcaster who specializes in fashion culture. Her publications include *Good Hair Days: A History of British Hairstyles* (1999), *Lingerie: A Lexicon of Style* (2000), *I DO: 100 Years of Wedding Fashion* (2001), *Stiletto* (2004) and *How to be Adored* (2010). Her passion for hair is borne out in her work as Cultural Trends Advisor for Vidal Sassoon's Advanced Academy, where she works closely on the development of new collections and lectures internationally on the latest hair trends. Caroline was awarded a visiting professorship at the University of the Arts, London.

PAUL DAVIES was born in 1961 in Colchester, and was educated at Bristol University and The Polytechnic of Central London during the 1980s. He presently lectures in Architecture at The Architectural Association, London, usually on the subject of Las Vegas, but with diversions into comparable interests in London. He is married to photographer Julie Cook; they live in Bethnal Green.

JOHN DAVIS has been Fellow in Modem History at The Queen's College, Oxford, since 1989, and works on the history of modern London. He has published *Reforming London: The London Government Problem, 1855–1900* (1988) and *A History of Britain, 1885–1939* (1999). He has published articles on Rachmanism and on the ILEA, and is currently working on Britain in the 1970s.

TOM DYCKHOFF is a leading critic and broadcaster on architecture. He studied geography at Christ Church, Oxford, and architectural history at The Bartlett, University College London. Since then he has worked for the Prince of Wales's Institute of Architecture, on *Perspectives* magazine, organized exhibitions at the RIBA, taught at The Bartlett and has been deputy editor of *Space* magazine. He writes regularly for the *Guardian*. His major television series *The Secret Life of Buildings* aired in 2011. When he grows up he wants to be an architect.

HELEN CAROLINE EVENDEN is a writer, curator and lecturer specializing in architecture and vehicle design. She is a lecturer and Carmen Research Fellow at the Royal College of Art, London. Her main areas of academic interest include architecture for the motorist and Parliament buildings. She has lectured internationally, and made contributions to magazines, radio and television programmes, including the *Today Programme*, *Design Week* and *Driven*.

ALLEN FISHER has been involved in performance and writing since 1962. A poet, painter, publisher, editor and art historian, he has produced more than 120 books of graphics, art documentation and poetry, the most popular of which have been *Place* (1974), *Brixton Fractals* (1985), *Gravity* (2004) and *Leans* (2007). He is Head of Arts at Manchester Metropolitan University. Examples of his work are in the Tate Collection.

MURRAY FRASER is Professor of Architecture and Global Culture at The Bartlett School of Architecture, UCL. His teaching and research covers architectural design, cultural theory, architectural history and leading-edge digital technology. He is author of *John Bull's Other Homes* (1996) and *Architecture and the Special Relationship* (2008), and has contributed to books such as *Intersections* (2000) and *Autopia* (2002).

CHARLIE GERE is Reader in New Media Research at Lancaster University. He is the author of *Digital Culture* (2002) and *Age, Time and Technology* (2006). His research on digital culture has appeared in a number of collections and academic journals.

ANDREW GIBSON is Research Professor of Modern Literature and Theory at Royal Holloway, University of London. He is a member of the Conseil Scientifique of the Collège International de Philosophie in Paris. His many publications include *James Joyce* (Reaktion 2006), *Samuel Beckett* (Reaktion 2010), *Beckett and Badiou* (2006) and *Intermittency: The Concept of Historical Reason in French Philosophy* (2012).

PAMELA CHURCH GIBSON is Reader in Cultural and Historical Studies at the London College of Fashion. She has published a number of essays on different aspects of cinema, including both the heritage film and the British 'costume drama'. She has co-edited a number of anthologies, including *The Oxford Guide to Film Studies* (1998). Her most recent book is *Fashion and Celebrity Culture* (2011).

DAVID GILBERT is Professor of Geography at Royal Holloway, University of London, specializing in the modern history of London. His research has examined the influence of imperialism on London and urban tourism, as well as the development of suburbia. Publications include *Imperial Cities: Landscape Space and Performance* (with Felix Driver, 2003), *Geographies of British Modernity* (with Brian Short and David Matless, 2003) and *Fashion's World Cities* (ed., 2006). He lives with his family in Ealing ('the Queen of the Suburbs').

FIONA HENDERSON is currently teaching at Deele College, Co. Donegal. Her doctoral research explored the changing tourist landscapes and practices portrayal in guidebooks to London, Paris and Berlin in the second half of the twentieth century. She published a chapter (with David Gilbert) in another edited collection on London entitled *Imagined Londons*.

HILDA KEAN is an Honorary Research Fellow at Ruskin College, Oxford, and course director of the MA in Public History. Recent books include *Seeing History: Public History in Britain Now* (with Paul Martin and Sally Morgan, 2000) and *People and Their Posts: Public History Today* (with Paul Ashton, 2009).

PATRICK KEILLER's films include *London* (85 mins, 1994) and *Robinson in Space* (82 mins, 1997). *Robinson in Space* was extended as a book in 1999. *The Dilapidated Dwelling*, a documentary for televisionon housing in the UK, was completed in 2000. His most recent film, *Robinson in Ruins* (101 mins), was released in 2010. His exhibition 'The Robinson Institute' opened at Tate Britain in March 2012.

SARAH KENT was an artist, lecturer and curator before becoming a critic, and is passionate about all aspects of art making. As visual arts editor of *Time Out* magazine she witnessed the transformation of the London art scene by Damien Hirst and his generation. She has written numerous catalogue essays about them for the Saatchi Gallery, and *Shark Infested Waters* (1994) is a survey of Young British Artists in the Saatchi Collection. Other books include *Women's Images of Men* (1990), *Composition* (1995) and *Jessica Rankin: So Many Echoes of Echoes* (2007).

JOE KERR is an architectural historian, writer and broadcaster. He is Head of the Critical and Historical Studies Programme at the Royal College of Art, London, and co-editor of *Strangely Familiar: Narratives of Architecture and the City* (1996), *The Unknown City: Contesting Architecture and Social Space* (2000) and *Autopia: Cars and Culture* (2002). He is currently writing a book on the curious story of London's wartime Lenin Memorial. He is also a London bus driver based at Tottenham Garage.

HANIF KUREISHI was born in Bromley, Kent, in 1954, the son of a Pakistani father and an English mother. His novels include *The Buddha of Suburbia* (1990), which won the Whitbread Book of the Year Award, *The Black Album* (1995), *Gabriel's Gift* (2001) and *Something to Tell You* (2008). He has also written short stories, plays and screenplays.

ROGER LUCKHURST is Professor of Modern and Contemporary Literature in the School of English and Humanities at Birkbeck College, University of London. His publications include *The Invention of Telepathy* (2002), *Science Fiction, Cultural History of Literature Series* (2005) and *The Trauma Question* (2008).

TOM MCCARTHY is a writer, artist and General Secretary of the International Necronautical Society, a semi-fictitious organization played out across the worlds of art, literature and media. His projects to date have included the reconstruction of a mafia shootout in a Dutch wind tunnel and the construction of a radio broadcasting unit in the ICA, London. His 'Report' *Navigation Was Always a Difficult Art* was published in 2002. His other publications include *Tintin and the Secret of Literature* (2009) and the novel *'C'* (2010).

ROD MENGHAM is Reader in Modern English Literature at the University of Cambridge. He is author of books on Charles Dickens, Emily Brontë and Henry Green, as well as of *The Descent of Language* (1993), and he has edited collections of essays on contemporary fiction, violence and avant-garde art, and the fiction of the 1940s. His poems have been published under the title *Unsung: New and Selected Poems* (2nd edn, 2001), and with photographs by Marc Atkins in *Ars Cameralis* (2009).

ROBERT MIGHALL has held research fellowships at Oxford and in London. His publications include *A Geography of Victorian Gothic Fiction* (1999) and editions of *The Picture of Dorian Gray* (2000) and *The Strange Case of Doctor Jekyll and Mr Hyde* (2001) for Penguin Classics. He has also written *Sunshine: A Cultural History of the Sun* (2008) and *John Keats: A Biography*. His research interests include London and the histories of sexology and crime. He is a Fellow of the Royal Society of Arts.

PANIKOS PANAYI, Professor of European History at De Montfort University, was born in London in 1962, the son of Greek Cypriot immigrants. He has published widely on the history of migration, ethnicity and racism. His most important books include *The Impact of Immigration: A Documentary History of the Effects and Experience of Immigrants and Refugees in Britain since 1945* (1999), *Outsiders: A History of European Minorities* (1999), *Spicing Up Britain: The Multicultural History of British Food* (2008) and *An Immigration History of Britain: Multicultural Racism since 1800* (2010).

MILE PHILLIPS OBE was born in Guyana and travelled to Britain as a child. He was brought up and educated in London, and is now one of its leading black writers. He portrays the city in *London Crossing* (2001), and discusses its role in remaking his identity.

NICHOLAS ROYLE was born in Manchester in 1963, but has lived in London for the last 20 years. He is the author of five novels – *Counterparts* (1993), *Saxophone Dreams* (1996), *The Matter of the Heart* (1997), *The Director's Cut* (2000) and *Antwerp* (2004) – and the short story collection *Mortality* (2006). He teaches creative writing at Manchester Metropolitan University.

SALMAN RUSHDIE was born in Bombay, India, and emigrated to Britain in 1965. Among his books are *Midnight's Children* (1981), which won the Booker Prize, and *The Satanic Verses* (1988), for which he received a *fatwa* on grounds of blasphemy from the Ayatollah Khomeini of Iran. His publications since include *Haroum and the Sea of Stories* (1990), a children's book, a book of essays, *Imaginary Homelands* (1991), *East West* (1994), *The Moor's Last Sigh* (1995), *The Ground Beneath Their Feet* (1999), *Fury* (2001), *Shalimar the Clown* (2005) and *The Enchantress of Florence* (2008).

MARK W. TURNER is Professor of English at King's College London, where he teaches nineteenth- and twentieth-century urban literature and queer culture. He is the author of *Trollope and the Magazines* (2000) and *Backward Glances: Cruising the*

Queer Streets of London and New York (2003), and is editor of the journal *Media History*.

KATIE WALES is Honorary Professor, Faulty of Arts, The University if Nottingham, and a Fellow of the Royal Society of Arts. She has written many articles on the English language and the media. Her books include *The Social and Cultural History of Nottingham English* (2006), *A Dictionary of Stylistics* (2001), *Personal Pronouns in Present-day English* (1996) and *The Language of James Joyce* (1994).

PATRICK WRIGHT is Professor of Literature and Visual and Material Culture at King's College London. He is the author of *On Living in an Old Country* (1985), *A Journey Through Ruins* (1991), *The Village that Died for England* (1995, enlarged edition 2003), *Tank: The Progress of a Monstrous War Machine* (2000) and *Iron Curtain: From Stage to Cold War* (2007).

ACKNOWLEDGEMENTS

The editors and publishers gratefully acknowledge permission to reprint copyright material in this book as follows:

HANIF KUREISHI, 'Wild Women, Wild Men', from *Dreaming and Scheming: Reflections on Writing and Politics: Collected Non Fiction, Essays and Teachings*. Copyright © Hanif Kureishi 2002. Reproduced by permission of Rogers, Coleridge & White Ltd, 20 Powis Mews, London W11 1JN.

MIKE PHILLIPS, 'The State of London', from his *London Crossings* (Continuum, 2001).

SALMAN RUSHDIE, 'An Unimportant Fire' from his *Imaginary Homelands: Essays and Criticism, 1981–1991* (Granta Books, 1991), copyright © Salman Rushdie 1981, 1982, 1983, 1984, 1985, 1986, 1987, 1988, 1990, 1991. Reproduced by permission of Penguin Books Ltd.

PATRICK WRIGHT, 'Down in the Dirt', from his *A Journey through Ruins* (1992), by permission of the author.

INDEX